# Tom Miller

D1312447

# Managed DirectX 9

## Graphics and Game Programming

# *KICK START*

**SAMS**

800 East 96th Street, Indianapolis, Indiana 46240

# Managed DirectX 9 Kick Start: Graphics and Game Programming

International Standard Book Number: 0-672-32596-9

Library of Congress Catalog Card Number: 2003111747

Printed in the United States of America

First Printing: October 2003

09 08          12 11 10 9

## Trademarks

All terms mentioned in this book that are known to be trademarks or service marks have been appropriately capitalized. Sams Publishing cannot attest to the accuracy of this information. Use of a term in this book should not be regarded as affecting the validity of any trademark or service mark.

## Warning and Disclaimer

Every effort has been made to make this book as complete and as accurate as possible, but no warranty or fitness is implied. The information provided is on an "as is" basis. The author and the publisher shall have neither liability nor responsibility to any person or entity with respect to any loss or damages arising from the information contained in this book or from the use of the CD or programs accompanying it.

## Bulk Sales

Sams Publishing offers excellent discounts on this book when ordered in quantity for bulk purchases or special sales. For more information, please contact

**U.S. Corporate and Government Sales**
**1-800-382-3419**
**corpsales@pearsontechgroup.com**

For sales outside of the U.S., please contact

**International Sales**
**international@pearsoned.com**

**Associate Publisher**
*Michael Stephens*

**Acquisitions Editor**
*Neil Rowe*

**Development Editor**
*Mark Renfrow*

**Managing Editor**
*Charlotte Clapp*

**Production Editor**
*Benjamin Berg*

**Indexer**
*Johnna VanHoose Dinse*

**Proofreader**
*Katie Robinson*

**Technical Editor**
*David Franson*

**Team Coordinator**
*Cindy Teeters*

**Interior and Cover Designer**
*Gary Adair*

**Page Layout**
*Ron Wise*

# Contents at a Glance

# Table of Contents

# Foreword

Since the release of the Microsoft DirectX 9.0 SDK, which included the initial release of DirectX for Managed Code, developers have been demanding a book dedicated to this technology. There have been a few attempts thus far, but none that will match the level of knowledge and expertise you will find in this book.

How can I say this? Easy! During the development of DirectX for Managed Code, I was the development lead responsible for the DirectX SDK. Included in this role was the management of the massive development team responsible for making DirectX for Managed Code a reality. Okay, so it was two people. Regardless, the one guy primarily responsible for the effort is the author of this book.

As Tom's manager I witnessed his work and dedication first hand. I can tell you, if there's one person who has depth of knowledge with managed code, DirectX, and the .NET Framework, it's Tom. The information you'll find in this book comes from the source responsible for the development of DirectX for Managed Code API itself. You won't find a more knowledgeable person in this area.

While this book covers every component of DirectX for Managed Code, the majority of it focuses on the most used API, Direct3D. It will cover everything from networking, audio, and input devices to progressive meshes, shaders, and character animation. If you're looking for the ultimate programmer's guide for developing DirectX for Managed Code applications, there's no need to look any further.

—*Bob Gaines*
*Microsoft Corporation—Lead Program Manager*

# About the Author

**Tom Miller** is the development lead for Managed DirectX, as well as the designer of the API. He has worked on the DirectX team for the last four years, including the SDK team writing samples, as well as the DirectX for Visual Basic team. Previously at Microsoft, he worked on the Visual Basic and Office teams.

# Dedication

*To my wife Tanya, my son Lucas, and my daughter Samantha.*
*Without you, this never would have been possible.*

# Acknowledgments

To Bob Gaines, my manager while Managed DirectX was under development, who always had the encouragement I needed.

To the rest of the Managed DirectX team: Adam Lonnberg, Dominic Riccetti, Randy Russel, Rich Sauer, and Rick Hoskinson. The hard work everyone put into the project really paid off.

To Phil Taylor, the program manager for Managed DirectX, who got me out of many meetings and allowed me to continue working.

To Jason Kepner, who helped with the review of the book, and did most of the original artwork for the book.

To the beta testers of DirectX9, whose invaluable feedback helped shape the look and feel of the final Managed DirectX API.

To the management in DirectX who believed in me enough to allow my vision of Managed DirectX to be realized.

To my mom Vicki, who raised me and gave me the work ethic that works so well for me now.

To my sister Jessica. She'd be upset if I didn't mention her, especially since I mentioned Mom.

And last, but certainly not least:

To my wife Tanya, my son Lucas, and my daughter Samantha. Thank you for encouraging me to write this book, and dealing with the long periods of time when I was too "busy working" to be much fun. I couldn't have done this without your support.

I've run out of people to thank, so I'll just thank everyone else for reading this book.

# We Want to Hear from You!

As the reader of this book, *you* are our most important critic and commentator. We value your opinion and want to know what we're doing right, what we could do better, what areas you'd like to see us publish in, and any other words of wisdom you're willing to pass our way.

As an associate publisher for Sams Publishing, I welcome your comments. You can email or write me directly to let me know what you did or didn't like about this book—as well as what we can do to make our books better.

*Please note that I cannot help you with technical problems related to the topic of this book. We do have a User Services group, however, where I will forward specific technical questions related to the book.*

When you write, please be sure to include this book's title and author as well as your name, email address, and phone number. I will carefully review your comments and share them with the author and editors who worked on the book.

Email:   feedback@samspublishing.com

Mail:     Michael Stephens
          Associate Publisher
          Sams Publishing
          800 East 96th Street
          Indianapolis, IN 46240 USA

For more information about this book or another Sams Publishing title, visit our Web site at www.samspublishing.com. Type the ISBN (excluding hyphens) or the title of a book in the Search field to find the page you're looking for.

# Introduction

DirectX is a rich multimedia API that gives developers the ability to write high-performance applications using a standardized set of interfaces. The first release of DirectX coincided with Windows 95, and was called the "Games SDK." Since then, more than eight new versions of the API have been released; however, these APIs were designed for developers who used C and C++. There was an entire group of developers who had no easy access to the functionality DirectX provided.

## The History of Managed DirectX

The first public release of Managed DirectX happened on December 20, 2002, with the release of DirectX 9; however, the project had been in development for quite some time. Late in the development cycle for DirectX 8.1, while I was working on DirectX for Visual Basic, I started playing with the first beta of Visual Studio.NET and the .NET runtime, and it was obvious to me that this was the future of development. I began working on a prototype of "DirectX.NET," which would eventually become Managed DirectX, during this time.

From the beginning, Managed DirectX was designed to be just as powerful as the "core" API, with little to no overhead. In the past, Visual Basic users of DirectX lacked the ability to develop applications of similar quality when compared to the core DirectX API. Some of this was due to the Visual Basic runtime itself, while some was due to the overhead of the wrapper DLLs. In DirectX 8, we tried to eliminate some of these performance bottlenecks by removing the wrapping layer for the most performance critical API, Direct3D. Instead of having a proxy DLL that did data marshalling, we moved the Direct3D API directly into a type library. While this did improve performance slightly, in many cases all it did was overly complicate the API, particularly for the Visual Basic developers we were targeting.

After the release of DirectX 8, it was apparent that the API was not very easy to use. The samples were hard to follow and the code didn't look like "normal" Visual Basic applications. Most Visual Basic developers found the API too complicated to use; C++ developers had no reason to switch since there was no benefit in it for them. We were popular with the home enthusiasts, but game studios weren't even aware we existed. Our new API needed to address these issues. It needed to be fast, it needed to be easy to use, and it needed to have a reason for developers to switch from the C++ code they had been writing. The concept for Managed DirectX was born; now we just needed to implement it.

At the Game Developers Conference (GDC) in San Jose in 2002, the first alpha of Managed DirectX was released. It was based on the DirectX 8.1 runtime, and written exclusively in C#. We had most of the core DirectX components in this release, including DirectMusic, which was excluded in the final Managed DirectX release. The only DirectX components not represented in this first alpha were DirectDraw and DirectShow, mainly due to the fact that we hadn't decided whether or not we really would include these components or not. Looking back at that first release, it still amazes me how far it's come. I hadn't really addressed any of the problems that the Visual Basic DLLs exposed yet; all I had really done was expose the DirectX API to C#. There was a one-to-one mapping of every function, constant, and structure in DirectX.

This release was immensely helpful to us. It demonstrated the feasibility of the Managed DirectX runtime, and the feedback we got was surprisingly positive. One of the first things this release showed us was that the performance of this layer was lacking immensely. In best-case scenarios, we could get performance matching the native API, but in even a simple scenario (such as the Cube Map sample), the managed version would run at about 40% of the frame rate that the C++ version did. We had our work cut out for us.

We spent the next few months getting ready for our next release, the first beta of DirectX 9. We addressed all the major performance bottlenecks, added DirectDraw support, removed DirectMusic support, and had begun our ease-of-use improvements. We also made sure we had developers familiar with C# and managed code on the beta list. They would actually use the API to gauge how much we really had made the API simpler. The feedback we received was quick, and unanimous. Performance was fine; the API design, on the other hand, left much to be desired. Managed DirectX looked nothing like other managed APIs; it looked like a COM API. All of the components in the .NET runtime had a similar look and feel, while the Managed DirectX DLLs were completely different. We had two goals for this project: Make it fast, and make it easy to use. While we had delivered on the former, it was evident we hadn't delivered the latter.

A total redesign of the API commenced directly after Beta1. We talked with the .NET runtime team, we talked to the beta users, we gathered feedback from any place we could think of to find out the things that were wrong with our current design, and went about fixing it. I wrote a set of design guidelines that all components would need to adhere to, and the task of actually making our current API follow these guidelines started. Some of the changes were simple to implement, such as casing changes. In DirectX (and COM in general), constants and structure names were normally described in all caps, in the .NET runtime, things were cased properly. Other changes were more in depth in nature, such as adding enumeration support to classes. We released Beta2 and anxiously awaited the feedback from our users.

Much to our relief, the feedback was much more positive. We had taken steps in the right direction, and the API was well on its way to fulfilling our goals. We had more tweaks here and there for the remainder of the beta cycle, further refining our guidelines, and our API. About a month before the final release of DirectX 9, one of the beta releases was posted publicly. This was only the DirectX runtime, not the complete SDK, but did include the Managed DirectX API as well. The buzz for Managed DirectX had been building for some time now, and this was most developers' first exposure to the API. Without any samples or documentation, would people still be able to use it? This was a litmus test for us. Not only did people figure out how to use it, people started using it then. The feedback we received was nothing but positive. People posted articles on Web sites describing how to use the API. When the final release was posted in December, we had done what we set out to do.

# Namespaces Included

The Managed DirectX API has a relatively obvious set of namespaces, breaking down the functionality into the various "core" components housed in DirectX. There is also the generic "Microsoft.DirectX" namespace that houses the common functionality. The full list of namespaces included in Managed DirectX is listed in Table 1.

### TABLE 1

**Managed DirectX Namespaces**

| | |
|---|---|
| Microsoft.DirectX | Parent namespace, holds all common code. |
| Microsoft.DirectX.Direct3D | Direct3D graphics API, as well as the D3DX helper library. |
| Microsoft.DirectX.DirectDraw | DirectDraw graphics API. |
| Microsoft.DirectX.DirectPlay | DirectPlay networking API. |
| Microsoft.DirectX.DirectSound | DirectSound audio API. |
| Microsoft.DirectX.DirectInput | DirectInput user input API. |
| Microsoft.DirectX.AudioVideoPlayback | Simple audio and video playback API. |
| Microsoft.DirectX.Diagnostics | Simple diagnostics API. |
| Microsoft.DirectX.Security | Underlying structure for DirectX code access security. |
| Microsoft.DirectX.Security.Permissions | Permission classes for DirectX code access security. |

As you can see, this encompasses most functionality included with DirectX. During the course of this book, we will deal extensively with the Direct3D namespace, but will cover all of the other areas as well.

# Getting Started

So now that we've got a little groundwork information, we have enough information to actually get started writing some Managed DirectX applications! Before you begin writing the next big game using Managed DirectX, there are a few things you need to have.

First, you will need a source code editor and the runtime environment. I would recommend Visual Studio.NET 2003, as that is what Microsoft supports. Regardless of what editor you use, you will need version 1.1 of the .NET runtime, which you can install from the included CD (it also comes automatically with Visual Studio.NET 2003).

Next you will need to have the DirectX 9.0 SDK Update developer runtime installed. I would recommend installing the DirectX 9.0 Software Development Kit Update located on the included CD. This will give you the developer runtime, as well as many other samples, and documentation on Managed DirectX.

The graphics samples in the first few chapters should run on just about any modern graphics card. However, later samples will require a more advanced video card, capable of using vertex and pixel shaders. The geForce3 and above should be sufficient for these samples; however, I would recommend a card capable of using the shader model 2.0 (Radeon 9700 and above).

Before we actually delve into Managed DirectX coding, there are some things it will be assumed you know. If you are new to programming in general, this book probably isn't for you. The book is targeted for developers who already have general programming experience and are looking for information on building rich multimedia applications using Managed DirectX. The code written in the text of this book will be C#, but the included CD will also contain versions of the code written in Visual Basic.NET.

The included CD contains the DirectX 9.0 SDK Update, as well as all of the source code discussed in this book, both in C# and Visual Basic.NET. You will also find the .NET runtime version 1.1 included as well. You can download the DirectX 9 SDK Update or the .NET runtime at http://msdn.microsoft.com as well.

With these things out of the way, we are ready to start using Managed DirectX. Now, we just need to figure out how to actually write the code for this next big game.

# PART I

# Beginning Graphics Concepts

# Introducing Direct3D

**1**

One of the most popular aspects of "rich multimedia" applications would be the addition of 3D graphics. With the processing power of today's modern GPU (graphics processing unit), realistic scenes can be rendered in real time. Have you ever been playing the latest 3D game and wondered, "How do they do that?," only to assume it must be too complicated? Managed Direct3D allows developers an easy and fast way to get complex (or simple) graphics and animations on the screen. In this chapter we will cover the following:

- Creating a default Direct3D device

- Rendering a triangle in both screen coordinates and in world space

- Adding a light to our triangle

## Getting Started

Before we begin developing our first Managed Direct3D application, we need to get our environment ready. To accomplish this, follow these steps:

1. The first thing we'll want to do will be to load Visual Studio.NET and create a new project.

2. Let's select the Visual C# projects area, and create a new Windows Application project. We will need a place to do our rendering, and the standard Windows Form that comes with this project works perfectly.

3. Name the project whatever you like and create the new project.

After the project is created, we will need to make sure the Managed DirectX references are added to the project so we can use the components. Click the Add References menu selection in the project menu, and add the Microsoft.DirectX as well as the Microsoft.DirectX.Direct3D reference. For now, that's all we'll need.

With the references now loaded into the project, we could get right into writing some Managed DirectX code, but before we do that, we should add two new items into our "using" clauses so we don't need to fully qualify everything we'll be using. You can do this by opening the code window for the main windows form in your application (by default form1.cs) and adding the following lines at the end of the using clauses:

```
using Microsoft.DirectX;
using Microsoft.DirectX.Direct3D;
```

While this step isn't necessary, it saves a lot of typing, since you won't need to fully qualify each item before using it. Now, we are ready to start writing our first Managed DirectX application.

# The Direct3D Device

The root of all drawing in Direct3D is the device class. You can think of this class as analogous to the actual graphics device in your computer. A device is the parent of all other graphical objects in your scene. Your computer may have zero or many devices, and with Managed Direct3D, you can control as many of them as you need.

There are three constructors that can be used to create a device. For now, we're only going to use one of them; however we will get to the others in later chapters. The one we're concerned about takes the following arguments:

```
public Device ( System.Int32 adapter , Microsoft.DirectX.Direct3D.DeviceType deviceType ,
    System.Windows.Forms.Control renderWindow , Microsoft.DirectX.Direct3D.CreateFlags
    behaviorFlags, Microsoft.DirectX.Direct3D.PresentParameters presentationParameters )
```

## UNDERSTANDING THE DEVICE CONSTRUCTOR OVERLOADS

The second overload for the device is identical to the first, with the exception of the renderWindow parameter, which takes an IntPtr for an unmanaged (or non-windows form) window handle. The final overload takes a single IntPtr that is the unmanaged COM pointer to the IDirect3DDevice9 interface. This can be used if you have a need to work with an unmanaged application from your managed code.

Now, what do all of these arguments actually mean, and how do we use them? Well, the first argument "adapter" refers to which physical device we want this class to represent. Each device in your computer has a unique adapter identifier (normally 0 through one less than the number of devices you have). Adapter 0 is always the default device.

The next argument, DeviceType, tells Direct3D what type of device you want to create. The most common value you will use here is DeviceType.Hardware, which means you want to use a hardware device. Another option is DeviceType.Reference, which will allow you to use the reference rasterizer, which implements all features of the Direct3D runtime, and runs extremely slowly. You would use this option mainly for debugging purposes, or to test features of your application that your card doesn't support.

The "renderWindow" argument binds a window to this device. Since the windows forms control class contains a window handle, it makes it easy to use a derived class as our rendering window. You can use a form, panel, or any other control-derived class for this parameter. For now, we'll use forms.

The next parameter is used to control aspects of the device's behavior after

### USING A SOFTWARE DEVICE

You should note that the reference rasterizer is only distributed with the DirectX SDK, so someone with only the DirectX runtime will not have this feature. The last value is DeviceType.Software, which will allow you to use a custom software rasterizer. Unless you know you have a custom software rasterizer, ignore this option.

creation. Most of the members of the CreateFlags enumeration can be combined to allow multiple behaviors to be set at once. Some of these flags are mutually exclusive, though, and I will get into those later. We will only use the SoftwareVertexProcessing flag for now. This flag specifies that we want all vertex processing to happen on the CPU. While this is naturally slower than having the vertex processing happen on the GPU, we don't know for sure whether or not your graphics card supports this feature. It's safe to assume your CPU can do the processing for now.

The last parameter of this constructor controls how the device presents its data to the screen. Every aspect of the device's presentation parameters can be controlled via this class. We will go into further details on this structure later, but right now, the only members we will care about are the "Windowed" member, and the SwapEffect member.

The windowed member is a Boolean value used to determine whether the device is in full screen mode (false), or windowed mode (true).

The SwapEffect member is used to control implied semantics for buffer swap behavior. If you choose SwapEffect.Flip, the runtime will create an extra back buffer, and copy whichever becomes the front buffer at presentation time. The SwapEffect.Copy is similar to Flip, but requires you to set the number of back buffers to 1. The option we'll select for now is SwapEffect.Discard, which simply discards the contents of the buffer if it isn't ready to be presented.

Now that we have this information, we can create a device. Let's go back to our code, and do this now. First we will need to have a device object that we can use for our application. We can add a new private member device variable. Include the following line in your class definition:

```
private Device device = null;
```

We will add a new function to our class called "InitializeGraphics" that will be where we can actually use the constructor we've discussed. Add the following code to your class:

```
/// <summary>
/// We will initialize our graphics device here
/// </summary>
public void InitializeGraphics()
{
    // Set our presentation parameters
    PresentParameters presentParams = new PresentParameters();

    presentParams.Windowed = true;
    presentParams.SwapEffect = SwapEffect.Discard;

    // Create our device
    device = new Device(0, DeviceType.Hardware, this,
        CreateFlags.SoftwareVertexProcessing, presentParams);
}
```

As you can see, this creates our presentation parameters argument, sets the members we care about (Windowed and SwapEffect), and then creates the device. We used 0 as the adapter identifier, since that is the default adapter. We created an actual hardware device, as opposed to the reference rasterizer or a software rasterizer. You'll notice we used the "this" keyword as our rendering window. Since our application, and in particular, this class, is a windows form, we simply use that. We also let the CPU handle the vertex processing as mentioned previously.

All of this is great, but currently, the code is never called, so let's change the main function of our class to actually call this method. Let's change the static main method that is created by default to the following:

```
static void Main()
{
    using (Form1 frm = new Form1())
    {
        // Show our form and initialize our graphics engine
        frm.Show();
        frm.InitializeGraphics();
        Application.Run(frm);
    }
}
```

We made a few changes to this function. First, we added the using statement around the creation of our form. This ensures that our form is disposed when the application leaves the scope of this block. Next, we added the Show command to the form. We do this to ensure that the window is actually loaded and displayed (and thus the window handle is created) before we try to create our device. We then call our function to handle our device creation, and use the standard run method for our application. You can compile this application now and run it. Congratulations, you've just successfully created your first Direct3D application!

Okay, so admittedly the application is pretty boring. While it does create a device, it doesn't actually do anything with it, so just by looking at the running application, you can't tell that it's any different from the "empty" C# project we originally created. Let's change that now, and actually render something on our screen.

The windows forms classes have a built-in way to determine when it is time to redraw themselves: using the OnPaint override (you can also hook the Paint event). Each time the window needs to be redrawn, this event will be fired. This seems like the perfect place to put our rendering code. We don't want to do anything amazingly fancy right now, so let's just clear the window to a solid color. Add the following code to your class definition:

```
protected override void OnPaint(System.Windows.Forms.PaintEventArgs e)
{
    device.Clear(ClearFlags.Target, System.Drawing.Color.CornflowerBlue, 1.0f, 0);
    device.Present();
}
```

We use the Clear method on the device to fill our window with a solid color. In this case, we use one of the predefined colors, namely CornflowerBlue. The first parameter of the clear method is what we want to actually clear; in this example, we are clearing the target window. We will get to other members of the ClearFlags enumeration at a later time. The second parameter is the color we are using to clear our target, and for now the last few parameters aren't that important. After the device has been cleared, we want to actually update the physical display. The present method will do this presentation. There are a few different overloads of this method; the one shown here presents the entire area of the device. We will discuss the other overloads later.

If you run the application now, you will notice that while running, the background color of the window is cornflower blue. You can resize the window or maximize it, and each time you do the entire window surface is filled with the cornflower blue color. While we can now see that something is going on with our device, it's still pretty boring. You could accomplish the same thing by setting the background color of the form in the designer. We need to draw something else to be impressive.

The basic object drawn in three dimensional graphics is the triangle. With enough triangles, you can represent anything, even smooth curved surfaces. So our first drawing will naturally need to be a single triangle. To simplify the act of drawing this triangle, we won't worry about dealing with things such as "world space" or "transforms" (which are topics we'll delve into shortly), but instead will draw a triangle using screen coordinates. So, in order to draw our amazing triangle, we will need two things. First, we will need some data construct that will hold the information about our triangle. Second, we will tell the device to actually draw it.

Luckily for us, the Managed DirectX runtime already has a construct to hold our triangle's data. There is a CustomVertex class in the Direct3D namespace that houses many of the common "vertex format" constructs used in Direct3D. A vertex format structure holds data in a format that Direct3D understands and can use. We will discuss more of these structures soon, but for now, we will use the TransformedColored structure for our triangle. This structure tells the Direct3D runtime that our triangle doesn't need to be transformed (that is, rotated or moved) since we will be specifying the coordinates in screen coordinates. It also includes a color component for each point (vertex) in the triangle. Go back to our OnPaint override, and add the following code after the clear call:

```
CustomVertex.TransformedColored[] verts = new CustomVertex.TransformedColored[3];
verts[0].SetPosition(new Vector4(this.Width / 2.0f, 50.0f, 0.5f, 1.0f));
verts[0].Color = System.Drawing.Color.Aqua.ToArgb();
verts[1].SetPosition(new Vector4(this.Width - (this.Width / 5.0f), this.Height -
    (this.Height / 5.0f), 0.5f, 1.0f));
verts[1].Color = System.Drawing.Color.Black.ToArgb();
verts[2].SetPosition(new Vector4(this.Width / 5.0f, this.Height - (this.Height / 5.0f)
    , 0.5f, 1.0f));
verts[2].Color = System.Drawing.Color.Purple.ToArgb();
```

Each member of the array we have created will represent one point in our triangle, thus the need to create three members. We then call the SetPosition method on each member of our array using a newly created Vector4 structure. The position for a transformed vertex includes the x and y positions in screen coordinates (relative to the windows 0, 0 origin), as well as the z position and rhw member (reciprocal of homogenous w). Each of these two members are ignored for our current sample. The Vector4 structure is a convenient way of holding this information. We then set each of the vertices' colors. Notice here that we need to call the ToArgb method of the standard colors we are using. Direct3D expects colors to be a 32-bit integer, and this method will convert the stock color into this format.

You'll notice that we use the current window's width and height to determine our triangle's coordinates as well. We do this just so the triangle resizes with the window.

Now that we have the data, we need to tell Direct3D that we want to draw our triangle, and how to draw it. We can do that by adding the following code below our clear call in the OnPaint override:

```
device.BeginScene();
device.VertexFormat = CustomVertex.TransformedColored.Format;
device.DrawUserPrimitives(PrimitiveType.TriangleList, 1, verts);
device.EndScene();
```

What the heck does that mean? Well, it's relatively simple. The BeginScene method lets Direct3D know that we are about to draw something and to be ready for it. Now that we've told Direct3D that we're going to draw something, we need to tell it what we're going to draw. This is what the VertexFormat property is for. This tells the Direct3D runtime which fixed function pipeline format we will be using. In our case, we are using the transformed and colored vertices pipeline. Don't worry if you don't necessarily understand what a "fixed function pipeline" is; we'll get to that soon.

The DrawUserPrimitives function is where the actual drawing takes place. So what exactly do the parameters mean? The first parameter is the type of primitive we plan on drawing. There are numerous different types available to us, but right now, we just want to draw a list of triangles, so we choose the TriangleList primitive type. The second parameter is the number of triangles we plan on drawing; for a triangle list this should always be the number of vertices in your data divided by three. Since we are only drawing one triangle, naturally, we use 1 here. The last parameter for this function is the data Direct3D will use to draw the triangle. Since we've already filled up our data, we're all set now. The last method, EndScene, just informs the Direct3D runtime that we are no longer drawing. You must call EndScene after every time you've called BeginScene.

Now compile and run our new application. You'll notice that our colored background now has a colored triangle as well. One important thing to note is that the colors at the points of the triangle are the colors we specified in our code, but on the inside of the triangle, the color fades from one color to another. Direct3D automatically interpolates the colors between the triangles for you. Feel free to modify the stock colors I've chosen to see this effect in action.

There are some things you may have noticed if you were playing around with the application. For example, if you resize the window smaller, it doesn't update its contents, but instead simply does nothing. The reason for this is that Windows does not consider shrinking a window a case where you need to repaint the entire window. After all, you've simply removed some data that was displayed; you didn't erase any data that was already there. Fortunately, there is a simple way around this. We can just tell Windows that we always need the window to be repainted. This can be accomplished easily by invalidating the window at the end of our OnPaint override.

```
this.Invalidate();
```

Uh oh, it appears we've broken our application! Running it now shows mainly a blank screen, and sometimes our triangle "flickers" onscreen. This effect is much more pronounced as you resize your window. This is no good; why did this happen? It turns out Windows is trying to be smart and redraws our current window form (the blank one) after invalidating our window. There is painting going on outside of our OnPaint override. This is easily fixed by changing the "style" of window we create. In the constructor for your form, replace the "TODO" section with the following line:

```
this.SetStyle(ControlStyles.AllPaintingInWmPaint | ControlStyles.Opaque, true);
```

Now when you run the application, everything works as expected. All we did was tell windows that we want *all* of the painting to happen inside our OnPaint override (WmPaint comes from the classic Win32 message), and that our window will not be transparent. This ensures that no extra painting from windows will occur, and everything will go through us. You may also notice that if you resize the window to where there is no visible client area, the application will throw an exception. You can change the minimum size property of the form if this really bothers you.

# Making Our Triangle Three Dimensional

Looking back at our application, it doesn't appear to be very three dimensional. All we did was draw a colored triangle inside a window, which could just as easily have been done with GDI. So, how do we actually draw something in 3D and have it look a little more impressive? Actually, it's relatively simple to modify our existing application to accommodate us.

If you remember, earlier when we were first creating the data for our triangle, we used something called *transformed* coordinates. These coordinates are already known to be in screen space, and are easily defined. What if we had some coordinates that weren't already transformed though? These untransformed coordinates make up the majority of a scene in a modern 3D game.

When we are defining these coordinates, we need to define each vertex in world space, rather than screen space. You can think of world space as an infinite three-dimensional Cartesian space. You can place your objects anywhere in this "world" you want to. Let's modify our application to draw an untransformed triangle now.

We'll first change our triangle data to use one of the untransformed vertex format types; in this case, all we really care about is the position of our vertices, and the color, so we'll choose CustomVertex.PositionColored. Change your triangle data code to the following:

```
CustomVertex.PositionColored[] verts = new CustomVertex.PositionColored[3];
verts[0].SetPosition(new Vector3(0.0f, 1.0f, 1.0f));
verts[0].Color = System.Drawing.Color.Aqua.ToArgb();
verts[1].SetPosition(new Vector3(-1.0f, -1.0f, 1.0f));
verts[1].Color = System.Drawing.Color.Black.ToArgb();
verts[2].SetPosition(new Vector3(1.0f, -1.0f, 1.0f));
verts[2].Color = System.Drawing.Color.Purple.ToArgb();
```

And change your VertexFormat property as well:

```
device.VertexFormat = CustomVertex.PositionColored.Format;
```

Now what's this? If you run the application, nothing happens; you're back to your colored screen, and nothing else. Before we figure out why, let's take a moment to describe the changes. As you can see, we've switched our data to use the PositionColored structure instead. This structure will hold the vertices in world space as well as the color of each vertex. Since these vertices aren't transformed, we use a Vector3 class in place of the Vector4 we used with the transformed classes, because transformed vertices do not have an rhw component. The members of the Vector3 structure map directly to the coordinates in world space; x, y, and z. We also need to make sure Direct3D knows we've changed the type of data we are drawing, so we change our fixed function pipeline to use the new untransformed and colored vertices by updating the VertexFormat property.

So why isn't anything displayed when we run our application? The problem here is that while we're now drawing our vertices in world space, we haven't given Direct3D any information on how it should display them. We need to add a camera to the scene that can define how to view our vertices. In our transformed coordinates, a camera wasn't necessary because Direct3D already knew where to place the vertices in screen space.

The camera is controlled via two different transforms that can be set on the device. Each transform is defined as a 4×4 matrix that you can pass in to Direct3D. The projection transform is used to define how the scene is projected onto the monitor. One of the easiest ways to generate a projection matrix is to use the PerspectiveFovLH function on the Matrix class. This will create a perspective projection matrix using the field of view, in a left-handed coordinate system.

What exactly is a left-handed coordinate system anyway, and why does it matter? In most Cartesian 3D coordinate systems, positive x coordinates move toward the right, while positive y coordinates move up. The only other coordinate left is z. In a left-handed coordinate system, positive z moves away from you, while in a right-handed coordinate system, positive z moves toward you. You can easily remember which coordinate system is which by taking either hand and having your fingers point toward positive x. Then twist and curl your fingers so they are now pointing to positive y. The direction your thumb is pointing is positive z. See Figure 1.1.

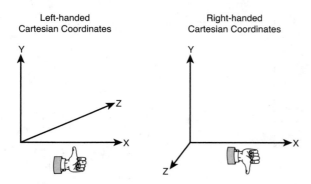

**FIGURE 1.1**   3D coordinate systems.

Direct3D uses a left-handed coordinate system. If you are porting code from a right-handed coordinate system, there are two things you need to do. First, flip the order of your triangles so they are ordered clockwise from front. This is done so back face culling works correctly. Don't worry; we'll get to back face culling soon. Second, use the view matrix to scale the world by –1 in the z direction. You can do this by flipping the sign of the M31, M32, M33, and M34 members of the view matrix. You can then use the RH versions of the matrix functions to build right-handed matrices.

Now, since we are creating a new application, we will just use the left-handed coordinate system that Direct3D expects. Here is the prototype for our projection matrix function:

```
public static Microsoft.DirectX.Matrix PerspectiveFovLH ( System.Single fieldOfViewY ,
    System.Single aspectRatio , System.Single znearPlane , System.Single zfarPlane )
```

The projection transform is used to describe the *view frustum* of the scene. You can think of the view frustum as a pyramid with the top of it cut off, with the inside of said pyramid being the viewable area of your scene. The two parameters in our function, the near and far planes, describe the limits of this pyramid, with the far plane making up the "base" of the pyramid structure, while the near plane is where we cut off the top. See Figure 1.2. The field of view parameter describes the angle at the point of the pyramid. See Figure 1.3. You can think of the aspect ratio just like the aspect ratio of your television; for example, a wide screen television has an aspect ratio of 1.85. You can normally figure this parameter out easily by dividing the width of your viewing area by the height. Only objects that are contained within this frustum are drawn by Direct3D.

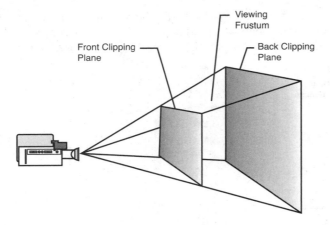

**FIGURE 1.2** Visualizing the viewing frustum.

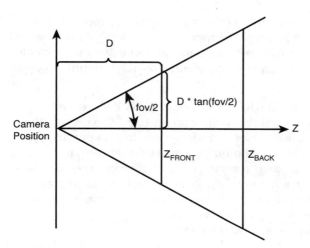

**FIGURE 1.3** Determining field of view.

Since we never set our projection transform, our view frustum never really existed, thus there was nothing really for Direct3D to draw. However, even if we did create our projection transform, we never created our view transform, which contains the information about the camera itself. We can easily do this with the look at function. The prototype for this function follows:

```
public static Microsoft.DirectX.Matrix LookAtLH(Microsoft.DirectX.Vector3 cameraPosition,
    Microsoft.DirectX.Vector3 cameraTarget , Microsoft.DirectX.Vector3 cameraUpVector )
```

This function is pretty self-explanatory. It takes three arguments that describe the properties of the camera. The first argument is the camera's position in world space. The next argument is the position in world space we want the camera to look at. The last argument is the direction that will be considered "up."

With the description of the projection transform and the view transform, Direct3D would now have enough information to display our newly drawn triangle, so let's go ahead and modify our code to get something displayed. We'll add a new function, "SetupCamera", into our OnPaint function just after our clear call. The body of this function will be

```
private void SetupCamera()
{
    device.Transform.Projection = Matrix.PerspectiveFovLH((float)Math.PI / 4,
        this.Width / this.Height, 1.0f, 100.0f);
    device.Transform.View = Matrix.LookAtLH(new Vector3(0,0, 5.0f), new Vector3(),
        new Vector3(0,1,0));
}
```

As you can see, we create our projection matrix and set that to our device's projection transform to let Direct3D know what our view frustum is. We then create our view matrix and set that to our device's view transform so Direct3D knows our camera information. Add a call to this function into OnPaint directly after the clear call, and we are now ready to run our application once more.

That doesn't seem right. Sure, we've got our triangle drawn now, but it's all black, even though we just specified which colors we wanted the triangle points to be. Once again, the problem lies in the difference between the pretransformed triangle we drew in our first application, and our nontransformed triangle now. In a nontransformed environment, by default Direct3D uses lighting to determine the final pixel color of each primitive in the scene. Since we have no lights defined in our scene, there is no external light shining on our triangle, so it appears black. We've already defined the color we want our triangle to appear, so for now, it's safe to simply turn off the lights in the scene. You can accomplish this easily by adding the following line to the end of your SetupCamera function call:

```
device.RenderState.Lighting = false;
```

## USING DEVICE RENDER STATES

There are many render states that can be used to control various stages in the rendering pipeline. We will discuss more of them in subsequent chapters.

Running the application now will show a triangle similar to our first pretransformed triangle. It seems we've done a lot of work to get back into the same position we were before we switched to our nontransformed triangles. What real benefit did we get from making these changes? Well, the major one is that we've got our triangle in a real three-dimensional world now, rather than just drawing them in screen coordinates. This is the first step in creating compelling 3D content.

So now that we've got our triangle drawn in our world, what could we do that would make it actually look like a three-dimensional world? Well, the easiest thing we could do would be to just rotate the triangle. So, how can you go about doing this? Luckily, it's quite simple; we simply have to modify the world transform.

The *world transform* on the device is used to transform the objects being drawn from model space, which is where each vertex is defined with respect to the model, to world space, where each vertex is actually placed in the world. The world transform can be any combination of translations (movements), rotations, and scales. Since we only want to rotate our triangle right now, we'll just create a single transform for this. There are many functions off the Matrix object that can be used to create these transforms. Add the following line to your SetupCamera function:

```
device.Transform.World = Matrix.RotationZ((float)Math.PI / 6.0f);
```

This tells Direct3D that the transform for each object drawn after this should use the following world transform, at least until a new world transform is specified. The world transform is created by rotating our objects on the z axis, and we pass in an angle to the function. The angle should be specified in radians, not degrees. There is a helper function, "Geometry.DegreeToRadians", in the Direct3DX library (which we'll add to our project later). We just picked this angle arbitrarily to show the effect. Running this application shows you the same triangle as before, but now rotated about its z axis.

Fancy, but still a little bland; let's spice it up by making the rotation happen continuously. Let's modify the world transform:

```
device.Transform.World = Matrix.RotationZ((System.Environment.TickCount / 450.0f)
    / (float)Math.PI);
```

Running our project now should show our triangle spinning around slowly about the z axis. It seems a little jumpy, but that is caused by the TickCount property. The TickCount property in the System class is a small wrapper on the GetTickCount method in the Win32 API, which has a resolution of approximately 15 milliseconds. This means that the number returned here will only update in increments of approximately 15, which causes this jumpy behavior. We can smooth out the rotation easily by having our own counter being incremented, rather than using TickCount. Add a new member variable called "angle" of type float. Then change your world transform as follows:

```
    device.Transform.World = Matrix.RotationZ(angle / (float)Math.PI);
    angle += 0.1f;
```

Now the triangle rotates smoothly around. Controlling rotation (or any movement) in this way is not a recommended tactic, since the variable is incremented based on the speed of the rendering code. With the rapid speed increases of modern computers, basing your rendering code on variables like this can cause your application to run entirely too fast on newer hardware, or even worse, entirely too slow on old hardware. We will discuss a better way to base your code on a much higher resolution timer later in the book.

Our spinning triangle still isn't all that impressive, though. Let's try to be real fancy and make our object spin on multiple axes at once. Luckily, we have just the function for that. Update our world transform like the following:

```
device.Transform.World = Matrix.RotationAxis(new Vector3(angle / ((float)Math.PI * 2.0f),
    angle / ((float)Math.PI * 4.0f), angle / ((float)Math.PI * 6.0f)),
    angle / (float)Math.PI);
```

The major difference between this line of code and the last is the new function we are calling, namely RotationAxis. In this call, we first define the axis we want to rotate around, and we will define our axis much like we do the angle, with a simple math formula for each component of the axis. We then use the same formula for the rotation angle. Go ahead and run this new application so we can see the results of our rotating triangle.

Oh no! Now our triangle starts to spin around, disappears momentarily, and then reappears, and continues this pattern forever. Remember earlier when back face culling was mentioned? Well, this is the perfect example of what back face culling really does. When Direct3D is rendering the triangles, if it determines that a particular face is not facing the camera, it is not drawn. This process is called *back face culling*. So how exactly does the runtime know if a particular primitive is facing the camera or not? A quick look at the culling options in Direct3D gives a good hint. The three culling options are none, clockwise, and counterclockwise. In the case of the clockwise or counterclockwise options, primitives whose vertices are wound in the opposite order of the cull mode are not drawn.

Looking at our triangle, you can see that the vertices are wound in a counterclockwise manner. See Figure 1.4. Naturally, we picked this order for our triangle because the counterclockwise cull mode is the default for Direct3D. You could easily see the difference in how the vertices are rendered by swapping the first and third index in our vertex list.

Now that we know how back face culling works, it's obvious that for our simple application, we simply don't want or need these objects to be culled at all. There is a simple render state that controls the culling mode. Add the following line to our SetupCamera function call:

```
device.RenderState.CullMode = Cull.None;
```

Now, when the application is run, everything works as we would have expected. Our triangle rotates around on the screen, and it does not disappear as it rotates. For the first time, our application actually looks like something in real 3D. Before we continue, though, go ahead and resize the window a little bit. Notice how the triangle behaves the same way, and looks the same regardless of window size?

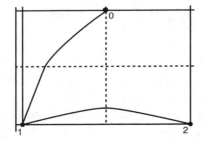

**FIGURE 1.4** Vertex winding order.

# Automatic Device Resets During a Resize

Anyone who's ever written a Direct3D application in C++ or DirectX for Visual Basic understands that normally, when the window of your application is resized, the device needs to be reset; otherwise, Direct3D will continue to render the scene at the same resolution as when the device was created, and the resulting image will be copied (and stretched to fit) onto the newly sized window. Managed DirectX is smart enough to realize when you've created your device with a Windows Form control, and can automatically reset the device for you when this control is resized. Naturally, you can revert back to the normal behavior and handle device resets yourself quite easily. There is an event attached to the device called "DeviceResizing", which occurs right before the automatic device reset code. By capturing this event, and setting the Cancel member of the EventArgs class passed in to true, you can revert to the default behavior. Add the following function to your sample:

```
private void CancelResize(object sender, CancelEventArgs e)
{
    e.Cancel = true;
}
```

As you can see, this function does nothing more than say yes, we do want to cancel this action. Now, we need to hook up this event handler to our device so it knows not to perform this action. Add the following line of code immediately after the device creation:

```
device.DeviceResizing += new CancelEventHandler(this.CancelResize);
```

Now run the application once more and after it starts, maximize the window. As you can easily see, the triangle, while still there and in the same spot, looks horrible. The edges are jagged, and it's just not very nice looking at all. Go ahead and delete the last two sections of code we added. The default behavior of Managed DirectX handles the device resizing for you, and we might as well take advantage of it.

# We've Got Camera and Action; What About Lights?

Now that we've got our single triangle drawn and spinning around, what else could make it even better? Why, lights of course! We mentioned lights briefly before, when our triangle turned completely black after we first moved over to our nontransformed triangles. Actually, we completely turned the lighting off in our scene. The first thing we need to do is to turn that back on, so change the lighting member back to true:

```
device.RenderState.Lighting = true;
```

You could just delete the line entirely since the default behavior for the device is to have lighting on; we'll just leave it as true for the sake of clarity. Running the application now, we see we're back to the black triangle again; it's just spinning around now. Maybe we should go ahead and define a light, and turn it on. You'll notice the device class has a lights array attached to it, with each member of the array holding the various light properties. We want to define the first light in the scene and turn it on, so let's add the following code into our OnPaint method just after our triangle definition code:

```
device.Lights[0].Type = LightType.Point;
device.Lights[0].Position = new Vector3();
device.Lights[0].Diffuse = System.Drawing.Color.White;
device.Lights[0].Attenuation0 = 0.2f;
device.Lights[0].Range = 10000.0f;
device.Lights[0].Commit();
device.Lights[0].Enabled = true;
```

So, what exactly do all those lines of code do? First, we define what type of light we want to display. We've picked a point light, which is a light that radiates light in all directions equally, much like a light bulb would. There are also directional lights that travel in a given direction infinitely. You could think of the sun as a directional light (yes, in reality the sun would be a point light since it does give off light in all directions; however, from our perspective on Earth, it behaves more like a directional light). Directional lights are only affected by the direction and color of the light and ignore all other light factors (such as attenuation and range), so they are the least computationally expensive light to use. The last light type would be the spot light, which like its name is used to define a spot light, much like you would see at a concert, highlighting the person on stage. Given the large number of factors in making up the spot light (position, direction, cone angle, and so on), they are the most computationally expensive lights in the system.

With that brief discussion on light types out of the way, we'll continue. Next we want to set the position of our point light source. Since the center of our triangle is at 0, 0, 0, we may as well position our light there as well. The parameterless constructor of Vector3 does this. We set the diffuse component of the light to a white color, so it will light the surface normally. We set the first attenuation property, which governs how the light intensity changes over distance. The range of the light is the maximum distance the light has any effect. Our range far exceeds our needs in this case. You can see the DirectX SDK (included on the CD) for more information on the mathematics of lights.

Finally, we commit this light to the device, and enable it. If you look at the properties of a light, you will notice one of them is a Boolean value called "Deferred". By default, this value is false, and you are therefore required to call Commit on the light before it is ready to be used. Setting this value to true will eliminate the need to call Commit, but does so at a performance penalty. Always make sure your light is enabled and committed before expecting to see any results from it.

Well, if you've run your application once more, you'll notice that even though we've got our light defined in the scene now, the triangle is still black. If our light is on, yet we see no light, Direct3D must not be lighting our triangle, and in actuality, it isn't. Well, why not? Lighting

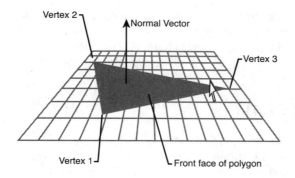

**FIGURE 1.5** Vertex normals.

calculations can only be done if each face in your geometry has a normal, which currently we don't have. What exactly is a normal, though? A *normal* is a perpendicular vector pointing away from the front side of a face; see Figure 1.5.

Knowing this, let's add a normal to our triangle so we can see the light in our scene. The easiest way to do this would be to change our vertex format type to something that includes a normal. There just so happens to be a structure built in for this as well. Change your triangle creation code to the following:

```
CustomVertex.PositionNormalColored[] verts=new CustomVertex.PositionNormalColored[3];
verts[0].SetPosition(new Vector3(0.0f, 1.0f, 1.0f));
verts[0].SetNormal(new Vector3(0.0f, 0.0f, -1.0f));
verts[0].Color = System.Drawing.Color.White.ToArgb();
verts[1].SetPosition(new Vector3(-1.0f, -1.0f, 1.0f));
verts[1].SetNormal(new Vector3(0.0f, 0.0f, -1.0f));
verts[1].Color = System.Drawing.Color. White.ToArgb();
verts[2].SetPosition(new Vector3(1.0f, -1.0f, 1.0f));
verts[2].SetNormal(new Vector3(0.0f, 0.0f, -1.0f));
verts[2].Color = System.Drawing.Color. White.ToArgb();
```

Plus we'll need to change the vertex format to accommodate our new data, so update the following as well:

```
device.VertexFormat = CustomVertex.PositionNormalColored.Format;
```

The only big change between this set of data and the last one is the addition of the normal and the fact that the color of each vertex is white. As you can see, we've defined a single normal vector for each vertex that points directly away from the front of the vertex. Since our vertices are all on the same z plane (1.0f), with varying coordinates on the x and y planes, the perpendicular vector would be facing the negative z axis alone. Running our application now, you will see our triangle is back, and appears lit. Try changing the color of the diffuse component to other values to see how the light affects the scene. Notice that if you set the color to red, the triangle appears red. Try playing with this member to see various ways the light changes.

One thing to remember is that the light is calculated per vertex, so with low polygon models (such as our single triangle), the lighting looks less than realistic. We will discuss more advanced lighting techniques, such as per pixel lighting, in later chapters. These lights produce a much more realistic scene.

# Device States and Transforms

Two items we've used in our sample code thus far that haven't been delved into are the various device states and transforms. There are three different state variables on the device: the render states, the sampler states, and the texture states. We've only used some of the render states thus far; the latter two are used for texturing. Don't worry; we'll get to texturing soon enough. The render state class can modify how Direct3D will do its rasterization of the scene. There are many different attributes that can be changed with this class, including lighting and culling, which we've used in our application already. Other options you can set with these render states include fill mode (such as wire frame mode) and various fog parameters. We will discuss more of these options in subsequent chapters.

As mentioned before, transformations are matrices used to convert geometry from one coordinate space to another. The three major transformations used on a device are the world, view, and projection transforms; however, there are a few other transforms that can be used. There are transforms that are used to modify texture stages, as well as up to 255 world matrices.

# Swapchains and RenderTargets

So what exactly is going on with the device that allows it to draw these triangles? Well, there are a few things implicit on a device that handle where and how items are drawn. Each device has an implicit swap chain, as well as a render target.

A swap chain is essentially a series of buffers used to control rendering. There is a back buffer, which is where any drawing on this swap chain occurs. When a swap chain that has been created with SwapEffect.Flip is presented, the back buffer data is "flipped" to the front buffer, which is where your graphics card will actually read the data. At the same time, a third buffer becomes the new back buffer, while the previous front buffer moves to the unused third buffer. See Figure 1.6 for details.

A true "flip" operation is implemented by changing the location of where the video card will read its data and swapping the old one with the current back buffer location. For DirectX 9, this term is used generically to indicate when a back buffer is being updated as the display. In windowed mode, these flip operations are actually a copy of the data, considering our device isn't controlling the entire display, but instead just a small portion of it. The end result is the same in either case, though. In full screen mode, using SwapEffect.Flip, the actual flip occurs; some drivers will also implement SwapEffect.Discard or SwapEffect.Copy with a flip operation in full screen mode.

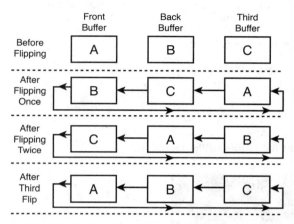

**FIGURE 1.6**    Back buffer chain during flips.

If you create a swap chain using SwapEffect.Copy or SwapEffect.Flip, it is guaranteed that any present call will not affect the back buffer of the swap chain. The runtime will enforce this by creating extra hidden buffers if necessary. It is recommended that you use SwapEffect.Discard to avoid this potential penalty. This mode allows the driver to determine the most efficient way to present the back buffer. It is worth noting that when using SwapEffect.Discard you will want to ensure that you clear the entire back buffer before starting new drawing operations. The runtime will fill the back buffer with random data in the debug runtime so developers can see if they forget to call clear.

The back buffer of a swap chain can also be used as a render target. Implicitly, when your device is created, there is a swap chain created, and the render target of the device is set to that swap chain's back buffer. A render target is simply a surface that will hold the output of the drawing operations that you perform. If you create multiple swap chains to handle different rendering operations, you will want to ensure that you update the render target of your device beforehand. We will discuss this more in later chapters.

> **USING MULTISAMPLING ON YOUR DEVICE**
>
> It is worth mentioning that if you plan on using anti-aliasing (or multisampling as it is called in Direct3D), you must use SwapEffect.Discard. Attempting to use any other option will fail.

# In Brief

We've covered the bare essentials for getting a triangle rendered, and then included code to make it spin around and get it lit inside our scene. In doing so, we've accomplished the following:

- Created a Direct3D device attached to our windows form

- Rendered a single colored triangle in our window

- Rotated our triangle around our scene

- Introduced a simple light to our scene

Compiling the code will show a window that looks much like Figure 1.7.

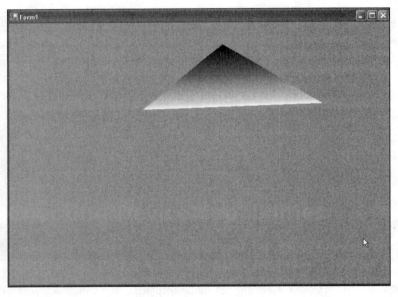

**FIGURE 1.7**   Spinning 3D triangle.

In our next chapter we'll look at how we can find out which options our device can support, and create our devices accordingly.

# Choosing the Correct Device

The number of possible permutations when creating a device is quite staggering. With all of the varying types of graphics cards available in the market today, knowing which features each of them support is simply not feasible. You will need to query the device itself to find out the features it supports. During this chapter, we will discuss

- Enumerating all of the adapters on a system.
- Enumerating supported formats for each device.
- Capabilities of the devices we are enumerating.

## Enumerating Your System's Adapters

Many systems today can support multiple monitors per machine. While it hasn't quite hit the "mainstream," having multiple monitors (*multimon* for short) can be quite useful, and is rapidly becoming more popular. With the higher-end graphics card supporting multimon natively, you can expect this feature to be used more exclusively. The latest cards from ATI, nVidia, and Matrox all have dual head support, which can allow multiple monitors to be attached to a single graphics card.

Direct3D devices are specified per adapter. In this case, you can think of an "adapter" as the actual graphics hardware that connects to the monitor. While the ATI Radeon 9700 is only one "physical" adapter, it has two monitor hookups (DVI and VGA), and thus has two adapters in Direct3D. You may not know which, or even how many, devices are on a system your game will be running on, so how can you detect them and pick the right one?

There is a static class in the Direct3D assemblies called "Manager" that can easily be used to enumerate adapters and device information, as well as retrieving the capabilities of the devices available on the system.

The very first property in the Manager class is the list of adapters in your system. This property can be used in multiple ways. It stores a "count" member that will tell you the total number of adapters on the system. Each adapter can be indexed directly (for example, Manager.Adapters[0]), and it can also be used to enumerate through each of the adapters on your system.

To demonstrate these features, a simple application will be written that will create a tree view of the current adapters on your system and the supported display modes that adapter can use. Load Visual Studio and follow these steps:

1. Create a new C# Windows Forms Project. You can name it anything you want; the sample code provided was named "Enumeration".

2. Add a reference to the Microsoft.DirectX.Direct3D and Microsoft.DirectX assemblies. Add using clauses for these assemblies as well.

3. In design view for the created windows form, add a TreeView control to your application. You will find the TreeView control in the toolbox.

4. Select the TreeView control on your form, and hit the F4 key (or right-click and choose Properties). In the properties of your TreeView, set the "Dock" parameter to "Fill". This will cause your TreeView to always fill up the entire window, even if it is resized.

Now, you should add a function that will scan through every adapter on the system, and provide a little information on the modes each one can support. The following function will do this work, so add it somewhere in your class:

```
/// <summary>
/// We will fill our tree view here
/// </summary>
public void LoadGraphics()
{
    foreach(AdapterInformation ai in Manager.Adapters)
    {
        TreeNode root = new TreeNode(ai.Information.Description);

        TreeNode driverInfo = new TreeNode(string.Format
            ("Driver information: {0} - {1}",
            ai.Information.DriverName,
            ai.Information.DriverVersion) );

        // Add the driver information to the root node
```

```
root.Nodes.Add(driverInfo);

// Get each display mode supported
TreeNode displayMode = new TreeNode(string.Format
    ("Current Display Mode: {0}x{1}x{2}",
    ai.CurrentDisplayMode.Width,
    ai.CurrentDisplayMode.Height,
    ai.CurrentDisplayMode.Format));

foreach(DisplayMode dm in ai.SupportedDisplayModes)
{
    TreeNode supportedNode = new TreeNode(string.Format
        ("Supported: {0}x{1}x{2}",
        dm.Width, dm.Height, dm.Format));

    displayMode.Nodes.Add(supportedNode);
}
// Add the display modes
root.Nodes.Add(displayMode);
// Add the root node
treeView1.Nodes.Add(root);
    }
}
```

While this may look like quite a bit of code, in reality what it's doing is quite simple. We can break it down to see exactly what's going on. First, we begin our enumeration of the adapters in the system. The foreach mechanism used in C# makes this loop amazingly simple. For each adapter in the system, this loop will run one time, and fill out the AdapterInformation structure for the given adapter.

Looking at the AdapterInformation structure itself, you will see that it has several members:

```
public struct AdapterInformation
{
int Adapter;
DisplayMode CurrentDisplayMode;
AdapterDetails Information;
AdapterDetails GetWhqlInformation();
DisplayModeEnumerator SupportedDisplayModes;
}
```

The adapter member refers to the adapter ordinal that you use when creating the device. The ordinal will be a zero-based index with the number of ordinals being equal to the number of adapters in your system. The two members of this structure that return AdapterDetails structures both return identical results, with one exception. In the "Information" member, Windows Hardware Quality Labs (WHQL) information isn't returned with the details, while it is in the GetWhqlInformation function. Retrieving this information can be quite expensive and take some time, thus the need to separate it out.

The AdapterDetails structure contains much information about the adapter itself, including its description and driver information. Applications can use this structure to make decisions based on certain hardware types, although this shouldn't ever be necessary.

The last two members of this structure return DisplayMode structures. These structures can be used to determine various types of display modes, and include the width and height of the display mode, as well as the refresh rate and the format being used. The CurrentDisplayMode member will return the information about the display mode currently in use on the adapter, while the SupportedDisplayModes will return a list of all of the display modes supported by this adapter.

So, we use the description of the device retrieved by the Information property to form our root node in our tree view. We then add a node that will contain the driver name and version number (also retrieved from the Information property) as a child of this root node. We also add a child containing the current display mode properties for the adapter.

We then add child nodes for every supported display mode for this adapter under the current display mode. Now, we just need to call this function during application startup, and we can run it. Modify the main function as follows:

```
using (Form1 frm = new Form1())
{
    frm.LoadGraphics();
    Application.Run(frm);
}
```

When running this application, you should see a window much like you see in Figure 2.1.

As you can see, this list contains a list of formats supported by the device. These formats can be used as a valid back buffer format when filling out your present parameter's structure. The format enumeration follows a pattern when naming the various formats supported. The pattern is a single letter followed by a number. The letter represents the type of data; the number is the number of bits of data being held. Some of the letters can be as follows:

- A—alpha
- X—unused
- R—red
- G—green

- B—blue
- L—luminance
- P—palette

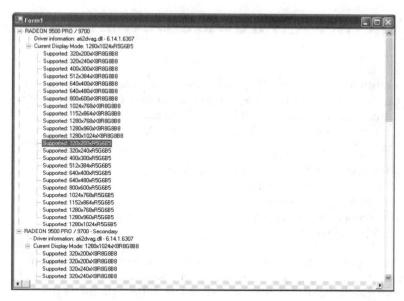

**FIGURE 2.1** A treeview of adapter modes.

The total sum of all the bits in the format determines the total size of the format. For example, a format that is X8R8G8B8 (as listed in Figure 2.1) would be a 32-bit format with 8 bits used in each red, green, and blue, with the remaining 8 bits unused.

So thus far, we've gathered enough information to get the adapter ordinal for the device we want to create, as well as the back buffer format we want to support. What about the other options in the device constructor? Well, luckily, the Manager class has all we need.

## VALID FORMATS FOR BACK BUFFERS AND DISPLAYS

While the list of formats is quite large, there are only a few that are valid and can be used as a back buffer or display format. The valid formats for a back buffer are

- A2R10G10B10
- A8R8G8B8
- X8R8G8B8
- A1R5G5B5
- X1R5G5B5
- R5G6B5

Display formats can be the same as the back buffer formats, with the exception of those that contain an alpha component. The only format that can be used for a display with alpha is A2R10G10B10, and even then that's only in full-screen mode.

Note that just because these formats are supported by Direct3D as valid back buffer formats, your adapter may not support them. In our sample, the only supported formats we received were X8R8G8B8 and R5G6B5.

# Determining Whether a Hardware Device Is Available

The manager class has a multitude of functions that can be used to determine the support your adapter has for a particular feature. For example, if you wanted to determine whether or not your device supported a particular format, and didn't want to enumerate all possible adapters and formats, you could use the manager class to make this determination. The following function can be used:

```
public static System.Boolean CheckDeviceType ( System.Int32 adapter ,
   Microsoft.DirectX.Direct3D.DeviceType checkType ,
   Microsoft.DirectX.Direct3D.Format displayFormat ,
   Microsoft.DirectX.Direct3D.Format backBufferFormat ,
   System.Boolean windowed , System.Int32 result )
```

This can be used to determine quickly whether your device supports the type of format you wish to use. The first parameter is the adapter ordinal you are checking against. The second is the type of device you are checking, but this will invariably be DeviceType.Hardware the majority of the time. Finally, you specify the back buffer and display formats, and whether or not you want to run in windowed or full screen mode. The final parameter is optional, and if used, will return the integer code (HRESULT in COM) of the function. The method will return true if this is a valid device type, and false otherwise.

This is quite useful if you know beforehand the only types of formats you will support. There isn't much of a need to enumerate through every possible permutation of device types and formats if you already know what you need.

## DETECTING FORMAT CONVERSION

It's important to note that in windowed mode, the back buffer format does not need to match the display mode format if the hardware can support the appropriate color conversion. While the CheckDeviceType method will return appropriate results regardless of whether or not this support is available, you can also use the CheckDeviceFormatConversion method off of the Manager class to detect this ability directly. Full-screen applications cannot do color conversion at all. You may also use Format.Unknown in windowed mode.

# Checking Device Capabilities

For every possible thing a device can do that may or may not be capable of happening purely in hardware, there is an item called a "capability," or "Cap" for short. There is a Caps structure in the Direct3D runtime that lists every possible capability a device can have. Once a device is created, you can use the "Caps" property of the device to determine the features it supports, but if you want to know the features the device can support before you've created it, then what? Naturally, there is a method in the Manager class that can help here as well.

Now to add a little code to our existing application that will get the capabilities of each adapter in our system. We can't add the list of capabilities to the current tree view because of the sheer number of capabilities included (there are hundreds of different capabilities that can be checked). The easiest way to show this data will be to use a text box.

Go ahead and go back to design view for our windows form, and switch the tree view's dock property from "Fill" to "Left". It's still the entire size of the window though, so cut the width value in half. Now, add a text box to the window, and set its dock member to "Fill". Also make sure "Multiline" is set to true and "Scrollbars" is set to "Both" for the text box.

Now you will want to add a hook to the application so that when one of the adapters is selected, it will update the text box with the capabilities of that adapter. You should hook the "AfterSelect" event from the tree view (I will assume you already know how to hook these events). Use the following code in the event handler function:

```
private void treeView1_AfterSelect(object sender,System.Windows.Forms.TreeViewEventArgs e)
{
    if (e.Node.Parent == null) // root node
    {
        // Get the device caps for this node
        textBox1.Text = e.Node.Text + " Capabilities: \r\n\r\n" + Manager.GetDeviceCaps
            (e.Node.Index, DeviceType.Hardware).ToString().Replace("\n", "\r\n");
    }
}
```

As you can see, this is relatively simple. For the root nodes (which happen to be our adapters), after they are selected we call the Manager.GetDeviceCaps function, passing in the adapter ordinal for the node (which happens to be the same as the index). The ToString member of this structure will return an extremely large list of all capabilities of this device. Running the application now will result in something like Figure 2.2.

Now, there are quite a few different capabilities that can be supported, as you can tell by the very large list that was generated. Anything that can be supported by a device is listed here. If you want to see if your device supports fogging, it's here. If you want to know the maximum simultaneous render targets, it's here as well. The Caps structure is broken down mainly into two groups of items. The first group is Boolean values that determine whether

**USING THE CAPS TO DETERMINE FIXED-FUNCTION FEATURES**

Many of the capabilities listed in the Caps structure pertain directly to the fixed function pipeline (for example, the MaxActiveLights member). If you are using the programmable pipeline, many of the capabilities will not apply to your scene. We will discuss the differences between the fixed function and programmable pipelines in later chapters.

a particular feature is supported; for example, the SupportsAlphaCompare member would be true if the device supports alpha compare. The other class of capabilities returns actual values, such as the MaxActiveLights member, which is naturally the maximum number of active lights you can have in a scene.

Throughout the book, we may discuss individual capabilities as we need them.

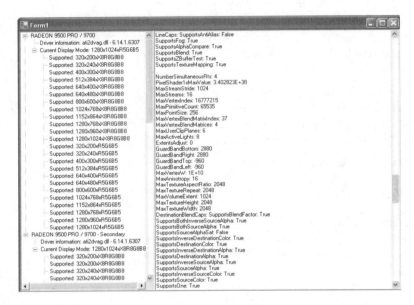

**FIGURE 2.2**   Device display mode and capabilities.

# In Brief

In this chapter, we learned how to pick the right graphics device for our applications. The items covered included

- Enumerating each adapter on your system

- Enumerating formats supported for your device

- Detecting the capabilities of the devices we are enumerating

In our next chapter we'll begin covering more efficient ways of rendering geometry, plus texturing for even more realistic scenes.

# Rendering Using Simple Techniques

The rendering done up to this point hasn't been done very efficiently. New lists of vertices were allocated every time the scene was rendered, and everything was stored in system memory. With modern graphics cards having an abundance of memory built into the card, you can get vast performance improvements by storing your vertex data in the video memory of the card. Having the vertex data stored in system memory requires copying the data from the system to the video card every time the scene will be rendered, and this copying of data can be quite time consuming. Removing the allocation from every frame could only help as well.

## Using Vertex Buffers

Direct3D has just the mechanism needed for this: vertex buffers. A vertex buffer, much like its name, is a memory store for vertices. The flexibility of vertex buffers makes them ideal for sharing transformed geometry in your scene. So how can the simple triangle application from Chapter 1, "Introducing Direct3D," be modified to use vertex buffers?

Creating a vertex buffer is quite simple. There are three constructors that can be used to do so; we will look at each one.

```
public VertexBuffer ( Microsoft.DirectX.Direct3D.Device device , System.Int32
    sizeOfBufferInBytes , Microsoft.DirectX.Direct3D.Usage usage ,
    Microsoft.DirectX.Direct3D.VertexFormats vertexFormat ,
    Microsoft.DirectX.Direct3D.Pool pool )

public VertexBuffer ( System.Type typeVertexType , System.Int32 numVerts ,
    Microsoft.DirectX.Direct3D.Device device ,
    Microsoft.DirectX.Direct3D.Usage usage ,
    Microsoft.DirectX.Direct3D.VertexFormats vertexFormat ,
    Microsoft.DirectX.Direct3D.Pool pool )
```

The various parameter values can be

- device—The Direct3D device you are using to create this vertex buffer. The vertex buffer will only be valid on this device.

- sizeOfBufferInBytes—The size you want the vertex buffer to be, in bytes. If you are using the constructor with this parameter, the buffer will be able to hold any type of vertex.

- typeVertexType—If you want your vertex buffer to only contain one type of vertex, you can specify that type here. This can be the type of one of the built-in vertex structures in the CustomVertex class, or it can be a user defined vertex type. This value cannot be null.

- numVerts—When specifying the type of vertex you want to store in your buffer, you must also specify the maximum number of vertices the buffer will store of that type. This value must be greater than zero.

- usage—Defines how this vertex buffer can be used. Not all members of the Usage type can be used when creating a vertex buffer. The following values are valid:

  - DoNotClip—Used to indicate that this vertex buffer will never require clipping. You must set the clipping render state to false when rendering from a vertex buffer using this flag.

  - Dynamic—Used to indicate that this vertex buffer requires dynamic memory use. If this flag isn't specified, the vertex buffer is static. Static vertex buffers are normally stored in video memory, while dynamic buffers are stored in AGP memory, so choosing this option is useful for drivers to determine where to store the memory. See the DirectX SDK documentation for more information on Dynamic usage.

  - Npatches—Used to indicate that this vertex buffer will be used to draw N-Patches.

  - Points—Used to indicate that this vertex buffer will be used to draw points.

- RTPatches—Used to indicate that this vertex buffer will be used to draw high order primitives.

- SoftwareProcessing—Used to indicate that vertex processing should happen in software. Otherwise, vertex processing should happen in hardware.

- WriteOnly—Used to indicate that this vertex buffer will never be read from. Unless you have a very good reason for needing to read vertex buffer data, you should always select this option. Data stored in video memory that does not include this option suffers a severe performance penalty.

- vertexFormat—Defines the format of the vertices that will be stored in this buffer. You can choose VertexFormat.None if you plan on having this be a generic buffer.

- pool—Defines the memory pool where you want the vertex buffer to be located. You must specify one of the following memory pool locations:

  - Default—The vertex buffer is placed in the memory pool most appropriate for the data it contains. This is normally in either video memory or AGP memory, depending on the usage parameter. Vertex buffers created in this memory pool will be automatically disposed before a device reset.

  - Managed—The vertex buffer's data is automatically copied to device accessible memory as needed. The data is also backed by a system memory buffer, and can always be locked.

  - SystemMemory—The vertex buffer's data is placed in system memory, where it is not accessible from the device.

  - Scratch—A system memory pool that is not bound by a device, and thus cannot be used by the device. It is useful for manipulating data without being bound to a particular device format.

In looking at the colored triangle application from Chapter 1, it should be relatively easy to move the triangle data into a vertex buffer. First, declare the vertex buffer member variable directly after our device:

```
private Device device = null;
private VertexBuffer vb = null;
```

Instead of creating the data every time the scene will be rendered, you will get greater

## CREATING VERTEX BUFFERS FROM UNMANAGED COM POINTERS

Much like the device, there is an overload for our vertex buffer that takes an IntPtr. This value is used to pass in the actual COM interface pointer for the unmanaged IDirect3DVertexBuffer9 interface. This is useful when you want to use a vertex buffer created from an external (unmanaged) source. Any fully managed application will never use this constructor, and this value cannot be null.

performance by doing this only once. You can do this immediately after the device has been created, so move the triangle creation code there:

```
// Create our device
device = new Device(0, DeviceType.Hardware, this, CreateFlags.SoftwareVertexProcessing
    , presentParams);

CustomVertex.PositionColored[] verts = new CustomVertex.PositionColored[3];
verts[0].SetPosition(new Vector3(0.0f, 1.0f, 1.0f));
verts[0].Color = System.Drawing.Color.Aqua.ToArgb();
verts[1].SetPosition(new Vector3(-1.0f, -1.0f, 1.0f));
verts[1].Color = System.Drawing.Color.Black.ToArgb();
verts[2].SetPosition(new Vector3(1.0f, -1.0f, 1.0f));
verts[2].Color = System.Drawing.Color.Purple.ToArgb();
vb = new VertexBuffer(typeof(CustomVertex.PositionColored), 3, device, Usage.Dynamic |
        Usage.WriteOnly, CustomVertex.PositionColored.Format, Pool.Default);
vb.SetData(verts, 0, LockFlags.None);
```

The only changes here are the two new lines after our triangle creation code. We first create a vertex buffer holding three members of the vertex structure type we've already declared. We want the buffer to be write-only, dynamic, and stored in the default memory pool for best performance. We then need to actually put our triangle list into our vertex buffer, and we accomplish this easily with the SetData method. This method accepts any generic object (much like DrawUserPrimitives) as its first member. The second member is the offset where we want to place our data, and since we want to fill in all of the data, we will use zero here. The last parameter is how we want the buffer locked while we are writing our data. We will discuss the various locking mechanisms shortly; for now, we don't care about how it's locked.

Compiling the application now will naturally give you a compile error since the DrawUserPrimitives call in OnPaint requires the "verts" variable. We need a way to tell Direct3D that we want to draw from our vertex buffer rather than the array we had declared before.

Naturally, this method does exist. We can call the SetStreamSource method from the device to have Direct3D read our vertex buffer when drawing our primitives. The prototypes for the two overloads of this function are

```
public void SetStreamSource ( System.Int32 streamNumber ,
    Microsoft.DirectX.Direct3D.VertexBuffer streamData ,
    System.Int32 offsetInBytes , System.Int32 stride )

public void SetStreamSource ( System.Int32 streamNumber ,
    Microsoft.DirectX.Direct3D.VertexBuffer streamData ,
    System.Int32 offsetInBytes )
```

The only difference between the two overloads is that one contains an extra member for the stride size of the stream. The first parameter is the stream number we will be using for this data. For now, we will always use zero as this parameter; however, we will discuss multiple streams in a later chapter. The second parameter is the vertex buffer that holds the data we want to use as our source. The third parameter is the offset (in bytes) into the vertex buffer that we want to be the beginning of the data Direct3D will draw from. The stride size parameter (which is only in one overload) is the size of each vertex in the buffer. If you've created your vertex buffer with a type, using the overload with this parameter isn't necessary.

Now replace the drawing call with the following code:

```
device.SetStreamSource(0, vb, 0);
device.DrawPrimitives(PrimitiveType.TriangleList, 0, 1);
```

As just described, we set stream zero to our vertex buffer, and since we want to use all of the data, we have our offset as zero as well. Notice that we've also changed the actual drawing call. Since we have all of our data in a vertex buffer, we no longer need to call the DrawUserPrimitives method because that function is only designed to draw user-defined data passed directly into the method. The more generic DrawPrimitives function will draw our primitives from our stream source. The DrawPrimitives method has three parameters, the first being the primitive type we've already discussed. The second parameter is the starting vertex in the stream. The last parameter is the number of primitives we will be drawing.

Even this simple demonstration of drawing a triangle with a vertex buffer shows approximately a 10% increase in performance based on frame rate. We will get into measuring performance and frame rates in later chapters. However, there is still a problem with this application that makes itself readily apparent when you attempt to resize your window. The triangle simply disappears as soon as your window is resized.

There are a few things going on here that are causing this behavior, and two of them have been mentioned briefly already. Remembering back to the previous chapter, we know that when our window is resized, our device is automatically reset. However, when a resource is created in the default memory pool (such as our vertex buffer), it is automatically disposed when the device is reset. So while our window is being resized, our device is being reset, and our vertex buffer disposed. One of the nifty features of Managed DirectX is that it will automatically re-create your vertex buffer for you after the device has been reset. However, there will be no data in the buffer, so the next time it's time to draw, nothing is shown.

The vertex buffer has an event we can capture, "created", that will inform us when it has been re-created and is ready to be filled with data. We should update our application to capture this event, and use that to fill our buffer with data. Add the following function to the application:

```
private void OnVertexBufferCreate(object sender, EventArgs e)
{
    VertexBuffer buffer = (VertexBuffer)sender;

    CustomVertex.PositionColored[] verts = new CustomVertex.PositionColored[3];
    verts[0].SetPosition(new Vector3(0.0f, 1.0f, 1.0f));
    verts[0].Color = System.Drawing.Color.Aqua.ToArgb();
    verts[1].SetPosition(new Vector3(-1.0f, -1.0f, 1.0f));
    verts[1].Color = System.Drawing.Color.Black.ToArgb();
    verts[2].SetPosition(new Vector3(1.0f, -1.0f, 1.0f));
    verts[2].Color = System.Drawing.Color.Purple.ToArgb();

    buffer.SetData(verts, 0, LockFlags.None);
}
```

This function has the standard event handler signature, taking in an object that is the item firing this event, plus the generic argument list. This event will never have an argument list, so you can safely ignore this member. We first get the vertex buffer that is firing this event by casting the sender member back to a vertex buffer. We then follow the exact same path we took last time by creating our data and calling SetData. We should replace the triangle creation code from our InitializeGraphics function now, and use the following two lines instead:

```
vb.Created += new EventHandler(this.OnVertexBufferCreate);
OnVertexBufferCreate(vb, null);
```

This code hooks the created event from the vertex buffer, and ensures that our OnVertexBufferCreate method is called whenever our vertex buffer has been created. Since the event hasn't been hooked up when the object is first created, we need to manually call our event handler function for the first time. Now run the application once more and try resizing the window.

## UNDERSTANDING RESOURCE LIFETIMES

All graphics resources will automatically be disposed if they are stored in video memory during a device reset; however, only vertex and index buffers will be re-created for you after the reset. Also note that all resources are also disposed when the device itself is disposed.

You've now successfully updated the simple triangle application from an inefficient one to a much more efficient one using video memory and vertex buffers. However, it still seems quite boring, a single triangle spinning around. Now, you can try to make something even more exciting. A common first thing to try would be to render a box, so it's time to do that. The code will get slightly more complicated now, but all the basic principles will still apply.

All geometry in a 3D scene is composed of triangles, so how would you render a box or cube? Well, to make a square you can use two triangles, and a box is composed of six squares. The only coordinates we really need are the eight corner vertices of the box, and we can create a box from those. Let's change our geometry creation code like in Listing 3.1:

**LISTING 3.1**    Creating a Cube

```
CustomVertex.PositionColored[] verts = new CustomVertex.PositionColored[36];

// Front face
verts[0] = new CustomVertex.PositionColored(-1.0f, 1.0f, 1.0f, Color.Red.ToArgb());
verts[1] = new CustomVertex.PositionColored(-1.0f, -1.0f, 1.0f, Color.Red.ToArgb());
verts[2] = new CustomVertex.PositionColored(1.0f, 1.0f, 1.0f, Color.Red.ToArgb());
verts[3] = new CustomVertex.PositionColored(-1.0f, -1.0f, 1.0f, Color.Red.ToArgb());
verts[4] = new CustomVertex.PositionColored(1.0f, -1.0f, 1.0f, Color.Red.ToArgb());
verts[5] = new CustomVertex.PositionColored(1.0f, 1.0f, 1.0f, Color.Red.ToArgb());

// Back face (remember this is facing *away* from the camera, so vertices should be
//    clockwise order)
verts[6] = new CustomVertex.PositionColored(-1.0f, 1.0f, -1.0f, Color.Blue.ToArgb());
verts[7] = new CustomVertex.PositionColored(1.0f, 1.0f, -1.0f, Color.Blue.ToArgb());
verts[8] = new CustomVertex.PositionColored(-1.0f, -1.0f, -1.0f, Color.Blue.ToArgb());
verts[9] = new CustomVertex.PositionColored(-1.0f, -1.0f, -1.0f, Color.Blue.ToArgb());
verts[10] = new CustomVertex.PositionColored(1.0f, 1.0f, -1.0f, Color.Blue.ToArgb());
verts[11] = new CustomVertex.PositionColored(1.0f, -1.0f, -1.0f, Color.Blue.ToArgb());

// Top face
verts[12] = new CustomVertex.PositionColored(-1.0f, 1.0f, 1.0f, Color.Yellow.ToArgb());
verts[13] = new CustomVertex.PositionColored(1.0f, 1.0f, -1.0f, Color.Yellow.ToArgb());
verts[14] = new CustomVertex.PositionColored(-1.0f, 1.0f, -1.0f, Color.Yellow.ToArgb());
verts[15] = new CustomVertex.PositionColored(-1.0f, 1.0f, 1.0f, Color.Yellow.ToArgb());
verts[16] = new CustomVertex.PositionColored(1.0f, 1.0f, 1.0f, Color.Yellow.ToArgb());
verts[17] = new CustomVertex.PositionColored(1.0f, 1.0f, -1.0f, Color.Yellow.ToArgb());

// Bottom face (remember this is facing *away* from the camera, so vertices should be
//    clockwise order)
verts[18] = new CustomVertex.PositionColored(-1.0f, -1.0f, 1.0f, Color.Black.ToArgb());
verts[19] = new CustomVertex.PositionColored(-1.0f, -1.0f, -1.0f, Color.Black.ToArgb());
verts[20] = new CustomVertex.PositionColored(1.0f, -1.0f, -1.0f, Color.Black.ToArgb());
verts[21] = new CustomVertex.PositionColored(-1.0f, -1.0f, 1.0f, Color.Black.ToArgb());
verts[22] = new CustomVertex.PositionColored(1.0f, -1.0f, -1.0f, Color.Black.ToArgb());
verts[23] = new CustomVertex.PositionColored(1.0f, -1.0f, 1.0f, Color.Black.ToArgb());
```

**LISTING 3.1** Continued

```
// Left face
verts[24] = new CustomVertex.PositionColored(-1.0f, 1.0f, 1.0f, Color.Gray.ToArgb());
verts[25] = new CustomVertex.PositionColored(-1.0f, -1.0f, -1.0f, Color.Gray.ToArgb());
verts[26] = new CustomVertex.PositionColored(-1.0f, -1.0f, 1.0f, Color.Gray.ToArgb());
verts[27] = new CustomVertex.PositionColored(-1.0f, 1.0f, -1.0f, Color.Gray.ToArgb());
verts[28] = new CustomVertex.PositionColored(-1.0f, -1.0f, -1.0f, Color.Gray.ToArgb());
verts[29] = new CustomVertex.PositionColored(-1.0f, 1.0f, 1.0f, Color.Gray.ToArgb());

// Right face (remember this is facing *away* from the camera, so vertices should be
   clockwise order)
verts[30] = new CustomVertex.PositionColored(1.0f, 1.0f, 1.0f, Color.Green.ToArgb());
verts[31] = new CustomVertex.PositionColored(1.0f, -1.0f, 1.0f, Color.Green.ToArgb());
verts[32] = new CustomVertex.PositionColored(1.0f, -1.0f, -1.0f, Color.Green.ToArgb());
verts[33] = new CustomVertex.PositionColored(1.0f, 1.0f, -1.0f, Color.Green.ToArgb());
verts[34] = new CustomVertex.PositionColored(1.0f, 1.0f, 1.0f, Color.Green.ToArgb());
verts[35] = new CustomVertex.PositionColored(1.0f, -1.0f, -1.0f, Color.Green.ToArgb());

buffer.SetData(verts, 0, LockFlags.None);
```

Now that is a lot of vertices to have to type in: 36 to be exact, but don't worry. You can load the source code located on the included CD. As mentioned already, the box will be made of 12 triangles, and each triangle has 3 vertices, which gives the vertex list. Running the code just as it is will throw an exception during the SetData call. Can you guess why? If you guessed that we never updated the original size of our vertex buffer, you were correct. There are a couple extra changes we want to make before we're ready to really run this. Update the lines represented as follows:

```
vb = new VertexBuffer(typeof(CustomVertex.PositionColored), 36, device, Usage.Dynamic
    | Usage.WriteOnly, CustomVertex.PositionColored.Format, Pool.Default);

device.Transform.World = Matrix.RotationYawPitchRoll(angle / (float)Math.PI, angle /
    (float)Math.PI * 2.0f, angle / (float)Math.PI);

device.DrawPrimitives(PrimitiveType.TriangleList, 0, 12);
```

The major thing we're doing is changing the size of the vertex buffer we've created to hold all the data we want to render. We've also changed the rotation somewhat to make the box spin a little crazier. Finally, we actually change our rendering call to render all 12 primitives, rather than the single triangle we had before. Actually, since our box is a fully formed 3D object that is completely filled, we no longer need to see the back-facing triangles. We can use the default culling mode in Direct3D (counterclockwise). Go ahead and remove the cull mode line from your source. You can try running the example now.

Terrific, we've now got a colorful box spinning around our screen. Each face of the box is a different color, and we can see each face of the box as it rotates without turning our back face culling off. If you wanted to render more than one box in a scene, hopefully you wouldn't create a series of vertex buffers, one for each box. There's a much easier way to do this.

We will draw a total of three boxes now, each side by side. Since our current camera settings have our first box taking up pretty much the entire scene, we should move our camera back a little first. Change the look at function as follows:

```
device.Transform.View = Matrix.LookAtLH(new Vector3(0,0, 18.0f), new Vector3(),
    new Vector3(0,1,0));
```

As you can see, we just moved the position of our camera back so we can see more of the scene. Running the application now will show you the same box spinning around; it will just appear smaller, since the camera is farther away now. In order to draw two more boxes on the sides of this one, we can reuse our existing vertex buffer, and just tell Direct3D to draw the same vertices again. Add the following lines of code after the call to DrawPrimitives:

```
device.Transform.World = Matrix.RotationYawPitchRoll(angle / (float)Math.PI, angle /
    (float)Math.PI / 2.0f, angle / (float)Math.PI * 4.0f) *
    Matrix.Translation(5.0f, 0.0f, 0.0f);
device.DrawPrimitives(PrimitiveType.TriangleList, 0, 12);

device.Transform.World = Matrix.RotationYawPitchRoll(angle / (float)Math.PI, angle /
    (float)Math.PI * 4.0f, angle / (float)Math.PI / 2.0f) *
    Matrix.Translation(-5.0f, 0.0f, 0.0f);
device.DrawPrimitives(PrimitiveType.TriangleList, 0, 12);
```

So, what exactly are we doing here? Direct3D already knows what type of vertices we are planning on drawing, due to the VertexFormat property we set to draw our first box. It also knows what vertex buffer to retrieve the data from due to the SetStreamSource function also used on the first box. So what does Direct3D need to know in order to draw a second (and third) box? The only information that is needed is where and what to draw.

Setting the world transform will "move" our data from object space into world space, so what are we using as our transformation matrix? First, we rotate much like we did in the SetupCamera function; although we use a slightly different rotation function, that's just so the boxes rotate at different angles. The second half of the world transform is new, though. We multiply a Matrix.Translation to our existing rotation matrix. A translation matrix provides a way to move vertices from one point to another in world space. Looking at our translation points, we want to move the second box five units to the right, while we are moving the third box five units to the left.

You will also notice that we multiply our two transformation matrices, which provides us with a cumulative transformation of the arguments. They are done in the order they are specified, so in this case, our vertices will be rotated first, then translated (moved) second. Translating and then rotating would provide very different results. It is important to remember the order of operations when you are transforming vertices.

The code included with the CD shows updated code that draws a total of nine boxes rather than the three shown here. See Figure 3.1.

**FIGURE 3.1**   Colored cubes.

# Texturing Our Objects

While rendering with colors and lights is quite exciting, objects don't look realistic enough if this is all we are using. The term "texture" when describing non-3D applications is usually in reference to the roughness of an object. Textures in a 3D scene are essentially flat 2D bitmaps that can be used to simulate a texture on a primitive. You might want to take a bitmap of grass to make a nice looking hill, or perhaps clouds to make a sky. Direct3D can render up to eight textures at a time for each primitive, but for now, let's just deal with a single texture per primitive.

Since Direct3D uses a generic bitmap as its texture format, any bitmap you load can be used to texture an object. How is the flat 2D bitmap converted into something that is drawn onto a 3D object, though? Each object that will be rendered in a scene requires texture coordinates, which are used to map each texel to a corresponding pixel on screen during rasterization. *Texel* is an abbreviation for texture element, or the corresponding color value for each address in a texture. The address can be thought of much like a row and column number, which are called "U" and "V" respectively. Normally, these values are scalar; that is the valid ranges for them go from 0.0 to 1.0. 0, 0 is located at the upper left corner of the texture, while 1, 1 would be located at the bottom right corner of the texture. The center of the texture would be located at 0.5, 0.5. See Figure 3.2.

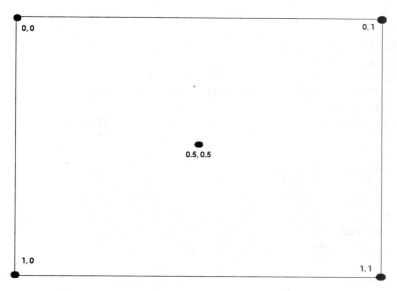

**FIGURE 3.2**  Visualizing texture coordinates.

In order to render our boxes with a texture, we must change the vertex format we are using to render our box, as well as the data we are passing down to the graphics card. We will replace the "color" component of our vertex data with texture coordinate data. While it's perfectly valid to have our object both colored and textured, for this exercise, we will simply use the texture to define the color of each primitive. Modify your vertex creation code as in Listing 3.2:

**LISTING 3.2** Textured Box Data

```
CustomVertex.PositionTextured[] verts = new CustomVertex.PositionTextured[36];

// Front face
verts[0] = new CustomVertex.PositionTextured(-1.0f, 1.0f, 1.0f, 0.0f, 0.0f);
verts[1] = new CustomVertex.PositionTextured(-1.0f, -1.0f, 1.0f, 0.0f, 1.0f);
verts[2] = new CustomVertex.PositionTextured(1.0f, 1.0f, 1.0f, 1.0f, 0.0f);
verts[3] = new CustomVertex.PositionTextured(-1.0f, -1.0f, 1.0f, 0.0f, 1.0f);
verts[4] = new CustomVertex.PositionTextured(1.0f, -1.0f, 1.0f, 1.0f, 1.0f);
verts[5] = new CustomVertex.PositionTextured(1.0f, 1.0f, 1.0f, 1.0f, 0.0f);

// Back face (remember this is facing *away* from the camera, so vertices should be
    clockwise order)
verts[6] = new CustomVertex.PositionTextured(-1.0f, 1.0f, -1.0f, 0.0f, 0.0f);
verts[7] = new CustomVertex.PositionTextured(1.0f, 1.0f, -1.0f, 1.0f, 0.0f);
verts[8] = new CustomVertex.PositionTextured(-1.0f, -1.0f, -1.0f, 0.0f, 1.0f);
verts[9] = new CustomVertex.PositionTextured(-1.0f, -1.0f, -1.0f, 0.0f, 1.0f);
verts[10] = new CustomVertex.PositionTextured(1.0f, 1.0f, -1.0f, 1.0f, 0.0f);
verts[11] = new CustomVertex.PositionTextured(1.0f, -1.0f, -1.0f, 1.0f, 1.0f);

// Top face
verts[12] = new CustomVertex.PositionTextured(-1.0f, 1.0f, 1.0f, 0.0f, 0.0f);
verts[13] = new CustomVertex.PositionTextured(1.0f, 1.0f, -1.0f, 1.0f, 1.0f);
verts[14] = new CustomVertex.PositionTextured(-1.0f, 1.0f, -1.0f, 0.0f, 1.0f);
verts[15] = new CustomVertex.PositionTextured(-1.0f, 1.0f, 1.0f, 0.0f, 0.0f);
verts[16] = new CustomVertex.PositionTextured(1.0f, 1.0f, 1.0f, 1.0f, 0.0f);
verts[17] = new CustomVertex.PositionTextured(1.0f, 1.0f, -1.0f, 1.0f, 1.0f);

// Bottom face (remember this is facing *away* from the camera, so vertices should be
    clockwise order)
verts[18] = new CustomVertex.PositionTextured(-1.0f, -1.0f, 1.0f, 0.0f, 0.0f);
verts[19] = new CustomVertex.PositionTextured(-1.0f, -1.0f, -1.0f, 0.0f, 1.0f);
verts[20] = new CustomVertex.PositionTextured(1.0f, -1.0f, -1.0f, 1.0f, 1.0f);
verts[21] = new CustomVertex.PositionTextured(-1.0f, -1.0f, 1.0f, 0.0f, 0.0f);
verts[22] = new CustomVertex.PositionTextured(1.0f, -1.0f, -1.0f, 1.0f, 1.0f);
verts[23] = new CustomVertex.PositionTextured(1.0f, -1.0f, 1.0f, 1.0f, 0.0f);

// Left face
verts[24] = new CustomVertex.PositionTextured(-1.0f, 1.0f, 1.0f, 0.0f, 0.0f);
verts[25] = new CustomVertex.PositionTextured(-1.0f, -1.0f, -1.0f, 1.0f, 1.0f);
verts[26] = new CustomVertex.PositionTextured(-1.0f, -1.0f, -1.0f, 1.0f, 0.0f);
verts[27] = new CustomVertex.PositionTextured(-1.0f, 1.0f, -1.0f, 0.0f, 1.0f);
```

**LISTING 3.2** Continued

```
verts[28] = new CustomVertex.PositionTextured(-1.0f, -1.0f, -1.0f, 1.0f, 1.0f);
verts[29] = new CustomVertex.PositionTextured(-1.0f, 1.0f, 1.0f, 0.0f, 0.0f);

// Right face (remember this is facing *away* from the camera, so vertices should be
    clockwise order)
verts[30] = new CustomVertex.PositionTextured(1.0f, 1.0f, 1.0f, 0.0f, 0.0f);
verts[31] = new CustomVertex.PositionTextured(1.0f, -1.0f, 1.0f, 1.0f, 0.0f);
verts[32] = new CustomVertex.PositionTextured(1.0f, -1.0f, -1.0f, 1.0f, 1.0f);
verts[33] = new CustomVertex.PositionTextured(1.0f, 1.0f, -1.0f, 0.0f, 1.0f);
verts[34] = new CustomVertex.PositionTextured(1.0f, 1.0f, 1.0f, 0.0f, 0.0f);
verts[35] = new CustomVertex.PositionTextured(1.0f, -1.0f, -1.0f, 1.0f, 1.0f);

buffer.SetData(verts, 0, LockFlags.None);
```

Obviously, the biggest change here is the data type being used to store the vertex list. The last two float values stored in each vertex are the u and v coordinates in a texture that will be used to render the primitive. Since each face of the box is a square, and the textures will be square as well, it makes good sense to map each square directly to the texture. You will notice that the vertex in the "upper left" corner of the primitive maps directly to 0, 0, the corresponding texel in the texture; just as the "bottom right" vertex maps directly to the 1, 1 texel. By doing this, each face of the square will hold the entire texture.

The application isn't quite ready for prime time yet. Running it as it is will end up throwing an exception because our vertex buffer was created for a different type of data. Modify the vertex buffer creation like the following:

```
vb = new VertexBuffer(typeof(CustomVertex.PositionTextured), 36, device, Usage.Dynamic
    ¦ Usage.WriteOnly, CustomVertex.PositionTextured.Format, Pool.Default);
```

I'm sure you guessed that would be the change needed. Let's make it a little easier to draw our boxes, though; all the lines of code there are just duplicated. Let's add a function to do the drawing for us:

```
private void DrawBox(float yaw, float pitch, float roll, float x, float y, float z,
        Texture t)
{
    angle += 0.01f;

    device.Transform.World = Matrix.RotationYawPitchRoll(yaw, pitch, roll) *
        Matrix.Translation(x, y, z);
    device.SetTexture(0, t);
    device.DrawPrimitives(PrimitiveType.TriangleList, 0, 12);
}
```

The first six parameters of this function are the same as we have been using to begin with. We pass in the yaw, pitch, and roll for our box rotation, plus the x, y, and z for our box translation. The last parameter is a new one, though; it will represent the texture we use when rendering this box. We will also call the SetTexture method on the device to tell Direct3D which texture we want to use when rendering this primitive. The first parameter of this method is the texture stage we are setting this texture on. You might remember a short while ago when I mentioned that you could render up to eight textures for a primitive; this first parameter is the index to those textures. Since we only have one set of texture coordinates, we will always use the first index, 0. Also notice that, since we are modifying our "angle" member variable and the world transform, you can remove those lines from the SetupCamera method.

Before we change our rendering code to call our new function, we first need to define some textures we will be using. The demo code on the CD includes three textures in the source project attached as resources. They are puck.bmp, ground.bmp, and banana.bmp. In the project menu, click Add Existing Item and add the three images to your project. Once each image has been added, you will need to view the properties of each, and change the "Build Action" item to "Embedded Resource". Since we will be using three textures, add three texture member variables to the application. Add the following below the declaration for our vertex buffer:

```
private Texture tex = null;
private Texture tex1 = null;
private Texture tex2 = null;
```

These will be the three textures we use for drawing our box. However, we still need to actually set these up to use the three bitmaps we have as embedded resources. Add the following code directly after your vertex buffer creation and data-filling code:

```
tex = new Texture(device, new Bitmap(this.GetType(), "puck.bmp"), 0, Pool.Managed);
tex1 = new Texture(device, new Bitmap(this.GetType(), "banana.bmp"), 0, Pool.Managed);
tex2 = new Texture(device, new Bitmap(this.GetType(), "ground.bmp"), 0, Pool.Managed);
```

This constructor for our texture takes four parameters. The first is the device we will be using to render this texture. All resources (textures, vertex buffers, and so on) in a scene will be associated with a device. The next parameter is the System.Drawing.Bitmap we will be using to get the data for this texture. In this case, we use the bitmap constructor to load our file from the resources. The third parameter here is the usage parameter, which we discussed briefly when speaking about vertex buffers. For now, we will use zero, since we're not that interested in the usage. The last parameter is the memory pool to store the texture in. For convenience, we will use the managed pool for now. The other constructors available for textures are

```
public Texture ( System.IntPtr lp , Microsoft.DirectX.Direct3D.Device device ,
    Microsoft.DirectX.Direct3D.Pool pool )

public Texture ( Microsoft.DirectX.Direct3D.Device device , System.Int32 width ,
    System.Int32 height , System.Int32 numLevels ,
    Microsoft.DirectX.Direct3D.Usage usage ,
    Microsoft.DirectX.Direct3D.Format format ,
    Microsoft.DirectX.Direct3D.Pool pool )

public Texture ( Microsoft.DirectX.Direct3D.Device device , System.IO.Stream data ,
    Microsoft.DirectX.Direct3D.Usage usage , Microsoft.DirectX.Direct3D.Pool pool )
```

The first constructor takes an IntPtr argument that is the unmanaged COM interface pointer for IDirect3DTexture9. This is used for interoperability with unmanaged code. The next constructor allows you to create a "blank" texture from scratch, specifying the height, width, and number of levels of detail, rather than reading these values from the file. The last constructor is very similar to the one we've used in our application, just using a stream rather than a bitmap object. This stream must be able to be loaded into a System.Drawing.Bitmap object for this constructor to work. There are other interesting functions for texture loading in the TextureLoader class, which we will get to in subsequent chapters.

Now that we've got our three textures defined and loaded with the bitmaps stored in our resources, let's update our drawing code to show our boxes with the textures. We can get rid of all the drawing code for our rendering function, and replace it with the following:

```
// Draw our boxes
DrawBox(angle / (float)Math.PI, angle / (float)Math.PI * 2.0f, angle / (float)Math.PI /
    4.0f, 0.0f, 0.0f, 0.0f, tex);
DrawBox(angle / (float)Math.PI, angle / (float)Math.PI / 2.0f, angle / (float)Math.PI *
    4.0f, 5.0f, 0.0f, 0.0f, tex1);
DrawBox(angle / (float)Math.PI, angle / (float)Math.PI * 4.0f, angle / (float)Math.PI /
    2.0f, -5.0f, 0.0f, 0.0f, tex2);
```

This should render each of the three boxes we already had, although now instead of each face being colored with a different color, each box should be textured. The sample code included on the CD will render a total of nine boxes. See Figure 3.3.

**FIGURE 3.3** Textured cubes.

# In Brief

In this chapter, our applications started using much more efficient rendering techniques, for example

- Using vertex buffers to store our vertex data, and drawing multiple primitives from the same buffer

- Creating textures for more realistic objects

- Including data in our vertex buffer to tell Direct3D where to render the texture on the primitives

In the next chapter we will begin discussing more advanced rendering techniques, including using index buffers, using other primitive types, and using depth buffers.

# More Rendering Techniques

Now that we have the basic rendering concepts down, we can focus more on rendering techniques that can help improve performance and make our scenes look even better. This chapter will focus on rendering techniques such as

- Using primitive types other than a list of triangles

- Using index buffers for more controlled rendering

- Using depth buffers for more realistic rendering

## Rendering Other Primitive Types

All of the code we've written thus far concentrated on drawing a single type of primitive, namely a list of triangles. However, there are actually numerous different primitive types we can draw. The following list describes these primitive types:

- PointList—This is a self-describing primitive type, as it will render the data as a list of points. You cannot use this primitive type if you are drawing indexed primitives (which we'll cover later in this chapter). See Figure 4.1.

- LineList—Renders each pair of vertices as individual lines. You must pass in an even number of vertices (at least two) when using this primitive type. See Figure 4.2.

- LineStrip—Renders the vertices as a single polyline. After the first line segment is drawn using the first two vertices, each subsequent line segment is drawn using the previous line's endpoint as its start point. You must pass in at least two vertices for this primitive type. See Figure 4.3.

- TriangleList—The primitive type we've been using thus far. Renders each set of three vertices as a single isolated triangle. Back face culling is determined by the current cull render state. See Figure 4.4.

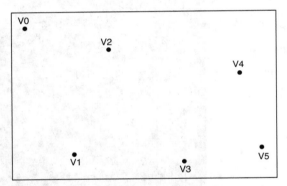

**FIGURE 4.1**    Point lists.

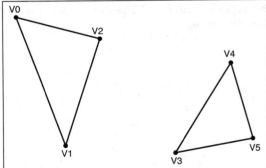

**FIGURE 4.2**    Line lists.

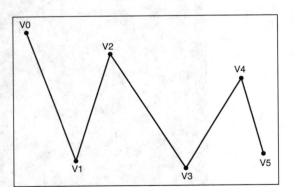

**FIGURE 4.3**    Line strips.

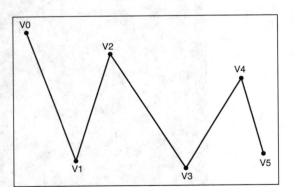

**FIGURE 4.4**    Triangle lists.

- TriangleStrip—A triangle strip draws each triangle after the first using the last two vertices of the triangle before it. The cull mode is automatically flipped on all even-numbered triangles. The cull mode is flipped on these triangles; since it is sharing the last two vertices of the previous triangle, the vertices will be wound the opposite direction. This is by far the most common primitive type for complex 3D objects. See Figure 4.5.

- TriangleFan—Similar to the TriangleStrip, but each triangle shares the same first vertex. See Figure 4.6.

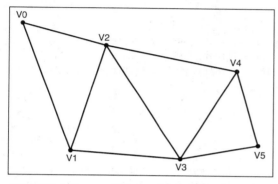

**FIGURE 4.5**   Triangle strips.

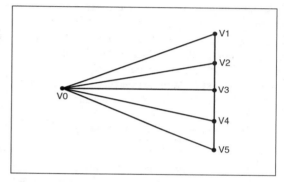

**FIGURE 4.6**   Triangle fan.

We can use the same vertex data to draw any of these types of primitives. Direct3D will interpret the vertex data differently depending on the type of primitive that you tell it will be drawn. Let's write a quick bit of code to draw each of the different primitive types.

The sample code on the CD was derived from the first vertex buffer sample we created in Chapter 3, "Rendering Using Simple Techniques." The changes made to the code will be outlined here. Since this code will not require our vertices to be moved, the world transform in SetupCamera was removed, as well as all references to the private "angle" member variable. The following constant was then added:

```
private const int NumberItems = 12;
```

Twelve was picked arbitrarily, but for a reason. Too many vertices, and the screen gets cluttered; however, we want to ensure we have a number of vertices that is both even and divisible by three. This is so both our LineList primitives and our TriangleList primitives can be rendered correctly. We next need to modify the vertex buffer creation and the OnVertexBufferCreate function as in Listing 4.1:

**LISTING 4.1**  Creating Random Vertices

```
vb = new VertexBuffer(typeof(CustomVertex.PositionColored), NumberItems, device,
    Usage.Dynamic | Usage.WriteOnly, CustomVertex.PositionColored.Format,
    Pool.Default);
// Create a list of vertices equal to the number of items
CustomVertex.PositionColored[] verts = new CustomVertex.PositionColored[NumberItems];

// Randomly select the position of this vertex..  Keep it within a range of 5.
for(int i = 0; i < NumberItems; i++)
{
    float xPos = (float)(Rnd.NextDouble() * 5.0f) - (float)(Rnd.NextDouble() * 5.0f);
    float yPos = (float)(Rnd.NextDouble() * 5.0f) - (float)(Rnd.NextDouble() * 5.0f);
    float zPos = (float)(Rnd.NextDouble() * 5.0f) - (float)(Rnd.NextDouble() * 5.0f);
    verts[i].SetPosition(new Vector3(xPos, yPos, zPos));
    verts[i].Color = RandomColor.ToArgb();
}
buffer.SetData(verts, 0, LockFlags.None);
```

There is nothing magical going on here. We modified our vertex buffer to hold the correct number of vertices (as defined by our NumberItems constant). We then modified our vertex creation function to plot the correct number of vertices in a random way. You can see the source code included on the CD for the definitions of "Rnd" and "RandomColor".

Now we need to modify our actual drawing calls. An easy way to show the difference in how these various primitive types interact with one another would be to have the code scroll through them sequentially. Let's have our drawing code do that every two seconds. An easy way to do this would be to check our current time (in ticks) versus the startup time. Add the following member variables into your declaration section:

```
private bool needRecreate = false;
// Timing information
private static readonly int InitialTickCount = System.Environment.TickCount;
```

The Boolean value will allow us to re-create our vertex buffer at the start of each "cycle," so we don't continue to display the same vertices over and over again. Replace the single DrawPrimitives call with the code section in Listing 4.2:

**LISTING 4.2**  Rendering Each Primitive Type

```
// We will decide what to draw based on primitives
int index = ((System.Environment.TickCount - InitialTickCount) / 2000) % 6;
switch (index)
{
```

**LISTING 4.2**   Continued

```
case 0: // Points
    device.DrawPrimitives(PrimitiveType.PointList, 0, NumberItems);
    if (needRecreate)
    {
        // After the primitives have been drawn, recreate a new set
        OnVertexBufferCreate(vb, null);
        needRecreate = false;
    }
    break;
case 1: // LineList
    device.DrawPrimitives(PrimitiveType.LineList, 0, NumberItems / 2);
    needRecreate = true;
    break;
case 2: // LineStrip
    device.DrawPrimitives(PrimitiveType.LineStrip, 0, NumberItems - 1);
    break;
case 3: // TriangleList
    device.DrawPrimitives(PrimitiveType.TriangleList, 0, NumberItems / 3);
    break;
case 4: // TriangleStrip
    device.DrawPrimitives(PrimitiveType.TriangleStrip, 0, NumberItems - 2);
    break;
case 5: // TriangleFan
    device.DrawPrimitives(PrimitiveType.TriangleFan, 0, NumberItems - 2);
    break;
}
```

This is a relatively self-explanatory section of code. Depending on which primitive type we are on in our cycle, we simply call DrawPrimitives with the appropriate type. You'll notice that for a list of points, we simply use the number of vertices as our primitive count, drawing one point for each vertex. LineList and TriangleList primitives draw isolated primitives, so our DrawPrimitives call with these types is the number of vertices divided by the number of vertices in a single primitive of the correct type: two or three respectively. For LineStrip primitives, given that each vertex after the second shares its starting point with the ending point of the previous line, you only need to draw one less than the current number of items. TriangleStrip and TriangleFan primitives behave the same way, but since there are three vertices in a triangle, with two shared, we use two less.

Running this application will show you first a series of points rendered on the screen, followed by a series of disjointed lines. Next these lines will connect to form a solid polyline, and then switch to a series of isolated triangles. Finally, these triangles will begin sharing vertices to form a strip, and then a fan. One thing you may notice is that the "points" may be small and hard to see. You can artificially "scale" these points by setting a render state. Add the following line to your SetupCamera function to scale each point to three times its normal size:

```
device.RenderState.PointSize = 3.0f;
```

You'll notice that the single points are now much larger than they were originally. Feel free to play with this render state. Now that we have the different types of primitives drawing correctly, let's investigate ways to lower the amount of memory usage of our data.

# Using Index Buffers

If you remember our first application rendering cubes, we created data for a total of 36 vertices. There were 2 triangles for each face of the cube; 6 faces multiplied by 2 triangles equals 12 primitives. Since each primitive has 3 vertices, we get our 36. However, in reality, there were only 8 different vertices being used; one for each corner of the cube.

Storing the same vertex data multiple times in a small application such as this may not seem like that big of a deal, but in a large-scale application where you're storing mass amounts of vertex data, saving room by not duplicating your vertices is nothing but a good thing. Luckily, Direct3D has a mechanism for sharing vertex data inside a primitive called index buffers.

Like its name implies, an *index buffer* is a buffer that stores indices into vertex data. The indices stored in this buffer can be 32-bit (integer data) or 16-bit (short data). Unless you really need more indices than provided by the short data type, stick with that as it is half the size of the integer data.

When using an index buffer to render your primitives, each index in your index buffer corresponds directly to a vertex stored in your vertex data. For example, if you were rendering a single triangle with the indices of 0, 1, 6, it would render the triangle using the vertices mapped to those indices. Let's modify our cube drawing application to use indices. First, modify our vertex data creation function as shown in Listing 4.3:

**LISTING 4.3**   Creating Vertices for Our Cube

```
vb = new VertexBuffer(typeof(CustomVertex.PositionColored), 8, device, Usage.Dynamic |
    Usage.WriteOnly, CustomVertex.PositionColored.Format, Pool.Default);

CustomVertex.PositionColored[] verts = new CustomVertex.PositionColored[8];

// Vertices
verts[0] = new CustomVertex.PositionColored(-1.0f, 1.0f, 1.0f, Color.Purple.ToArgb());
```

**LISTING 4.3** Continued

```
verts[1] = new CustomVertex.PositionColored(-1.0f, -1.0f, 1.0f, Color.Red.ToArgb());
verts[2] = new CustomVertex.PositionColored(1.0f, 1.0f, 1.0f, Color.Blue.ToArgb());
verts[3] = new CustomVertex.PositionColored(1.0f, -1.0f, 1.0f, Color.Yellow.ToArgb());
verts[4] = new CustomVertex.PositionColored(-1.0f, 1.0f, -1.0f, Color.Gold.ToArgb());
verts[5] = new CustomVertex.PositionColored(1.0f, 1.0f, -1.0f, Color.Green.ToArgb());
verts[6] = new CustomVertex.PositionColored(-1.0f, -1.0f, -1.0f, Color.Black.ToArgb());
verts[7] = new CustomVertex.PositionColored(1.0f,-1.0f,-1.0f, Color.WhiteSmoke.ToArgb());
buffer.SetData(verts, 0, LockFlags.None);
```

As you can see, we dramatically lowered the amount of vertex data, by only storing the 8 vertices that make up the corners of the cube. Now, we still want to draw 36 vertices, just with different orders of these 8 vertices. Since we know what our vertices are now, what are the 36 indices to these vertices that we would need to use to draw our cube? Looking at our previous application, we could compare each of the 36 vertices used, and find the appropriate index in our new list. Add our list of indices, shown in Listing 4.4, to the declaration section:

**LISTING 4.4** The Box Index Buffer Data

```
private static readonly short[] indices = {
    0,1,2, // Front Face
    1,3,2, // Front Face
    4,5,6, // Back Face
    6,5,7, // Back Face
    0,5,4, // Top Face
    0,2,5, // Top Face
    1,6,7, // Bottom Face
    1,7,3, // Bottom Face
    0,6,1, // Left Face
    4,6,0, // Left Face
    2,3,7, // Right Face
    5,2,7 // Right Face
};
```

The index list is broken down to three for each triangle we will be drawing, for ease of reading. As you can see, the front face is created by using two triangles. The first triangle uses vertices 0, 1, and 2, while the second triangle uses vertices 1, 3, and 2. Similarly, for the right face, the first triangle uses vertices 2, 3, and 7, while the second triangle uses 5, 2, and 7. All of the back face culling winding rules will still apply when using indices as well.

However, just having the list of indices doesn't really help us until we update our application to use them. For this, you will need to create an index buffer. Add the following line after the declaration for our vertex buffer:

```
private IndexBuffer ib = null;
```

This object will be used to store our indices and give Direct3D access to them. This object is remarkably similar to the vertex buffer object we've already created; it just will store indices instead. Let's instantiate this object and fill it with data. After the instantiation of the vertex buffer, add the code in Listing 4.5:

**LISTING 4.5**   Creating the Index Buffer

```
ib = new IndexBuffer(typeof(short), indices.Length,device,Usage.WriteOnly,Pool.Default);
ib.Created += new EventHandler(this.OnIndexBufferCreate);
OnIndexBufferCreate(ib, null);

private void OnIndexBufferCreate(object sender, EventArgs e)
{
    IndexBuffer buffer = (IndexBuffer)sender;
    buffer.SetData(indices, 0, LockFlags.None);
}
```

You'll notice that the constructor for the index buffer mirrors that of the vertex buffer. The only difference is the restrictions of the type parameter. As mentioned earlier, you can only use the short (System.Int16) or integer (System.Int32) data types for the index data. We also hook the created event and call our hook function for the first run. We then simply fill our index buffer with the data we needed.

Now, we just need to fix our rendering code to actually use this data. If you remember, there was a function called "SetStreamSource" to tell Direct3D which vertex buffer to use when rendering. Of course, there's a similar item for index buffers, however this time it's simply a property since there can only be one type of index buffer in use at a time. Immediately after our SetStreamSource call, set this property:

```
device.Indices = ib;
```

Now that Direct3D knows about our index buffer, we need to modify our drawing calls. Currently, our drawing calls are trying to draw 12 primitives (36 vertices) from our vertex buffer, which will naturally fail since it only holds 8 vertices. Add the DrawBox function back:

```
private void DrawBox(float yaw, float pitch, float roll, float x, float y, float z)
{
    angle += 0.01f;
```

```
device.Transform.World = Matrix.RotationYawPitchRoll(yaw, pitch, roll) *
    Matrix.Translation(x, y, z);
device.DrawIndexedPrimitives(PrimitiveType.TriangleList, 0, 0, 8, 0,
    indices.Length / 3);
}
```

We've changed our drawing call from DrawPrimitives to DrawIndexedPrimitives. Let's look at the prototype for this function:

```
public void DrawIndexedPrimitives ( Microsoft.DirectX.Direct3D.PrimitiveType primitiveType
    , System.Int32 baseVertex , System.Int32 minVertexIndex , System.Int32 numVertices ,
    System.Int32 startIndex , System.Int32 primCount )
```

The first parameter is the same as the previous function, the type of primitives we will be drawing. The baseVertex parameter is the offset from the start of the index buffer to the first vertex index. The minVertexIndex is the minimum vertex index for vertices in this call. The numVertices member is relatively self-explanatory (the number of vertices used during this call); however, it is starting from the baseVertex + minVertexIndex parameters. The startIndex member refers to the location in the array to start reading vertices. The last parameter stays the same (the number of primitives to draw).

So, as you can see, we are simply drawing our 8 vertices, using our index buffer to render 12 primitives for our cube. Now let's remove our DrawPrimitives calls and replace them with calls into our DrawBox method, shown in Listing 4.6:

**LISTING 4.6**  Drawing Boxes

```
// Draw our boxes
DrawBox(angle / (float)Math.PI, angle / (float)Math.PI * 2.0f, angle / (float)Math.PI /
    4.0f, 0.0f, 0.0f, 0.0f);
DrawBox(angle / (float)Math.PI, angle / (float)Math.PI / 2.0f, angle / (float)Math.PI *
    4.0f, 5.0f, 0.0f, 0.0f);
DrawBox(angle / (float)Math.PI, angle / (float)Math.PI * 4.0f, angle / (float)Math.PI /
    2.0f, -5.0f, 0.0f, 0.0f);

DrawBox(angle / (float)Math.PI, angle / (float)Math.PI * 2.0f, angle / (float)Math.PI /
    4.0f, 0.0f, -5.0f, 0.0f);
DrawBox(angle / (float)Math.PI, angle / (float)Math.PI / 2.0f, angle / (float)Math.PI *
    4.0f, 5.0f, -5.0f, 0.0f);
DrawBox(angle / (float)Math.PI, angle / (float)Math.PI * 4.0f, angle / (float)Math.PI /
    2.0f, -5.0f, -5.0f, 0.0f);

DrawBox(angle / (float)Math.PI, angle / (float)Math.PI * 2.0f, angle / (float)Math.PI /
    4.0f, 0.0f, 5.0f, 0.0f);
```

**LISTING 4.6**   Continued

```
DrawBox(angle / (float)Math.PI, angle / (float)Math.PI / 2.0f, angle / (float)Math.PI *
    4.0f, 5.0f, 5.0f, 0.0f);
DrawBox(angle / (float)Math.PI, angle / (float)Math.PI * 4.0f, angle / (float)Math.PI /
    2.0f, -5.0f, 5.0f, 0.0f);
```

Running this application now will render very colorful cubes spinning around your scene.

The reason each vertex in our list has a different color is to visually show one of the "drawbacks" to using index buffers to share vertices. When the vertices are shared across multiple primitives, *all* of the vertex data is shared, including colors and normal data. When determining whether you can really share these vertices, you must first determine if sharing this data can cause lighting or color errors (since lighting calculations are based on the normal data). You can see that each corner of the cube is rendered in the color for its vertex, and the faces of the cube are interpolated from the colors of its vertices.

# Using Depth Buffers

A *depth buffer* (often referred to as a z-buffer or a w-buffer) is how Direct3D stores "depth" information for rendering. This depth information is used during rasterization to determine how pixels block (occlude) each other. Currently, our application has no depth buffer associated with it, so no pixels are occluded during rasterization. However, we have no pixels that are occluded anyway, so let's try to draw a few more cubes that will actually overlap some of our existing cubes. Add the following DrawBox calls to the end of our existing DrawBox calls:

```
DrawBox(angle / (float)Math.PI, angle / (float)Math.PI * 2.0f, angle / (float)Math.PI /
    4.0f, 0.0f, (float)Math.Cos(angle), (float)Math.Sin(angle));
DrawBox(angle / (float)Math.PI, angle / (float)Math.PI / 2.0f, angle / (float)Math.PI *
    4.0f, 5.0f, (float)Math.Sin(angle), (float)Math.Cos(angle));
DrawBox(angle / (float)Math.PI, angle / (float)Math.PI / 2.0f, angle / (float)Math.PI /
    2.0f, -5.0f, (float)Math.Cos(angle), (float)Math.Sin(angle));
```

All we are really doing here is having three extra cubes spin around the three center horizontal cubes. Running this application, you can easily see the cubes overlapping, but you can't visually see where one cube ends and the other begins. It appears as if the cubes are simply a blob. This is where a depth buffer comes in handy.

Adding a depth buffer to our application is actually quite an easy task. Do you remember the presentation parameters we passed in to our device constructor? Well, this is where we include our depth buffer information. There are two new parameters we will need to fill out to include a depth buffer with our device:

```
public Microsoft.DirectX.Direct3D.DepthFormat AutoDepthStencilFormat [get,  set]
public bool EnableAutoDepthStencil [get,  set]
```

## SHOP TALK

### SAVING MEMORY WITH INDEX BUFFERS

So how exactly does using an index buffer save memory for our application? Let's compare the relatively simple cube applications, both with and without using the index buffer. In the first scenario, we created a vertex buffer holding 32 vertices of type CustomVertex.PositionColored. This structure happens to be 16 bytes (4 bytes each for x, y, z, and color). Multiply this size by the number of vertices, and you can see our vertex data consists of 576 bytes of data.

Now, compare this with the index buffer method. We only use 8 vertices (of the same type), so our vertex data size is 128 bytes. However, we are also storing our index data as well, so what is the size of that? We are using short indices (2 bytes each) and we are using 36 of them. So our index data alone is 72 bytes, combined with our vertex data we have a total size of 200 bytes.

Compare that to our original size of 576 bytes, and we have a remarkable 65% reduction in memory usage. Extrapolate these numbers out for very large scenes, and the possible memory saved using index buffers can be quite substantial.

Setting "EnableAutoDepthStencil" to true will turn on the depth buffer for your device, using the depth format specified in the AutoDepthStencilFormat member. Valid values of the DepthFormat enumeration for this member are listed in Table 4.1:

### TABLE 4.1

**Possible Depth Formats**

| VALUE | DESCRIPTION |
| --- | --- |
| D16 | A 16-bit z-buffer bit depth. |
| D32 | A 32-bit z-buffer bit depth. |
| D16Lockable | A 16-bit z-buffer bit depth that is lockable. |
| D32FLockable | A lockable format where depth value is represented by a standard IEEE floating point number. |
| D15S1 | A 16-bit z-buffer bit depth using 15 bits for depth channel, with the last bit used for the stencil channel (stencil channels will be discussed later). |
| D24S8 | A 32-bit z-buffer bit depth using 24 bits for depth channel, with the remaining 8 bits used for the stencil channel. |
| D24X8 | A 32-bit z-buffer bit depth using 24 bits for depth channel, with the remaining 8 bits ignored. |
| D24X4S4 | A 32-bit z-buffer bit depth using 24 bits for depth channel, with 4 bits used for the stencil channel, and the remaining 4 bits ignored. |
| D24FS8 | A non-lockable format that contains 24 points of depth (as a floating point) and 8 bits for the stencil channel. |

## SHOP TALK

### PICKING THE RIGHT DEPTH BUFFER

Nearly every graphics card on the market today supports a z-buffer; however, depending on the circumstances, using this depth buffer can have its drawbacks. When calculating the depth of a pixel, Direct3D will place the pixel somewhere in the z-buffer range (normally from 0.0f to 1.0f), but this placement is rarely uniform across the entire range. The ratio of the near and far plane directly affects the distribution pattern of your z-buffer.

For example, if your near plane is 1.0f, and your far plane is 100.0f, 90% of the range will be used in the first 10% of your depth buffer. If you had a large "outdoor" scene, it wouldn't be uncommon to have much larger far planes. In the previous example, if your far plane was 1000.0f, 98% of the range would be used in the first 2% of the depth buffer. This could cause "artifacts" on distant objects, which may or may not matter in your application.

Using a w-buffer depth buffer eliminates this problem, but has its own downfalls as well. It's possible for artifacts to appear on near objects rather than distant objects when using a w-buffer. Also, it's worth noting that there isn't as much support in graphics cards for w-buffers as there is for z-buffers.

One last comment on depth buffers. For greater performance when rendering using depth buffers, it's best to render items from front (highest z) to back (lowest z). During scene rasterization, Direct3D can quickly reject a pixel that is already occluded and skip the drawing completely. This is naturally not the case when we're rendering data with alpha components, but since we haven't gotten that far yet, we'll skip that until later.

Larger depth buffers can naturally store much more depth data, at the expense of performance. Unless you know you need a very large depth buffer, stick with smaller values. Most modern graphics cards will support a minimum of a 16-bit depth buffer, so add that to the present parameters structure:

```
presentParams.EnableAutoDepthStencil = true;
presentParams.AutoDepthStencilFormat = DepthFormat.D16;
```

Perfect, now our device has a depth buffer. Let's see what difference it makes in our application. Go ahead and run it now.

Well, something must be broken because that isn't what we were supposed to see. What happened to our cubes? Why did adding a depth buffer to our device suddenly cause all of our rendering to break? Interestingly enough, it's because our depth buffer was never "cleared," so it was in an invalid state. We are already clearing our device, and it's an easy fix to clear our depth buffer at the same time. Modify your clear call as follows:

```
device.Clear(ClearFlags.Target | ClearFlags.ZBuffer, Color.CornflowerBlue, 1.0f, 0);
```

Running the application now produces desired results. You can easily see how the cubes are separated, and the depth buffer is now functioning normally.

# In Brief

In this chapter we covered more advanced rendering techniques, including

- Using index buffers to eliminate the need for duplicating vertices and lower our overall memory usage
- The differences between each of the various primitive types and how to use each of them
- Depth buffers, and how to use them

In the next chapter we will start rendering real objects loaded from files. It's time to move on to meshes.

# Rendering with Meshes

**5**

During this chapter we will

- Discuss and use the Mesh object.

- Get introduced to materials.

- Draw common objects as meshes.

- Use meshes to load and render external files.

## Defining the Mesh

While there are many times when you may want to manually create vertex and index data, it's also common to want to load existing vertex data from an external source, such as a file. A common file format holding this data is an .X file. In the previous chapters, large portions of the code were there just to create simple objects that were to be rendered. While for the simple cubes and triangles, it wasn't all that bad, imagine trying to write similar code that was creating an object that had tens of thousands of vertices instead of the 36 that were used for the cube. The amount of time and effort to write this code would be substantial.

Luckily there is an object in Managed DirectX that can encapsulate storing and loading vertex and index data, namely the Mesh. Meshes can be used to store any type of graphical data, but are mainly used to encapsulate complex models. Meshes also contain several methods used to enhance performance of rendering these objects. All mesh objects will contain a vertex buffer and an index buffer like we've already used, plus will also contain an attribute buffer that we'll discuss later in this chapter.

The actual mesh object resides in the Direct3D Extensions library (D3DX). Currently, we've only had references to the main Direct3D assembly, so before we can use this mesh object, we'll first need to add a reference to the Microsoft.DirectX.Direct3DX.dll assembly to our project. Now, let's try to create our rotating box application using the mesh object.

After you make sure you have the correct references loaded in your solution, you should add a member variable for your mesh. You would place this in the same spot you put your vertex buffer and index buffer member variables before:

```
private Mesh mesh = null;
```

There are three constructors for creating a mesh; however, currently none of these will be needed. There are several static methods on the Mesh class that we can use to create or load various models. One of the first you'll notice is the "Box" method, which, as its name implies, creates a mesh that contains a box. Considering that's what we want to render right now, that looks perfect. Place the following code after your device creation method:

```
mesh = Mesh.Box(device, 2.0f, 2.0f, 2.0f);
```

This method will create a new mesh that contains the vertices and indices to render a cube with a height, width, and depth of 2.0f. This is the same size cube we created manually with our vertex buffer before. We've reduced all of that creation code we had down to one line; it doesn't get much easier than that.

Now that we've got our mesh created, though, do we render it the same way, or do we need to do something different? When rendering our cube before, we needed to call SetStreamSource to let Direct3D know which vertex buffer to read data from, as well as setting the indices and vertex format property. None of this is required when rendering a mesh.

## DRAWING WITH A MESH

Saying the methods you used when drawing the cube before aren't necessary isn't entirely accurate. The mesh stores the vertex buffer, index buffer, and vertex format being used internally. When the mesh is rendered, it will automatically set the stream source, as well as the indices and vertex format properties for you.

Now that our mesh has been created, what do we need to do in order to render it onscreen? Meshes are broken up into a group of subsets (based on the attribute buffer, which we'll discuss shortly) and there is a method "DrawSubset" we can use for rendering. Let's modify our DrawBox function as follows:

```
private void DrawBox(float yaw, float pitch, float roll, float x, float y, float z)
{
    angle += 0.01f;

    device.Transform.World = Matrix.RotationYawPitchRoll(yaw, pitch, roll) *
        Matrix.Translation(x, y, z);
    mesh.DrawSubset(0);
}
```

As you can see, we've replaced our call to DrawIndexedPrimitives with a single call to DrawSubset. The generic primitives created by the Mesh class (such as Mesh.Box) will always have a single subset that is zero based. This is all we need to do in order for our application to run; amazingly simple. Go ahead and check it out now.

Well, we've got our nine spinning cubes again, but, boy, are they all pure white. If you looked at the vertex format of the vertices created in the mesh (you can do something as simple as looking at the VertexFormat property on the mesh), you'll see that the only data stored in this mesh is position and normal data. There is no color stored in the mesh, and since we've turned lighting off, it renders everything in white.

If you remember from Chapter 1, "Introducing Direct3D," lighting only works when there is normal data stored for our vertices, and since there is some normal data for our cube, maybe we should just turn lighting back on. The default lighting value for a device is enabled, so you can either remove the line setting it to false, or set it to true.

Well, we've successfully turned our white cubes into black cubes now. Hopefully you guessed this is because we have no lights in our scene, so everything is "dark," thus rendered black. Now rather than specifying specific lights, wouldn't it be great if we could just have a constant light around our entire scene? Welcome to ambient lighting.

Ambient lights provide a constant source of light for a scene. All objects in the scene will be lit exactly the same way since ambient light isn't dependent on any factors that the other lighting methods are (such as position, direction, or attenuation). You don't even really need normal data in order to use an ambient light. Ambient light is highly efficient, but doesn't produce "realistic" results. For now, though, it will produce sufficient results. Add the following line where your lighting render state was:

```
device.RenderState.Ambient = Color.Red;
```

The ambient light in a scene is globally defined by the ambient render state, which takes in a color. In this case, we want our "global" light to take on a red color so that we can see the effects easily. Running the application now, you might expect to see nine spinning red cubes, but no, they are still black. What else could be missing?

# Using Materials and Lighting

So what's different now than when we were first using lights? The only major difference (other than the fact that we are using a mesh) is the lack of color in our vertex data. This *is* the cause of the light "failing" now.

In order for Direct3D to correctly calculate the color of a particular point on a 3D object, it must not only know the color of the light, but how that object will reflect the color of that light. In the real world if you shine a red light on a light blue surface, that surface will appear a soft purple color. You need to describe how our "surface" (our cube) reflects light.

In Direct3D, materials describe this property. You can specify how the object will reflect ambient and diffuse lighting, what the specular highlights (discussed later) will look like, and whether the object appears to emit light at all. Add the following code to your DrawBox call (before the DrawSubset call).

```
Material boxMaterial = new Material();
boxMaterial.Ambient = Color.White;
boxMaterial.Diffuse = Color.White;
device.Material = boxMaterial;
```

Here we create a new material, and set its ambient and diffuse color values to white. Using white means we will reflect *all* ambient and diffuse lighting that hits these objects. We then use the Material property on the device so that Direct3D knows which material to use while rendering its data.

Running the application now shows us the red cubes spinning around that we expected to see before. Modifying the ambient light color will change the color of every cube in the scene. Modifying the ambient color component of the material will change how the light is reflected off of the object. Changing the material to a color with absolutely no red in it (such as green) will cause the object to once again render black. Changing the material to a color with some red (for example, gray) will cause the object to appear a darker gray.

There are actually quite a few stock objects you can use when using mesh files. Use any of the following methods for creating these meshes (each of the stock mesh functions requires the device as the first parameter):

```
mesh = Mesh.Box(device, 2.0f, 2.0f, 2.0f);
```

## *SHOP TALK*

### USING MORE REALISTIC LIGHTING

As you can tell, the cubes don't look very realistic when rendered in this way. You can't even see where the "corners" of the cube are; it just looks like a blob of red in a cube-like shape. This is due to how ambient light affects the scene. If you remember, ambient light will calculate lighting the same for every vertex in a scene, regardless of normal, or any parameter of the light. See Figure 5.1.

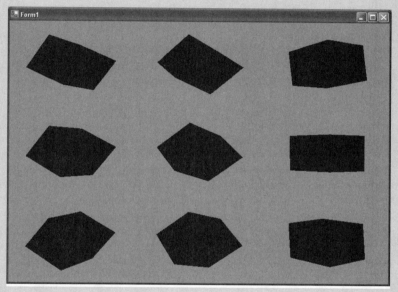

**FIGURE 5.1**  Ambient light with no shading.

To make a more realistic-looking cube, we will need to add a real light to our scene. Comment out the ambient light line and add the following lines below it:

```
device.Lights[0].Type = LightType.Directional;
device.Lights[0].Diffuse = Color.DarkBlue;
device.Lights[0].Direction = new Vector3(0, -1, -1);
device.Lights[0].Commit();
device.Lights[0].Enabled = true;
```

This will create a dark blue directional light pointing in the same direction the camera is facing. Running the application now will result in the cubes (now dark blue) much more realistically shaded as they spin around. You can see that the faces directly in the path of the light have the full color applied, while faces not directly in the path of the light are shaded darker (possibly even completely black). See Figure 5.2.

*SHOP TALK*

**FIGURE 5.2**   Cubes shaded realistically using directional lights.

Uses a left-handed coordinate system to create a box.

| | |
|---|---|
| Width | Specify the size of the box along the x-axis. |
| Height | Specify the size of the box along the y-axis. |
| Depth | Specify the size of the box along the z-axis. |

```
mesh = Mesh.Cylinder(device, 2.0f, 2.0f, 2.0f, 36, 36);
```

Uses a left-handed coordinate system to create a cylinder.

| | |
|---|---|
| Radius1 | The radius of the cylinder on the negative z end. This value should be greater than or equal to 0.0f. |
| Radius2 | The radius of the cylinder on the positive z end. This value should be greater than or equal to 0.0f. |
| Length | Length of the cylinder on the z-axis. |
| Slices | The number of slices along the main axis (larger value will add more vertices). |
| Stacks | The number of stacks along the main axis (larger value will add more vertices). |

```
mesh = Mesh.Polygon(device, 2.0f, 8);
```

Uses a left-handed coordinate system to create a polygon.

Length      The length of each side of the polygon
Sides       Number of sides this polygon will have  `mesh = Mesh.Sphere(device, 2.0f, 36, 36);`

Uses a left-handed coordinate system to create a sphere.

Radius      Radius of the created sphere. This value should be greater than or equal to 0.
Slices      The number of slices along the main axis (larger value will add more vertices)
Stacks      The number of stacks along the main axis (larger value will add more vertices)

```
mesh = Mesh.Torus(device, 0.5f, 2.0f, 36, 18);
```

Uses a left-handed coordinate system to create a torus.

InnerRadius    Inner radius of the created torus. This value should be greater than or equal to 0.
OutterRadius   Inner radius of the created torus. This value should be greater than or equal to 0.
Sides          Number of sides in a cross section of the torus. This value must be greater than or equal to three.
Rings          Number of rings in a cross section of the torus. This value must be greater than or equal to three.

```
mesh = Mesh.Teapot(device);
```

Uses a left-handed coordinate system to create a teapot (yes a teapot). See Figure 5.3.

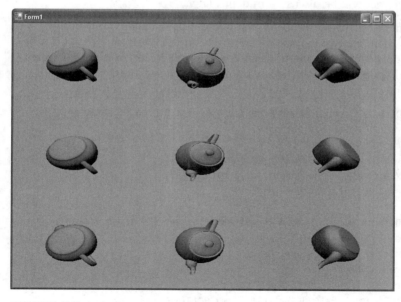

**FIGURE 5.3**    The intrinsic teapot mesh.

Each of these methods also has a second overload that can return adjacency information. Adjacency information is returned as three integers per face that specify the three neighbors of each face in the mesh.

# Using Meshes to Render Complex Models

Rendering teapots can be quite exciting, but it's not often you make a game with nothing but teapots. Most meshes are created by artists using a modeling application. If your modeling application supports exporting to the X file format, you're in luck!

## CONVERTING COMMON MODELING FORMATS TO THE X FILE FORMAT

The DirectX SDK (included on the CD) includes several conversion utilities for the most popular modeling applications out there. Using these conversion tools allows you to easily use your high-quality models in your applications.

There are a few types of data stored in a normal x file that can be loaded while creating a mesh. There is naturally the vertex and index data that will be required to render the model. Each of the subsets of the mesh will have a material associated with it. Each material set can contain texture information as well. You can also get the High Level Shader Language (HLSL) file that should be used with this mesh while loading the file. HLSL is an advanced topic that will be discussed in depth later.

Much like the static methods on the Mesh object that allowed us to create our generic "simple" primitive types, there are two main static methods on the mesh object that can be used to load external models. These two methods are Mesh.FromFile and Mesh.FromStream. The methods are essentially identical, with the stream method having more overloads for dealing with the size of the stream. The root overload for each method is as follows:

```
public static Microsoft.DirectX.Direct3D.Mesh FromFile ( System.String filename ,
    Microsoft.DirectX.Direct3D.MeshFlags options ,
    Microsoft.DirectX.Direct3D.Device device ,
    Microsoft.DirectX.Direct3D.GraphicsStream adjacency ,
    out Microsoft.DirectX.Direct3D.ExtendedMaterial[] materials ,
    Microsoft.DirectX.Direct3D.EffectInstance effects )


public static Microsoft.DirectX.Direct3D.Mesh FromStream ( System.IO.Stream stream ,
    System.Int32 readBytes ,
    Microsoft.DirectX.Direct3D.MeshFlags options ,
    Microsoft.DirectX.Direct3D.Device device ,
    Microsoft.DirectX.Direct3D.GraphicsStream adjacency ,
    out Microsoft.DirectX.Direct3D.ExtendedMaterial[] materials ,
    Microsoft.DirectX.Direct3D.EffectInstance effects )
```

The first parameter(s) are the source of the data we will be using to load this mesh. In the FromFile case, this is a string that is the filename of the mesh we wish to load. In the stream case, this is the stream, and the number of bytes we wish to read for the data. If you wish to read the entire stream, simply use the overload that does not include the readBytes member.

The MeshFlags parameter controls where and how the data is loaded. This parameter may be a bitwise combination of the values found in Table 5.1.

**TABLE 5.1**

**Mesh Flags Enumeration Values**

| PARAMETER | VALUE |
| --- | --- |
| MeshFlags.DoNotClip | Use the Usage.DoNotClip flag for vertex and index buffers. |
| MeshFlags.Dynamic | Equivalent to using both IbDynamic and VbDynamic. |
| MeshFlags.IbDynamic | Use Usage.Dynamic for index buffers. |
| MeshFlags.IbManaged | Use the Pool.Managed memory store for index buffers. |
| MeshFlags.IbSoftwareProcessing | Use the Usage.SoftwareProcessing flag for index buffers. |
| MeshFlags.IbSystemMem | Use the Pool.SystemMemory memory pool for index buffers. |
| MeshFlags.IbWriteOnly | Use the Usage.WriteOnly flag for index buffers. |
| MeshFlags.VbDynamic | Use Usage.Dynamic for vertex buffers. |
| MeshFlags.VbManaged | Use the Pool.Managed memory store for vertex buffers. |
| MeshFlags.VbSoftwareProcessing | Use the Usage.SoftwareProcessing flag for vertex buffers. |
| MeshFlags.VbSystemMem | Use the Pool.SystemMemory memory pool for vertex buffers. |
| MeshFlags.VbWriteOnly | Use the Usage.WriteOnly flag for vertex buffers. |
| MeshFlags.Managed | Equivalent to using both IbManaged and VbManaged. |
| MeshFlags.Npatches | Use the Usage.NPatches flag for both index and vertex buffers. This is required if the mesh will be rendered using N-Patch enhancement. |
| MeshFlags.Points | Use the Usage.Points flag for both index and vertex buffers. |
| MeshFlags.RtPatches | Use the Usage.RtPatches flag for both index and vertex buffers. |
| MeshFlags.SoftwareProcessing | Equivalent to using both IbSoftwareProcessing and VbSoftwareProcessing. |
| MeshFlags.SystemMemory | Equivalent to using both IbSystemMem and VbSystemMem. |
| MeshFlags.Use32Bit | Use 32-bit indices for the index buffer. While possible, normally not recommended. |
| MeshFlags.UseHardwareOnly | Use hardware processing only. |

The next parameter is the device we will be using to render this mesh. Since resources must be associated with a device, this is a required parameter.

The adjacency parameter is an "out" parameter, meaning it will be allocated and passed to you after the function has finished working. This will return the adjacency information for the mesh, stored as three integer values for each face of the mesh, that will specify the three neighbors.

## READING ADJACENCY INFORMATION FROM THE RETURNED GRAPHICSSTREAM

The adjacency information returned to you from the mesh creation routines will come from a GraphicsStream class. You can get a local copy of the adjacency data with this small snippet of code:

```
int[] adjency = adjBuffer.Read(typeof(int),
mesh.NumberFaces * 3);
```

This will create an array of three integers per face storing the adjacency information that is easier to access than the native GraphicsStream class.

The extended material parameter is also an out parameter that will return an array of information about the different subsets in the mesh. The ExtendedMaterial class holds both the normal Direct3D material, as well as a string that can be used to load a texture. This string is normally the filename or resource name of the texture; however, since the loading of the texture is done by the application, this can be any user-provided string data.

Finally, we have the EffectInstance parameter, which describes the HLSL shader file and values that will be used for this mesh. There are actually multiple overloads for each of these methods that take varying combinations of these parameters. Always pick the one that has only the information you want and need.

Now that seems like quite a bit to chew on just to load and render a mesh, but in reality it's not that bad. It looks slightly intimidating at first, but once you actually see the code, it really isn't all that bad. Let's start writing some of that code now.

First, we'll need to make sure we have member variables that will store our materials and textures for the different subsets of the mesh. Add the following variables after your mesh declaration:

```
private Material[] meshMaterials;
private Texture[] meshTextures;
```

Since there can possibly be many different subsets in this mesh, you will need to store an array of both textures and materials, one for each subset. Now let's actually take a look at some code to load a mesh; create a function called "LoadMesh" that looks like Listing 5.1:

**LISTING 5.1**    Loading a Mesh from a File

```
private void LoadMesh(string file)
{
    ExtendedMaterial[] mtrl;

    // Load our mesh
    mesh = Mesh.FromFile(file, MeshFlags.Managed, device, out mtrl);

    // If we have any materials, store them
    if ((mtrl != null) && (mtrl.Length > 0))
```

**LISTING 5.1** Continued

```
    {
        meshMaterials = new Material[mtrl.Length];
        meshTextures = new Texture[mtrl.Length];

        // Store each material and texture
        for (int i = 0; i < mtrl.Length; i++)
        {
            meshMaterials[i] = mtrl[i].Material3D;
            if ((mtrl[i].TextureFilename != null) && (mtrl[i].TextureFilename !=
                string.Empty))
            {
                // We have a texture, try to load it
                meshTextures[i] = TextureLoader.FromFile(device, @"..\..\" +
                    mtrl[i].TextureFilename);
            }
        }
    }
}
```

Okay, so it looks a little more scary than the simple things we've done before, but really it's not. It's actually quite simple. First, we declare our ExtendedMaterial array that will store the information about the subsets of this mesh. Then, we simply call the FromFile method to load our mesh. We don't necessarily care about the adjacency or HLSL parameters now, so we use the overload that doesn't have them.

After our mesh has been loaded, we want to store the material and texture information for the various subsets. After we make sure there really are different subsets, we finally allocate our local material and texture arrays using the number of subsets as our size. We then loop through each of our ExtendedMaterial array members, and store the material in our local copy. If there is texture information included in this material subset, we use the TextureLoader.FromFile function to create our texture. This function only takes two parameters, the device and the filename of the texture and is *much* faster than going through System.Drawing.Bitmap like we did before.

In order to draw this mesh, you will need to add the following method to your application:

```
private void DrawMesh(float yaw, float pitch, float roll, float x, float y, float z)
{
    angle += 0.01f;

    device.Transform.World = Matrix.RotationYawPitchRoll(yaw, pitch, roll) *
        Matrix.Translation(x, y, z);
```

```
for (int i = 0; i < meshMaterials.Length; i++)
{
    device.Material = meshMaterials[i];
    device.SetTexture(0, meshTextures[i]);
    mesh.DrawSubset(i);
}
}
```

If you notice, we've kept the same basic signature as we had with our DrawBox method. Then, in order to draw the mesh, you will loop through each of the materials and perform the following steps:

1. Set the stored material as the material on the device.

2. Set the texture on the device to the stored texture. Even if there is no stored texture, setting the texture to null is completely valid and correct in that case.

3. Call DrawSubset passing in our subset id.

Perfect, now we've got all we really need to load a mesh and render it onscreen. The source code on the accompanying CD uses the model "tiny.x" that ships with the DirectX SDK as its test model for this application. In order to render this model, we added the following after device creation:

```
// Load our mesh
LoadMesh(@"..\..\tiny.x");
```

We then need to modify our camera information because the tiny model is anything but tiny. It is actually quite large, and we need to zoom our camera way out. Replace the view and projection transforms as follows:

```
device.Transform.Projection = Matrix.PerspectiveFovLH((float)Math.PI / 4, this.Width /
    this.Height, 1.0f, 10000.0f);
device.Transform.View = Matrix.LookAtLH(new Vector3(0,0, 580.0f), new Vector3(),
    new Vector3(0,1,0));
```

As you can see, we increased the length of the far plane, and moved the position of the camera pretty far back. Now, the only thing left to do is actually call DrawMesh during your render loop:

```
DrawMesh(angle / (float)Math.PI, angle / (float)Math.PI * 2.0f, angle /
    (float)Math.PI / 4.0f, 0.0f, 0.0f, 0.0f);
```

You may also want to turn the lights back to white now. You don't want to see your mesh rendered with a blue tint to it. Running the application would give you results similar to Figure 5.4.

**FIGURE 5.4**   A mesh rendered from a file.

Now we're getting somewhere. This is beginning to look much nicer than our cubes spinning around.

# In Brief

In this chapter we covered meshes, including

- Using the Mesh object
- Using materials
- Using meshes to draw common objects
- Using meshes to load and render external files

In our next chapter, we will explore optimizations that we can make to mesh data, and more advanced features of the mesh.

# Using Managed DirectX to Write a Game

# 6

## Choosing the Game

While many of the more advanced features of 3D programming haven't been discussed yet, there has been enough basic ground covered to write a simple 3D game. You will use the knowledge gained thus far, plus add a few new things.

Before we actually begin writing a game, it would be a good idea to come up with a plan. We will need to know the type of game we will be writing, the basic features it will hold, and so on. Given the limited set of topics we've covered this far, we obviously can't create something overly complex.

Instead, a simple game will be written. One of the first demo games for MS-DOS was called "Donkey," in which the user controlled a car, and the goal was to avoid the donkeys in the road. Sounds simple enough; this chapter will make a 3D version, without the donkeys. We'll call this game "Dodger."

Before we begin actually writing some code, though, we need to spend a little bit of time planning and designing our game. What will we need for the game, and what do we want to do while playing it? Well, obviously, we'll need a car class to control our vehicle. Then it might be a good idea to have a class to control the obstacles we will be trying to avoid. Plus, we'll need our main game engine class that will do all of the rendering, and keep it all together.

If you were attempting to create a commercial game that you wanted to be published and sold in stores, you would spend a lot of time coming up with a game proposal. Game proposals are in-depth documents that detail the vast majority of the game concepts and features. Given that the scope of this book is intended to cover the actual development work, and not necessarily the steps that you would need to take in order to get it published, this exercise will be skipped.

Another recommended document that is normally required before development work starts is the technical specification (*spec* for short). This includes a mildly detailed list of all the classes, plus the methods and properties the classes will implement. It may also contain UML diagrams that show the relationships between the objects. The goal of the spec is to sit down and really think about the design of your application before you start writing any code. Again, since the focus of this book is on the code, the spec for this project will be omitted as well. I would recommend that you always spend some time coming up with a spec before writing any code.

# Writing the Game

You can jump right into Visual Studio and get the project started. Create a new C# Windows Application project called "Dodger". The default name of the form that has been created for you is Form1. Replace each instance of Form1 with DodgerGame, which is the name of the class that the code in this chapter will represent. You'll want to add references to the three Managed DirectX assemblies you've been using in your projects thus far, and include a using statement for them in your code file. You should set this project up much like you did most of the others. You will have a private Direct3D device variable and should modify your constructor as follows:

```
public DodgerGame()
{
    this.Size = new Size(800,600);
    this.Text = "Dodger Game";

    this.SetStyle(ControlStyles.AllPaintingInWmPaint | ControlStyles.Opaque, true);
}
```

This will set the window size to 800×600 (which should be plenty good enough), and establish the window title and the style, so the rendering code will work normally. Then you should modify the entry point for the application by replacing the main method with the one found in Listing 6.1.

**LISTING 6.1**   Main Entry Point for Your Game

```
static void Main()
{
    using (DodgerGame frm = new DodgerGame())
    {
        // Show our form and initialize our graphics engine
        frm.Show();
        frm.InitializeGraphics();
        Application.Run(frm);
    }
}
```

This should be familiar; it's essentially the same code you've used to start all of the examples thus far. You create the windows form, show it, initialize the graphics engine, and then run the form, and thus the application. Inside the InitializeGraphics function, though, is where you will start to make some changes. Add the method found in Listing 6.2 to your application.

**LISTING 6.2**   Initializing Your Graphics Components

```
/// <summary>
/// We will initialize our graphics device here
/// </summary>
public void InitializeGraphics()
{
    // Set our presentation parameters
    PresentParameters presentParams = new PresentParameters();

    presentParams.Windowed = true;
    presentParams.SwapEffect = SwapEffect.Discard;
    presentParams.AutoDepthStencilFormat = DepthFormat.D16;
    presentParams.EnableAutoDepthStencil = true;

    // Store the default adapter
    int adapterOrdinal = Manager.Adapters.Default.Adapter;
    CreateFlags flags = CreateFlags.SoftwareVertexProcessing;

    // Check to see if we can use a pure hardware device
    Caps caps = Manager.GetDeviceCaps(adapterOrdinal, DeviceType.Hardware);

    // Do we support hardware vertex processing?
    if (caps.DeviceCaps.SupportsHardwareTransformAndLight)
        // Replace the software vertex processing
```

**LISTING 6.2**   Continued

```
        flags = CreateFlags.HardwareVertexProcessing;

    // Do we support a pure device?
    if (caps.DeviceCaps.SupportsPureDevice)
        flags |= CreateFlags.PureDevice;

    // Create our device
    device = new Device(adapterOrdinal, DeviceType.Hardware, this, flags, presentParams);
    // Hook the device reset event
    device.DeviceReset += new EventHandler(this.OnDeviceReset);
    this.OnDeviceReset(device, null);
}
```

At first you create the presentation parameters structure much like you've done before, ensuring that you have a depth buffer. However, what's next is new. First, you store the adapter's ordinal, which you get from the default adapter. The creation flags that will be used when creating the device are also stored, and you default to software vertex processing much like all of our examples have used thus far.

However, most modern-day graphics cards can support vertex processing on the actual graphics hardware. Why would you want to spend valuable CPU time doing something the graphics card can do much faster anyway? The easiest answer is that you don't; however, you don't currently know whether or not the adapter being used supports this feature. This brings us to the next section of code.

You will now get and store the capabilities (*Caps* for short) of the device *before* you actually create it, so you can determine the flags you want to use for creating the device. Since you will be creating a hardware device, these Caps are the only set you will store. You may remember back from Chapter 2, "Choosing the Correct Device," when we displayed the entire list of capabilities of the device, that the structure is huge and broken up into many different sections. The section of interest right now is the DeviceCaps section, which stores the Caps specific to a driver.

When you want to check to see whether a particular feature is supported, you can simply check the Boolean value that maps to this feature: If it is true, the feature is supported; otherwise, it is not. You first check to see whether hardware transform and lighting is supported on this device. If it is, you can create the device with the hardware vertex processing flag, so we assign this to our stored flags instead. You then check to see whether you can create a pure device (which can only be created if hardware vertex processing is enabled), and if you can, you do a bitwise OR of the flags, adding this feature as well. The most efficient type of device you can create is a pure hardware device, so if these options are available to you, you should use them.

You then create your device using the flags you've stored, so depending on your graphics cards capabilities, you may have a pure hardware device, or some other variation. If you remember when you were using our vertex buffers and needed to hook the created event for when the device was reset, there is a similar situation here. Whenever the device is reset, you will want to set all of the default state of the device. You should hook the device's reset event, and then call it the initial time to set the state. The event handler method can be found in Listing 6.3. Add this method to your application.

**LISTING 6.3**  *Setting Default Device State*

```
private void OnDeviceReset(object sender, EventArgs e)
{
    device.Transform.Projection = Matrix.PerspectiveFovLH((float)Math.PI / 4,
        (float)this.Width / (float)this.Height, 1.0f, 1000.0f);

    device.Transform.View = Matrix.LookAtLH(new Vector3(0.0f, 9.5f, 17.0f), new Vector3(),
        new Vector3(0,1,0));

    // Do we have enough support for lights?
    if ((device.DeviceCaps.VertexProcessingCaps.SupportsDirectionalLights) &&
        ((unit)device.DeviceCaps.MaxActiveLights > 1))
    {
        // First light
        device.Lights[0].Type = LightType.Directional;
        device.Lights[0].Diffuse = Color.White;
        device.Lights[0].Direction = new Vector3(1, -1, -1);
        device.Lights[0].Commit();
        device.Lights[0].Enabled = true;
        // Second light
        device.Lights[1].Type = LightType.Directional;
        device.Lights[1].Diffuse = Color.White;
        device.Lights[1].Direction = new Vector3(-1, 1, -1);
        device.Lights[1].Commit();
        device.Lights[1].Enabled = true;

    }
    else
    {
        // Hmm.. no light support, let's just use
        // ambient light
        device.RenderState.Ambient = Color.White;
    }
}
```

Once again, the beginning of this function is pretty similar to things you've done before. You set up the camera by setting the view and projection transforms on your device. For this game, there will be a static non-moving camera, so this will only need to be done once after each device reset (all device-specific state is lost during a reset).

Using ambient light isn't preferred since we've already seen that the ambient light isn't overly realistic, so a directional light would be better. However, you can't be sure if the device actually supports these lights. Once the device has been created, you will no longer need to use the Caps structure that was stored before, since the device maintains this information for you. If the device can support directional lights, and can support more than one of them, you will use them; otherwise, you can default to an ambient light. It may not be all that realistic, but it's better than an all black scene.

Finally, you need to override the OnPaint function to enable your rendering, much like you've done before. You don't need to do much yet; just get something rendered. Add the following function:

## USING ONLY THE LIGHTS YOU NEED

Rather than the all-or-nothing approach used in the code here, you could instead perform a "layered" check of the light support. In this scenario, you would first detect if at least one light was supported, and if so, turn that light on. Then you could check if a second light was supported, and turn that one on if so. This enables you to have a fallback case (one light) even for devices that don't have the support you want (two lights). This example wouldn't look very good with only one directional light, so the layered check wasn't done. If it was, though, it would look something like this:

```
// Do we have enough support for lights?
if ((device.DeviceCaps.VertexProcessingCaps.SupportsDirectionalLights) &&
    ((unit)device.DeviceCaps.MaxActiveLights > 0))
{
    // First light
    device.Lights[0].Type = LightType.Directional;
    device.Lights[0].Diffuse = Color.White;
    device.Lights[0].Direction = new
Vector3(1, -1, -1);
    device.Lights[0].Commit();
    device.Lights[0].Enabled = true;
    if ((unit)device.DeviceCaps.MaxActiveLights > 1))
    {
    // Second light
        device.Lights[1].Type = LightType. Directional;
        device.Lights[1].Diffuse = Color.White;
        device.Lights[1].Direction = new Vector3(-1, 1, -1);
        device.Lights[1].Commit();
        device.Lights[1].Enabled = true;
    }
}
```

```
protected override void OnPaint(System.Windows.Forms.PaintEventArgs e)
{
    device.Clear(ClearFlags.Target ¦ ClearFlags.ZBuffer, Color.Black, 1.0f, 0);

    device.BeginScene();
    device.EndScene();

    device.Present();

    this.Invalidate();
}
```

Nothing new here, unless you consider the background color being black new or exciting. Now you can get ready to put in the first game play object, the road. The source code on the CD includes a .X file that will hold the road mesh data, so naturally we will need to declare the variables for the road mesh:

```
// Game board mesh information
private Mesh roadMesh = null;
private Material[] roadMaterials = null;
private Texture[] roadTextures = null;
```

You will also use a variation of the load mesh function you wrote in the previous chapter. The major differences here are that it will be static, since it will need to be called from more than one class, and you will pass in all the material and texture information rather than relying on the class level variables that were used before. Add the method from Listing 6.4 to your code.

**LISTING 6.4**   Generic Mesh Loading Routine

```
public static Mesh LoadMesh(Device device, string file, ref Material[] meshMaterials,
    ref Texture[] meshTextures)
{
    ExtendedMaterial[] mtrl;

    // Load our mesh
    Mesh tempMesh = Mesh.FromFile(file, MeshFlags.Managed, device, out mtrl);

    // If we have any materials, store them
    if ((mtrl != null) && (mtrl.Length > 0))
    {
        meshMaterials = new Material[mtrl.Length];
        meshTextures = new Texture[mtrl.Length];

        // Store each material and texture
        for (int i = 0; i < mtrl.Length; i++)
```

**LISTING 6.4    Continued**

```
        {
            meshMaterials[i] = mtrl[i].Material3D;
            if ((mtrl[i].TextureFilename != null) && (mtrl[i].TextureFilename !=
                string.Empty))
            {
                // We have a texture, try to load it
                meshTextures[i] = TextureLoader.FromFile(device, @"..\..\" +
                    mtrl[i].TextureFilename);
            }
        }
    }

    return tempMesh;
}
```

This function has already been discussed in depth before, so there's no need to go into it once more. You will use this function to load the road's mesh, and you should do this in the device reset event function. At the end of that function, add the following code:

```
// Create our road mesh
roadMesh = LoadMesh(device, @"..\..\road.x", ref roadMaterials, ref roadTextures);
```

Make sure you have copied the road mesh and texture file to your source code location. This code will load our road mesh, including the textures, and store the textures, materials, and mesh. Now, you will want to render this road mesh more than once per frame; you should create a function to do the rendering. Add the following function to your code:

```
private void DrawRoad(float x, float y, float z)
{
    device.Transform.World = Matrix.Translation(x, y, z);
    for (int i = 0; i < roadMaterials.Length; i++)
    {
        device.Material = roadMaterials[i];
        device.SetTexture(0, roadTextures[i]);
        roadMesh.DrawSubset(i);
    }
}
```

You should recognize this function, since it's remarkably similar to the one used to render the mesh before. You translate the mesh into the correct position and render each subset. The plan for rendering the road is to render two sections at a time: the section the car is currently driving on and the section immediately after that. In all actuality, the car will not be moving at all; we will instead move the road.

The reasoning behind doing it this way is two-fold. First, if the car was moved every frame, you would also need to move the camera every frame to keep up with it. That's just extra calculations you don't need. Another reason is precision: If you let the car move forward, and the player was good, eventually the car would be so far into the "world" that you could lose floating point precision, or worse overflow the variable. Since the "world" will not have any boundaries (there won't be any way to "win" the game), you keep the car in the same relative position, and move the road below it.

Naturally, you will need to add some variables for controlling the road. Add the following class level variables and constants:

```
// Constant values for the locations
public const float RoadLocationLeft = 2.5f;
public const float RoadLocationRight = -2.5f;
private const float RoadSize = 100.0f;
private const float MaximumRoadSpeed = 250.0f;
private const float RoadSpeedIncrement = 0.5f;


// Depth locations of the two 'road' meshes we will draw
private float RoadDepth0 = 0.0f;
private float RoadDepth1 = -100.0f;
private float RoadSpeed = 30.0f;
```

The mesh being used for the road is a known commodity. It is exactly 100 units long and 10 units wide. The size constant reflects the actual length of the road, while the two location constants mark the center of the lanes on either side of the road. The last two constants are designed to control the actual gameplay (once it is implemented). The maximum road speed you want to allow the game to get to is 250 units per second, and every time you increment the speed, you will want to increment it one half of a unit.

Finally, you need to maintain the depth location of the two road sections. You should initialize the first section at zero, with the second section initialized directly at the end of the first (notice that this is the same as the road size variable). With the basic variables and constants needed to draw (and move) the road, let's add the calls to do the actual drawing. You will want to draw the road first, so immediately after your BeginScene call in your rendering function, add the two DrawRoad calls:

```
// Draw the two cycling roads
DrawRoad(0.0f, 0.0f, RoadDepth0);
DrawRoad(0.0f, 0.0f, RoadDepth1);
```

Running the application now, you can see that the road is definitely being drawn; however, the "asphalt" of the road looks extremely pixilated. The cause of this pixilation is the way Direct3D determines the color of a pixel in the rendered scene. When one texel happens to cover more than one pixel on the screen, the pixels are run through a magnify filter to compensate. When there can be multiple texels covering a single pixel, they are run through a minifying filter. The default filter for both minification and magnification is a Point filter, which simply uses the nearest texel as the color for that pixel. This is the cause of our pixilation.

Now, there are multiple different ways to filter our textures; however, the device may or may not support them. What you really want is a filter that can interpolate between the texels to give a more smooth look to the road texture. In the OnDeviceReset function, add the code found in Listing 6.5.

**LISTING 6.5**    Implementing Texture Filtering

```
// Try to set up a texture minify filter, pick anisotropic first
if (device.DeviceCaps.TextureFilterCaps.SupportsMinifyAnisotropic)
{
    device.SamplerState[0].MinFilter = TextureFilter.Anisotropic;
}
else if (device.DeviceCaps.TextureFilterCaps.SupportsMinifyLinear)
{
    device.SamplerState[0].MinFilter = TextureFilter.Linear;
}

// Do the same thing for magnify filter
if (device.DeviceCaps.TextureFilterCaps.SupportsMagnifyAnisotropic)
{
    device.SamplerState[0].MagFilter = TextureFilter.Anisotropic;
}
else if (device.DeviceCaps.TextureFilterCaps.SupportsMagnifyLinear)
{
    device.SamplerState[0].MagFilter = TextureFilter.Linear;
}
```

As you can see here, you first detect whether your device can support anisotropic filtering for minification or magnification. If it can, you use that filter for both filters. If it cannot, you next see whether the device supports a linear filter for both, and use that if it's available. If neither of these is available, you should do nothing and live with the pixilation of the road. Assuming your card supports one of these filtering methods, running the application now will show a much less-pixilated road.

Now the road is in the middle of the screen, but it's not yet moving. You will need a new method that will be used to update the game state, and do nifty things like moving the road and detecting when the car has collided with an obstacle. You should call this function as the first thing you do in your OnPaint method (before the Clear method):

```
// Before this render, we should update any state
OnFrameUpdate();
```

You will also need to add this method to your application. Add the method from Listing 6.6 to your code.

**LISTING 6.6** Per Frame Updates

```
private void OnFrameUpdate()
{
    // First, get the elapsed time
    elapsedTime = Utility.Timer(DirectXTimer.GetElapsedTime);

    RoadDepth0 += (RoadSpeed * elapsedTime);
    RoadDepth1 += (RoadSpeed * elapsedTime);

    // Check to see if we need to cycle the road
    if (RoadDepth0 > 75.0f)
    {
        RoadDepth0 = RoadDepth1 - 100.0f;
    }

    if (RoadDepth1 > 75.0f)
    {
        RoadDepth1 = RoadDepth0 - 100.0f;
    }
}
```

This function will get much larger before the game is finished, but for now, all you really want it to do is move the road. Ignoring the elapsed time (which I'll get to briefly), the only thing this function currently does is move the road and then remove road sections you've already passed, and place them at the end of the current road section. When determining the amount of movement the road should have, we use the current road speed (measured in units per second), and multiply that by the amount of elapsed time (measured in seconds), to get the "fraction" of movement this frame should have. You will also need to include the reference to the elapsedTime variable in your declaration section:

```
private float elapsedTime = 0.0f;
```

## SHOP TALK

### USING REAL-TIME TO MOVE OBJECTS

Why do we need the time? For the sake of argument, let's say you decided to just increment the road position a constant amount for every frame. On your computer, it runs just perfectly, so why wouldn't it run just as well on other systems? So you try it out on your buddy's system, which happens to be quite a bit slower than yours. What's this? The road seems to be moving amazingly slow. Trying it out

*SHOP TALK*

on a machine faster than yours shows the road moves much faster than it should as well.

The reason for this is that you are doing your calculations based on frame rate. For example, let's say on your system, you run at a near constant 60 frames per second. So when doing your calculations, you base everything off of this static frame rate. However, machines that only run at 40 frames per second, or faster ones that run at say 80 frames per second, will naturally provide different results. Since it should be a goal that your game runs identically on *every* system (as far as speed is concerned), using frame rate to do your calculations should always be avoided.

A better way to deal with this problem is to define your movements and calculations per some unit of time. For example, our maximum road speed constant is defined as 250 units per second. Our first goal would be to retrieve the amount of time that has passed since our last "update." The .NET Runtime has a built-in property (tick count) that can be used to determine the current tick count of the system, but this has its problems; mainly the low resolution of the timer. This property will only update approximately every 15 milliseconds, so on a system where you are running a high frame rate (above 60 frames per second), the movement will appear choppy, since the times used won't be smooth.

The DirectX SDK includes a class called DirectXTimer that uses a high-resolution timer (usually 1 millisecond) if it's available on your machine. If this timer isn't available on your machine, it will revert back to the tick count. The examples in this book will use this timer as the mechanism for timing. It already includes the code for a high-precision timer, so why should we reinvent the wheel?

# Adding a Movable Car into Your Scene

Now that you have the road rendering, as well as moving through the scene, you should add the object the player will interact with: the car. You could simply put the car variables and constants and code into the main class where we have the road sections, but that just wouldn't be very modular. You will want to maintain the car code separately and in its own class. Create the car class now. From the project menu, select the Add New Item option, and choose to add a new class, named "Car". Make sure you include the using clauses for the Managed DirectX references in this new code file that has been created for you.

What will the car class need to do? Since the car will remain stationary while everything moves below it, the car will not need to move backward or forward. However, given that the car will need to dodge any obstacles in the road, it will need to be able to move left or right. It will also need to be able to render itself. Given this information, you should add the following set of variables in your class:

```
// Car constants
public const float Height = 2.5f;
public const float Depth = 3.0f;
public const float SpeedIncrement = 0.1f;
private const float Scale = 0.85f;
```

```
// Car data information
private float carLocation = DodgerGame.RoadLocationLeft;
private float carDiameter;
private float carSpeed = 10.0f;
private bool movingLeft = false;
private bool movingRight = false;

// Our car mesh information
private Mesh carMesh = null;
private Material[] carMaterials = null;
private Texture[] carTextures = null;
```

These will control everything you need to control for your car. You have constants for the height and depth of the car, which will remain static (since you are only moving left or right). The speed at which the car's lateral movement can change is also constant. The final constant is because the car's model is slightly larger than the side of the road, so you will need to scale the model down slightly.

The non-constant data in the car class is relatively self-explanatory. You have the current location of the car on the road, which we will default to the left side. You have the diameter of the car, which will be used when it is time to determine when it has collided with an obstacle. You have the current lateral speed of the car (since the road can increase in speed, the car movement speed should increase as well). Of course, you also have our two Boolean variables that determine which direction you are moving, if at all. Lastly, the mesh data is stored.

The constructor for the car class will need to create the mesh object (and its associated structures) and calculate the diameter of the car. Replace the default constructor created for you with the code found in Listing 6.7.

## LISTING 6.7    Creating a Car Class

```
/// <summary>
/// Create a new car device, and load the mesh data for it
/// </summary>
/// <param name="device">D3D device to use</param>
public Car(Device device)
{
    // Create our car mesh
    carMesh = DodgerGame.LoadMesh(device, @"..\..\car.x", ref carMaterials,
ref carTextures);

    // We need to calculate a bounding sphere for our car
    VertexBuffer vb = carMesh.VertexBuffer;
    try
```

**LISTING 6.7** Continued

```
    {
        // We need to lock the entire buffer to calculate this
        GraphicsStream stm = vb.Lock(0, 0, LockFlags.None);
        Vector3 center; // We won't use the center, but it's required
        float radius = Geometry.ComputeBoundingSphere(stm,
            carMesh.NumberVertices, carMesh.VertexFormat, out center);

        // All we care about is the diameter.  Store that
        carDiameter = (radius * 2) * Scale;
    }
    finally
    {
        // No matter what, make sure we unlock and dispose this vertex
        // buffer.
        vb.Unlock();
        vb.Dispose();
    }
}
```

Creating the mesh is simple, since it's the exact same method you used when creating the road's mesh, just with different variable names. Calculating the diameter of the car (which is next), though, is new and exciting code. What you are really doing is calculating the bounding sphere (the sphere that completely contains all of the points in your mesh) for the car. The Geometry class contains this function, but it requires that you pass in the vertex data you wish to calculate the bounding sphere for.

What you need is to get the vertex data from the mesh. You already know that the vertex data is stored in vertex buffers, so you can use the vertex buffer that's stored in the mesh. In order to read the data from the vertex buffer, you will need to call the lock method. You will learn about the various methods from the vertex buffer in the next chapter; for now, this method will just return all of the vertex data to you in a stream. You can then use the ComputeBoundingSphere method to get the "center" of this mesh and the radius of the sphere. Since you don't care about the center of the mesh, and want to store the diameter, you can just double the radius and store that. However, since you are scaling down the mesh, you should also scale down the diameter. Finally (in your finally block no less), you make sure the vertex buffer we were using has been unlocked and disposed.

Now you should add a method to do the drawing of your car. Since you are storing the location of the car in the class, the only thing you will need for this method is the device to use for the drawing. This method will be strikingly similar to the DrawRoad call, with the only differences being the variables used and the fact that we scale the mesh before translating it. Add the following code:

```csharp
/// <summary>
/// Render the car given the current properties
/// </summary>
/// <param name="device">The device used to render the car</param>
public void Draw(Device device)
{
    // The car is a little bit too big, scale it down
    device.Transform.World = Matrix.Scaling(Scale,
        Scale, Scale) *  Matrix.Translation(carLocation, Height, Depth);

    for (int i = 0; i < carMaterials.Length; i++)
    {
        device.Material = carMaterials[i];
        device.SetTexture(0, carTextures[i]);
        carMesh.DrawSubset(i);
    }
}
```

Before you actually use the car class, though, you will need to make the private variables you may need access to publicly available. Add this public property list to your car class:

```csharp
// Public properties for car data
public float Location
{
    get { return carLocation; }
    set { carLocation = value; }
}
public float Diameter
{
    get { return carDiameter; }
}
public float Speed
{
    get { return carSpeed; }
    set { carSpeed = value; }
}
public bool IsMovingLeft
{
    get { return movingLeft; }
    set { movingLeft = value; }
}
public bool IsMovingRight
```

```
{
    get { return movingRight; }
    set { movingRight = value; }
}
```

Now, you will need to add a variable to maintain the car class in the main game engine. Add the following somewhere in your variable declaration section of DodgerGame:

```
// Car
private Car car = null;
```

Since you use the device as a parameter to the constructor of the car, you can't actually create the car class until the device has been created. A good place to put the car's creation would be in the OnDeviceReset method. Immediately after creating the road mesh add the following to create your car object:

```
// Create our car
car = new Car(device);
```

Now that you have the car object created, you can update the rendering method to include the car drawing method. After the two DrawRoad methods being called in the OnPaint method, add a call to your draw method from the car object:

```
// Draw the current location of the car
car.Draw(device);
```

Now you have the car rendered on your moving road. How can you control the movement of the car from one side of the road to the other, though? Ignoring the mouse for now, you can assume that the user has a keyboard, and they will use the keyboard to control the car. The arrow keys make perfect sense for this control, so you should use them. Override the OnKeyDown method in the DodgerGame class as seen in Listing 6.8.

**LISTING 6.8**    Handling Keystrokes

```
/// <summary>
/// Handle key strokes
/// </summary>
protected override void OnKeyDown(System.Windows.Forms.KeyEventArgs e)
{
    // Handle the escape key for quiting
    if (e.KeyCode == Keys.Escape)
    {
        // Close the form and return
        this.Close();
```

**LISTING 6.8**   Continued

```
            return;
    }

    // Handle left and right keys
    if ((e.KeyCode == Keys.Left) || (e.KeyCode == Keys.NumPad4))
    {
        car.IsMovingLeft = true;
        car.IsMovingRight = false;
    }
    if ((e.KeyCode == Keys.Right) || (e.KeyCode == Keys.NumPad6))
    {
        car.IsMovingLeft = false;
        car.IsMovingRight = true;
    }
    // Stop moving
    if (e.KeyCode == Keys.NumPad5)
    {
        car.IsMovingLeft = false;
        car.IsMovingRight = false;
    }
}
```

Nothing strange is going on here. If the Escape key is pressed, the game will be ended by closing the form. If the left or right key is pressed, you set the appropriate "moving" variable true, while setting the opposite moving variable false. If the 5 key on the number pad is pressed, you stop movement of the car completely. So now, running the application and pressing these keys will cause the variables controlling the car to update, but the car itself will not move. You need to add an update function to the car as well. Add the method found in Listing 6.9 into your car class.

**LISTING 6.9**   Updating Car Movements

```
/// <summary>
/// Update the cars state based on the elapsed time
/// </summary>
/// <param name="elapsedTime">Amount of time that has elapsed</param>
public void Update(float elapsedTime)
{
    if (movingLeft)
    {
        // Move the car
```

LISTING 6.9    Continued

```
            carLocation += (carSpeed * elapsedTime);
            // Is the car all the way to the left?
            if (carLocation >= DodgerGame.RoadLocationLeft)
            {
                movingLeft = false;
                carLocation = DodgerGame.RoadLocationLeft;
            }
        }

        if (movingRight)
        {
            // Move the car
            carLocation -= (carSpeed * elapsedTime);
            // Is the car all the way to the right?
            if (carLocation <= DodgerGame.RoadLocationRight)
            {
                movingRight = false;
                carLocation = DodgerGame.RoadLocationRight;
            }
        }
    }
}
```

This method takes in the elapsed time so that you can maintain the same movement on all computers much like you do with the road. The function itself is quite simple. If one of the movement variables is true, you will move the appropriate direction (based on the elapsed time). You then detect whether you've moved all the way to the correct location, and if you have, you will stop the movement completely. However, this method isn't being called currently, so you will need to update the OnFrameUpdate method in the DodgerGame class to include calling this method. Add the following line to the end of that method:

```
// Now that the road has been 'moved', update our car if it's moving
car.Update(elapsedTime);
```

# Adding Obstacles

Congratulations. This is the first interactive 3D graphics application you've created. The effect of simulating car movement has been achieved.  While you know that it's really the road that is moving below the car, it appears as if the car is speeding down the road. You've got half of the gameplay options implemented already. What you need now are the obstacles that you will be trying to avoid. Much like you added the car class, add a new class called "Obstacle". Make sure you add the using clauses for the Managed DirectX references for this code file as well.

Rather than using the same mesh for every obstacle, it would be nice to have a little variety in the obstacle list: in both type of obstacle as well as color. You can use the stock objects that can be created from the mesh object to vary the types of mesh, and you can use the materials to vary the colors. You should add the constants and variables needed for the obstacle class from Listing 6.10.

**LISTING 6.10**   Obstacle Constants

```
// Object constants
private const int NumberMeshTypes = 5;
private const float ObjectLength = 3.0f;
private const float ObjectRadius = ObjectLength / 2.0f;
private const int ObjectStacksSlices = 18;

// obstacle colors
private static readonly Color[] ObstacleColors = {
        Color.Red, Color.Blue, Color.Green,
        Color.Bisque, Color.Cyan, Color.DarkKhaki,
        Color.OldLace, Color.PowderBlue, Color.DarkTurquoise,
        Color.Azure, Color.Violet, Color.Tomato,
        Color.Yellow, Color.Purple, Color.AliceBlue,
        Color.Honeydew, Color.Crimson, Color.Firebrick };

// Mesh information
private Mesh obstacleMesh = null;
private Material obstacleMaterial;
private Vector3 position;
private bool isTeapot;
```

As you can see from the first constant, there will be five different mesh types (sphere, cube, torus, cylinder, and teapot). The majority of these mesh types will have either a length parameter or a radius parameter. Since you will want the obstacles to be similarly sized, you should use constants for these parameters. Many of the mesh types also have extra parameters that control the number of triangles included in the mesh (stacks, slices, rings, and so forth). The last constant will be used for these parameters. Increase this value for more triangles (and a higher level of detail), decrease it for less.

The list of colors that is next is where you will pick your color for the mesh. I've randomly selected these colors, but you can feel free to add, remove, or change any of the colors in this list. You'll notice that you aren't storing an array of materials, nor are you storing textures for our meshes in this class. You know the default mesh types only contain one subset with no textures or materials, so this extra information isn't necessary.

Since the obstacles should be "lying" on the road as the player drives by, and you know in reality that it's the road that is moving (not the player), you will also need to ensure that the obstacles move with the world. You therefore maintain a position for the obstacle that will be updated every frame as the road moves. Finally, since you can't control the size of a teapot during creation, you need to know if we're using a teapot obstacle so that you can scale it to the correct size.

Replace the class constructor of the Obstacle class with the following new one:

```
public Obstacle(Device device, float x, float y, float z)
{
    // Store our position
    position = new Vector3(x, y, z);

    // It's not a teapot
    isTeapot = false;

    // Create a new obstacle
    switch (Utility.Rnd.Next(NumberMeshTypes))
    {
        case 0:
            obstacleMesh = Mesh.Sphere(device, ObjectRadius, ObjectStacksSlices,
                ObjectStacksSlices);
            break;
        case 1:
            obstacleMesh = Mesh.Box(device, ObjectLength, ObjectLength, ObjectLength);
            break;
        case 2:
            obstacleMesh = Mesh.Teapot(device);
            isTeapot = true;
            break;
        case 3:
            obstacleMesh = Mesh.Cylinder(device, ObjectRadius, ObjectRadius, ObjectLength,
                ObjectStacksSlices, ObjectStacksSlices);
            break;
        case 4:
            obstacleMesh = Mesh.Torus(device, ObjectRadius / 3.0f, ObjectRadius / 2.0f,
                ObjectStacksSlices, ObjectStacksSlices);
            break;
    }
```

```
// Set the obstacle color
obstacleMaterial = new Material();
Color objColor = ObstacleColors[Utility.Rnd.Next(ObstacleColors.Length)];
obstacleMaterial.Ambient = objColor;
obstacleMaterial.Diffuse = objColor;
}
```

You'll notice the use of the "Rnd" property on a utility class here. The source for this function is included on the CD, and is unimportant to the implementation of this function. Its goal is to simply return random numbers. The constructor for our obstacle stores the default position of the obstacle, and defaults to a non-teapot mesh (since there is only one case where it will be a teapot). It then randomly selects one of the mesh types and creates that mesh. Finally, it selects a random color from the list and uses that as the material color for the obstacles.

Before you're ready to get the obstacles into your game engine, though, there are a couple other things you will need to do. First, you need to have a function to update your objects' position to match the road. Add the following method:

```
public void Update(float elapsedTime, float speed)
{
    position.Z += (speed * elapsedTime);
}
```

Again, you pass in the elapsed time to ensure that we maintain the same behavior on machines of different speeds. You also pass in the current speed of the road, so the objects will be moving as if they are lying on the road. With the obstacles being updated, you also need a method to do the rendering. Much like the car's draw method, you will need one for your obstacle as well. Add the method found in Listing 6.11 to your obstacle class.

**LISTING 6.11**   Drawing Obstacles

```
public void Draw(Device device)
{
    if (isTeapot)
    {
        device.Transform.World = Matrix.Scaling(ObjectRadius, ObjectRadius, ObjectRadius)
            * Matrix.Translation(position);
    }
    else
    {
        device.Transform.World = Matrix.Translation(position);
    }
    device.Material = obstacleMaterial;
```

LISTING 6.11    Continued

```
        device.SetTexture(0, null);
        obstacleMesh.DrawSubset(0);
}
```

Since the teapot mesh isn't correctly scaled after creation, if you are rendering one of those, you should first scale the teapot, and then move it into position. You then set the material for your color, set the texture to null, and draw the mesh.

Obviously, you will want to have more than one obstacle on the road at a time. What you need is an easy way to add and remove obstacles from the game engine. Using an array is a possibility, but not the greatest since it makes resizing the array a bit difficult. You should just make a collection class for storing your obstacles. Add the class found in Listing 6.12 to the end of your obstacle code file.

LISTING 6.12    Obstacles Collection Class

```
public class Obstacles : IEnumerable
{
    private ArrayList obstacleList = new ArrayList();

    /// <summary>
    /// Indexer for this class
    /// </summary>
    public Obstacle this[int index]
    {
        get
        {
            return (Obstacle)obstacleList[index];
        }
    }

    // Get the enumerator from our arraylist
    public IEnumerator GetEnumerator()
    {
        return obstacleList.GetEnumerator();
    }

    /// <summary>
    /// Add an obstacle to our list
    /// </summary>
    /// <param name="obstacle">The obstacle to add</param>
    public void Add(Obstacle obstacle)
```

**LISTING 6.12**   Continued

```
    {
        obstacleList.Add(obstacle);
    }

    /// <summary>
    /// Remove an obstacle from our list
    /// </summary>
    /// <param name="obstacle">The obstacle to remove</param>
    public void Remove(Obstacle obstacle)
    {
        obstacleList.Remove(obstacle);
    }

    /// <summary>
    /// Clear the obstacle list
    /// </summary>
    public void Clear()
    {
        obstacleList.Clear();
    }
}
```

You will need to put a using clause for System.Collections at the top of your code file for this to compile correctly. This class contains an indexer for direct access to an obstacle, an enumerator so that the foreach construct works, and the three methods you will care about: add, remove, and clear. With this base functionality in your obstacles code file, you're ready to add obstacles to your engine.

First, you will need a variable that you can use to maintain the list of current obstacles in the scene. Add the following variable into the DodgerGame class:

```
// Obstacle information
private Obstacles obstacles;
```

Now you need a function you can use to fill up the next road section with new obstacles. Use the following code for this:

```
/// <summary>
/// Add a series of obstacles onto a road section
/// </summary>
/// <param name="minDepth">Minimum depth of the obstacles</param>
private void AddObstacles(float minDepth)
```

```
{
    // Add the right number of obstacles
    int numberToAdd = (int)((RoadSize / car.Diameter - 1) / 2.0f);
    // Get the minimum space between obstacles in this section
    float minSize = ((RoadSize / numberToAdd) - car.Diameter) / 2.0f;

    for (int i = 0; i < numberToAdd; i++)
    {
        // Get a random # in the min size range
        float depth = minDepth - ((float)Utility.Rnd.NextDouble() * minSize);
        // Make sure it's in the right range
        depth -= (i * (car.Diameter * 2));

        // Pick the left or right side of the road
        float location = (Utility.Rnd.Next(50) > 25)?RoadLocationLeft:RoadLocationRight;

        // Add this obstacle
        obstacles.Add(new Obstacle(device, location, ObstacleHeight, depth));
    }
}
```

This function will be the starting point for getting obstacles into the game. It first calculates the number of obstacles to add in this road section. It has to make sure that there will be enough room between obstacles for the car to fit; otherwise, the game wouldn't be very fair. After it calculates the number of obstacles needed for the road and the minimum space between obstacles, it adds them randomly to the road. It then adds them to the current list of obstacles. You'll notice the ObstacleHeight constant used when creating a new obstacle. The definition for this is

```
private const float ObstacleHeight = Car.Height * 0.85f;
```

Three things left before the obstacles are in the scene: You need to add a call into our obstacle addition method somewhere, you need to make sure you call the update function on each obstacle in the scene, and you need to render the obstacles. Since you will need a method to reset all the member variables back to defaults in order to start a new game, you should just create that function now, and use this method to be our initial call to AddObstacles. Add the method found in Listing 6.13.

**LISTING 6.13** Loading Default Game Options

```
/// <summary>
/// Here we will load all the default game options
/// </summary>
```

**LISTING 6.13** Continued

```
private void LoadDefaultGameOptions()
{
    // Road information
    RoadDepth0 = 0.0f;
    RoadDepth1 = -100.0f;
    RoadSpeed = 30.0f;
    // Car data information
    car.Location = RoadLocationLeft;
    car.Speed = 10.0f;
    car.IsMovingLeft = false;
    car.IsMovingRight = false;

    // Remove any obstacles currently in the game
    foreach(Obstacle o in obstacles)
    {
        // Dispose it first
        o.Dispose();
    }
    obstacles.Clear();

    // Add some obstacles
    AddObstacles(RoadDepth1);

    // Start our timer
    Utility.Timer(DirectXTimer.Start);
}
```

This method takes the various member variables of the classes you might care about and resets them to the defaults. It also takes any existing obstacles in the list, disposes them, and clears the list before refilling the list with new obstacles. It finally starts the timer. You should add the call to this function after you've created the device in the InitializeGraphics method. Do *not* add this function into the OnDeviceReset method; you only want to call this function when a new game is being started.

```
// Load the default game options
LoadDefaultGameOptions();
```

Now you need to add the call to update the obstacles into the OnFrameUpdate method. You want to update every obstacle every frame, so you will need to enumerate them. Add the following into the OnFrameUpdate method before the car's update method:

```
// Move our obstacles
foreach(Obstacle o in obstacles)
{
    // Update the obstacle, check to see if it hits the car
    o.Update(elapsedTime, RoadSpeed);
}
```

The last step before having the obstacles in the game engine would be to actually render them. In your OnPaint method, immediately after the car's draw method, you should add similar code for rendering your obstacles:

```
// Draw any obstacles currently visible
foreach(Obstacle o in obstacles)
{
    o.Draw(device);
}
```

Try running the game now! As you speed down the road, you pass a few obstacles, but then what's this? It seems that after you pass the first few obstacles, no more ever appear. If you remember correctly, the AddObstacles method only adds the obstacles to one section of road, and you are constantly moving the road sections, yet you never call the method again for these "new" road sections. Update the section of code you use to add new road sections as follows:

```
// Check to see if we need to cycle the road
if (RoadDepth0 > 75.0f)
{
    RoadDepth0 = RoadDepth1 - 100.0f;
    AddObstacles(RoadDepth0);
}

if (RoadDepth1 > 75.0f)
{
    RoadDepth1 = RoadDepth0 - 100.0f;
    AddObstacles(RoadDepth1);
}
```

Now things are looking more promising. You have the car speeding down the road, flying by obstacles (and at least currently, flying through obstacles). The obstacles themselves seem a little boring though. You should add a little movement to them. You can make them rotate around as you speed toward them! First, you'll need to add a few new member variables to the obstacle class to control the rotation:

```
// Rotation information
private float rotation = 0;
private float rotationspeed = 0.0f;
private Vector3 rotationVector;
```

The speed they rotate and the axis they rotate on should be random so that they appear to all be moving differently. This can be easily accomplished by adding the following two lines at the end of the obstacle class constructor:

```
rotationspeed = (float)Utility.Rnd.NextDouble() * (float)Math.PI;
rotationVector = new Vector3((float)Utility.Rnd.NextDouble(),
    (float)Utility.Rnd.NextDouble(),(float)Utility.Rnd.NextDouble());
```

Two things left to do before the obstacles will rotate correctly. First you need to include the rotation into the update function as follows:

```
rotation += (rotationspeed * elapsedTime);
```

Nothing unusual here; simply increase the rotation based on the elapsed time and the current (randomly selected) rotation speed. Finally, you will need to actually add a rotation into your world transform so that the obstacles are rendered rotating. Update the two world transform calls as follows:

```
if (isTeapot)
{
    device.Transform.World = Matrix.RotationAxis(rotationVector, rotation)
        * Matrix.Scaling(ObjectRadius, ObjectRadius, ObjectRadius)
        * Matrix.Translation(position);
}
else
{
    device.Transform.World = Matrix.RotationAxis(rotationVector, rotation)
        * Matrix.Translation(position);
}
```

Running the game now, you can see the obstacles spinning around randomly as you speed toward them. What's the next step? Well, it would be great if the car would actually collide with the obstacles, and you could keep a score to see how well you've done. Once you start adding the score, you'll also need to maintain game state. Add the following member variables to your main engine in the DodgerGame class:

```
// Game information
private bool isGameOver = true;
```

```
private int gameOverTick = 0;
private bool hasGameStarted = false;
private int score = 0;
```

All of the game's information is stored here. You know whether or not the game is over, whether the game has started for the first time, the last time the game was over, and the current score of the user playing the game. That's all well and good, but what do you need to actually do with all of this? You should start with the score, since that's what the player is going to care most about anyway. Every time the player passes an obstacle, you will want to increase the score. However, you also want to make the game harder as it progresses, so you should also increase the road's speed so that the obstacles come at the player even faster. First things first: Add a line to reset the score in the LoadDefaultGameOptions so that when a new game is started, the player won't start with points:

```
car.IsMovingRight = false;
score = 0;
```

Now, in the OnFrameUpdate method, before you actually move the obstacles, add the following code:

```
// Remove any obstacles that are past the car
// Increase the score for each one, and also increase
// the road speed to make the game harder.
Obstacles removeObstacles = new Obstacles();
foreach(Obstacle o in obstacles)
{
    if (o.Depth > car.Diameter - (Car.Depth * 2))
    {
        // Add this obstacle to our list to remove
        removeObstacles.Add(o);
        // Increase roadspeed
        RoadSpeed += RoadSpeedIncrement;

        // Make sure the road speed stays below max
        if (RoadSpeed >= MaximumRoadSpeed)
        {
            RoadSpeed = MaximumRoadSpeed;
        }

        // Increase the car speed as well
        car.IncrementSpeed();

        // Add the new score
```

```
        score += (int)(RoadSpeed * (RoadSpeed / car.Speed));
    }
}
// Remove the obstacles in the list
foreach(Obstacle o in removeObstacles)
{
    obstacles.Remove(o);
    // May as well dispose it as well
    o.Dispose();
}
removeObstacles.Clear();
```

What you want to do here is get a list of obstacles that you've already passed (this "list" should only contain one obstacle at a time). For each obstacle in this list, you will want to increase the score, as well as increase the road speed to raise difficulty, and increase the car's movement speed (although not as much as you increase the road's speed). After all that has been completed, you remove these obstacles from the real obstacle list. As you can see, a formula using the current road speed is used when calculating the score, so that as you get farther along, you will get more points. You'll also notice a method we use for the car that we haven't implemented yet. Nothing fancy here:

```
/// <summary>
/// Increment the movement speed of the car
/// </summary>
public void IncrementSpeed()
{
    carSpeed += SpeedIncrement;
}
```

Now you will need to add a new method to determine when the car has actually hit one of the obstacles. You should add this check into the obstacle class. Add the following method there:

```
public bool IsHittingCar(float carLocation, float carDiameter)
{
    // In order for the obstacle to be hitting the car,
    // it must be on the same side of the road and
    // hitting the car

    if (position.Z > (Car.Depth - (carDiameter / 2.0f)))
    {
        // are we on the right side of the car
        if ((carLocation < 0) && (position.X < 0))
```

```
        return true;

    if ((carLocation > 0) && (position.X > 0))
        return true;
    }
    return false;
}
```

Pretty simple stuff here; you check to see if the car is at the same depth as the obstacle and can hit it, and if it is, and it's on the same side of the road, return true. Otherwise, the car and obstacle haven't hit, so you can return false. With this code in now, you need to implement this into the game engine. Replace the obstacle update code with this new and improved code:

```
// Move our obstacles
foreach(Obstacle o in obstacles)
{
    // Update the obstacle, check to see if it hits the car
    o.Update(elapsedTime, RoadSpeed);
    if (o.IsHittingCar(car.Location, car.Diameter))
    {
        // If it does hit the car, the game is over.
        isGameOver = true;
        gameOverTick = System.Environment.TickCount;
        // Stop our timer
        Utility.Timer(DirectXTimer.Stop);
    }
}
```

Now, after you update each obstacle, you check to see if it is hitting the car. If it is, the game is over. You set the game settings, and stop the timer.

# Implementing the Finishing Touches

Currently, you don't do anything with these state variables. You should implement the game-over logic first. You will force the player to hit any key to start the game. After the game is over (you've crashed), there will be a slight pause (approximately one second), and then hitting any key will start the game once again. The first thing you'll need to make sure is that while the game is over, you don't update any other state. So the very first lines in OnFrameUpdate should be

```
// Nothing to update if the game is over
if ((isGameOver) || (!hasGameStarted))
    return;
```

Now you need to handle the keystrokes to restart the game. At the very end of your OnKeyDown override, you can add this logic:

```
if (isGameOver)
{
    LoadDefaultGameOptions();
}


// Always set isGameOver to false when a key is pressed
isGameOver = false;
hasGameStarted = true;
```

This is the behavior you want. Now, when the game is over, and the player presses a key, a new game is started with the default game options. You can remove the call to LoadDefaultGameOptions from InitializeGraphics now if you want to, since it will be called as soon as you press a key to start a new game. However, you still don't have the code that will cause the slight pause after you crash. You can add that to your OnKeyDown override as well; you should do it directly after checking for Escape:

```
// Ignore keystrokes for a second after the game is over
if ((System.Environment.TickCount - gameOverTick) < 1000)
{
    return;
}
```

This will ignore any keystrokes (except Escape to quit) for a period of one second after the game is over. Now, you can actually play the game! There's definitely something missing, though. You're maintaining a score, but there is nothing in the game that tells the user anything. You will need to rectify that. There is a Font class in the Direct3D namespace that can be used to draw some text; however, there is also a Font class in the System.Drawing namespace, and these two class names will collide if you attempt to use "Font" without fully qualifying it. Luckily, you can alias with the using statement as follows:

```
using Direct3D = Microsoft.DirectX.Direct3D;
```

Now each font you create can be a different color, but must be a unique size and family. You will want to draw two different types of text for this game, so you will need two different fonts. Add the following variables to the DodgerGame class:

```
// Fonts
private Direct3D.Font scoreFont = null;
private Direct3D.Font gameFont = null;
```

You will need to initialize these variables, but can't do so until the device has been created. You should do this after the device creation code. This does not need to happen in the OnDeviceReset event since these objects will automatically handle the device reset for you. Just add these lines to the end of the InitializeGraphics method:

```
// Create our fonts
scoreFont = new Direct3D.Font(device, new System.Drawing.Font("Arial", 12.0f,
    FontStyle.Bold));
gameFont = new Direct3D.Font(device, new System.Drawing.Font("Arial", 36.0f,
    FontStyle.Bold | FontStyle.Italic));
```

You've created two fonts of different sizes, but of the same family: Arial. Now you need to update the rendering method to draw the text. You will want the text to be drawn last, so after the car's draw method, add the following:

```
if (hasGameStarted)
{
    // Draw our score
    scoreFont.DrawText(null, string.Format("Current score: {0}", score),
        new Rectangle(5,5,0,0), DrawTextFormat.NoClip, Color.Yellow);
}

if (isGameOver)
{
    // If the game is over, notify the player
    if (hasGameStarted)
    {
        gameFont.DrawText(null, "You crashed. The game is over.", new Rectangle(25,45,0,0),
            DrawTextFormat.NoClip, Color.Red);
    }
    if ((System.Environment.TickCount - gameOverTick) >= 1000)
    {
        // Only draw this if the game has been over more than one second
        gameFont.DrawText(null, "Press any key to begin.", new Rectangle(25,100,0,0),
            DrawTextFormat.NoClip, Color.WhiteSmoke);
    }
}
```

The DrawText method will be discussed in depth in a later chapter, so for now, just know that it does what its name implies. It draws text. As you can see here, once the game has been started the first time, you will always show the current score. Then, if the game is over, and it has been started for the first time already, you notify the player that they have crashed. Finally, if the game has been over for a second or longer, let the player know that pressing a key will start a new game.

Wow! Now you've got a full-fledged game in the works. You can play, see your score increase, see your game end when you crash, and start over and play again. What's left? Well, it would be awesome if you could store the highest scores we've achieved so far.

## SHOP TALK

### ADDING HIGH SCORES

First off, we will need a place to store the information for the high scores. We will only really care about the name of the player as well as the score they achieved, so we can create a simple structure for this. Add this into your main games namespace:

```
/// <summary>
/// Structure used to maintain high scores
/// </summary>
public struct HighScore
{
    private int realScore;
    private string playerName;
    public int Score { get { return realScore; } set { realScore = value; } }
    public string Name { get { return playerName; } set { playerName = value; } }
}
```

Now we will also need to maintain the list of high scores in our game engine. We will only maintain the top three scores, so we can use an array to store these. Add the following declarations to our game engine:

```
// High score information
private HighScore[] highScores = new HighScore[3];
private string defaultHighScoreName = string.Empty;
```

All we need now is three separate functions. The first will check the current score to see if it qualifies for inclusion into the high score list. The next one will save the high score information into the registry, while the last one will load it back from the registry. Add these methods to the game engine:

```
/// <summary>
/// Check to see what the best high score is.  If this beats it,
/// store the index, and ask for a name
/// </summary>
private void CheckHighScore()
```

```
{
    int index = -1;
    for (int i = highScores.Length - 1; i >= 0; i--)
    {
        if (score >= highScores[i].Score) // We beat this score
        {
            index = i;
        }
    }

    // We beat the score if index is greater than 0
    if (index >= 0)
    {
        for (int i = highScores.Length - 1; i > index ; i--)
        {
            // Move each existing score down one
            highScores[i] = highScores[i-1];
        }
        highScores[index].Score = score;
        highScores[index].Name = Input.InputBox("You got a high score!!",
            "Please enter your name.", defaultHighScoreName);
    }
}

/// <summary>
/// Load the high scores from the registry
/// </summary>
private void LoadHighScores()
{
    Microsoft.Win32.RegistryKey key =
        Microsoft.Win32.Registry.LocalMachine.CreateSubKey(
        "Software\\MDXBoox\\Dodger");

    try
    {
        for(int i = 0; i < highScores.Length; i++)
        {
            highScores[i].Name = (string)key.GetValue(
                string.Format("Player{0}", i),  string.Empty);

            highScores[i].Score = (int)key.GetValue(
```

```csharp
                        string.Format("Score{0}", i),  0);
            }
            defaultHighScoreName = (string)key.GetValue(
                "PlayerName", System.Environment.UserName);
        }
        finally
        {
            if (key != null)
            {
                key.Close(); // Make sure to close the key
            }
        }
    }


    /// <summary>
    /// Save all the high score information to the registry
    /// </summary>
    public void SaveHighScores()
    {
        Microsoft.Win32.RegistryKey key =
            Microsoft.Win32.Registry.LocalMachine.CreateSubKey(
            "Software\\MDXBoox\\Dodger");

        try
        {
            for(int i = 0; i < highScores.Length; i++)
            {
                key.SetValue(string.Format("Player{0}", i), highScores[i].Name);
                key.SetValue(string.Format("Score{0}", i), highScores[i].Score);
            }
            key.SetValue("PlayerName", defaultHighScoreName);
        }
        finally
        {
            if (key != null)
            {
                key.Close(); // Make sure to close the key
            }
        }
    }
```

*SHOP TALK*

I won't delve too much into these functions since they deal mainly with built-in .NET classes and have really nothing to do with the Managed DirectX code. However, it is important to show where these methods get called from our game engine.

The check for the high scores should happen as soon as the game is over. Replace the code in OnFrameUpdate that checks if the car hits an obstacle with the following:

```
if (o.IsHittingCar(car.Location, car.Diameter))
{
    // If it does hit the car, the game is over.
    isGameOver = true;
    gameOverTick = System.Environment.TickCount;
    // Stop our timer
    Utility.Timer(DirectXTimer.Stop);
    // Check to see if we want to add this to our high scores list
    CheckHighScore();
}
```

You can load the high scores at the end of the constructor for the main game engine. You might notice that the save method is public (while the others were private). This is because we will call this method in our main method. Replace the main method with the following code:

```
using (DodgerGame frm = new DodgerGame())
{
    // Show our form and initialize our graphics engine
    frm.Show();
    frm.InitializeGraphics();
    Application.Run(frm);
    // Make sure to save the high scores
    frm.SaveHighScores();
}
```

The last thing we need to do is actually show the player the list of high scores. We will add this into our rendering method. Right before we call the end method on our game font, add this section of code to render our high scores:

```
// Draw the high scores
gameFont.DrawText(null, "High Scores: ", new Rectangle(25,155,0,0),
    DrawTextFormat.NoClip, Color.CornflowerBlue);

for (int i = 0; i < highScores.Length; i++)
{
    gameFont.DrawText(null, string.Format("Player: {0} : {1}", highScores[i].Name,
        highScores[i].Score),
```

SHOP TALK

```
new Rectangle(25,210 + (i * 55),0,0), DrawTextFormat.NoClip,
        Color.CornflowerBlue);
}
```

Take a moment to pat yourself on the back. You've just finished your first game.

## In Brief

- Use the mesh classes to render the game objects.
- Check certain device capabilities.
- Basic user input.
- Design a scoring system.
- Putting it all together.

See if you can beat my best score in Figure 6.1.

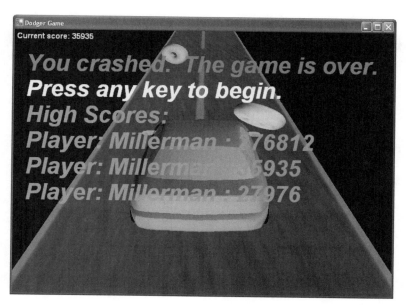

**FIGURE 6.1**    The completed game.

In the next chapter, we will discuss using advanced mesh features.

# PART II

# Intermediate Graphics Concepts

# Using Advanced Mesh Features

During the course of this chapter, we will discuss the more advanced features the mesh object contains, including

- Optimizing the mesh data
- Simplifying meshes
- Creating meshes with new vertex data components
- Welding vertices together

## Cloning Mesh Data

So you've finally gotten your mesh loaded and rendered in your scene. The scene has a few lights, and yet your mesh just appears completely black. Glancing at the properties of your mesh, you notice the vertex format doesn't include normal data, which as we already know is required for lighting calculations.

What we need is a simple way to take all of the mesh data we already have, and simply add the normal data to it. If you guessed that there is already a mechanism for this, then you've guessed correctly. Look at Listing 7.1:

**LISTING 7.1**    Ensuring That Your Mesh Contains Normal Data

```
// Check if mesh doesn't include normal data
if ((mesh.VertexFormat & VertexFormats.Normal) != VertexFormats.Normal)
{
    Mesh tempMesh = mesh.Clone(mesh.Options.Value,
        mesh.VertexFormat | VertexFormats.Normal, device);
    tempMesh.ComputeNormals();
    // Replace existing mesh
    mesh.Dispose();
    mesh = tempMesh;
}
```

Here we take an existing mesh object we've created named "mesh", and check to see if it already includes normal data. The VertexFormat property returns a list of VertexFormats that are combined via a bitwise OR, so we use our bitwise AND operator to determine whether the normal bit is set. If it is not, we then create a second temporary mesh via the Clone method on our original mesh. The Clone method has three overloads:

```
public Microsoft.DirectX.Direct3D.Mesh Clone (
    Microsoft.DirectX.Direct3D.MeshFlags options ,
    Microsoft.DirectX.Direct3D.GraphicsStream declaration ,
    Microsoft.DirectX.Direct3D.Device device )

public Microsoft.DirectX.Direct3D.Mesh Clone (
    Microsoft.DirectX.Direct3D.MeshFlags options ,
    Microsoft.DirectX.Direct3D.VertexElement[] declaration ,
    Microsoft.DirectX.Direct3D.Device device )

public Microsoft.DirectX.Direct3D.Mesh Clone (
    Microsoft.DirectX.Direct3D.MeshFlags options ,
    Microsoft.DirectX.Direct3D.VertexFormats vertexFormat ,
    Microsoft.DirectX.Direct3D.Device device )
```

In our example, we used the final overload. In each of the overloads, the first and last parameters are the same. The options parameter allows the newly created mesh object to have a different set of options than the original mesh did. If you want to keep the same options in the new mesh, then you can do what we've done in our example code above, using the existing options from the original mesh; however, you can also change them. Say you wanted the new mesh to reside in system memory rather than managed memory. Any of the MeshFlags that are available during mesh creation are also available during cloning.

The last parameter of the clone method is the device the new mesh will be created on. In many instances, this device will be the same device you used to create the original mesh, but it is possible to clone a mesh to an entirely different device. For example, let's say you were writing an application that was multiple-monitor aware, and had each monitor running in full-screen mode. While your mesh object was on your first monitor, and being rendered there, it isn't necessary to have an "instance" of this mesh on the secondary monitor. If the mesh now needs to be rendered on the secondary monitor as well, you can easily clone it to the new device, and have it available there as well. Our preceding example simply used the existing device we already had.

The middle parameter determines how the data will actually be rendered. In the overload we use, we pass in the vertex format of the newly cloned mesh (which can be different from the original). In each of the other overloads, the parameter is intended to be the vertex declaration of the newly created mesh. Vertex declarations are used in the programmable pipeline, which hasn't been covered yet, but they are essentially a much more powerful version of the fixed function vertex format options.

As you can see, there is also a helper function on the mesh class that can automatically compute the normals of a mesh. There are three overloads for this helper function as well. There is the parameter-less one we used, as well as two others that take in a single parameter for the adjacency information, either as an array of integers, or as a GraphicsStream. If you have the adjacency information, feel free to use it.

You can use the mesh's cloning ability to create new instances of the same mesh on a new device, or to change the options of an already created mesh. You can use it to create a mesh with new vertex format items, or even to remove existing vertex format data from your mesh. If the mesh you have currently doesn't meet your needs, you can probably clone it into a more suitable version.

## Optimizing Mesh Data

Cloning a mesh isn't the only way to enhance an existing mesh. Meshes can also be optimized in multiple ways. The Optimize function on a mesh is similar to the clone method, in that it can generate a new mesh with different options; however it can also perform optimizations during the generation of this new mesh. You cannot use the Optimize function to add or remove vertex data or clone to a new device though. Look at the main overload for the Optimize method:

```
public Microsoft.DirectX.Direct3D.Mesh Optimize (
    Microsoft.DirectX.Direct3D.MeshFlags flags ,
    int[] adjacencyIn , out int[] adjacencyOut ,
    out int[] faceRemap ,
    out Microsoft.DirectX.Direct3D.GraphicsStream vertexRemap )
```

Each of the four overloads for this method takes this set of arguments, or simply the flags and adjacency in information. Note, that the adjacencyIn parameter can be used as an array of integers (as shown above), or as a GraphicsStream.

The flags parameter is used to determine how the new mesh can be created. This member can be one or more flags from the MeshFlags enumeration (excluding the Use32Bit or the WriteOnly flags). However, there are numerous Optimize flags in this enumeration that can be used specifically for this function. See Table 7.1:

**TABLE 7.1**

**Mesh Optimization Options**

| | |
|---|---|
| MeshFlags.OptimizeCompact | Reorders the faces in the mesh to remove unused vertices and faces. |
| MeshFlags.OptimizeAttrSort | Reorders the faces of the mesh so that there are fewer attribute state changes (i.e., materials), which can enhance DrawSubset performance. |
| MeshFlags.OptimizeDeviceIndependent | Using this option affects the vertex cache size by specifying a default cache size that works well on legacy hardware. |
| MeshFlags.OptimizeDoNotSplit | Using this flag specifies that vertices should not be split if they are shared between attribute groups. |
| MeshFlags.OptimizeIgnoreVerts | Optimize faces only; ignore vertices. |
| MeshFlags.OptimizeStripeReorder | Using this flag will reorder the faces to maximize the length of adjacent triangles. |
| MeshFlags.OptimizeVertexCache | Using this flag will reorder the faces to increase the cache hit rate of the vertex caches. |

## OPTIMIZING MESHES IN PLACE

What if you don't want to create a whole new mesh though? You don't really want to change the various creation flags; you just want the benefits of the optimizations. There is a near identical method on the mesh object called "OptimizeInPlace" that takes the same parameters, with only two differences. The flags parameter *must* be one of the optimization flags (you cannot change any of the creation flags), and this method has no return value. All of the optimizations will happen directly on the mesh that calls this method.

The adjacencyIn parameter is also required, and can either be an integer array containing three integers per face that specify the three neighbors for each face in the mesh, or a graphics stream containing this same data.

If you choose one of the two overloads that has more than those two overloads, the last three parameters are all data that will be returned to you via an out parameter. The first member of this returned data will be the new adjacency information returned to you. The second member will be the new index for each face in the mesh. The final member will be a graphics stream that contains the new index for each vertex. Many applications will not require this information, and can skip using these overloads.

The following small section of code shows sorting a mesh by its attribute buffer, and ensuring that it is in managed memory:

```
// Compact our mesh
Mesh tempMesh = mesh.Optimize
➥(MeshFlags.Managed |
    MeshFlags.OptimizeAttrSort |
    ➥MeshFlags.OptimizeDoNotSplit, adj);
mesh.Dispose();
mesh = tempMesh;
```

# Simplifying Existing Meshes

> ## GENERATING ADJACENCY INFORMATION
>
> You may notice that many of the advanced methods of the mesh take in adjacency information. You can get this information during mesh creation, but what if you are receiving a mesh that has already been created? There is a method on the mesh object "GenerateAdjacency" that you can use to get this information. The first parameter to this function is a float value that you can use to specify that vertices whose position differ by less than this amount will be treated as coincident. The second parameter is an integer array that will be filled with the adjacency information. This array must be at least three * mesh.NumberFaces.

Now let's say that your artist has just given you a mesh for "prop" that resides in differing locations in your scene, depending on which level you are on. It some levels, the mesh is way in the background, and doesn't need to be nearly as detailed as in other levels where it is right up close to the character. You could ask your artist to make you two different models, a high detailed one, and a low detailed one, but if the artist is already swamped with work, why not just use some of the built-in simplification our mesh class can provide.

Simplifying a mesh is the act of taking an existing mesh, using a set of provided weights, and trying to remove as many faces or vertices as possible to achieve a lower-detail mesh. However, before a mesh can be simplified, it must first be cleaned.

Cleaning a mesh is performed by adding another vertex where two fans of triangles share the same vertex. Let's look at the overloads for the clean method:

```
public static Microsoft.DirectX.Direct3D.Mesh Clean (
    Microsoft.DirectX.Direct3D.Mesh mesh ,
    Microsoft.DirectX.Direct3D.GraphicsStream adjacency ,
    Microsoft.DirectX.Direct3D.GraphicsStream adjacencyOut ,
    out System.String errorsAndWarnings )
```

You'll notice that much like the earlier functions, this one takes as a parameter in the mesh we are going to clean, as well as the adjacency information. However, you'll also notice that the adjacencyOut parameter is always required as well. The most common technique is to use the adjacency in graphics stream you get from the mesh creation as both the adjacencyIn and adjacencyOut parameter for the cleaning. There is also a string that can be returned to notify you of any errors or warnings encountered when cleaning the mesh. You should also note that the adjacency parameters can be either the graphics streams as shown above, or arrays of integers.

To show the dramatic simplification that can be achieved using these techniques, I took the MeshFile example that we wrote in Chapter 5, "Rendering with Meshes," and decided to use this as the starting point for our simplification. First, I turned on wire-frame mode so you could see the effect the simplification has on the vertices more easily. I added the following line in the SetupCamera function:

```
device.RenderState.FillMode = FillMode.WireFrame;
```

Next, as we've just discussed, the mesh needs to be cleaned. Since we need to know the mesh's adjacency information for the cleaning, we need to modify the mesh creation code in LoadMesh as follows:

```
ExtendedMaterial[] mtrl;
GraphicsStream adj;

// Load our mesh
mesh = Mesh.FromFile(file, MeshFlags.Managed, device, out adj, out mtrl);
```

The only real change was the addition of the adj variable, which will hold our adjacency information. We then called the overload for FromFile that returned this data. Now we just need to make the actual call to Clean, so at the end of the LoadMesh function, we can add the following code to clean our mesh:

```
// Clean our main mesh
Mesh tempMesh = Mesh.Clean(mesh, adj, adj);
// Replace our existing mesh with this one
mesh.Dispose();
mesh = tempMesh;
```

Before we update our code to do the actual simplification of this mesh, we should first look at the actual Simplify method, and its various overloads:

```
public static Microsoft.DirectX.Direct3D.Mesh Simplify (
    Microsoft.DirectX.Direct3D.Mesh mesh ,
    int[] adjacency ,
    Microsoft.DirectX.Direct3D.AttributeWeights vertexAttributeWeights ,
    float[] vertexWeights , System.Int32 minValue ,
    Microsoft.DirectX.Direct3D.MeshFlags options )
```

Once again, the structure of this method should seem similar. The mesh we are going to simplify is the first parameter, followed by the adjacency (which can be specified as either an integer array or a graphics stream).

The AttributeWeights structure used for the next parameter is used to set the weights for the various values used when simplifying the mesh. Most applications should use the overloads that do not take this member, since the default structure will only consider geometric and normal adjustment. It is only in special cases that other members would need to be modified. The default values for this structure if you do not pass it in would be

```
AttributeWeights weights = new AttributeWeights();
weights.Position = 1.0f;
weights.Boundary = 1.0f;
weights.Normal = 1.0f;
weights.Diffuse = 0.0f;
weights.Specular = 0.0f;
weights.Binormal = 0.0f;
weights.Tangent = 0.0f;
weights.TextureCoordinate = new float[]
{0.0f, 0.0f, 0.0f, 0.0f, 0.0f, 0.0f, 0.0f, 0.0f };
```

The next member is a list of weights for each vertex. If you pass in null for this member, it is assumed that each weight will be 1.0f.

The minValue member is the minimum number of faces or vertices (depending on the flags you pass in) you want to try to simplify the mesh to. The lower this value, the lower the details of the resulting mesh; however, you should note that just because this call may succeed does not mean that the exact minimum value has been reached. This member is intended to be a desired minimum, not an absolute minimum.

The final parameter to this function can only be one of two flags. If you want to simplify the number of vertices, you should pass in MeshFlags.SimplifyVertex. Otherwise, if you want to simplify the indices, use MeshFlags.SimplifyFace.

Now we should add the code to simplify the mesh we used in our MeshFile example. We will want to keep both the original (cleaned) mesh, as well as the simplified mesh to toggle between them, so let's add a new member variable to store our simplified mesh:

```
private Mesh simplifiedMesh = null;
```

Next, you should actually create the simplified mesh. At the end of the LoadMesh function, add this small section of code:

```
// Get our new simplified mesh
simplifiedMesh = Mesh.Simplify(mesh, adj, null, 1, MeshFlags.SimplifyVertex);

Console.WriteLine("Number of vertices in original mesh: {0}",
    mesh.NumberVertices);
Console.WriteLine("Number of vertices in simplified mesh: {0}",
    simplifiedMesh.NumberVertices);
```

Here you are trying to simplify the huge mesh down to a single vertex. Talk about low resolution meshes; you can't get much lower than that. Then you print out the number of vertices before and after the simplification to the output window. Running the application now won't actually show you the simplified mesh yet, but it will show you the number of vertices of the two meshes:

```
Number of vertices in original mesh: 4445
Number of vertices in simplified mesh: 391
```

We may not have simplified our mesh down to one vertex like we asked for, but we did simplify it down to 8.8% of its original size. For objects off in the distance, you probably couldn't tell the difference between the high resolution and the low resolution models anyway; you may as well save the triangles for something more useful.

Now let's update the code so that we can actually see the result of this simplification. We will want to toggle between the normal and simplified mesh, so first we should add a Boolean variable to maintain the current mesh we are rendering:

```
private bool isSimplified = false;
```

Next, we should update our rendering code to render the correct subset depending on the value of our Boolean. In the OnPaint overload, update the following code:

```
device.Material = meshMaterials[i];
device.SetTexture(0, meshTextures[i]);
if (!isSimplified)
{
    mesh.DrawSubset(i);
}
else
{
    simplifiedMesh.DrawSubset(i);
}
```

Notice that even though we may be rendering the full normal mesh, or the simplified one, the material and texture both stay the same. The only change we make is which mesh we call DrawSubset on. The only thing left to do is to have a way to actually toggle our Boolean value. You should make it toggle when the space bar is pressed; add the following method:

```
protected override void OnKeyPress(KeyPressEventArgs e)
{
    if (e.KeyChar == ' ')
    {
        isSimplified = !isSimplified;
    }
}
```

When you first run the example now, you see the full mesh rendered in wire-frame mode. There are quite a few vertices in this mesh; looking at the face alone, it almost looks solid, there are so many vertices. Now, hit the space bar and watch all of those vertices disappear. The effect is quite noticeable when the camera is close to the object, but what if the object was far away? Add another Boolean variable to control the camera distance:

```
private bool isClose = true;
```

Now update the SetupCamera function to have the camera up close or far away depending on this Boolean variable:

```
if (isClose)
{
    device.Transform.View = Matrix.LookAtLH(new Vector3(0,0, 580.0f), new Vector3(),
        new Vector3(0,1,0));
}
else
{
    device.Transform.View = Matrix.LookAtLH(new Vector3(0,0, 8580.0f), new Vector3(),
        new Vector3(0,1,0));
}
//device.RenderState.FillMode = FillMode.WireFrame;
```

As you can see, the camera is positioned 8,000 units further back if the camera isn't "close." You'll also notice that I turned off wire-frame mode here. Since most games aren't played in wire-frame mode, this will give you a more realistic view of what your players would see. The last thing we need to do is to have a way to toggle the camera. We will use the "m" key for this. Add the following to the end of the OnKeyPress override:

```
if (e.KeyChar == 'm')
{
    isClose = !isClose;
}
```

Run the example once more. While the camera is still close, hit the space bar a few times. Now, hit the "m" key to move the camera far away from the object. Hit the space bar a few more times; notice that the effect is much less dramatic? See if you can really tell if the meshes in Figure 7.1 and Figure 7.2 are that different.

**FIGURE 7.1**   Up close and high resolution mesh.

**FIGURE 7.2**   Far away and low resolution mesh.

This technique can be used quite effectively to lower the resolution of your meshes when it's not feasible to have your artist create multiple copies of the same mesh.

*SHOP TALK*

## SAVING MESHES

If you haven't noticed, performing this simplification operation is costly. Compare the startup time of our original MeshFile application with this new one. Even if it isn't feasible for your artist to create separate low resolution meshes, you also don't want to force the user to wait through the timely simplification process.

So what's a good middle ground? Why not do the simplification in a tool that is *not* part of the main game, which can save the newly simplified mesh into its own file? This frees your artist up to continue working on high-quality art, and allows the game to load the data it needs quickly without performing all of the simplification calculations each time it needs to.

If we wanted to save our simplified version of the mesh we've been using, we could add code similar to this:

```
// Save our simplified mesh for later use
// First we need to generate the adjacency for this mesh
int[] simpleAdj = new int[simplifiedMesh.NumberFaces * 3];
simplifiedMesh.GenerateAdjacency(0.0f, simpleAdj);
using (Mesh cleanedMesh = Mesh.Clean(simplifiedMesh,
        simpleAdj, out simpleAdj))
{
    cleanedMesh.Save(@"..\..\simple.x", simpleAdj,
        mtrl, XFileFormat.Text);
}
```

You'll notice that we never did get any adjacency information for our simplified mesh. Since we'll need that, we simply generate it. It's important to realize that the act of simplification normally makes a mesh unclean once more. An unclean mesh cannot be saved, so we need to first clean our newly simplified mesh. We do this in a using clause because we want our cleaned mesh to be disposed once we're done with it.

There are actually eight different overloads for the Save method, but they are all remarkably similar. Four of the overloads save the data into a stream you pass in, while the other four will save them to a file. We choose the file overload as you can see here. Each of the overloads takes in the adjacency and materials used for the mesh; we simply reuse the adjacency we just generated and the materials from the original mesh. The adjacency information can once again be specified as either an array of integers or a graphics stream. Half of the overloads take an EffectInstance structure that deals with High Level Shader Language effect files that we'll discuss later.

The final parameter for the save function is the type of file format you want to save it as. There is the text format, the binary format, and the compressed format. Choose whichever suits your needs best.

# Welding Vertices in a Mesh

Another way to simplify vertices with much less control, but at a much higher speed, is to weld similar vertices together. There is a method on the mesh class, "WeldVertices", that can be used to weld together vertices that are replicated and have equal attribute values. The method prototypes contain the following:

```
public void WeldVertices ( Microsoft.DirectX.Direct3D.WeldEpsilonsFlags flags ,
    Microsoft.DirectX.Direct3D.WeldEpsilons epsilons ,
    Microsoft.DirectX.Direct3D.GraphicsStream adjacencyIn ,
    Microsoft.DirectX.Direct3D.GraphicsStream adjacencyOut ,
    out int[] faceRemap ,
    Microsoft.DirectX.Direct3D.GraphicsStream vertexRemap )
```

The last four parameters have already been discussed at length, so we won't delve into those here once more. They are the same as they were in the clean function we've discussed previously. The first two parameters, however, control how the various vertices are welded together. The first parameter can be one or more of the values found in Table 7.2:

### TABLE 7.2

**Flags for Welding Vertices**

| | |
|---|---|
| WeldEpsilonsFlags.WeldAll | Welds all vertices marked by adjacency as being overlapping. |
| WeldEpsilonsFlags.WeldPartialMatches | If the given vertex is within the epsilon value given by the WeldEpsilons structure, modify the partially matched vertices to be identical. If all components are equal, then remove one of the vertices. |
| WeldEpsilonsFlags.DoNotRemoveVertices | Can only be used if WeldPartialMatches is specified. Only allows modification of vertices, but not removal. |
| WeldEpsilonsFlags.DoNotSplit | Can only be used if WeldPartialMatches is specified. Does not allow the vertices to be split. |

The WeldEpsilons structure itself is strikingly similar to the AttributeWeights structure used for simplifying a mesh. The only difference is there is a new member for this structure that controls the tessellation factor. Tessellating a mesh is the act of changing the level of detail in the model by either removing triangles, or splitting a single triangle into two or more smaller triangles. All other members remain the same.

To show the effect of using this method, we'll once again modify the existing MeshFile example to weld its vertices together. Since this is really only one call that operates in place, there isn't much code we will need to add. The first time a key is pressed we will do the weld, so replace the OnKeyPress method with the following:

```
protected override void OnKeyPress(KeyPressEventArgs e)
{
    Console.WriteLine("Before: {0}", mesh.NumberVertices);
    mesh.WeldVertices(WeldEpsilonsFlags.WeldAll, new WeldEpsilons(), null, null);
    Console.WriteLine("After: {0}", mesh.NumberVertices);
}
```

Running the example now and pressing the space bar will result in the following text output:

```
Before: 4432
After: 3422
```

Not quite the 91% reduction we got when simplifying, but it was *much* faster than before. However, did you notice how the texture coordinates changed when you hit the space bar? This was caused by the removal of some of the vertices in that area. Up close, it's quite noticeable, but at a distance, once again, it's hardly obvious unless you're looking for it.

## SHOP TALK

### VALIDATING YOUR MESH

Wouldn't it be great if there was a way to detect whether or not your mesh needed cleaning or was ready to be optimized? Naturally, there is. The mesh class has a method, "Validate", which contains four different overloads. One of the overloads looks like the following:

```
public void Validate ( Microsoft.DirectX.Direct3D.GraphicsStream adjacency ,
        System.String errorsAndWarnings )
```

There are also overloads that support integer arrays as the adjacency information, plus you can use the functions with or without the errors parameter.

If the mesh is valid, this method will succeed, and the errors output string (if specified) will be System.String.Empty. If the mesh isn't valid (for example, invalid indices), then the behavior is dependant on whether or not the errors output string is specified. If it is, the function will return the errors in the mesh in this string, but succeed. If it is not, the function will throw an exception.

Using the Validate method before any simplification or optimization methods can help eliminate any unnecessary failures of those methods.

# Making Lots of Little Meshes Out of One Big One

Rather than just removing vertices from your mesh, what if you actually wanted to split your one large mesh into many different pieces? Let's once again take our MeshFile example and modify it slightly to split the one large mesh into smaller, more manageable meshes.

When you split a mesh up, you will take the existing single mesh and turn it into an array of meshes that can be used to do the rendering. For this example, you will maintain both the original mesh as well as the split mesh so that you can see them both rendered and compare them.

First, you will need to declare an array of meshes to hold the split mesh. You will also need some Boolean variables to control how and which meshes are being rendered. Add the following variables to your declaration section:

```
// Split information
private Mesh[] meshes = null;
private bool drawSplit = false;
private bool drawAllSplit = false;
private int index = 0;
private int lastIndexTick = System.Environment.TickCount;
```

These variables will hold the entire list of newly created meshes after the split, as well as the flag on whether or not you are drawing the original or split mesh (you should default to the original). If you are drawing the split mesh, there is a second flag to see whether you are drawing all of the split meshes in the array, or a single one at a time; again, you should default to a single one at a time. You will need to maintain the current index of the mesh you are drawing (in case you are drawing one at a time), plus a "mini-timer" to determine when to switch to the next mesh (if you are drawing one at a time).

With the variable declarations out of the way, we can create our array of meshes. Directly after the LoadMesh call in InitializeGraphics, add the following section of code:

```
meshes = Mesh.Split(mesh, null, 1000, mesh.Options.Value);
```

We should take a look at the various parameters the split function takes. There are two overloads, so we will look at the most complete one:

```
public static Microsoft.DirectX.Direct3D.Mesh[] Split (Mesh mesh , int[] adjacencyIn ,
    System.Int32 maxSize , MeshFlags options ,
    out GraphicsStream adjacencyArrayOut ,
    out GraphicsStream faceRemapArrayOut ,
    out GraphicsStream vertRemapArrayOut )
```

As you can see, the call takes in the mesh we want to split as the first parameter. The adjacency is the next parameter (you can pass null as we've done above if you don't care about this member). The third parameter is the maximum number of vertices you want each of the newly created meshes to have. In our previous example, we want a maximum of 1,000 vertices per new mesh. The options parameter is used to specify the flags for each of the newly created meshes. The final three out parameters all return the information about each of the new meshes in a stream. We will use the overloads without this information.

With our newly created array of meshes, we now need a way to specify which meshes we will be drawing: the original or the array. Before we can do that, though, we need a way to toggle between them. We will use the same keys we used earlier: the space bar and "m". Replace the OnKeyPress method with the following code:

```
protected override void OnKeyPress(KeyPressEventArgs e)
{
    if (e.KeyChar == ' ')
    {
        drawSplit = !drawSplit;
    }
    else if (e.KeyChar == 'm')
    {
        drawAllSplit = !drawAllSplit;
    }
}
```

Here we toggle whether to draw the original mesh or the split mesh, as well as toggling whether to draw individual members of the split mesh, or the whole thing. Now, we should update the DrawMesh method to actually use these variables. Replace the contents of this method with the code in Listing 7.2.

**LISTING 7.2**    Rendering Your Split Meshes

```
if ((System.Environment.TickCount - lastIndexTick) > 500)
{
    index++;
    if (index >= meshes.Length)
        index = 0;

    lastIndexTick = System.Environment.TickCount;
}
device.Transform.World = Matrix.RotationYawPitchRoll(yaw, pitch, roll) *
    Matrix.Translation(x, y, z);
for (int i = 0; i < meshMaterials.Length; i++)
{
    device.Material = meshMaterials[i];
    device.SetTexture(0, meshTextures[i]);
    if (drawSplit)
```

LISTING 7.2   Continued

```
    {
        if (drawAllSplit)
        {
            foreach(Mesh m in meshes)
                m.DrawSubset(i);
        }
        else
        {
            meshes[index].DrawSubset(i);
        }
    }
    else
    {
        mesh.DrawSubset(i);
    }
}
```

In this updated function, we now increment our index over half of a second, and ensure that we wrap if it happens to go over the length of our split array. Then, if we are drawing the split mesh, we check if we are drawing the entire thing, or a single member, and behave accordingly. Otherwise, we draw the original mesh.

Running this example now will start it rendering the original un-split mesh. Hit the space bar, though, and it starts rendering each of the split meshes individually. If you hit the "m" key while in this mode, it will render *all* of the split meshes simultaneously. Can you tell the difference between rendering the original mesh, and rendering the entire array of split meshes?

# In Brief

In this chapter, we learned just about everything there is to know about the standard mesh class, including

- Optimizing mesh data

- Simplifying meshes

- Creating meshes with new vertex data components

- Welding vertices together

In the next chapter, we will explore the resources available in Direct3D in depth, and the more advanced features of them.

# Understanding Resources

Resources are the backbone of rendering complex objects in Direct3D. During the course of this chapter, we will discuss the more advanced features of these resources, including

- Static and dynamic resources

- Updating the buffers included in meshes

- Uses of the various locking flags

- Using unsafe mode for maximum performance

## Starting with the Resource Class

The Resource class is relatively small, and is the base class for all resources in Direct3D, so it may be a good idea to start this section with a list of each method, and what it's intended to be used for. You will never actually create or use the Resource class itself, since it is an abstract class, but you may find yourself using these methods on your other resource classes. See Table 8.1 for the methods on the resource class:

## TABLE 8.1

**Resource Class Methods and Properties**

| PROPERTY OR METHOD | DESCRIPTION |
| --- | --- |
| Device | Read-only property that will return the device this resource was created with. |
| Type | Read-only property that returns the type of resource this is. Valid return values for this property are in the ResourceType enumeration. |
| Priority | Read-write property that returns the priority of this resource. Priorities only matter when dealing with resources that reside in the managed memory pool. They are used to determine when a resource can be removed from memory. The lower the priority, the faster a resource can be removed. By default, all managed resources have a priority of 0, and all non-managed resources will always have a priority of 0. There is also a SetPriority method, which returns the old priority after setting the new one. |
| PreLoad | Use this method to indicate that a managed resource will be needed shortly. This will allow Direct3D to move your resource into video memory before it is actually needed. It's important to note, that if you are already using more video memory than you have, this method will silently do nothing. |
| PrivateData members | There are three members that allow you to get and set private data for each of your resources. This data is never used by Direct3D and can be used by your application as you see fit. |

As you can see, the resource class deals mainly with enhancing managed resources performance. While not listed in the chart above, or the resource class, it's important to note that each resource in Direct3D will also have a usage, as well as a memory pool (defined in the Usage and Pool enumerations). These properties define how the resource is used, and where it is located in memory (be it system memory, video memory, or AGP memory).

Resources all have a way to allow the CPU to access the data it stores, normally by a mechanism called Locking. In our examples thus far, we've filled our buffers with single "SetData" calls, and created our textures from files; however, it is possible to retrieve the data, or only set small subsections of that data, via locking these resources. We will discuss locking in this chapter briefly. Let's look at the first resource we were introduced to.

# Using the Vertex and Index Buffers

Vertex buffers are the main data structure used by Direct3D to store vertices, while the Index buffers are the same for indices. These classes derive from the Resource class, and thus inherit those methods, plus add a few of their own.

The first new property is a description of the buffer. The structure returned from this property will tell you everything you need to know about how the buffer was created, including the format, the usage, the memory pool, the size, and the vertex format. While it may be true that you would already know this information if you were creating the buffers yourself, this is very useful information if you are simply receiving the buffers from an external source that you know nothing about.

## SHOP TALK

### STATIC AND DYNAMIC BUFFERS

Before getting into the last two methods that reside on the buffers, now seems like the perfect time to discuss the differences between static and dynamic buffers. The concepts here apply equally well to both vertex and index buffers.

So, obviously the first question would be, "What is the difference between a static and a dynamic buffer?" As luck would have it, I happen to have an answer for that. If the buffer was created with the usage flag Usage.Dynamic, the buffer is a dynamic buffer; any other buffer is a static buffer. Static buffers are designed for items that do not change very often, while dynamic buffers are more easily used for buffers that have constantly changing data. You can see where the names come from.

Just because a buffer is static, though, doesn't mean it cannot be modified. However, locking a static buffer while that buffer is already in use can have a very significant performance penalty. Before the data can be modified, the GPU needs to finish reading the current set of data, which can be very time consuming. Doing this several times in the same frame is even worse, because now you've eliminated the buffering the driver can do, and you are forcing your GPU to sit around idling waiting for you to finish modifying your buffer's data. Graphics cards are extremely powerful today; you do not want them idling when they could be busy drawing triangles.

If you expect your buffer's data to be modified frequently, it should be created with Usage.Dynamic. This flag allows Direct3D to optimize the pipeline for frequent data modification. You will receive no speed enhancements by specifying a buffer as dynamic, and then never modifying it; as a matter of fact, it will be slower than if you simply made a static buffer to begin with.

Always know the amount of "churn" you expect on your buffers per frame and create accordingly. For maximum performance, it is recommended that you have one large static vertex buffer for each vertex format you wish to render. It's sometimes not feasible to have only these static buffers, though, and in those cases, the dynamic buffers are there for you.

# Locking Our Buffers

The locking mechanism seems to be one of the most misunderstood calls in Direct3D, particularly in Managed DirectX. How to do the locks, and do them fast seems to be a particularly tough question for people to grasp.

Before we get to that, though, what exactly is "locking" the buffer? It is simply the act of allowing your CPU to access a range of data in your resource. Since you cannot talk directly to the graphics hardware, there needs to be a way to allow you to manipulate vertex data from your application, and the locking mechanism is it. Look at the various lock overloads that exist for our vertex and index buffers (they take the same parameters):

```
public System.Array Lock ( System.Int32 offsetToLock ,
    Microsoft.DirectX.Direct3D.LockFlags flags )

public System.Array Lock ( System.Int32 offsetToLock , System.Type typeVertex ,
    Microsoft.DirectX.Direct3D.LockFlags flags , params int[] ranks )

public Microsoft.DirectX.Direct3D.GraphicsStream Lock ( System.Int32 offsetToLock ,
    System.Int32 sizeToLock , Microsoft.DirectX.Direct3D.LockFlags flags )
```

As you can see, there are three overloads available when attempting to lock our buffers. We should start with the first one, since it is the simplest. This overload is only available if you created your buffer via the constructor that takes a System.Type and a number of vertices or indices. In actuality, this overload really just calls the next overload with the data you passed in from the constructor.

The next two overloads are where things get interesting. The first parameter of each is the offset (in bytes) at which you want to start the lock. If you wish to lock the entire buffer, you will naturally want to start this member at zero. You'll notice the first two overloads each return an array, which can be extremely useful since it will return the data to you in an easy-to-use form. In the second overload, the second parameter is the base type of the array you wish to be returned. The last parameter is used to determine the size of the array that is returned.

This "ranks" parameter seems to throw everyone for a loop for some reason, so let's look at it in depth for a moment. Let's assume you had a vertex buffer that had nothing but position data in it (Vector3), and it had 1,200 vertices in it. If you wanted to lock this buffer into a Vector3 array of 1,200 items, the lock call would look like this:

```
Vector3[] data = (Vector3[])vb.Lock(0, typeof(Vector3), LockFlags.None, 1200);
```

This call will result in a single dimension array of 1,200 Vector3s. Now let's say for some reason you wanted to have a two-dimensional array of 600 vertices each. That lock call would look like

```
Vector3[,] data = (Vector3[,])vb.Lock(0, typeof(Vector3), LockFlags.None, 600, 600);
```

Notice the extra parameter? The ranks parameter is actually a parameter array. It can and will create up to a three-dimensional array of data to return back to you. You should use this parameter to specify exactly how large of an array you wish to get back.

LockFlags will be covered with the last overload, but first I want to point out some of the drawbacks of using either of the overloads that return an array. First and foremost, we should talk about performance. Assuming you have created a vertex buffer with the "default" options, and no lock flags, when this method is called, the following things happen:

- Vertex data is locked; memory location of data is stored.
- A new array of the correct type is allocated, given the size specified in the ranks parameter.
- The data is copied from the locked memory location to our new buffer.
- This buffer is returned to the user, who then modifies it as needed.
- When the Unlock method is finally called, there is another copy of data from the array back into the locked memory location.
- Finally, the vertex data is unlocked.

It's not hard to understand how and why this method could be quite a bit slower than you might expect given all that it's doing. It's possible to remove one of the two copies, by either specifying Usage.WriteOnly when creating the buffer (eliminates the first copy), or by specifying the LockFlags.ReadOnly flag when locking (eliminates the second copy), but it isn't possible to remove both. What could you do with a ReadOnly/WriteOnly buffer anyway?

The last overload is the most powerful. It also has a new parameter the others don't, namely the size of the data we want to lock. In the other overloads, this value is calculated during the call (sizeof(type) * NumberRanks). If you are using this overload, simply pass in the size of the data you wish to lock (in bytes). If you want to lock the entire buffer, pass in zero for the first two parameters of this method.

This overload will return a GraphicsStream class that will allow you to directly manipulate the locked data, without any extra memory allocations for the arrays, without any extra memory copies. You can do exactly what it is you want to do with the memory. There are multiple methods on the GraphicsStream object that allow you to "write" your data to this memory, but this isn't where you can get the big speed boosts. You get the big speed boosts manipulating the memory directly.

I don't want to sound like I'm suggesting that the locking functions that return arrays are amazingly slow. They are very convenient and when used properly, almost as fast as the overloads that return the stream. However, when you are looking to pull every ounce of performance out of your system, using the graphics stream is the way to go.

# Controlling How Buffers Are Locked

Last, we need to talk about the flags you can use when locking the buffer. The only valid flags when locking a vertex buffer are

- LockFlags.None

- LockFlags.Discard

- LockFlags.NoOverwrite

- LockFlags.NoDirtyUpdate

- LockFlags.NoSystemLock

- LockFlags.ReadOnly

Obviously, when using no lock flags, the default locking mechanism is used. However, if you want more control over your locking, the other flags can be used for a variety of options.

The "Discard" flag can only be used on dynamic buffers. For Vertex and Index buffers, the entire buffer will be discarded, and a new chunk of memory will be returned to you in case there is anything else still accessing the old memory. This flag is useful if you are filling a vertex buffer dynamically. Once the vertex buffer has been filled completely, you lock with discard. It is often used in combination with the next flag.

The "NoOverwrite" flag (which is also only valid on dynamic buffers) tells Direct3D that you will not overwrite any data in the vertex or index buffer. Using the flag will allow the call to return immediately, and continue to use the buffer. If you do not use this flag, the lock call will not return until any rendering is currently finished. Since you may not overwrite any of the data currently in this buffer, it is only useful for appending vertices to a buffer.

A common use of these two flags comes from a large buffer you are filling dynamically. As you keep adding new data into your buffer, you continue to use the NoOverwrite flag until the buffer is full. At that time, your next lock will use the Discard flag to flush the buffer and start over. We can look at Listing 8.1, an excerpt of code from the Point Sprites sample that ships with the DirectX SDK.

**LISTING 8.1**    Portion of PointSprites Example

```
if (++numParticlesToRender == flush)
{
    // Done filling this chunk of the vertex buffer.  Lets unlock and
    // draw this portion so we can begin filling the next chunk.

    vertexBuffer.Unlock();

    dev.DrawPrimitives(PrimitiveType.PointList, baseParticle,
            numParticlesToRender);

    // Lock the next chunk of the vertex buffer.  If we are at the
```

**LISTING 8.1**   Continued

```
    // end of the vertex buffer, LockFlags.Discard the vertex buffer and start
    // at the beginning.  Otherwise, specify LockFlags.NoOverWrite, so we can
    // continue filling the VB while the previous chunk is drawing.
    baseParticle += flush;

    if (baseParticle >= discard)
        baseParticle = 0;

    vertices = (PointVertex[])vertexBuffer.Lock(baseParticle *
        DXHelp.GetTypeSize(typeof(PointVertex)), typeof(PointVertex),
        (baseParticle != 0) ? LockFlags.NoOverwrite : LockFlags.Discard,
        flush);
    count = 0;

    numParticlesToRender = 0;
}
```

In this excerpt, we detect whether or not it's time to "flush" our data (a call to DrawPrimitives). If it is, we unlock our buffer and render. Then we detect whether or not we are at the end of our buffer (baseParticle >= discard), and finally lock our buffer once more. We start locking at the end of the buffer, passing in the NoOverwrite flag, unless baseParticle is zero, in which case we lock at the beginning of the buffer, and use the Discard flag. This allows us to continue to add new point sprites to our scene until our buffer is full, at which time we discard our old buffer and start using a new one.

With the two "complex" flags out of the way, we can discuss the remaining flags now. The easiest of these is the "ReadOnly" flag, which as its name implies tells Direct3D that you will not write to the buffer. When dealing with the lock overloads that return arrays, this also has the benefit of not copying the data you've updated when you finally call Unlock.

The NoDirtyUpdate flag prevents any change in the "dirty" status of the resource. Without this flag, locking a resource will automatically add a dirty region to that resource.

The last of the flags probably won't be used all that often. Normally, when you lock a resource in video memory, a systemwide critical section is reserved, not allowing any display mode changes while the lock is in effect. Using the NoSystemLock flag disables this feature. This is only useful for lock operations you expect to take quite some time, and only if you still need speedy system speed. Using this flag often isn't recommended.

Naturally, after you've called lock, you must tell Direct3D that you're done with the lock at some time. The unlock method is used for this. There are no parameters for this function, and unlock *must* be called every time you call lock. Rendering will fail if there are any unlocked buffers.

# Using Texture Resources

All of the texture resources in Managed DirectX derive from a single BaseTexture class, which itself derives from the Resource class. There are a few new methods on the BaseTexture object that are covered in Table 8.2.

**TABLE 8.2**

**Base Texture Methods**

| PROPERTY OR METHOD | DESCRIPTION |
|---|---|
| LevelCount | This read-only property specifies the number of levels this texture has. For example, a mipmapped texture (described in the sidebar "Dissecting Mipmaps") would have the number of mipmaps as its level count. |
| GenerateMipSubLevels | This method will automatically generate the mipmap sublevels we've just mentioned for you. It will use the next property to determine the filtering mode to use when creating these levels. |
| AutoGenerateFilterType | This read-write property describes how the mipmap sublevels are generated automatically. It takes a member of the TextureFilter enumeration, and will automatically re-create any mipmap sublevels if the filter type is changed. The default filter type for mipmap level generation is TextureFilter.Linear unless the driver does not support that mode, in which case it will use TextureFilter.Point. If the device does not support the selected filter type, this property set will throw an exception. All filter values are valid with the exception of "None". You can see the TextureFilterCaps member of the Caps structure to determine which filter types are supported by your device. |
| LevelOfDetail | Another read-write property that determines the most detailed level of detail for managed textures. |

*SHOP TALK*

**DISSECTING MIPMAPS**

So what is this mipmap we keep talking about? Simply put, a mipmap is a chain of textures, with the first member of that chain being the most highly detailed texture. For each subsequent member of that chain, the size is reduced by one power of 2. For example, assuming that you have an original "high resolution" texture of 256×256, the next level in that mipmap would be 128×128, followed then by 64×64, and so on. Mipmap chains are used by Direct3D to control the quality of the rendered textures, at the expense of needing more memory to store the mipmaps. When objects are up close, the high-quality versions of the textures are used; when objects are far away, the lower-resolution textures are used instead.

When creating a texture, one of the parameters used specifies the number of levels you wish to have in this texture. This number of levels corresponds directly to the mipmap chain. Specifying zero for this parameter will cause Direct3D to automatically create a set of mipmaps from your original texture resolution all the way down to a final 1×1 texture in your mipmap chain. In our example above, using 0 for this parameter on a texture that has an original size of 256×256 will create a chain of nine textures: 256×256, 128×128, 64×64, 32×32, 16×16, 8×8, 4×4, 2×2, and 1×1.

When calling the SetTexture function, Direct3D will automatically filter between the various textured mipmaps, based on the currently set MipFilter property on the sampler states class. If you remember our Dodger game we wrote in Chapter 6, you'll remember we set the minify and magnify filters for our road textures. It is the same concept here for the mipmap filters.

# Locking Textures and Getting Descriptions

Just like the vertex and index buffers earlier, each of the texture types also has a locking mechanism, and a way to determine the features it uses. In addition to these methods, textures also have two new features that the geometry resources do not: namely, dirty regions and a "backing" object. Before we get into those, let's explore the locking mechanism for textures.

The locking mechanism for textures is remarkably similar to locking our geometry buffers, with two differences. The first is the lock calls take in a "level" parameter, which is naturally the mipmap level you wish to perform this lock operation on. The second is the rectangle (or box for volume textures) you wish to perform the lock on. You can use the overloads that do not specify this member to lock the entire texture surface.

When dealing with cube textures, there is one extra parameter that is needed: the face of the cube map you wish to lock. You can use a value from the CubeMapFace enumeration for this parameter.

You may also notice that some of the overloads for LockRectangle can return a pitch parameter as an out. If you need to know the amount of data in each row, this is what the pitch will provide you. If you specify this parameter, it will return the number of bytes in a row of blows.

While the texture locks can take in a type parameter for locking specific types of data, the textures themselves only store color information. If you wish to use one of the overloads that use a type, you should ensure that type is the same size as the pixel format of the texture; for example, a 32-bit pixel format should be locked with an integer, while a 16-bit pixel format should be locked with a short.

We should look at an example of locking a texture now. We will use the MeshFile example we've already looked at as the basis for this example. We'll remove the texture that is currently used for rendering the model, and replace it with one we generate dynamically for our application. We will want to have two modes for this texture, one that is "cycling" the textures, and one that is purely random. We will need the following variables to be declared for this:

```
private uint texColor = 0;
private bool randomTextureColor = false;
```

We plan on having a 32-bit pixel format for our texture, so we store our cycling color in a 32-bit format (uint) as well. We also want to specify whether we are creating random texture colors, or using the cycling texture, thus the need for the Boolean. Now, we should create the method that will do the actual texture locking and updating. In order to show the differences between the array methods, and the unsafe methods, we will do both. The array method is shown in Listing 8.2.

**LISTING 8.2**   Filling a Texture with an Array

```
private void FillTexture(Texture t, bool random)
{
    SurfaceDescription s = t.GetLevelDescription(0);
    Random r = new Random();
    uint[,] data = (uint[,])t.LockRectangle(typeof(uint), 0,
        LockFlags.None, s.Width, s.Height);

    for (int i = 0; i < s.Width; i++)
    {
        for (int j = 0; j < s.Height; j++)
        {
            if (random)
            {
                data[i,j] = (uint)Color.FromArgb(
                    r.Next(byte.MaxValue),
                    r.Next(byte.MaxValue),
                    r.Next(byte.MaxValue)).ToArgb();
            }
            else
            {
                data[i,j] = texColor++;
                if (texColor >= 0x00ffffff)
                    texColor = 0;
            }
        }
    }

    t.UnlockRectangle(0);
}
```

So what is going on in this code? You take an existing texture, and first get the description of the texture. You do this in order to get the width and size of the data so that you know how much data will need to be filled. Since you know the width and height of the data, you will lock into a two dimensional array (of size width/height). You want to lock into an unsigned integer (since you are using a 32-bit pixel format), and don't care about any lock flags. Since you will only create one level of the mipmap chain, you will lock level zero.

After the texture is locked, we will go through every member of the returned array and update its color, either to a random value or to a value we increment every time (our "cycling" color). Finally, after this data is all updated, we unlock our texture and we are finished.

Now, what would the unsafe version of this method look like? Actually, quite similar, and that code is shown in Listing 8.3.

**LISTING 8.3**    Filling a Texture with Unsafe Code

```
private unsafe void FillTextureUnsafe(Texture t, bool random)
{
    SurfaceDescription s = t.GetLevelDescription(0);
    Random r = new Random();
    uint* pData = (uint*)t.LockRectangle(0,
        LockFlags.None).InternalData.ToPointer();

    for (int i = 0; i < s.Width; i++)
    {
        for (int j = 0; j < s.Height; j++)
        {
            if (random)
            {
                *pData = (uint)Color.FromArgb(
                    r.Next(byte.MaxValue),
                    r.Next(byte.MaxValue),
                    r.Next(byte.MaxValue)).ToArgb();
            }
            else
            {
                *pData = texColor++;
                if (texColor >= 0x00ffffff)
                    texColor = 0;
            }
            pData++;
        }
    }

    t.UnlockRectangle(0);
}
```

Notice that the only differences in this function are the declaration of unsafe, and how we've updated our data? We lock the buffer into a graphics stream, and use the "InternalData" member (which is an IntPtr) to get the actual pointer to the data we wish to manipulate. We manipulate the data directly via the pointer, and finally unlock our texture.

In order to compile this method, you will need to turn on the capability to compile unsafe code in your project properties. In the Configuration Properties section, set the Allow Unsafe Code Blocks to true.

Now that you've got the function to fill the texture with fancy color data, you should update the LoadMesh function to not attempt to create the textures via a file, but instead use the function. Replace the material code in the LoadMesh method with the following:

```
// Store each material and texture
for (int i = 0; i < mtrl.Length; i++)
{
    meshMaterials[i] = mtrl[i].Material3D;
    meshTextures[i] = new Texture(device,
                256, 256, 1, 0, Format.X8R8G8B8 ,Pool.Managed);
#if (UNSAFE)
    FillTextureUnsafe(meshTextures[i], randomTextureColor);
#else
    FillTexture(meshTextures[i], randomTextureColor);
#endif
}
```

As you can see, we no longer attempt to load a texture from a file. For each texture in our array, we create a new texture using pixel format X8R8G8B8 (a 32-bit format). We create a 256×256 texture, with only one level, so there are no mipmap levels after the first. We then fill our texture using the method we just wrote. You'll notice I have the fill texture method wrapped in an #if statement. You can define Unsafe in your code file to use that method instead.

## ROTATING BY FRAMERATE

There is one thing I want to point out that reinforces something I mentioned before: Do you notice how the speed of the model's rotation changes when you hit a key and have the random texture color? This is because the model's movement is dependent on the frame rate, rather than a system timer.

With the texture now being created via our function, you can run the application and notice the model looks quite colorful. However, it once again appears "blocky," and the textures are staying constant. We should call our fill texture method every frame. We might as well fix the blocky look of our texture as well. Replace the SetupCamera function with the one in Listing 8.4:

**LISTING 8.4**    Setting Camera Options

```
private void SetupCamera()
{
    device.Transform.Projection = Matrix.PerspectiveFovLH((float)Math.PI / 4,
        this.Width / this.Height, 1.0f, 10000.0f);
    device.Transform.View = Matrix.LookAtLH(new Vector3(0,0, 580.0f),
        new Vector3(), new Vector3(0,1,0));

    device.RenderState.Lighting = false;

    if (device.DeviceCaps.TextureFilterCaps.SupportsMinifyAnisotropic)
        device.SamplerState[0].MinFilter = TextureFilter.Anisotropic;
    else if (device.DeviceCaps.TextureFilterCaps.SupportsMinifyLinear)
        device.SamplerState[0].MinFilter = TextureFilter.Linear;

    if (device.DeviceCaps.TextureFilterCaps.SupportsMagnifyAnisotropic)
        device.SamplerState[0].MagFilter = TextureFilter.Anisotropic;
    else if (device.DeviceCaps.TextureFilterCaps.SupportsMagnifyLinear)
        device.SamplerState[0].MagFilter = TextureFilter.Linear;

    foreach(Texture t in meshTextures)
#if (UNSAFE)
    FillTextureUnsafe(t, randomTextureColor);
#else
    FillTexture(t, randomTextureColor);
#endif
}
```

We turned lighting off so we can see the beauty of our colors without them being "shaded" by the lighting. We also turned on a texture filter (if it is supported) to remove the blocky look of the texture. The last thing we need to do is have a way to turn on the "random" texture colors. We'll just use any keypress as a toggle between the two texture modes. Add the following:

```
protected override void OnKeyPress(KeyPressEventArgs e)
{
    randomTextureColor = !randomTextureColor;
}
```

Using the random color option produces an almost animated effect. It almost looks like the snow you see on the television when there's no reception. See Figure 8.1.

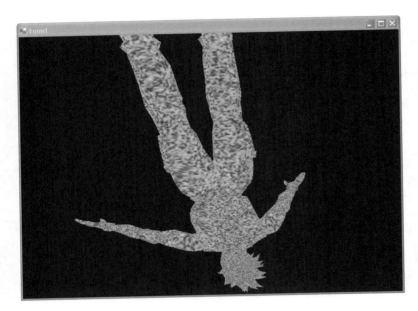

**FIGURE 8.1**   A snowy texture.

# In Brief

In this chapter we talked in depth about the resources available in a Direct3D application and how they can be used, including

- Static and dynamic resources
- Updating the buffers included in meshes
- Uses of the various locking flags
- Using unsafe mode for maximum performance

In our next chapter, we will begin looking at the more complex mesh types available to us.

# Using the Other Mesh Types

## Simplifying Meshes

We spent a good amount of time understanding the basic Mesh class that is included in the extensions library; however, there are actually three other mesh types we haven't looked at yet. During the course of this chapter we will explore these remaining objects.

You've already looked at creating a simplified mesh by using the Simplify method on the mesh class. Since the common case for using a simplified mesh is to show a less-detailed version of a model, in any given scene, it's probably not a great idea to store multiple versions of a mesh, particularly if you're not even going to be using some of them.

The SimplificationMesh object can be used to encapsulate the process of simplifying a mesh. However, you can't actually use the object to do the rendering; you must first get an actual mesh from the simplification mesh. If you remember the simplified example before, there were two "modes" for the example. One mode was an up-close mode that displayed the model before it was simplified. There was also a "far away" mode that displayed the same model in the distance with many fewer faces and vertices. You will do something similar now, except allowing the model to gradually go into the distance.

Rather than starting with the simplify mesh sample we did in Chapter 7, "Using Advanced Mesh Features," it will be easier if we simply start with the example we did in Chapter 5, "Rendering with Meshes," for loading a mesh from a file. We will simply add our code to this example instead. The first thing we will need is a declaration for our SimplificationMesh object, as well as a variable to control our camera's position. Add the following variables:

```
private SimplificationMesh simplifiedMesh = null;
private float cameraPos = 580.0f;
```

Storing the camera's depth position as a variable will allow us to easily change where the camera is located. You will also need to update the view transform to actually use the correct position as well. In the SetupCamera method, update the view transform as follows:

```
device.Transform.View = Matrix.LookAtLH(new Vector3(0,0, cameraPos),
    new Vector3(), new Vector3(0,1,0));
```

Obviously since the SetupCamera method is called every frame, any update we make to this variable will update the camera as well, which is what we want. This simplification mesh variable is obviously where we store the data to simplify our mesh. If you notice, we don't have any extra mesh objects. Anytime we simplify our mesh, we will simply replace it with the "new" one.

We will need to modify the LoadMesh method in order to make sure our mesh is cleaned and our simplification mesh object is created correctly. We will need to replace this method with the one in Listing 9.1:

LISTING 9.1    Creating a Simplification Mesh

```
private void LoadMesh(string file)
{
    ExtendedMaterial[] mtrl;
    GraphicsStream adj;

    // Load our mesh
    mesh = Mesh.FromFile(file, MeshFlags.Managed, device, out adj, out mtrl);

    // If we have any materials, store them
    if ((mtrl != null) && (mtrl.Length > 0))
    {
        meshMaterials = new Material[mtrl.Length];
        meshTextures = new Texture[mtrl.Length];

        // Store each material and texture
        for (int i = 0; i < mtrl.Length; i++)
        {
            meshMaterials[i] = mtrl[i].Material3D;
```

**LISTING 9.1**  Continued

```
            if ((mtrl[i].TextureFilename != null) &&
                (mtrl[i].TextureFilename != string.Empty))
            {
                // We have a texture, try to load it
                meshTextures[i] = TextureLoader.FromFile(device, @"..\..\" +
                    mtrl[i].TextureFilename);
            }
        }
    }

    // Clean our main mesh
    Mesh tempMesh = Mesh.Clean(mesh, adj, adj);
    // Replace our existing mesh with this one
    mesh.Dispose();
    mesh = tempMesh;

    // Create our simplification mesh
    simplifiedMesh = new SimplificationMesh(mesh, adj);
}
```

As you see, we will need to maintain the adjacency information for both the cleaning and our simplification mesh. Once our mesh has been loaded and our textures created (if any existed), we will clean our mesh preparing it for simplification. We then create our simplification mesh object from the newly cleaned mesh.

Actually, we don't really need to do anything else, since the mesh will draw just fine now. However, we want to add some code that will allow us to move our mesh farther from the camera, and lower the detail of the mesh as we do so. We will allow the keyboard to control this "movement," so we will add the override in Listing 9.2:

**LISTING 9.2**  KeyPress Event Handler

```
protected override void OnKeyPress(KeyPressEventArgs e)
{
    if (e.KeyChar == '+')
    {
        cameraPos += (MoveAmount * 2);
        simplifiedMesh.ReduceFaces(mesh.NumberFaces - MoveAmount);
        simplifiedMesh.ReduceVertices(mesh.NumberVertices - MoveAmount);
        mesh.Dispose();
        mesh = simplifiedMesh.Clone(simplifiedMesh.Options.Value,
```

LISTING 9.2    Continued

```
                simplifiedMesh.VertexFormat, device);
    }
    if (e.KeyChar == 'w')
        device.RenderState.FillMode = FillMode.WireFrame;

    if (e.KeyChar == 's')
        device.RenderState.FillMode = FillMode.Solid;
}
```

You'll notice that we are using an undefined constant here to control the amount of movement each keypress will activate. You can define the constant as you see fit; the value I used was

```
private const int MoveAmount = 100;
```

In this method, if the "w" key is pressed, we switch to wire-frame mode, which allows an easier viewing of the actual triangles being drawn. Pressing "s" will switch back to the solid fill. If the "+" key is pressed, we will move our camera away from our model somewhat (based on our constant) to simulate "moving away" from the model. With the model farther away now, we then reduce the number of faces and vertices by our specified constant amount. We then dispose of the original mesh. We will want to use the clone of our simplified mesh to do the drawing in the rendering method, so we replace our original mesh with this clone.

Running the application now, you can press the "+" key a few times and switch between wire-frame and solid mode, and probably not be able to tell the difference as the model gets farther away (which is entirely the point). However, to show that something is actually being done, let's add some text to our rendered scene to show the number of faces and vertices for the mesh being rendered. Add the following variable to control our font:

```
private Microsoft.DirectX.Direct3D.Font font = null;
```

We will also need to initialize our font object before we can actually use it to draw any text. After the call to LoadMesh in the IntializeGraphics method, add this initialization code:

```
// Create our font
font = new Microsoft.DirectX.Direct3D.Font(device, new System.Drawing.Font
    ("Arial", 14.0f, FontStyle.Bold | FontStyle.Italic));
```

Feel free to change the options here and create a different type of font, or a different size or style. Finally, all we need to do is draw some text. Immediately after the call to the DrawMesh method, you can add this code:

```
font.DrawText(null, string.Format("Number vertices in mesh: {0}",
    mesh.NumberVertices), new Rectangle(10, 10, 0, 0),
    DrawTextFormat.NoClip, Color.BlanchedAlmond);

font.DrawText(null, string.Format("Number faces in mesh: {0}",
    mesh.NumberFaces), new Rectangle(10, 30, 0, 0),
    DrawTextFormat.NoClip, Color.BlanchedAlmond);
```

Now it's easy to see as you move your model farther away that the number of vertices and faces being drawn is being reduced. You should see something similar to Figure 9.1 after hitting the "+" key a few times.

**FIGURE 9.1**    A simplified mesh.

One of the first problems you may notice with this application is that we can't seem to regain any of the lost vertices. Sure, we can simplify the mesh just fine, but what if we wanted to bring the model closer to us once more? There is no RaiseVertices method, and using the ReduceVertices method and passing in a larger number of vertices has no effect. The SimplificationMesh objects are designed to simplify meshes, and that is all; there is no going back. Progressive meshes were designed to handle this case.

# Controlling the Level of Detail with Progressive Meshes

There are cases where you'd only want to simplify a mesh (for example, imagine a model for a rocket you've fired). However, if you are only simplifying, it means the object's detail never needs to be increased, which isn't as common as the cases where you may need to progressively lower *or* raise the level of detail. I'm sure you can see where the name of the progressive mesh came from.

To show the behavior of the progressive meshes, we will write a similar application to the one we wrote for the simplification mesh a moment ago. However, instead of just simplifying, we will also allow you to raise the level of detail by bringing the model closer to the camera as well. Once again we will start with the example to load a mesh from a file.

The ProgressiveMesh class derives from the BaseMesh class just like the Mesh class does. You can use the progressive mesh class to draw your objects, unlike the SimplificationMesh object. Knowing this, we can replace the declaration for your mesh object with this one:

```
private ProgressiveMesh progressiveMesh = null;
```

You will also need to replace each instance of the old mesh variable with the new progressiveMesh variable. With the new variable name and type, we obviously need to update the LoadMesh method, since our code won't even compile right now. We will use a similar method; we will just generate our progressive mesh at the end. Use the code shown in Listing 9.3.

**LISTING 9.3**   Loading a Progressive Mesh

```
private void LoadMesh(string file)
{
    ExtendedMaterial[] mtrl;
    GraphicsStream adj;

    // Load our mesh
    using(Mesh mesh = Mesh.FromFile(file, MeshFlags.Managed, device,
                out adj, out mtrl))
    {

        // If we have any materials, store them
        if ((mtrl != null) && (mtrl.Length > 0))
        {
            meshMaterials = new Material[mtrl.Length];
            meshTextures = new Texture[mtrl.Length];
```

**LISTING 9.3**   Continued

```
        // Store each material and texture
        for (int i = 0; i < mtrl.Length; i++)
        {
            meshMaterials[i] = mtrl[i].Material3D;
            if ((mtrl[i].TextureFilename != null) &&
                (mtrl[i].TextureFilename != string.Empty))
            {
                // We have a texture, try to load it
                meshTextures[i] = TextureLoader.FromFile(device,
                    @"..\..\" + mtrl[i].TextureFilename);
            }
        }
    }


    // Clean our main mesh
    using(Mesh tempMesh = Mesh.Clean(mesh, adj, adj))
    {
        // Create our progressive mesh
        progressiveMesh = new ProgressiveMesh(tempMesh, adj,
            null, 1, MeshFlags.SimplifyVertex);

        // Set the initial mesh to the max
        progressiveMesh.NumberFaces = progressiveMesh.MaxFaces;
        progressiveMesh.NumberVertices = progressiveMesh.MaxVertices;
    }
  }
}
```

Notice that we use two temporary mesh objects to generate our progressive mesh. We use the cleaned mesh to do the actual generation of our progressive mesh. The fourth parameter is the important one for the progressive mesh constructor: It is the minimum number of vertices or faces we want in the generated mesh, depending on the MeshFlags option you pass in (either SimplifyFace or SimplifyVertex). Naturally, this is just an approximation, and even if it's not possible to simplify the mesh to that degree, this method should still succeed.

You'll also notice that immediately we set the number of vertices and facesto the maximum values. Generating the mesh leaves it simplified. Setting the number of faces and/or vertices on a progressive mesh will update the current level of detail used to render the mesh. Since we want to initially start out at full detail, we naturally update the number of faces and vertices to their maximums.

To get the application to compile, you'll need to change the DrawSubset call in your DrawMesh method as follows:

```
progressiveMesh.DrawSubset(i);
```

Running the application now, you should notice that it behaves exactly as the original sample did. Our model spins around and is fully detailed. Now, we need to handle our keypresses and camera movement. We will use code similar to what we used in our simplification mesh example. You will need the declarations for the camera position variable and the move amount constant:

```
private float cameraPos = 580.0f;
private const int MoveAmount = 100;
```

You'll once again need to modify your view transform to allow the camera position to be updated. Replace the view transform line with the following:

```
device.Transform.View = Matrix.LookAtLH(new Vector3(0,0, cameraPos),
    new Vector3(), new Vector3(0,1,0));
```

Finally, you'll need to handle the keystrokes and react accordingly. Use the override in Listing 9.4:

**LISTING 9.4**    KeyPress Event Handler

```
protected override void OnKeyPress(KeyPressEventArgs e)
{
    if (e.KeyChar == '+')
    {
        cameraPos += (MoveAmount * 2);
        progressiveMesh.NumberVertices =
            ((BaseMesh)progressiveMesh).NumberVertices - MoveAmount;

        progressiveMesh.NumberFaces =
            ((BaseMesh)progressiveMesh).NumberFaces - MoveAmount;
    }
    if (e.KeyChar == '-')
    {
        cameraPos -= (MoveAmount * 2);
        progressiveMesh.NumberVertices =
            ((BaseMesh)progressiveMesh).NumberVertices + MoveAmount;

        progressiveMesh.NumberFaces =
            ((BaseMesh)progressiveMesh).NumberFaces + MoveAmount;
    }
```

**LISTING 9.4** Continued

```
    if (e.KeyChar == 'w')
        device.RenderState.FillMode = FillMode.WireFrame;

    if (e.KeyChar == 's')
        device.RenderState.FillMode = FillMode.Solid;
}
```

Once again, we allow you to switch between wire-frame mode and solid mode by pressing the "w" or "s" key. We also keep the "+" key as our "decrease level of detail" key. When the "+" key is pressed, we move our camera farther away, and update the number of vertices and faces. You'll notice that when we are attempting to actually *get* the number of faces or vertices, we must first cast our progressive mesh to a BaseMesh object. Since the set property exists on the progressive mesh object, while the get property exists on the base object, this cast is necessary.

We also added the capability to increase our level of detail now as well. Naturally, we used the "−" key for this operation. It essentially does the exact opposite of what the "+" keys does. It moves the camera closer, and increases the number of vertices and faces in the mesh.

It would also be nice to add some rendered text to the application to show the number of vertices and meshes currently being rendered. Rather than repeat the code here, you can look earlier in this chapter for the declaration and initialization of a font variable. Once those are in your application, you can use the following in your rendering method:

### STORING MULTIPLE LEVELS OF DETAIL

It's common to store multiple meshes of varying levels of detail rather than having one large progressive mesh controlling the entire range of details. If you look at the Progressive Mesh sample that ships with the DirectX SDK, you will see an example of this implementation. You can use the TrimByFaces and TrimByVertices methods on the progressive mesh object to change the level of details that any particular progressive mesh supports.

```
font.DrawText(null, string.Format("Number vertices in mesh: {0}",
    ((BaseMesh)progressiveMesh).NumberVertices), new Rectangle(10, 10, 0, 0),
    DrawTextFormat.NoClip, Color.BlanchedAlmond);

font.DrawText(null, string.Format("Number faces in mesh: {0}",
    ((BaseMesh)progressiveMesh).NumberFaces), new Rectangle(10, 30, 0, 0),
    DrawTextFormat.NoClip, Color.BlanchedAlmond);
```

# Rendering Patch Meshes

Simplifying meshes is a common practice, but what about the times when the meshes you've got are already too simple? You have enough triangle bandwidth to display even more vertices in your mesh. While it may not be common to want to increase the detail of a model, it is possible, and patch meshes are the way. Most modern 3D graphics modeling programs have a concept of a type of patch mesh, or some type of high order primitives such as NURBS or subdivided surfaces.

The objective of this book is not to explain the theory behind understanding patch meshes, so we will not get into that. What we want to do is to understand how to use them, and how they can increase a model's level of detail. To do this, we will create a small application that loads a model and allows us to subdivide the vertices to make a more complex model.

Once again, we will start with the file load mesh example from Chapter 5. We keep doing this because it sets up the majority of the "state" for us to get started. You will need the models from the included CD for this example as well. The code on the included CD uses two of the models that are included in the DirectX SDK (tiger.x and cube.x), plus a small sphere model you will find on the CD. Make sure you copy the texture for the tiger model (tiger.bmp) as well. You will need the following variables added:

```
private float tessLevel = 1.0f;
private const float tessIncrement = 1.0f;
private string filename = @"..\..\sphere.x";
private Microsoft.DirectX.Direct3D.Font font = null;
```

You will have our current tessellation level (which is initially set to 1.0f), as well as how much we will increment this level each time. Feel free to manipulate this constant, but for now, the default value will do nicely. We will also need to store the name of the current model we are loading, as well as a font to draw the text during rendering.

You will also want to change the SetupCamera method since the last one was set up for a very large model, while the ones being used for this example are quite a bit smaller. Update the method as follows:

```
private void SetupCamera()
{
    device.Transform.Projection = Matrix.PerspectiveFovLH(
        (float)Math.PI / 4, this.Width / this.Height, 1.0f, 100.0f);

    device.Transform.View = Matrix.LookAtLH(new Vector3(0,0, 5.0f),
        new Vector3(), new Vector3(0,1,0));

    device.Lights[0].Type = LightType.Directional;
    device.Lights[0].Diffuse = Color.DarkKhaki;
```

```
device.Lights[0].Direction = new Vector3(0, 0, -1);
device.Lights[0].Commit();
device.Lights[0].Enabled = true;

}
```

This simply sets the camera and our light up. It's not very efficient to call this every single frame, but for clarity, we will do so for this example. Of course, we *should* be checking to see whether our graphics card supports directional lighting as well, but for this simple example, we will assume it exists as well.

Instead of using a single LoadMesh call (like we've done before) to get our mesh ready, replace the call to that method with the following few calls:

```
// Create our patch mesh
CreatePatchMesh(filename, tessLevel);

// Create our font
font = new Microsoft.DirectX.Direct3D.Font(device, new System.Drawing.Font
    ("Arial", 14.0f, FontStyle.Bold | FontStyle.Italic));

// Default to wireframe mode first
device.RenderState.FillMode = FillMode.WireFrame;
```

Obviously here we will be creating our patch mesh, along with our font. We also switch our fill mode to wire-frame by default, since it is much easier to see the new triangles appearing in wire-frame mode. However, we don't have the method to create our patch mesh defined yet, so we should add that now. See Listing 9.5:

**LISTING 9.5**  Creating a Patch Mesh

```
private void CreatePatchMesh(string file, float tessLevel)
{
    if (tessLevel < 1.0f) // Nothing to do
        return;

    if (mesh != null)
        mesh.Dispose();

    using (Mesh tempmesh = LoadMesh(file))
    {
        using (PatchMesh patch = PatchMesh.CreateNPatchMesh(tempmesh))
        {
            // Calculate the new number of faces/vertices
            int numberFaces = (int)(tempmesh.NumberFaces
```

**LISTING 9.5**    Continued

```
                    * Math.Pow(tessLevel, 3));
            int numberVerts = (int)(tempmesh.NumberVertices
                * Math.Pow(tessLevel, 3));

            mesh = new Mesh(numberFaces, numberVerts, MeshFlags.Managed
                ¦ MeshFlags.Use32Bit, tempmesh.VertexFormat, device);

            // Tessellate the patched mesh
            patch.Tessellate(tessLevel, mesh);
        }
    }
}
```

If the tessellation level we are currently using is less than 1.0f (the default), there is nothing to do in this method, so we simply return immediately. Otherwise, we get ready to create our new tessellated mesh. Since we will be replacing the existing mesh if it exists, we will first dispose of that one. What's this though? Our current LoadMesh method doesn't return any values; we should update that as shown in Listing 9.6:

**LISTING 9.6**    Loading a Mesh with Normal Data

```
private Mesh LoadMesh(string file)
{
    ExtendedMaterial[] mtrl;

    // Load our mesh
    Mesh mesh = Mesh.FromFile(file, MeshFlags.Managed, device,
                out mtrl);

    // If we have any materials, store them
    if ((mtrl != null) && (mtrl.Length > 0))
    {
        meshMaterials = new Material[mtrl.Length];
        meshTextures = new Texture[mtrl.Length];

        // Store each material and texture
        for (int i = 0; i < mtrl.Length; i++)
        {
            meshMaterials[i] = mtrl[i].Material3D;
            if ((mtrl[i].TextureFilename != null) &&
                (mtrl[i].TextureFilename != string.Empty))
            {
```

**LISTING 9.6**   Continued

```
                // We have a texture, try to load it
                meshTextures[i] = TextureLoader.FromFile(device,
                    @"..\..\" + mtrl[i].TextureFilename);
            }
        }
    }

    if ((mesh.VertexFormat & VertexFormats.Normal) != VertexFormats.Normal)
    {
        // We must have normals for our patch meshes
        Mesh tempMesh = mesh.Clone(mesh.Options.Value,
            mesh.VertexFormat | VertexFormats.Normal, device);

        tempMesh.ComputeNormals();

        mesh.Dispose();
        mesh = tempMesh;
    }
    return mesh;
}
```

There isn't anything here that we haven't seen before. We create our mesh (via a local variable). If there are no normals in our mesh, we clone the mesh and compute the normals, since they are required for the tessellation of our patch mesh. Finally, we return the created mesh (with the normals).

**THE USING STATEMENT**

You'll notice that for both the returned mesh and the patch mesh we create in this method, we use the "using" keyword. In case you are unaware, this causes the object in the using clause to be automatically disposed when it leaves the scope of the clause.

We then create a new patch mesh object based on the newly returned mesh. Since we will use the patch mesh object to tessellate into a new mesh, we need to know the number of new vertices and faces this mesh will need to have. After we've calculated that and created the new mesh, we finally tessellate our patch mesh into this newly created mesh. You'll notice that we are using the MeshFlags.Use32Bit flag as well. Since it's entirely possible we could get a very large mesh returned back after tessellation, we want to make sure we can support the largest meshes we can.

In reality, we are ready to run this application now. It will be pretty boring, though. First, let's add our text to the rendered scene. After the call to draw our mesh, add the following:

```
font.DrawText(null, string.Format
    ("Number Vertices: {0}\r\nNumber Faces: {1}",
    mesh.NumberVertices, mesh.NumberFaces),
```

```
        new Rectangle(10,10,0,0),
        DrawTextFormat.NoClip, Color.Black);
```

Finally, all we need now is a way to change models and increase (or decrease) the amount of tessellation. We will use the override in Listing 9.7:

**LISTING 9.7**   KeyPress Event Handler

```
protected override void OnKeyPress(KeyPressEventArgs e)
{
    if (e.KeyChar == '+')
    {
        tessLevel += tessIncrement;
        CreatePatchMesh(filename, tessLevel);
    }
    if (e.KeyChar == '-')
    {
        tessLevel -= tessIncrement;
        CreatePatchMesh(filename, tessLevel);
    }
    if (e.KeyChar == 'c')
    {
        filename = @"..\..\cube.x";
        tessLevel = 1.0f;
        CreatePatchMesh(filename, tessLevel);
    }
    if (e.KeyChar == 'o')
    {
        filename = @"..\..\sphere.x";
        tessLevel = 1.0f;
        CreatePatchMesh(filename, tessLevel);
    }
    if (e.KeyChar == 't')
    {
        filename = @"..\..\tiger.x";
        tessLevel = 1.0f;
        CreatePatchMesh(filename, tessLevel);
    }
    if (e.KeyChar == 'w')
        device.RenderState.FillMode = FillMode.WireFrame;

    if (e.KeyChar == 's')
        device.RenderState.FillMode = FillMode.Solid;


}
```

We will use the old mainstays of "w" and "s" to switch between wire-frame and solid fill modes, respectively. We will also use the "+" and "–" keys to increase and decrease the tessellation level, much like we did for our progressive mesh example. We finally use the "c" key to switch to a cube model, the "t" key to switch to the tiger model, and the "o" key to switch back to the sphere model. Try running the example now and switching between the various models and tessellation levels.

# Seeing the Tessellation Levels

You can see the difference in the following figures:

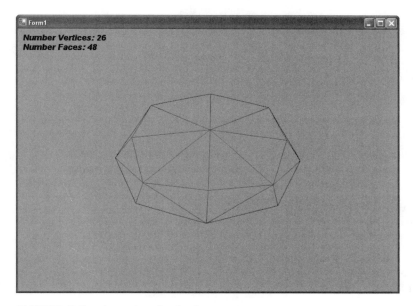

**FIGURE 9.2**   A very low-detail sphere.

As you can see here, this "sphere" doesn't look much like a sphere. Hardly any triangles are being drawn, it looks all blocky in solid fill modes, and it's just not very realistic. However, if we just split each triangle into multiple triangles (subdivide) a few times, it looks much better.

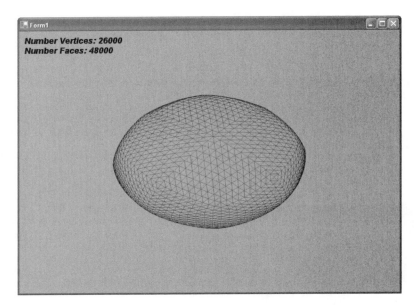

**FIGURE 9.3**   Adding detail to the sphere.

The sphere looks much more like a sphere now than it did before. Each triangle has been tessellated quite a few times, and the effect makes the sphere look much more realistic.

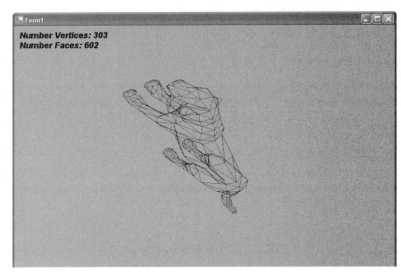

**FIGURE 9.4**   The normal detail of the tiger.

You can see how the tiger looks somewhat blocky, although the texture definitely helps hide some of this. However, it's still obvious if you're looking for it. Increasing the tessellation will remove this blockiness.

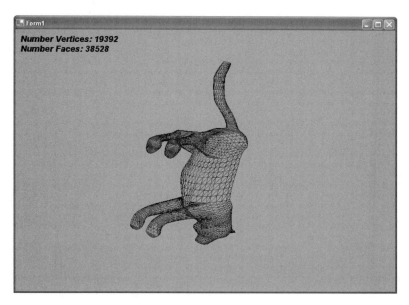

**FIGURE 9.5**    A very highly detailed tiger.

With the increased tessellation, you can see that the blockiness has disappeared.

# In Brief

We covered the rest of the mesh types in this chapter, including

- Simplification meshes
- Progressive meshes
- Patch meshes

In our next chapter, we will explore some of the other classes in the extensions library, including lines, environment maps, and rendering to textures.

# Using the Helper Classes

## Drawing Lines

Drawing simple line types was actually covered back in Chapter 4, "More Rendering Techniques," when dealing with primitive types, as there is a primitive type for a line list or a line strip that can be easily used. However, when drawing these types of lines, you cannot have lines with varying widths, or lines that are anti-aliased (unless the whole scene is).

Depending on the type of application you are trying to write, drawing lines can be a very common occurrence, or something that you simply never have to do. However, with the ease of the Line class, it's a simple matter to draw them anytime they're necessary. To show the simplicity of drawing some lines, we will write a quick example to draw a random number of lines on the screen continuously.

Go ahead and create a new project, and get it ready for writing some Direct3D code. This includes adding the references to the assemblies, as well as including the using clauses for the namespaces. Go ahead and create a private variable for the device, and set the window style for our rendering as well. No need to put the code necessary for these items here, as we've done them quite a few times by now.

Lines can be drawn in either pre-transformed coordinates (that is, screen coordinates) or in world space. For this example, we will only care about the lines drawn in screen space, so our device will not need to have a depth buffer. Use the method found in Listing 10.1 to initialize the graphics.

**LISTING 10.1**   Initializing Your Device

```
public void InitializeGraphics()
{
    // Set our presentation parameters
    PresentParameters presentParams = new PresentParameters();

    presentParams.Windowed = true;
    presentParams.SwapEffect = SwapEffect.Discard;

    // Create our device
    device = new Device(0, DeviceType.Hardware, this,
        CreateFlags.SoftwareVertexProcessing, presentParams);
}
```

This code is just like we've seen before, only without the depth buffer. Now, our rendering function will be the painting override just like we've done for each example thus far:

```
protected override void OnPaint(System.Windows.Forms.PaintEventArgs e)
{
    device.Clear(ClearFlags.Target, Color.Black, 1.0f, 0);

    device.BeginScene();
    //Draw some lines
    DrawRandomLines();
    device.EndScene();
    device.Present();

    // Let them show for a few seconds
    System.Threading.Thread.Sleep(250);
    this.Invalidate();
}
```

Once again, there is nothing overly spectacular here. We clear our device, begin the scene, make our call to draw some lines, end the scene, and present it. Finally, we sleep for a quarter of a second so that we can actually *see* the lines being drawn, and start the whole loop over again. Naturally, our draw lines method hasn't been defined yet. Use the one found in Listing 10.2.

**LISTING 10.2**   Drawing Random Lines

```
private void DrawRandomLines()
{
    Random r = new Random();
    int numberLines = r.Next(50);
    using (Line l = new Line(device))
    {
        for (int i = 0; i < numberLines; i++)
        {
            int numVectors = 0;
            while (numVectors < 2)
                numVectors = r.Next(4);

            Vector2[] vecs = new Vector2[numVectors];
            for(int inner = 0; inner < vecs.Length; inner++)
            {
                vecs[inner] = new Vector2(r.Next(this.Width),
                    r.Next(this.Height));
            }
            // Color
            Color c = Color.FromArgb(r.Next(byte.MaxValue),
                r.Next(byte.MaxValue), r.Next(byte.MaxValue));

            int width = 0;

            while (width == 0)
                width = r.Next(this.Width / 100);

            // Set the width
            l.Width = width;

            // Should they be antialiased?
            l.Antialias = r.Next(50) > 25 ? true : false;

            // Draw the line
            l.Begin();
            l.Draw(vecs, c);
            l.End();
        }
    }
}
```

Each time this method is called, you first decide a random number of lines to draw (up to a maximum of 50 of them). You then create a single line object to draw each line. You could create a new line object for each line, or you could just create one "global" one to use for all lines, but this way makes the code very easy to read.

Now, you randomly pick the number of points in this line, ensuring that there are at least two. After you've determined the total number of points this line will have, you can pick a random location for each point based on the start and end point based on the windows width and height. You also pick a random color for the line, and a random width. The width is also based on the window width. The anti-alias mode is then selected randomly as well. If this value ends up being false, the lines (particularly lines of greater-than-one width) will appear "jagged." If this value is true, the lines will appear much smoother.

Finally, you are actually ready to draw a line. Wrap the Draw call around the calls to Begin and End to let Direct3D know that we are drawing a line.

While you didn't actually use these options for this example, there are other properties you can use while drawing your lines. There is a GlLines Boolean property that determines whether the OpenGL-style lines should be used (the default value for this option is false). You can also use the DrawTransform method to draw lines in 3D space instead of the screen coordinates used here.

Now, you'll just need to update your main method as follows:

```
static void Main()
{
    using (Form1 frm = new Form1())
    {
        // Show our form and initialize our graphics engine
        frm.Show();
        frm.InitializeGraphics();
        Application.Run(frm);
    }
}
```

Running this application should fill your screen with a wide array of constantly changing lines. Some will be thin, some will be thick, some will be jagged, and some will be smooth. Sometimes there will be many, other times just a few. See Figure 10.1.

**FIGURE 10.1**    Random lines across the screen.

# Drawing Text

Again, drawing text is something that has already been done. However you just did the bare minimum before; we will delve a little deeper into the methods now. In the previous examples, there has been a Font object both in the Microsoft.DirectX.Direct3D namespace, as well as the System.Drawing namespace. You must distinguish between them, so in order to help facilitate this, you should use the following using clause:

```
using Direct3D = Microsoft.DirectX.Direct3D;
```

This will allow us to the use the Direct3D alias instead of having to type the entire namespace out. With that, let's go ahead and create a new project for our text drawing example. Make sure you add the references and the using clauses to the project (including the previous one). Also, ensure that you have a private variable for our device, and the window style set correctly for our rendering. With those items done, add the following variables:

```
private Direct3D.Font font = null;
private Mesh mesh = null;
private Material meshMaterial;
private float angle = 0.0f;
```

Here we are declaring a font that will allow us to draw text on the screen, as well as a mesh and that mesh's material. The mesh will actually be simple text that has been extruded and is a 3D mesh rather than the simple 2D text we'll be drawing as well. The angle parameter we've used before will allow the 3D text to rotate around based on frame rate. We now need to initialize the graphics with the method found in Listing 10.3.

**LISTING 10.3**    Initializing Your Graphics for Font Drawing

```
public void InitializeGraphics()
{
    // Set our presentation parameters
    PresentParameters presentParams = new PresentParameters();

    presentParams.Windowed = true;
    presentParams.SwapEffect = SwapEffect.Discard;
    presentParams.AutoDepthStencilFormat = DepthFormat.D16;
    presentParams.EnableAutoDepthStencil = true;

    // Create our device
    device = new Device(0, DeviceType.Hardware, this,
        CreateFlags.SoftwareVertexProcessing, presentParams);
    device.DeviceReset += new System.EventHandler(this.OnDeviceReset);
    OnDeviceReset(device, null);

    // What font do we want to use?
    System.Drawing.Font localFont = new System.Drawing.Font
        ("Arial", 14.0f, FontStyle.Italic);

    // Create an extruded version of this font
    mesh = Mesh.TextFromFont(device, localFont, "Managed DirectX",
            0.001f, 0.4f);

    // Create a material for our text mesh
    meshMaterial = new Material();
    meshMaterial.Diffuse = Color.Peru;

    // Create a font we can draw with
    font = new Direct3D.Font(device, localFont);
}
```

We create a hardware device with a depth buffer here, and hook the DeviceReset event. Since we will only need to set our lights and camera up once per device reset, we will put that code in the event handler (we'll get to that in a moment). Finally, we create a System.Drawing.Font that we will use as the basis for both our 2D and 3D text items. I picked a 14-point Arial font, but feel free to pick any valid font on your system. We first create our 3D extruded mesh from the font. We will use the string "Managed DirectX" to extrude. You will need an entirely new mesh for every different string you want to render

**RENDERING EXTRUDED TEXT**

Make sure that 3D extruded text is really what you want when you are deciding what to render. Drawing some 2D text can be done with two simple triangles, while drawing 3D extruded text can take thousands of triangles.

in 3D. We then set our material to any color we want and create our 2D font.

You will want to set up the camera and lights in the event handler method that you've used here as well, so define that like this:

```
private void OnDeviceReset(object sender, EventArgs e)
{
    Device dev = (Device)sender;
    dev.Transform.Projection = Matrix.PerspectiveFovLH(
        (float)Math.PI / 4, this.Width / this.Height, 1.0f, 100.0f);

    dev.Transform.View = Matrix.LookAtLH(new Vector3(0,0, -9.0f),
        new Vector3(), new Vector3(0,1,0));

    dev.Lights[0].Type = LightType.Directional;
    dev.Lights[0].Diffuse = Color.White;
    dev.Lights[0].Direction = new Vector3(0, 0, 1);
    dev.Lights[0].Commit();
    dev.Lights[0].Enabled = true;
}
```

The camera and lights are really only for the 3D extruded text. The 2D text has all been pre-transformed and lit, so these options aren't necessary. However, the extruded text is actually a real 3D model, so in order to have it look correct we create our camera and light. Let's add a method to draw this 3D extruded text now:

```
private void Draw3DText(Vector3 axis, Vector3 location)
{
    device.Transform.World = Matrix.RotationAxis(
        axis, angle) *
        Matrix.Translation(location);
    device.Material = meshMaterial;
    mesh.DrawSubset(0);

    angle += 0.01f;
}
```

As you can see here, we pass in the location of the mesh in world space, and the axis we want it to rotate on. This method is similar to the DrawMesh method we've used in previous examples, as it simply sets the material and draws the first mesh subset. In this extruded mesh, we know there will only ever be one subset. We also increase our angle parameter. Controlling the "animation" this way makes the movement be controlled by frame rate, which we already know is a bad thing, but for readability we will use this method. Now, let's add our method to draw some 2D text:

```
private void Draw2DText(string text, int x, int y, Color c)
{
    font.DrawText(null, text, new Rectangle(x, y,
        this.Width , this.Height ),
        DrawTextFormat.NoClip | DrawTextFormat.ExpandTabs |
        DrawTextFormat.WordBreak , c);
}
```

Here we pass in the actual text we want to render, as well as the position (in screen coordinates) where we want the upper left corner of the text to reside. The last parameter is naturally the color. You'll notice now that in our call to DrawText, we include the width and height of the window in the rectangle we pass in. We do this because we've also passed in the WordBreak flag, which will cause automatic word wrapping to occur if the text starts to run past the end of the bounding rectangle. We also want any tabs in the text to be expanded as well, and the text not to be clipped.

With the two main methods for rendering our text in place, we now only need to include our OnPaint override (see Listing 10.4):

**LISTING 10.4**  Rendering Your Text

```
protected override void OnPaint(System.Windows.Forms.PaintEventArgs e)
{
    device.Clear(ClearFlags.Target | ClearFlags.ZBuffer, Color.Black, 1.0f, 0);

    device.BeginScene();

    Draw2DText("Here's some text", 10, 10, Color.WhiteSmoke);
    Draw2DText("Here's some text\r\nwith\r\nhard\r\nline breaks",
        100, 80, Color.Violet);

    Draw2DText("This\tis\tsome\ttext\twith\ttabs.",
        this.Width / 2, this.Height - 80 , Color.RoyalBlue);

    Draw2DText("If you type enough words in a single sentence, " +
        "you may notice that the text begins to wrap.  Try resizing " +
        "the window to notice how the text changes as you size it.",
```

**LISTING 10.4**  Continued

```
            this.Width / 2 + this.Width / 4, this.Height / 4 , Color.Yellow);

    // Draw our two spinning meshes
    Draw3DText(new Vector3(1.0f, 1.0f, 0.0f),
        new Vector3(-3.0f, 0.0f, 0.0f));

    Draw3DText(new Vector3(0.0f, 1.0f, 1.0f),
        new Vector3(0.0f, -1.0f, 1.0f));

    device.EndScene();

    device.Present();
    this.Invalidate();
}
```

You'll notice that at first, we draw simple text like we've done before; just a short sentence in the upper left. Next we draw some new text with actual hard line breaks. We expect this text to be rendered with these line breaks. After that we draw some words that are separated with tabs instead of spaces. Since we included the ExpandTabs flag, these will be expanded when rendered. Finally, we draw one very large sentence. There are no hard line breaks in this sentence, but we fully expect it to have the word wrap feature invoked on it. Finally, add your main method:

```
static void Main()
{
    using (Form1 frm = new Form1())
    {
        // Show our form and initialize our graphics engine
        frm.Show();
        frm.InitializeGraphics();
        Application.Run(frm);
    }
}
```

Running the application now will render some text that looks like what you see in Figure 10.2.

Feel free to resize this window like the text asks you to. You'll notice that as the window size changes, the text wraps in different ways. You'll also notice even the text that doesn't wrap initially can start wrapping.

### ENHANCING FONT PEFORMANCE

The Font class draws its text based on textures that it creates to hold the rendered letters. Rendering these letters to a texture happens via GDI, and can potentially be slow. It may be wise to call the two preload methods on the font class during startup to ensure you don't hit these load times during runtime. You can call PreloadCharacters to load a specific set of characters, or PreloadText to load a specific string.

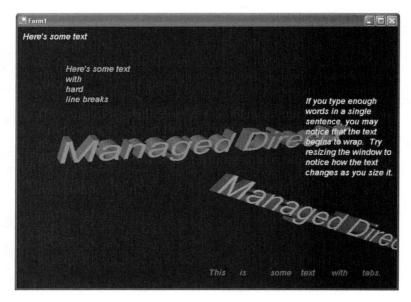

**FIGURE 10.2** Rendered text.

# Rendering to Surfaces

Have you ever been playing a game, such as a racing game, and seen how you can turn on a "rear-view" mirror? Possibly you've played one of the kart racing games where there is a billboard showing the race in the background? These effects are normally achieved by rendering the same scene (most times with a different camera) into a texture. Actually, despite sounding somewhat difficult, this is in reality quite simple to do. You can once again take the example for loading a mesh from a file from Chapter 5, "Rendering with Meshes," and update it for this example.

We will naturally need to declare a new texture that we will be rendering to, among other things, so add the following declarations:

```
private Texture renderTexture = null;
private Surface renderSurface = null;
private RenderToSurface rts = null;
private const int RenderSurfaceSize = 128;
```

Here we have declared the texture we will be rendering to, the actual surface we will be rendering to (which we will actually just get from the texture), and the helper class for rendering to a surface. We've also declared the size of the surfaces we'll be creating. In the InitializeGraphics method, we will want to hook the device reset event to give us a place to create our textures and surfaces, so replace the device constructor call with this:

```
device = new Device(0, DeviceType.Hardware, this,
        CreateFlags.SoftwareVertexProcessing, presentParams);
device.DeviceReset +=new EventHandler(OnDeviceReset);
OnDeviceReset(device, null);
```

Now, add the actual event handler found in Listing 10.5.

**LISTING 10.5**  Setting Default Options on Your Device

```
private void OnDeviceReset(object sender, EventArgs e)
{
    Device dev = (Device)sender;

    if (dev.DeviceCaps.VertexProcessingCaps.SupportsDirectionalLights)
    {
        uint maxLights = (uint)dev.DeviceCaps.MaxActiveLights;
        if (maxLights > 0)
        {
            dev.Lights[0].Type = LightType.Directional;
            dev.Lights[0].Diffuse = Color.White;
            dev.Lights[0].Direction = new Vector3(0, -1, -1);
            dev.Lights[0].Commit();
            dev.Lights[0].Enabled = true;
        }

        if (maxLights > 1)
        {
            dev.Lights[1].Type = LightType.Directional;
            dev.Lights[1].Diffuse = Color.White;
            dev.Lights[1].Direction = new Vector3(0, -1, 1);
            dev.Lights[1].Commit();
            dev.Lights[1].Enabled = true;
        }

    }

    rts = new RenderToSurface(dev, RenderSurfaceSize, RenderSurfaceSize,
        Format.X8R8G8B8, true, DepthFormat.D16);
```

**LISTING 10.5** Continued

```
        renderTexture = new Texture(dev, RenderSurfaceSize, RenderSurfaceSize, 1,
            Usage.RenderTarget, Format.X8R8G8B8, Pool.Default);

        renderSurface = renderTexture.GetSurfaceLevel(0);
}
```

Here, we will actually do our checks as we're supposed to. We will first detect whether the device supports directional lights. If it does, we will begin turning on our lights, assuming it supports enough active lights. We will have two directional lights, one shining toward the front of our model, the other shining toward the back.

After our lights have been created and turned on, we will create our helper class using the size of our constant. You'll notice that many of the parameters for this constructor match items you'd find in the device's presentation parameters. This example is just using well-known members, but it may be useful to actually use the same values from your present parameters structure.

Lastly, we create our texture. Notice that we've specified the usage to be a render target, since we plan on rendering to this texture soon. We also use the same format here as we did for our helper class. All render target textures *must* be in the default memory pool as we've done here. We also get the actual surface from the texture and store that as well.

Since we've got our lights set up in the device reset event handler, you should go ahead and remove them from the SetupCamera method already existing in this example. Now you will need to add a new method to render into our surface. You should use the method found in Listing 10.6.

**LISTING 10.6** Rendering to a Surface

```
private void RenderIntoSurface()
{
    // Render to this surface
    Viewport view = new Viewport();
    view.Width = RenderSurfaceSize;
    view.Height = RenderSurfaceSize;
    view.MaxZ = 1.0f;

    rts.BeginScene(renderSurface, view);

    device.Clear(ClearFlags.Target | ClearFlags.ZBuffer, Color.DarkBlue, 1.0f,
        0);
    device.Transform.Projection = Matrix.PerspectiveFovLH((float)Math.PI / 4,
```

**LISTING 10.6**   Continued

```
        this.Width / this.Height, 1.0f, 10000.0f);

    device.Transform.View = Matrix.LookAtLH(new Vector3(0,0, -580.0f),
        new Vector3(), new Vector3(0, 1,0));

    DrawMesh(angle / (float)Math.PI, angle / (float)Math.PI * 2.0f,
        angle / (float)Math.PI / 4.0f, 0.0f, 0.0f, 0.0f);

    DrawMesh(angle / (float)Math.PI, angle / (float)Math.PI / 2.0f,
        angle / (float)Math.PI * 4.0f, 150.0f, -100.0f, 175.0f);

    rts.EndScene(Filter.None);
}
```

This looks quite a bit like our normal rendering method. We have a begin scene call, an end scene call, we set our camera transforms, and we draw our meshes. This looks similar because it is similar. When we render to a texture, we really do need to render the items of the scene we want to have shown in the texture. In our case, you'll notice our camera is just about the same, except it is on the other side of the model, so we should be seeing "behind" the model in our rendered texture. You'll also notice that we're rendering two models in this scene. We do this to give off the "fake" effect that there are two models in the world, and in the default view you can only see the one since the second is behind the camera. However, in the secondary view, with the camera facing the other way, you can see both models.

You'll notice that the BeginScene method takes the surface that we will be rendering to as an argument. Since we are using the surface we've retrieved from our texture, any updates to this surface will be reflected in our texture. The EndScene method allows you to pass in a mipmap filter that you wish to apply to the surface. Rather than worrying about the device capabilities, we will use no filtering for this example. One last thing to notice is that we've changed the clear color for our textured scene. We do this to show the obvious difference between the "real" scene, and the "other" scene.

Naturally, we will need to modify our rendering method slightly as well. First, we will want to render the scene to our texture before we even start rendering it for our main window. Add a call to our method as the very first item in your OnPaint method:

```
RenderIntoSurface();
```

Finally, we will want to actually put the texture on the screen somehow. There is another helper class called the Sprite that we will discuss in a later chapter, but we will use it here since it allows an easy mechanism to draw a texture in screen coordinates. Add the following section of code before your end scene method:

```
using (Sprite s = new Sprite(device))
{
    s.Begin(SpriteFlags.None);
    s.Draw(renderTexture, new Rectangle(0, 0, RenderSurfaceSize,
        RenderSurfaceSize),  new Vector3(0, 0, 0), new Vector3(0, 0, 1.0f),
        Color.White);
    s.End();
}
```

This code simply renders the entire texture's surface onto the screen in the upper left corner. Running the application now should show you something similar to what you see in Figure 10.3.

**FIGURE 10.3**    Rendering to a surface.

# Rendering Environment Maps

Environment mapping is a technique that can be used to simulate a highly reflective surface. You may see this effect in racing games, where a bright shiny car "reflects" the clouds above it, or where a "new" ice hockey rink seems to reflect the players as they skate on it. A common way to implement these environment maps is to use a cube texture (a six-sided texture), and we will show this technique now.

Before we begin looking at this code specifically, you will once again need to create a new project and get it ready for coding (including adding the references, the device variable, and setting the window style). We will also need two of the meshes that ship with the DirectX SDK, the car model and the skybox2 model (and associated textures). Once that has been done, add the following variable declarations:

```
private Mesh skybox = null;
private Material[] skyboxMaterials;
private Texture[] skyboxTextures;

private Mesh car = null;
private Material[] carMaterials;
private Texture[] carTextures;

private CubeTexture environment = null;
private RenderToEnvironmentMap rte = null;
private const int CubeMapSize = 128;
private readonly Matrix ViewMatrix = Matrix.Translation(0.0f, 0.0f, 13.0f);
```

Here we've declared the two meshes we will need to draw, the sky box (our "environment"), and the object we want to reflect this environment on[md]in our case, the car. We also need to have the cube texture that will store the environment and the helper class for rendering the environment map.

Since not all cards support cube textures, we will need to detect whether your card supports these before we can continue with the example. You will need a new graphics initialization method to handle this. Use the one found in Listing 10.7.

**LISTING 10.7**   Initializing Your Device for Environment Mapping

```
public bool InitializeGraphics()
{
    // Set our presentation parameters
    PresentParameters presentParams = new PresentParameters();

    presentParams.Windowed = true;
    presentParams.SwapEffect = SwapEffect.Discard;
    presentParams.AutoDepthStencilFormat = DepthFormat.D16;
    presentParams.EnableAutoDepthStencil = true;
```

LISTING 10.7   Continued

```
        // Create our device
        device = new Device(0, DeviceType.Hardware, this,
                CreateFlags.SoftwareVertexProcessing, presentParams);
        device.DeviceReset +=new EventHandler(OnDeviceReset);
        OnDeviceReset(device, null);

        // Do we support cube maps?
        if (!device.DeviceCaps.TextureCaps.SupportsCubeMap)
            return false;

        // Load our meshes
        skybox = LoadMesh(@"..\..\skybox2.x", ref skyboxMaterials,
                ref skyboxTextures);
        car = LoadMesh(@"..\..\car.x", ref carMaterials, ref carTextures);

        return true;
}
```

The only major difference between this and our others is the fact that it returns a Boolean value identifying whether it succeeded or not. It hooks the device reset event and uses a new LoadMesh method as well. Before we look at those methods, though, we will need to update our main method to handle the return value of this method:

```
static void Main()
{
    using (Form1 frm = new Form1())
    {
        // Show our form and initialize our graphics engine
        frm.Show();
        if (!frm.InitializeGraphics())
        {
            MessageBox.Show("Your card does not support cube maps.");
            frm.Close();
        }
        else
        {
            Application.Run(frm);
        }
    }
}
```

You can see there is nothing unusual here. Now, let's look at our mesh loading method. Again, it's similar to our previous methods. After loading the mesh, materials and textures, it ensures that the data controls normal information (and adds it if not). It then returns the resulting mesh. Use the code found in Listing 10.8.

**LISTING 10.8**   Loading a Mesh with Normal Data

```
private Mesh LoadMesh(string file,ref Material[] meshMaterials,ref Texture[] meshTextures)
{
    ExtendedMaterial[] mtrl;

    // Load our mesh
    Mesh mesh = Mesh.FromFile(file, MeshFlags.Managed, device, out mtrl);

    // If we have any materials, store them
    if ((mtrl != null) && (mtrl.Length > 0))
    {
        meshMaterials = new Material[mtrl.Length];
        meshTextures = new Texture[mtrl.Length];

        // Store each material and texture
        for (int i = 0; i < mtrl.Length; i++)
        {
            meshMaterials[i] = mtrl[i].Material3D;
            if ((mtrl[i].TextureFilename != null) &&
                (mtrl[i].TextureFilename != string.Empty))
            {
                // We have a texture, try to load it
                meshTextures[i] = TextureLoader.FromFile(device, @"..\..\" +
                    mtrl[i].TextureFilename);
            }
        }
    }
    if ((mesh.VertexFormat & VertexFormats.Normal) != VertexFormats.Normal)
    {
        // We must have normals for our patch meshes
        Mesh tempMesh = mesh.Clone(mesh.Options.Value,
            mesh.VertexFormat | VertexFormats.Normal, device);

        tempMesh.ComputeNormals();

        mesh.Dispose();
```

**LISTING 10.8**   Continued

```
        mesh = tempMesh;
    }
    return mesh;
}
```

Now, much like our last example, we will need to create a render target surface to hold the environment map. We will do this in our reset event handler method:

```
private void OnDeviceReset(object sender, EventArgs e)
{
    Device dev = (Device)sender;

    rte = new RenderToEnvironmentMap(dev, CubeMapSize, 1,
        Format.X8R8G8B8, true, DepthFormat.D16);

    environment = new CubeTexture(dev, CubeMapSize, 1,
        Usage.RenderTarget, Format.X8R8G8B8, Pool.Default);
}
```

Here we've created both our helper class and our cube texture. The larger the size you pass in (in our case the CubeMapSize constant), the more detailed the environment map is. In many cases, it may be more efficient for you to store the environment map statically, in which case you could simply load the cube texture from a file (or some other data source). However, we want to show the environment map being created dynamically based on the rendered scene, thus we create our render target textures.

Much like our last example where we rendered our scene into a single texture, this example will also require multiple renderings of our scene. In this case though, we will need to render it a total of six extra times (once for each face of our cube map). Add the method in Listing 10.9 to your application to handle rendering to the environment map.

**LISTING 10.9**   Rendering Your Environment Map

```
private void RenderSceneIntoEnvMap()
{

    // Set the projection matrix for a field of view of 90 degrees
    Matrix matProj;
    matProj = Matrix.PerspectiveFovLH((float)Math.PI * 0.5f, 1.0f,
        0.5f, 1000.0f);

    // Get the current view matrix, to concat it with the cubemap view vectors
```

**LISTING 10.9**   Continued

```
Matrix matViewDir = ViewMatrix;
matViewDir.M41 = 0.0f; matViewDir.M42 = 0.0f; matViewDir.M43 = 0.0f;

// Render the six cube faces into the environment map
if (environment != null)
    rte.BeginCube(environment);

for (int i = 0; i < 6; i++)
{
    rte.Face((CubeMapFace) i , 1);

    // Set the view transform for this cubemap surface
    Matrix matView = Matrix.Multiply(matViewDir,
            GetCubeMapViewMatrix((CubeMapFace) i));

    // Render the scene (except for the teapot)
    RenderScene(matView, matProj, false);
}

rte.End(1);
}
```

There's quite a bit going on in this method. First, we create a projection matrix with a field of view of 90 degrees, since the angles between each cube face happen to be 90 degrees. We then get the view matrix we've stored for this application and modify the last row so that we can combine this with the view matrices for each face.

Next, we call the BeginCube method on our helper class, letting it know we will be creating an environmental cube map. There are also other methods this helper class has that allow different types of environment maps to be created, including BeginHemisphere, BeginParabolic (which each use two surfaces, one for positive z, the other for negative z), and BeginSphere (which uses a single surface).

With the environment map ready to be rendered, we then start a loop for each face in our cube map. For each face, we first call the Face method, which is analogous to the BeginScene method we've used for our device, and texture renders. It signals that the last "face" has been completed, and a new one is ready to be rendered. We then combine the current view matrix with one we retrieve from the GetCubeMapViewMatrix method. The definition for this method is found in Listing 10.10.

LISTING 10.10   Getting the View Matrix

```
private Matrix GetCubeMapViewMatrix(CubeMapFace face)
{
    Vector3 vEyePt = new Vector3(0.0f, 0.0f, 0.0f);
    Vector3 vLookDir = new Vector3();
    Vector3 vUpDir = new Vector3();

    switch (face)
    {
        case CubeMapFace.PositiveX:
            vLookDir = new Vector3(1.0f, 0.0f, 0.0f);
            vUpDir   = new Vector3(0.0f, 1.0f, 0.0f);
            break;
        case CubeMapFace.NegativeX:
            vLookDir = new Vector3(-1.0f, 0.0f, 0.0f);
            vUpDir   = new Vector3(0.0f, 1.0f, 0.0f);
            break;
        case CubeMapFace.PositiveY:
            vLookDir = new Vector3(0.0f, 1.0f, 0.0f);
            vUpDir   = new Vector3(0.0f, 0.0f,-1.0f);
            break;
        case CubeMapFace.NegativeY:
            vLookDir = new Vector3(0.0f,-1.0f, 0.0f);
            vUpDir   = new Vector3(0.0f, 0.0f, 1.0f);
            break;
        case CubeMapFace.PositiveZ:
            vLookDir = new Vector3(0.0f, 0.0f, 1.0f);
            vUpDir   = new Vector3(0.0f, 1.0f, 0.0f);
            break;
        case CubeMapFace.NegativeZ:
            vLookDir = new Vector3(0.0f, 0.0f,-1.0f);
            vUpDir   = new Vector3(0.0f, 1.0f, 0.0f);
            break;
    }

    // Set the view transform for this cubemap surface
    Matrix matView = Matrix.LookAtLH(vEyePt, vLookDir, vUpDir);
    return matView;
}
```

As you can see, we simply modify the view parameters based on which face we are looking at, and return the view matrix based on these vectors. Finally, after we've done all that, we render the entire scene without the shiny car (the false parameter to the RenderScene method). There's a lot going on in this method as well. Add the code found in Listing 10.11.

**LISTING 10.11**   Rendering Your Full Scene

```
private void RenderScene(Matrix View, Matrix Project, bool shouldRenderCar)
{
    // Render the skybox first
    device.Transform.World = Matrix.Scaling(10.0f, 10.0f, 10.0f);
    Matrix matView = View;
    matView.M41 = matView.M42 = matView.M43 = 0.0f;

    device.Transform.View = matView;
    device.Transform.Projection = Project;

    device.TextureState[0].ColorArgument1 = TextureArgument.TextureColor;
    device.TextureState[0].ColorOperation = TextureOperation.SelectArg1;
    device.SamplerState[0].MinFilter = TextureFilter.Linear;
    device.SamplerState[0].MagFilter = TextureFilter.Linear;
    device.SamplerState[0].AddressU = TextureAddress.Mirror;
    device.SamplerState[0].AddressV = TextureAddress.Mirror;

    // Always pass Z-test, so we can avoid clearing color and depth buffers
    device.RenderState.ZBufferFunction = Compare.Always;
    DrawSkyBox();
    device.RenderState.ZBufferFunction = Compare.LessEqual;

    // Render the shiny car
    if (shouldRenderCar)
    {
        // Render the car
        device.Transform.View = View;
        device.Transform.Projection = Project;

        using (VertexBuffer vb = car.VertexBuffer)
        {
            using (IndexBuffer ib = car.IndexBuffer)
            {
                // Set the stream source
                device.SetStreamSource(0, vb, 0,
                    VertexInformation.GetFormatSize(car.VertexFormat));

                // And the vertex format and indices
                device.VertexFormat = car.VertexFormat;
```

**LISTING 10.11**   Continued

```
            device.Indices = ib;

            device.SetTexture(0, environment);
            device.SamplerState[0].MinFilter = TextureFilter.Linear;
            device.SamplerState[0].MagFilter = TextureFilter.Linear;

            device.SamplerState[0].AddressU = TextureAddress.Clamp;
            device.SamplerState[0].AddressV = TextureAddress.Clamp;
            device.SamplerState[0].AddressW = TextureAddress.Clamp;

            device.TextureState[0].ColorOperation =
                TextureOperation.SelectArg1;
            device.TextureState[0].ColorArgument1 =
                TextureArgument.TextureColor;

            device.TextureState[0].TextureCoordinateIndex =
                (int)TextureCoordinateIndex.CameraSpaceReflectionVector;

            device.TextureState[0].TextureTransform =
                TextureTransform.Count3;

            device.Transform.World = Matrix.RotationYawPitchRoll(
                angle / (float)Math.PI, angle / (float)Math.PI * 2.0f,
                angle / (float)Math.PI / 4.0f);

            angle += 0.01f;

            device.DrawIndexedPrimitives(PrimitiveType.TriangleList,
                0, 0, car.NumberVertices, 0, car.NumberFaces);
        }
    }
  }
}
```

Now that's a method. The first thing we will want to do is render the skybox. Since we know the skybox is a little smaller than we will need initially, we will scale it to 10 times its size. We then set the texture and sampler states necessary to render the skybox textures (feel free to look at MSDN help for further explanations on these states).

If you'll notice, we never cleared the device. Since we don't want to call this for every face we render, before we render the sky box (which we know will have the farthest depth of anything in our scene), we set the render state so that the depth buffer will always pass while the skybox is rendering. With that out of the way, we render the skybox and switch the depth buffer function back to normal. The skybox rendering method should look familiar:

```
private void DrawSkyBox()
{
    for (int i = 0; i < skyboxMaterials.Length; i++)
    {
        device.Material = skyboxMaterials[i];
        device.SetTexture(0, skyboxTextures[i]);
        skybox.DrawSubset(i);
    }
}
```

With the skybox now rendered, we need to decide if we'll be rendering the car as well, based on the passed in parameter. If we do, then we need to reset the view and projection transforms. Now, since we want to control the automatic texture coordinate generation here, we will not use the DrawSubset method on our mesh. Instead, we will use the vertex buffer and index buffer directly, and call DrawIndexedPrimitives on our device instead. Once we've got these two buffers, we need to ensure that our device is ready to render the mesh.

First, we set the stream source to the vertex buffer from our mesh. We set the vertex format to the correct format based on our mesh as well, and set the index buffer to the indices property. Lastly, we set the cube texture into the first stage before we set up our remaining state and draw our primitives.

The really important items here are these lines:

```
device.TextureState[0].TextureCoordinateIndex =
    (int)TextureCoordinateIndex.CameraSpaceReflectionVector;

device.TextureState[0].TextureTransform = TextureTransform.Count3;
```

Since we don't have texture coordinates defined in our car mesh (and actually, even if we did), the first line says that rather than using any defined texture coordinates, instead use the reflection vector (transformed into camera space) as the texture coordinates. These are automatically generated in the fixed function pipeline based on the vertex position and normal, which is why we needed to ensure that our mesh had normals. Lastly, since we are using a 3D cube map, the texture transform tells the texture to expect 3D texture coordinates.

With the texture coordinates out of the way, we can then update our world transform (by just using a crazy rotation algorithm) and make our call to draw our primitives. Our application is almost ready for running, but first we need to add our rendering method:

```
protected override void OnPaint(System.Windows.Forms.PaintEventArgs e)
{
    RenderSceneIntoEnvMap();
    device.BeginScene();
```

```
RenderScene(ViewMatrix, Matrix.PerspectiveFovLH((float)Math.PI / 4,
        this.Width / this.Height, 1.0f, 10000.0f), true);
device.EndScene();
device.Present();
this.Invalidate();
}
```

For each render, first we render our environment map, and then we actually begin our "real" scene, and render it once more, this time including the car. With this, the application is ready for prime time.

After running the application, you should see a shiny reflective car spinning around the sky, much like in Figure 10.4.

**FIGURE 10.4**   A car with an environment map

# In Brief

- Drawing lines
- Drawing text
- Rendering to textures
- Rendering environment maps

In our next chapter, we will get into advanced graphics concepts and begin to talk about vertex and pixel shaders.

# PART III

# Advanced Graphics Concepts

# Introducing the Programmable Pipeline with the High Level Shader Language

Up to this point, you've been using the fixed-function pipeline to do all of your rendering. Back in the "old days" (before the release of DirectX 8.0) this was the only way to render anything. The fixed-function pipeline is essentially a set of rules and behaviors that govern how particular types of data will be rendered. While sufficient for many things, it lacks the control some developers need to fully take advantage of the features they plan on using. For example, all lighting in the fixed-function pipeline is done per vertex, rather than per pixel. With the rendering pipeline "fixed," there was no way to change the behavior of many rendering options, such as lights.

Enter DirectX 8.0 and the programmable pipeline. A revolutionary feature that first shipped with this release allowed the developers to control most every aspect of the pipeline. They could control the vertex processing with a new feature called "Vertex Shaders," and they could control the pixel processing with the aptly named "Pixel Shaders." These shader programs were quite powerful, but they were also not very easy to use. The syntax of the language resembled assembly, and it became apparent that something easier was needed.

In DirectX 9 the High Level Shader Language (HLSL) was released. HLSL was a simple C-like language that could be compiled into real shader code, but was much easier for the developers to read, maintain, and author. The full power of the programmable pipeline was still available in a much easier to use package. In this chapter the basic features of the High Level Shading Language will be covered, including

- Using the programmable pipeline.

- Transforming vertices.

- Using pixel shaders.

# Rendering a Single Triangle Without Using the Fixed-function Pipeline

What exactly is the "fixed-function pipeline" that has been mentioned several times so far in this chapter? The fixed-function pipeline controls exactly how vertices are rendered, how they are transformed, how they are lit, everything. When you set the vertex format property on the device, you are telling the device that you want to render these vertices in a certain way, based on what the vertex format is.

One of the major drawbacks of this design is that for every single feature that a graphics card needs to have exposed, a corresponding fixed-function API must be designed and implemented. With the power of graphics hardware increasing quite rapidly (quicker than CPU chips for example), the number of these APIs would quickly get out of hand. Even if it were ideal to have this large number of hard-to-understand APIs, there is still the underlying issue of the developer not really knowing what's going on under the covers. If there's one thing that most developers (particularly game developers) want, it's complete control.

One of the first applications this book discussed was a single triangle spinning around the screen. This was quite simple to do using the fixed-function pipeline, but now you will see what it would take to use the programmable pipeline instead. Go ahead and create a new windows form application and get it ready for this graphics program by declaring the device variable, as well as the window style. You will then need the following variables added:

```
private VertexBuffer vb = null;
private Effect effect = null;
private VertexDeclaration decl = null;

// Our matrices
private Matrix worldMatrix;
private Matrix viewMatrix;
private Matrix projMatrix;
private float angle = 0.0f;
```

Naturally, you will store the vertex data in the vertex buffer. Since you will not be using the transforms from the device, you will also need to store each of these transformation matrices to use in the programmable pipeline. The second and third variables here are completely new, though. The Effect object is the main object you will use when dealing with HLSL. The vertex declaration class is similar in use to the vertex format enumeration in the fixed-function pipeline. It informs the Direct3D runtime about the size and types of data it will be reading from the vertex buffer.

Since this application will be using a relatively new feature of graphics cards (namely the programmable pipeline), it's entirely possible that your graphics card will not support it. If that is the case, you will want to switch to the reference device that ships with the DirectX SDK. The reference device implements the entire API in software, albeit very slowly. You will need a more robust initialization routine for this, so use the one found in Listing 11.1.

**LISTING 11.1**    Initializing Graphics with a Fallback

```
public bool InitializeGraphics()
{
    // Set our presentation parameters
    PresentParameters presentParams = new PresentParameters();

    presentParams.Windowed = true;
    presentParams.SwapEffect = SwapEffect.Discard;
    presentParams.AutoDepthStencilFormat = DepthFormat.D16;
    presentParams.EnableAutoDepthStencil = true;

    bool canDoShaders = true;
    // Does a hardware device support shaders?
    Caps hardware = Manager.GetDeviceCaps(0, DeviceType.Hardware);
    if (hardware.VertexShaderVersion >= new Version(1, 1))
    {
        // Default to software processing
        CreateFlags flags = CreateFlags.SoftwareVertexProcessing;

        // Use hardware if it's available
        if (hardware.DeviceCaps.SupportsHardwareTransformAndLight)
            flags = CreateFlags.HardwareVertexProcessing;

        // Use pure if it's available
        if (hardware.DeviceCaps.SupportsPureDevice)
            flags |= CreateFlags.PureDevice;

        // Yes, Create our device
        device = new Device(0, DeviceType.Hardware, this, flags, presentParams);
```

**LISTING 11.1**    Continued

```
    }
    else
    {
        // No shader support
        canDoShaders = false;

        // Create a reference device
        device = new Device(0, DeviceType.Reference, this,
            CreateFlags.SoftwareVertexProcessing, presentParams);
    }

    // Create our vertex data
    vb = new VertexBuffer(typeof(CustomVertex.PositionOnly), 3, device,
        Usage.Dynamic ¦ Usage.WriteOnly, CustomVertex.PositionOnly.Format,
        Pool.Default);

    vb.Created += new EventHandler(this.OnVertexBufferCreate);
    OnVertexBufferCreate(vb, null);

    // Store our project and view matrices
    projMatrix = Matrix.PerspectiveFovLH((float)Math.PI / 4,
        this.Width / this.Height, 1.0f, 100.0f);

    viewMatrix = Matrix.LookAtLH(new Vector3(0,0, 5.0f), new Vector3(),
        new Vector3(0,1,0));

    // Create our vertex declaration
    VertexElement[] elements = new VertexElement[]
            {
                new VertexElement(0, 0, DeclarationType.Float3,
                DeclarationMethod.Default,
                DeclarationUsage.Position, 0),
                VertexElement.VertexDeclarationEnd
            };

    decl = new VertexDeclaration(device, elements);
    return canDoShaders;
}
```

The code here assumes the default adapter (ordinal zero) is the adapter you will be using to render the scene. If this isn't the case, feel free to modify this code to suit your graphics card.

For the sake of clarity, this code omitted a more robust enumeration routine and chose the default adapter. Before you can actually create the device, though, you will want to check the capabilities of the device that will be created, so you get the Caps structure.

In this application, you will only be using the programmable pipeline to render processed vertices, so you will need to ensure that the card can support at the very least the first generation vertex shaders. As new versions of the API are released, vertex and pixel shaders can have one or more generations added to them as a new "version" of the shader language. For example, the DirectX 9 release allows you to use vertex and pixel shaders up to version 3.0 (although currently there are no cards that support these versions). The first generation shader was naturally 1.0; however in DirectX 9, this version is obsolete, and has been replaced with version 1.1, which is what you can test against here.

Assuming the card does have this capability, you then want to create the "best" type of device possible. You default to software vertex processing, but if the device can support hardware processing and a pure device, you should use those instead. If the card does not have the capability to use shaders, you will instead use the reference device, which supports all features of the runtime, just very slowly.

Next you will need to create the vertex buffer, which should be quite familiar by now. You will want to render a single triangle, and you will only include the position of the vertices. The event handler method is as follows:

```
private void OnVertexBufferCreate(object sender, EventArgs e)
{
    VertexBuffer buffer = (VertexBuffer)sender;

    CustomVertex.PositionOnly[] verts = new CustomVertex.PositionOnly[3];
    verts[0].SetPosition(new Vector3(0.0f, 1.0f, 1.0f));
    verts[1].SetPosition(new Vector3(-1.0f, -1.0f, 1.0f));
    verts[2].SetPosition(new Vector3(1.0f, -1.0f, 1.0f));

    buffer.SetData(verts, 0, LockFlags.None);
}
```

Once the vertex buffer has been created, you will need to store the view and projection transformations for later use. You create these transformations in exactly the same way as you did before; the only difference is that now you won't be using the device's transform property to store this data.

Finally, you've come to the vertex declaration. The vertex declaration will tell Direct3D all of the information it needs to know about the vertices that will be passed on to the programmable pipeline. When creating the vertex declaration object, you pass in the device that will be used, as well as an array of vertex elements, each of which will describe one component of the vertex data. Take a look at the constructor for a vertex element:

```
public VertexElement ( System.Int16 stream , System.Int16 offset ,
    Microsoft.DirectX.Direct3D.DeclarationType declType ,
    Microsoft.DirectX.Direct3D.DeclarationMethod declMethod ,
    Microsoft.DirectX.Direct3D.DeclarationUsage declUsage ,
    System.Byte usageIndex )
```

The first parameter is the stream where the vertex data will be used. When calling SetStreamSource on the device, the first parameter is the stream that the vertex buffer passed in will be associated with. Thus far, you have stored all of the data in one vertex buffer on one stream; however, it is entirely possible to render a single object with data from multiple different vertex buffers assigned to different streams. Since you will only have one vertex buffer at stream zero, you will use that value for this parameter.

The second parameter is the offset into buffer where this data is stored. In this case, there is only one data type that the vertex buffer contains, so this will naturally be zero. However, if there were multiple components, each one would need to be offset accordingly. For example, if the first component was position (three float values), with the second component the normal (also three float values), the first component would have an offset of 0 (since it's the first component in the buffer), while the normal component would have an offset of 12 (four bytes for each of the three floats).

The third parameter is used to inform Direct3D of the type of data that will be used here. Since you are simply using the position, you can use the Float3 type here (this type will be discussed later in the chapter).

The fourth parameter describes the method in which this declaration will be used. In the majority of cases (unless you are using high order primitives), you will use Default as was done here.

The fifth parameter describes the usage of the component, such as position, normal, color, and so on. The three floats will be used to describe position. The final parameter modifies the usage data to allow you to specify multiple usage types. In most cases, you will use zero here as well.

It's important to note that your vertex element array *must* have VertexElement.VertexDeclarationEnd as its last member. So, for the simple vertex declaration, you will use stream number zero, having three floats, which represent the position of the vertices. With the vertex element array created, you can create the vertex declaration object. Finally, you will return a Boolean value; true if a hardware device that can use shaders, false if this is a reference device.

With the initialization method out of the way, you will need to call it and handle the return value. Update the main method as follows:

```
static void Main()
{
    using (Form1 frm = new Form1())
    {
        // Show our form and initialize our graphics engine
        frm.Show();
        if (!frm.InitializeGraphics())
        {
            MessageBox.Show("Your card does not support shaders.  " +
                "This application will run in ref mode instead.");
        }
        Application.Run(frm);
    }
}
```

So what's really left? Rendering the scene, and that's about it right? You will use the same rendering method used throughout the book, so override the OnPaint method as follows:

```
protected override void OnPaint(System.Windows.Forms.PaintEventArgs e)
{
    device.Clear(ClearFlags.Target | ClearFlags.ZBuffer, Color.CornflowerBlue, 1.0f, 0);

    UpdateWorld();
    device.BeginScene();

    device.SetStreamSource(0, vb, 0);
    device.VertexDeclaration = decl;
    device.DrawPrimitives(PrimitiveType.TriangleList, 0, 1);

    device.EndScene();

    device.Present();

    this.Invalidate();
}
```

After clearing the device, you will need to call the update world method, which does nothing more than increment the angle variable and modify the stored world matrix:

```
private void UpdateWorld()
{
    worldMatrix = Matrix.RotationAxis(new Vector3(angle / ((float)Math.PI * 2.0f),
```

```
            angle / ((float)Math.PI * 4.0f), angle / ((float)Math.PI * 6.0f)),
            angle / (float)Math.PI);

    angle += 0.1f;
}
```

With that done, the rest of the code looks familiar, with the exception being that you set the vertex declaration property rather than the vertex format property. Running this application as it is, though, will get you nothing more than a pretty cornflower blue screen. Why, you may ask? The Direct3D runtime simply has no idea what you want it to do. You need to actually write a "program" for the programmable pipeline.

Add a new blank text file to your project called simple.fx. You will use this file to store the HLSL program. Once this file has been created, add the following HLSL code to the file:

```
// Shader output, position and diffuse color
struct VS_OUTPUT
{
    float4 pos  : POSITION;
    float4 diff : COLOR0;
};

// The world view and projection matrices
float4x4 WorldViewProj : WORLDVIEWPROJECTION;
float Time = 1.0f;

// Transform our coordinates into world space
VS_OUTPUT Transform(
    float4 Pos  : POSITION)
{
    // Declare our return variable
    VS_OUTPUT Out = (VS_OUTPUT)0;

    // Transform our position
    Out.pos = mul(Pos, WorldViewProj);
    // Set our color
    Out.diff.r = 1 - Time;
    Out.diff.b = Time * WorldViewProj[2].yz;
    Out.diff.ga = Time * WorldViewProj[0].xy;

    // Return
    return Out;
}
```

As you can see, the HLSL code is remarkably similar to the C (and C#) language. First, examine what this small section of code is actually doing. First you declare a structure that will hold the output data of the vertex program. The declarations of the variables are slightly different than normal, however. A semantic has been added to each variable. Semantics are tags that will indicate the usage class of the variable: in this case, the position and first color.

You may wonder why both the position and color are in the output structure when the vertex buffer only contains position data. Since the output structure contains both position and color data (along with the corresponding semantics), Direct3D will know to render with the new data returned from the vertex program, instead of using the data stored in the vertex buffer.

Next you have the two "global" variables; the combination of the world, view, and projection matrices, along with a time variable to animate the color of the triangle. You will need to update each of these parameters every frame while the application is running.

Finally, you have the actual vertex program method. As you can see, it returns the structure you've already created and takes in as an argument the position of the vertices. This method will be run for every vertex in the vertex buffer (all three of them in this case). Notice that the input variable also has the semantic to let Direct3D know the type of data it's dealing with.

Once inside the method, the code is quite simple. You declare a variable that you will be returning: Out. You transform the position by multiplying the input position by the transformation matrix that is stored. You use the mul intrinsic function here because the matrix is a float4x4, while the position is a float4. Using the standard multiply operator will fail with a type mismatch.

After that, you use a simple formula to set each component of the color to a constantly changing value. Notice how you are setting different components of the color in each line, with the red being set first, then the blue, then the green and alpha. With the position and color values having been set, you can return the now filled structure.

## SHOP TALK

### DECLARING VARIABLES IN HLSL AND INTRINSIC TYPES

You will notice that you are using some intrinsic types that don't exist in the C or C# languages, namely float4 and float4x4. The scalar types that HLSL supports are

- bool—true or false
- int—A 32-bit signed integer
- half—A 16-bit floating point value
- float—A 32-bit floating point value
- double—A 64-bit floating point value

*SHOP TALK*

Variable declarations of these types will behave just as they would in the C# language: a single variable of that type. However, adding a single integer value to the end of one of these scalar types will declare a "vector" type. These vector types can be used like a vector, or like an array. For example, look at a declaration similar to one used in the code:

```
float4 pos;
```

This declares a Vector4 to hold a position. If you wanted a 2D vector instead, you could declare this as

```
float2 someVector;
```

You can access the members of this variable like an array, such as

```
pos[0] = 2.0f;
```

You can also access this type much like a vector in your C# code, such as

```
pos.x = 2.0f;
```

You can access one or more of the vector components in this way. This is called "swizzling." You may use the vector components of xyzw, as well as the color components of rgba; however, you may not mix and match these in the same swizzle. For example, these lines are valid (even if they don't do anything):

```
pos.xz = 0.0f;
pos.rg += pos.xz;
```

However, this line is not:

```
pos.xg = 0.0f;
```

The xg swizzle isn't valid since it's mixing both the vector and color components.

Variables can also have modifiers much like they do in C and C#. You can declare constants much like you would normally:

```
const float someConstant = 3.0f;
```

You can share variables among different programs:

```
shared float someVariable = 1.0f;
```

See the DirectX SDK documentation for more information on the HLSL if needed.

# Rendering Shader Programs with Techniques

Now that you have the vertex program written, how can you actually use it? There isn't an "entry point" into the vertex program, just a method somewhere. How do you get this method called, though? Quite simply, you can use something called a "technique." A technique consists of one to many passes, where each pass can set device state and set the vertex and pixel shaders to use your HLSL code. Look at the technique you can use for this application. Add this to your simple.fx file:

```
technique TransformDiffuse
{
    pass P0
    {
        CullMode = None;

        // shaders
        VertexShader = compile vs_1_1 Transform();
        PixelShader  = NULL;
    }
}
```

Here, you've declared a technique called TransformDiffuse, since this method will transform the vertices and add a diffuse color. This name is purely decorative and has no real purpose. In this technique, one pass has been defined. The cull mode is set to none, so you can see both the front and back of the single triangle. If you remember back to the original sample, you had to do this in the actual C# code. However, passes can be thought of as an excellent place to store (and update) device state, so it makes plenty of sense to add this here.

Next, you will want to use the vertex program for the vertices that will be rendered here, so the method is compiled using the vs_1_1 target. This target string should be used based on what you know your device supports. Since you already know your device supports at least vertex shader 1.1 (based on the capabilities check), you can use this target. If you were using vertex shader 2.0, the target would be vs_2_0. Pixel shader targets are defined such as ps_2_0.

Since there are no pixel programs, you can set the pixel shader member to null here, and that's the end of the pass. Nothing much going on, but now you will need to update the actual C# code to use this technique and pass.

First, you will use the Effect object that has been declared, since this is the main object used when dealing with your HLSL code. Add the following to the InitializeGraphics method (after device creation):

```
// Create our effect
effect = Effect.FromFile(device, @"..\..\simple.fx", null, ShaderFlags.None,
    null);
effect.Technique = "TransformDiffuse";
```

As you see, you are creating the effect object from a file (the one you've just created). You also set the technique here since only one technique will be used for the entire program. This effect object will be used for all of your dealings with the HLSL code you've written thus far. If you remember, you had two variables that needed to be updated each frame. Add the following code to the end of the UpdateWorld method:

```
Matrix worldViewProj = worldMatrix * viewMatrix * projMatrix;
effect.SetValue("Time", (float)Math.Sin(angle / 5.0f));
effect.SetValue("WorldViewProj", worldViewProj);
```

Here, you take the stored matrices and combine them, and update the variables in the HLSL code. This method is called every frame, so the variables will be updated this often as well. The only thing you have left to do is actually update the rendering to draw using the vertex program. Update your DrawPrimitives call as follows:

```
int numPasses = effect.Begin(0);
for (int i = 0; i < numPasses; i++)
{
    effect.Pass(i);
    device.DrawPrimitives(PrimitiveType.TriangleList, 0, 1);
}

effect.End();
```

Since the technique has already been selected for this effect, when it's time to render, you need to call the Begin method. The flags for this method allow you to choose to not save a particular state, but for this example aren't very important. The method will also return the number of passes in the current technique. Even though there is only one pass in the technique this example is using, it is a good idea to set up a loop similar to the one here to ensure that you render each technique as it was intended. Before you do any drawing, though, you need to call the Pass method on the effect object. The single parameter this takes is the pass index you will be rendering. This method gets the device ready to render the pass indicated, updates the device state, and sets the vertex and pixel shader methods. Finally, you simply draw the primitives just as you did before.

Once your rendering has been completed, you will need to call End on the effect, just like you called Begin earlier. This signals that (for now) you are done with this effect object. Running the application now should show you a rotating triangle that is consistently changing color. See Figure 11.1.

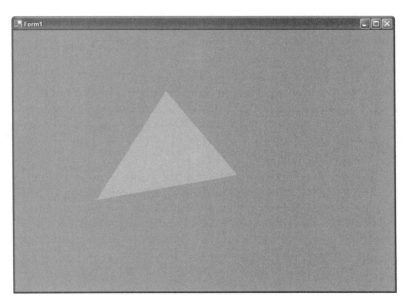

**FIGURE 11.1**    Rotating colorful triangle.

# Rendering Meshes Using the Programmable Pipeline

The simple triangle example is just that: simple. It's rare that you would use a vertex program on a single triangle in a real-world example, so instead of using this example, you should switch to rendering an entire mesh. Go ahead and replace the variables for the vertex declaration and the vertex buffer with this one for the mesh:

```
private Mesh mesh = null;
```

One nice thing about the mesh objects is that when they are rendered, they will automatically set the vertex declaration, so you don't need to worry about it. Naturally, you'll need to remove all instances in the code that dealt with either the vertex buffer or vertex declaration, as well. You will also need to update the initialize method to create the mesh. After the device and effect objects have been created, add the following code:

```
// Create our cylinder
mesh = Mesh.Cylinder(device, 1.5f, 1.5f, 1.5f, 36, 36);
```

Finally, you'll need to change the drawing method. Replace the DrawPrimitives call with the DrawSubset method on the mesh:

```
mesh.DrawSubset(0);
```

As you can see, there's nothing really special you need to do. Running this application now will cause a (very flat-looking) cylinder to be rendered with the same cycling colors our triangle had. The cylinder doesn't look much like a cylinder, though, since it's shaded with the same color everywhere. If you remember when this was discussed before, you simply added a directional light, and everything looked wonderful.

Using the lighting properties that you used before would defeat the purpose of this chapter, since those lights are implemented as part of the fixed-function pipeline. Since the goal is to show off the programmable pipeline, you can just update the HLSL code to render a single white directional light. First, you'll need a variable to describe the direction of the light. Add the following variable to your HLSL code:

```
// The direction of the light in world space
float3 LightDir = {0.0f, 0.0f, -1.0f};
```

Now you can simply replace the existing method with the following:

```
// Transform our coordinates into world space
VS_OUTPUT Transform(
    float4 Pos    : POSITION,
    float3 Normal : NORMAL )
{
    // Declare our return variable
    VS_OUTPUT Out = (VS_OUTPUT)0;

    // Transform the normal into the same coord system
    float4 transformedNormal = mul(Normal, WorldViewProj);

    // Set our color
    Out.diff.rgba = 1.0f;
    Out.diff *= dot(transformedNormal, LightDir);

    // Transform our position
    Out.pos = mul(Pos, WorldViewProj);

    // Return
    return Out;
}
```

You'll notice that another parameter has been included in the method, namely the normal data. You'll need to make sure that any vertices you run through this technique have normal data; otherwise, this will cause an error. The cylinder created by the Mesh class already contains this information, so you're fine here. Next, you will need to transform the normal data into the same coordinate system that the vertices will be in. You can't have lighting calculations for a certain set of vertices be performed on data in a different coordinate system; it just wouldn't make sense.

If you looked at any of the mathematics of lighting section in the DirectX SDK documentation, you'll know that a directional light is simply calculated by taking the dot product between the normal of the vertex and the direction of the light, and multiplying that by the color of the light. You can set your rgba swizzle to 1.0f, and do this calculation to get the final color of the cylinder.

The application should now render a white cylinder rotating around. The cylinder should look much more realistic and properly shaded now that you've added your own lighting calculations. It should appear similar to Figure 11.2.

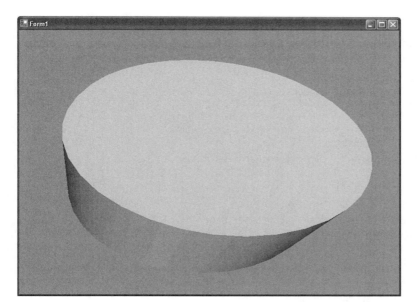

**FIGURE 11.2**   Shaded cylinder using the programmable pipeline.

Feel free to change the color of the light to see different effects. What if you changed it from a white light to a purple light?

# Using HLSL to Write a Pixel Shader

So far you've manipulated the vertices and written vertex programs, but that's only half the fun when dealing with the programmable pipeline. What about the color of each individual pixel? For this example, we will take the MeshFile example you wrote back in Chapter 5, "Rendering with Meshes," and update it to use the programmable pipeline instead. This one is being used because not only does it render vertices, but they are colored from a texture where a pixel shader could be used.

After loading this project, you will need to make a few changes to the source to begin using the programmable pipeline. First, you will need the variables to store the transformations and effect object, so add those:

```
private Effect effect = null;
// Matrices
private Matrix worldMatrix;
private Matrix viewMatrix;
private Matrix projMatrix;
```

You will also need to update the initialization method to handle picking the reference device if shader support isn't available. Replace the method with the method found in Listing 11.2.

**LISTING 11.2**   Initializing Graphics with Fallback

```
public bool InitializeGraphics()
{
    // Set our presentation parameters
    PresentParameters presentParams = new PresentParameters();

    presentParams.Windowed = true;
    presentParams.SwapEffect = SwapEffect.Discard;
    presentParams.AutoDepthStencilFormat = DepthFormat.D16;
    presentParams.EnableAutoDepthStencil = true;


    bool canDoShaders = true;
    // Does a hardware device support shaders?
    Caps hardware = Manager.GetDeviceCaps(0, DeviceType.Hardware);
    if ((hardware.VertexShaderVersion >= new Version(1, 1)) &&
        (hardware.PixelShaderVersion >= new Version(1, 1)))
    {
        // Default to software processing
        CreateFlags flags = CreateFlags.SoftwareVertexProcessing;
```

**LISTING 11.2**    Continued

```
        // Use hardware if it's available
        if (hardware.DeviceCaps.SupportsHardwareTransformAndLight)
            flags = CreateFlags.HardwareVertexProcessing;

        // Use pure if it's available
        if (hardware.DeviceCaps.SupportsPureDevice)
            flags |= CreateFlags.PureDevice;

        // Yes, Create our device
        device = new Device(0, DeviceType.Hardware, this, flags, presentParams);
    }
    else
    {
        // No shader support
        canDoShaders = false;

        // Create a reference device
        device = new Device(0, DeviceType.Reference, this,
            CreateFlags.SoftwareVertexProcessing, presentParams);
    }

    // Create our effect
    effect = Effect.FromFile(device, @"..\..\simple.fx", null, ShaderFlags.None, null);
    effect.Technique = "TransformTexture";

    // Store our project and view matrices
    projMatrix = Matrix.PerspectiveFovLH((float)Math.PI / 4,
        this.Width / this.Height, 1.0f, 10000.0f);

    viewMatrix = Matrix.LookAtLH(new Vector3(0,0, 580.0f), new Vector3(),
        new Vector3(0,1,0));

    // Load our mesh
    LoadMesh(@"..\..\tiny.x");

    return canDoShaders;
}
```

This is similar to the initialization method that was used earlier in this chapter, although this checks not only for vertex shader support, but also pixel shader support. Don't try to run this example yet, since you haven't created the HLSL file yet. Since the initialization now returns a Boolean, the main method will need updating as well. Simply use the same method you used earlier in this chapter for this one.

Since the SetupCamera method is using nothing but the fixed-function pipeline for transformations and lighting, you can eliminate that method completely from this source. Naturally, you'll also need to remove the call in your OnPaint override as well. The last code change you will need to make is to replace the DrawMesh method with one that will use HLSL to render. Replace the method with the one found in Listing 11.3.

**LISTING 11.3**    Drawing a Mesh with the HLSL

```
private void DrawMesh(float yaw, float pitch, float roll, float x, float y, float z)
{
    angle += 0.01f;

    worldMatrix = Matrix.RotationYawPitchRoll(yaw, pitch, roll)
        * Matrix.Translation(x, y, z);

    Matrix worldViewProj = worldMatrix * viewMatrix * projMatrix;
    effect.SetValue("WorldViewProj", worldViewProj);

    int numPasses = effect.Begin(0);
    for (int iPass = 0; iPass < numPasses; iPass++)
    {
        effect.Pass(iPass);
        for (int i = 0; i < meshMaterials.Length; i++)
        {
            device.SetTexture(0, meshTextures[i]);
            mesh.DrawSubset(i);
        }
    }
    effect.End();
}
```

Since this method is called every frame, this is where you will combine the transformation matrices and update the HLSL code with this variable. You then render each subset of the mesh for every pass in the technique. However, you currently haven't declared your HLSL for this application yet, so go ahead and add a new blank file called "simple.fx" to hold the HLSL and add the code found in Listing 11.4.

**LISTING 11.4**    HLSL Code for Rendering a Textured Mesh

```
// The world view and projection matrices
float4x4 WorldViewProj : WORLDVIEWPROJECTION;
sampler TextureSampler;

// Transform our coordinates into world space
void Transform(
    in float4 inputPosition : POSITION,
    in float2 inputTexCoord : TEXCOORD0,
    out float4 outputPosition : POSITION,
    out float2 outputTexCoord : TEXCOORD0
    )
{
    // Transform our position
    outputPosition = mul(inputPosition, WorldViewProj);
    // Set our texture coordinates
    outputTexCoord = inputTexCoord;
}

void TextureColor(
 in float2 textureCoords : TEXCOORD0,
 out float4 diffuseColor : COLOR0)
{
    // Get the texture color
    diffuseColor = tex2D(TextureSampler, textureCoords);
};

technique TransformTexture
{
    pass P0
    {
        // shaders
        VertexShader = compile vs_1_1 Transform();
        PixelShader  = compile ps_1_1 TextureColor();
    }
}
```

You'll notice pretty quickly that things were done differently for these shader programs. Rather than store the return values in a structure, you've simply added out parameters to the method declaration itself. For the vertex program, you only really care about the position (which is transformed) and the texture coordinates (which will simply be passed on).

The second method is the pixel shader. It accepts the texture coordinates for this pixel and returns the color this pixel should be rendered. For this case, you simply want to use the default color of the texture at this coordinate, so use the tex2D intrinsic method. This samples the texture at a given set of coordinates and returns the color at that point. For this example case, you can simply pass this on. This is about as simple as you can get for a pixel shader, and will render the mesh color just as the textures say, much like you see in Figure 11.3.

**FIGURE 11.3**    Mesh rendered using HLSL.

This pixel shader doesn't really do anything you haven't seen with the fixed-function pipeline, though. You should do something else that may make it a little more exciting. While you're at it, you should make more than one technique for this HLSL program. Add the following to your HLSL code:

```
void InverseTextureColor(
 in float2 textureCoords : TEXCOORD0,
 out float4 diffuseColor : COLOR0)
{
    // Get the inverse texture color
    diffuseColor = 1.0f - tex2D(TextureSampler, textureCoords);
};

technique TransformInverseTexture
```

```
{
    pass P0
    {
        // shaders
        VertexShader = compile vs_1_1 Transform();
        PixelShader  = compile ps_1_1 InverseTextureColor();
    }
}
```

This code here is similar to the first pixel shader, with the only difference being that you are subtracting the sampled color from 1.0f. Since 1.0f is considered "fully on" for a color, subtracting from this number will produce the inverse color for this pixel. You have also created a new technique whose only difference is the pixel shader method you call. Now, you should update the main C# code to allow switching between these two techniques. You should override the key press event and use the number keys to switch between them:

```
protected override void OnKeyPress(KeyPressEventArgs e)
{
    switch (e.KeyChar)
    {
        case '1':
            effect.Technique = "TransformTexture";
            break;
        case '2':
            effect.Technique = "TransformInverseTexture";
            break;
    }
    base.OnKeyPress (e);
}
```

Run the application now and press the 2 key. Notice how the mesh is now rendered so that it looks like a negative? See Figure 11.4.

How do you think you could add new techniques to mask out the blue color from the rendered mesh? What about only rendering the blue color of the mesh? See the code on the included CD for examples of how to accomplish these tasks.

**FIGURE 11.4** Mesh rendered with inverse colors using HLSL.

# In Brief

- Using the programmable pipeline.
- Transforming vertices.
- Using pixel shaders.

In our next chapter, we will get into more advanced HLSL concepts.

# Using the High Level Shader Language

In dealing with the programmable pipeline and the High Level Shader Language thus far, the possibilities of what can be accomplished have barely been touched. The items completed up to this point include basic functionality that exists in the fixed-function pipeline, but nothing more advanced. With the open-ended nature of the programmable pipeline, these advanced features that don't exist in the fixed-function pipeline should be the tasks you try to accomplish.

During this chapter you will look a little more deeply into HLSL, and how you can use this technology to implement features that are impossible (or difficult) in the fixed-function pipeline. Advanced features that will be discussed in this chapter include

- Simple vertex animation

- Simple color animation

- Texture blending

- Lighting models with textures

- The difference between per-vertex lighting and per-pixel lighting

# Using Simple Formulas to Simulate Animation

Rather than wasting space here duplicating the same code that has already been covered, you should copy the code that was used to render the cylinder in the previous chapter. This code will be modified slightly to show how easily simple animation can be added once you've begun using the programmable pipeline. This example will be modified to allow the mesh to "wobble" as it's being rendered.

Once the code has been loaded from the previous example, the first thing you'll want to do is to switch to using a sphere rather than the cylinder. It's not that this update wouldn't work with the cylinder; it would. However, the sphere happens to just look better. Replace the cylinder creation code with this:

```
// Create our sphere
mesh = Mesh.Sphere(device, 3.0f, 36, 36);
```

Since the sphere's size is larger than the cylinder that was being rendered before, you will also need to update the view matrix. You'll need to move the camera position back some, as in the following:

```
viewMatrix = Matrix.LookAtLH(new Vector3(0,0, 9.0f), new Vector3(),
    new Vector3(0,1,0));
```

With that, you should be able to run the application and see a (quite boring) spinning sphere being lit by a single directional light. What do you think could be done to make the sphere perform some simple animation? In your shader code, replace the single line that does transformation with the following code:

```
// Store our local position
float4 tempPos = Pos;
// Make the sphere 'wobble' some
tempPos.y += cos(Pos + (Time * 2.0f));
// Transform our position
Out.pos = mul(tempPos, WorldViewProj);
```

You'll notice that the Time variable is used in this example once more. Since that variable wasn't used in the example this was based on, you will need to add it to your shader code:

```
float Time = 0.0f;
```

In addition, you will need to update the variable every frame, so in your main code at the end of the UpdateWorld method, add the following code to update this variables value:

```
effect.SetValue("Time", angle);
```

So what exactly does the shader code accomplish? First, the input position of the vertex is stored in a temporary variable. Then the y component of this variable is modulated by adding the cosine of the current position of the vertex added with the constantly updating Time variable. Since the cosine method will always be within the range of -1 to 1, the effect will repeat indefinitely. With the vertex now being updated to simulate our animation, the temporary variable is used to perform the transformation rather than the original input position.

While this updated code does look a lot nicer than the boring old sphere, there's yet another easy thing you can do to make it look even better. Why not add some "animating" color as well? Replace the Out.diff initialization code with the following:

```
// Set our color
Out.diff = sin(Pos + Time);
```

Obviously, this code is based directly on the vertex animation code that was just done. The only major difference is the use of the sine method rather than cosine. You can see a major difference in the quality of the rendered scene while the application is running, though. This just goes to show you how you can quickly turn a "boring" sphere into something exciting. HLSL allows you to quickly change the way your scene is rendered with little to no changes to your main code.

# Determining Color by Blending Textures

In the real world, not very many applications will use simple pseudo-randomly generated colors when rendering models. Models are normally generated with highly detailed textures, and occasionally quite a few of them. What if there were a scenario where you needed to blend two or more textures for your model? Sure, you could do that with the fixed-function pipeline, but what if the model was something like "tiny.x", which most of the code in this book uses? This model only uses a single texture, so how will you use two textures blended together?

Once again, for brevity, you should use the code example written in the previos chapter that rendered the textured mesh. This will focus on adding a second texture and writing the code to blend between the two textures to calculate a final color.

## UNDERSTANDING THE PIXEL SHADER INSTRUCTION SET LIMIT

Since you will be manipulating a pixel shader in this code, one thing you may notice is that the amount of available "instructions" you can use in a 1.1 pixel shader code segment is extremely limited. For pixel shaders before version 1.4, you are limited to 12 instructions for the entire shader program, which obviously isn't very much. For version 1.4, the limit is raised to 28 (in two phases) but that's still not much. You are also limited to 8 constants in these shader programs. Pixel shader version 2.0 and higher has the capability to perform much more complex operations and have much higher instruction and constant counts. You can check the capabilities for your card to find out how many of each are supported.

Knowing this limitation, the code for the texture blending here will be shown in two sepa-rate ways: one with an extremely simple pixel shader that can be used on cards that support versions 1.1, and another more complex version that can be used on cards that support version 2.0 and above. You will need a relatively new graphics card in order to support this feature set.

Naturally, you should start with the 1.1 version since it's obviously simpler. Before you get to the actual shader code, though, you will need to make a few updates to the actual code. For one thing, you need a second texture to do the blending. Add the following texture variable for your second texture into your class:

```
private Texture skyTexture;
```

Also, since you know that the model you will be loading only has one material and one texture, you may want to remove the need for using arrays of materials and textures. The code included on the CD has done this, and the remaining code for this example will assume it has been completed.

You will now need to create a second texture that will be used to blend into your model. This example will assume that you've copied the skybox_top.JPG texture that ships with the DirectX SDK into your application folder. Feel free to use a different texture that suits your mood if you want. Once you have decided on the second texture, you will need to create it. The perfect place would be where the original texture is created in the LoadMesh method. Replace the single texture creation line with this:

```
// We have a texture, try to load it
meshTexture = TextureLoader.FromFile(device, @"..\..\" +
    mtrl[i].TextureFilename);
skyTexture = TextureLoader.FromFile(device, @"..\..\skybox_top.JPG");
```

If you've chosen a different texture file, you will want to use that filename instead. With the second texture created, the code to do the blending between the two can now be written. Add the following variables to your shader code:

```
float Time;

Texture meshTexture;
Texture skyTexture;

sampler TextureSampler = sampler_state { texture = <meshTexture>;
    mipfilter = LINEAR; };
sampler SkyTextureSampler = sampler_state { texture = <skyTexture>;
    mipfilter = LINEAR; };
```

The Time variable has been used often enough that it doesn't need explaining. The two texture variables are new, though. Rather than calling SetTexture on the device to assign these textures to a stage, the shader code will maintain the textures and sample them appropriately. Feel free to remove your SetTexture calls from your application, since they will be redundant anyway.

The two sampler variables are used internally in the shader to determine how a texture is sampled. In this case, each texture is sampled based on the actual texture and uses a linear mipmap filter. You could also include items such as minify and magnify filters, along with various clamping types in these sampler states. For this case, the mipmap filter is enough.

Before you can use the two texture variables, you'll need to actually set them to something. In your main code's initialization routine, add the following after your mesh has been loaded:

```
effect.SetValue("meshTexture", meshTexture);
effect.SetValue("skyTexture", skyTexture);
```

Your textures should have been created when your mesh was loaded, so they should be valid at this point. However, even though the model has been loaded and there are now two sets of textures that have been created, it doesn't eliminate a basic problem. The model itself only has a single set of texture coordinates. Use the following vertex shader program in place of the one already in use:

```
// Transform our coordinates into world space
void TransformV1_1(
    in float4 inputPosition : POSITION,
    in float2 inputTexCoord : TEXCOORD0,
    out float4 outputPosition : POSITION,
    out float2 outputTexCoord : TEXCOORD0,
    out float2 outputSecondTexCoord : TEXCOORD1
    )
{
    // Transform our position
    outputPosition = mul(inputPosition, WorldViewProj);
    // Set our texture coordinates
    outputTexCoord = inputTexCoord;
    outputSecondTexCoord = inputTexCoord;
}
```

As you see here, the shader code accepts as inputs a position and a single set of texture coordinates. However, as outputs, it not only returns the transformed position, it also passes on the input texture coordinate to both sets of output texture coordinates. Essentially, the code has duplicated the texture coordinates for each vertex. Now you can replace the pixel shader program with the following:

```
void TextureColorV1_1(
 in float4 P : POSITION,
 in float2 textureCoords : TEXCOORD0,
 in float2 textureCoords2 : TEXCOORD1,
 out float4 diffuseColor : COLOR0)
{
    // Get the texture color
    float4 diffuseColor1 = tex2D(TextureSampler, textureCoords);
    float4 diffuseColor2 = tex2D(SkyTextureSampler, textureCoords2);
    diffuseColor = lerp(diffuseColor1, diffuseColor2, Time);
};
```

Here the shader takes as inputs the position and both sets of texture coordinates that were returned from the vertex shader, and outputs the color that should be rendered for this pixel. In this case, you sample each of the two loaded textures (with identical texture coordinates), and then perform a linear interpolation on them (the lerp intrinsic function). The value of the Time variable will determine how much of each texture is actually visible at a time. You've never actually set the Time variable anywhere in your application, though. In your mesh drawing method, you can do that like this:

```
effect.SetValue("Time", (float)Math.Abs(Math.Sin(angle)));
```

You may be wondering something like "Why do the math here; wouldn't the shader be a better place to do this math?" You certainly want more of your math to be performed by the graphics card than by the CPU, since the graphics card will be *much* better at it. However, in this case the pixel shader instruction count has limited what you can do. Allowing the shader code to do the math for you here will not allow the shader to run on cards that only support pixel shader 1.1.

Before testing our texture blending, one more thing needs to be done. The function names for the vertex and pixel programs have been changed, so the technique is no longer valid. Replace with the following:

```
technique TransformTexture
{
    pass P0
    {
        // shaders
        VertexShader = compile vs_1_1 TransformV1_1();
        PixelShader  = compile ps_1_1 TextureColorV1_1();
    }
}
```

The technique name itself didn't change, so you should be able to run the application now. You should notice that the model is textured normally at startup, but quickly blends into a sky texture (assuming you used the texture this example has), and then blends back to the model texture. It repeats this until the application is closed.

What if your card supported pixel shader 2.0, though? The code here should be updated to support both the "older" pixel shader 1.1 hardware, as well as the new and improved pixel shader 2.0 hardware. First, add a variable to your main code so that you'll know if your card supports pixel shader 2.0:

```
private bool canDo2_0Shaders = false;
```

The example code will assume that the card does not support pixel shader 2.0 initially. After your device has been created in your initialization method, you should check to see if pixel shader 2.0 can be used. Make sure you do this before you've created your Effect object:

```
canDo2_0Shaders = device.DeviceCaps.PixelShaderVersion >= new Version(2, 0);
```

Since you'll be adding a second technique to handle the second set of shaders, you will need to determine which technique you will use based on the highest shader model you can support. Update this line with the following:

```
effect.Technique = canDo2_0Shaders ? "TransformTexture2_0" : "TransformTexture";
```

In this case, if 2.0 shader models are supported, the application will use that technique; otherwise, it will use the technique you've already written. Before you actually write this new technique, though, there is one more update you should make. Replace the line that sets the Time variable with the following:

```
if (canDo2_0Shaders)
{
    effect.SetValue("Time", angle);
}
else
{
    effect.SetValue("Time", (float)Math.Abs(Math.Sin(angle)));
}
```

Notice that with the more advanced shader program, the math will be moved to the graphics card? Since the instruction count is higher and can support the operations needed, this makes perfect sense. Now you'll need to add the actual new shader code, so add the code found in Listing 12.1 to your HLSL code.

LISTING 12.1   Shader Model 2.0 Texture Blend

```
// Transform our coordinates into world space
void TransformV2_0(
    in float4 inputPosition : POSITION,
    in float2 inputTexCoord : TEXCOORD0,
    out float4 outputPosition : POSITION,
    out float2 outputTexCoord : TEXCOORD0
    )
{
    // Transform our position
    outputPosition = mul(inputPosition, WorldViewProj);
    // Set our texture coordinates
    outputTexCoord = inputTexCoord;
}

void TextureColorV2_0(
 in float4 P : POSITION,
 in float2 textureCoords : TEXCOORD0,
 out float4 diffuseColor : COLOR0)
{
    // Get the texture color
    float4 diffuseColor1 = tex2D(TextureSampler, textureCoords);
    float4 diffuseColor2 = tex2D(SkyTextureSampler, textureCoords);
    diffuseColor = lerp(diffuseColor1, diffuseColor2, abs(sin(Time)));
};

technique TransformTexture2_0
{
    pass P0
    {
        // shaders
        VertexShader = compile vs_1_1 TransformV2_0();
        PixelShader  = compile ps_2_0 TextureColorV2_0();
    }
}
```

The first thing you should notice is that the vertex shader has gotten much simpler. Instead of duplicating the texture coordinates, the code simply transforms the position and passes on the original set of coordinates. There is absolutely nothing fancy about the vertex program.

The pixel shader looks much simpler as well. It no longer expects two sets of texture coordinates, instead choosing to use the same set of texture coordinates to sample the two different textures. In older pixel shader models (anything before 2.0), the shader was only allowed to "read" the texture coordinates one time. Sampling two textures with the same set of coordinates would cause two reads and naturally not be allowed, so this type of operation wasn't possible with the previous shader. You should also notice that the same formula is used to determine the interpolation level regardless of how the math is done in the shader code. The only differences in the technique are the function names (obviously) and the fact that the pixel shader is compiled with the target of ps_2_0.

You shouldn't be able to tell the difference in the application regardless of which shader is actually running. Many applications today need to support the latest and greatest features of the graphics card to look visually stunning. However, until the minimum requirements rise quite a bit, there will need to be these fallback cases that approximate the visually stunning high-end machines the best they can.

# Lighting Textures

In the previous chapter, simple directional lighting was discussed for a cylinder. The cylinder that was used for that example wasn't textured, and so far the lighting calculations have only been performed in the vertex programs. You can just as easily perform these lighting operations in your pixel shader code as well.

Like the previous example, we will use the simple mesh rendering example from the previous chapter as our starting point. In this section you will take that existing sample and add a colored light to the scene in our pixel shader.

The first step to making this update will be to add the following declarations to your shader code:

```
float4x4 WorldMatrix : WORLD;
float4 DiffuseDirection;

Texture meshTexture;
sampler TextureSampler = sampler_state { texture = <meshTexture>; mipfilter = LINEAR; };

struct VS_OUTPUT
{
    float4 Pos : POSITION;
    float2 TexCoord : TEXCOORD0;
    float3 Light : TEXCOORD1;
    float3 Normal : TEXCOORD2;
};
```

You'll notice that not only are you storing the combined world, view, and projection matrices, but there is another variable to store the world matrix itself. You'll understand why this is necessary when the shader code itself is discussed. There is also a variable to hold the direction of the light. Much like the previous example, there is a texture and a sampler state stored for reading the texture.

The output structure is quite different than anything seen yet. Not only are the position and texture coordinates passed on, but there are two new texture coordinate members that will be passed on as well. In reality, these members will not really be texture coordinates at all; they are just what will be used to transfer the necessary data from the vertex shader to the pixel shader.

You'll also need to actually update the values of these members. In your mesh drawing routing, you are already setting the WorldViewProj variable, so that is the perfect place for the following:

```
effect.SetValue("WorldMatrix", worldMatrix);
effect.SetValue("DiffuseDirection", new Vector4(0, 0, 1, 1));
```

The texture variable will also need to be set. In your initialization routine after your mesh (and texture) has been loaded, add the following:

```
effect.SetValue("meshTexture", meshTexture);
```

With those simple items out of the way, you're ready to update the shader code to perform the lighting. You should pick a color other than white for this light so that it's obvious the work is being done. Before looking at the pixel shader code, you should examine the vertex shader:

```
// Transform our coordinates into world space
VS_OUTPUT Transform(
    float4 inputPosition : POSITION,
    float3 inputNormal : NORMAL,
    float2 inputTexCoord : TEXCOORD0
    )
{
    //Declare our output structure
    VS_OUTPUT Out = (VS_OUTPUT)0;
    // Transform our position
    Out.Pos = mul(inputPosition, WorldViewProj);
    // Store our texture coordinates
    Out.TexCoord = inputTexCoord;
    // Store our light direction
    Out.Light = DiffuseDirection;
    // Transform the normals into the world matrix and normalize them
```

```
    Out.Normal = normalize(mul(inputNormal, WorldMatrix));

    return Out;
}
```

At first, this shader begins much like ones that have been used previously, albeit with more inputs. First, the position is transformed and the input texture coordinates stored. Next, however, the light direction is placed into the second texture coordinate set. You may notice that the light direction is a float4, while the texture coordinate is a float3. This implicitly implies the xyz swizzle on the larger component. Given that the diffuse direction is essentially a 3D vector and the w component is ignored anyway, this is perfect.

The normals will also need to be stored in the third set of texture coordinates. Before this can be done, though, the normals themselves must be transformed into the correct coordinate system, in this case the world's system. Without this step, the lighting calculations would be way off. You cannot perform math operations on objects in different coordinate systems. The newly transformed normals are normalized and stored in the third texture coordinate set.

With all the data needed to correctly light the model and its textures, you can add the following pixel shader code:

```
float4 TextureColor(
 float2 textureCoords : TEXCOORD0,
 float3 lightDirection : TEXCOORD1,
 float3 normal : TEXCOORD2) : COLOR0
{
    // Get the texture color
    float4 textureColor = tex2D(TextureSampler, textureCoords);
    // Make our diffuse color purple for now
    float4 diffuseColor = {1.0f, 0.0f, 1.0f, 1.0f};

    // Return the combined color after calculating the effect of
    // the diffuse directional light
    return textureColor * (diffuseColor * saturate(dot(lightDirection, normal)));
};
```

As you see, the pixel shader takes as inputs all of the sets of texture coordinates returned from the vertex shader and will return the color for this pixel. The first step is to naturally sample the current texture. Next, a light color is set (in this case a purple color). To calculate the intensity of this light at the pixel, you take the dot product of the light's direction with the normal, much like what was done in the vertex shader case earlier. The saturate intrinsic method clamps the return value to the range of zero to one, so there won't be any overly bright or overly dark colors. Finally, the final color is calculated by multiplying the current texture color by the diffuse lighting component.

While an extremely simple example, this is a much more common occurrence. Running the application, you should see the normal model rendered with a purple tint to it.

# Adding Specular Highlights

Another type of lighting that hasn't been discussed yet is specular highlighting. Specular highlighting makes an object appear "shiny" and much more realistic when being rendered. It's possible to use the lighting objects in the fixed-function pipeline to enable specular highlights; however, these highlights will be calculated per-vertex. This example will show how to accomplish this with the programmable pipeline instead.

Like the other examples in this chapter, this one will be based on an earlier section of code; in this case, the lit cylinder example you wrote in the previous chapter. This code already handles the diffuse lighting case, which should stay in this updated example to show the differences between the two lighting models.

While the cylinder object will show off the features that this example is trying to, a better object to use is the teapot. Change your main code from loading a cylinder to loading a teapot:

```
// Load our mesh
mesh = Mesh.Teapot(device);
```

Since this example will also be showing multiple different effects and allowing you to switch between them, you will want to have something to notify the user of the current state. You should declare a font variable to allow the user to be notified during the rendered scene:

```
// Out font
private Direct3D.Font font = null;
```

You may as well initialize the font variable directly after your teapot has been created as well:

```
//Create our font
font = new Direct3D.Font(device, new System.Drawing.Font("Arial", 12.0f));
```

With these things out of the way, you should now add the constants and variables you will need into your shader code:

```
float4x4 WorldViewProj : WORLDVIEWPROJECTION;
float4x4 WorldMatrix : WORLD;
float4 DiffuseDirection;
float4 EyeLocation;

// Color constants
```

```
const float4 MetallicColor = { 0.8f, 0.8f, 0.8f, 1.0f };
const float4 AmbientColor = { 0.05f, 0.05f, 0.05f, 1.0f };
```

The combined world, view, and projection matrix variable has been used in each example for transforming the vertices. The single world matrix will once again be used to transform the normals of each vertex. The diffuse direction member will allow the application to define the direction of the light, rather than having it hard coded in the shader like before. The last variable is the location of the eye. Specular highlights are calculated by determining a reflection between the normal and the eye.

You'll also notice there are two constants declared. Since metal is normally shiny, the example will use a color that resembles a metallic material for our diffuse light. An ambient color is also declared, although for this example it is essentially a non-factor. It's only been included for completeness of the lighting mathematic formulas.

For this example, the per-vertex lighting output structure only needs to be concerned with the position and color of each vertex, so declare the structure as follows:

```
struct VS_OUTPUT_PER_VERTEX
{
    float4 Position : POSITION;
    float4 Color : COLOR0;
};
```

Before the shader code for the specular highlighting, you need to update our diffuse lighting shader. There will be a separate shader for each lighting model. Replace your diffuse lighting shader with the following:

```
VS_OUTPUT_PER_VERTEX TransformDiffuse(
    float4 inputPosition : POSITION,
    float3 inputNormal : NORMAL,
    uniform bool metallic
    )
{
    //Declare our output structure
    VS_OUTPUT_PER_VERTEX Out = (VS_OUTPUT_PER_VERTEX)0;

    // Transform our position
    Out.Position = mul(inputPosition, WorldViewProj);

    // Transform the normals into the world matrix and normalize them
    float3 Normal = normalize(mul(inputNormal, WorldMatrix));

    // Make our diffuse color metallic for now
```

```
float4 diffuseColor = MetallicColor;

if(!metallic)
    diffuseColor.rgb = sin(Normal + inputPosition);

// Store our diffuse component
float4 diffuse = saturate(dot(DiffuseDirection, Normal));

// Return the combined color
Out.Color = AmbientColor + diffuseColor * diffuse;

return Out;
}
```

You'll notice there's a new input in this shader, a Boolean value declared with the "uniform" attribute. The uniform modifier is used to tell Direct3D that this variable can be treated as a constant, and cannot be changed during a draw call.

Once the shader actually starts, things appear pretty similar. First, the position is transformed, and then the normal is transformed. The diffuse color is then set to the constant metallic color that was declared earlier.

The next statement is something that hasn't been discussed before: namely, flow control. HLSL supports numerous flow control mechanisms in your shader code, including if statements like above, as well as loops such as the do loop, the while loop, and the for loop. Each of the flow control mechanisms has syntax similar to the equivalent statements in C#.

## SHOP TALK

### UNDERSTANDING FLOW CONTROL ON OLDER SHADER MODELS

Older shader models do not natively support flow control, or branching. In order to facilitate this, when generating the actual shader code, the HLSL compiler may actually unwind a loop, or execute all branches of if statements. This is something you need to be aware of, particularly if you are already writing a complex shader that is stretching the limits of the instruction count. Take a simple loop such as

```
for(int i = 0; i<10; i++)
{
    pos.y += (float)i;
}
```

Even though there is only a single statement in the line, this shader code once unwound would take up a whopping 20 instructions (at least). When your instruction count limit is 12 (like for pixel shader 1.1), this simple loop wouldn't be able to be compiled.

If the metallic variable is true, then the metallic color is kept for the light. However, if it is false, the color is switched to an "animating" color much like the first example in this chapter. Finally, the color returned is based on the directional light formula that's been used numerous times.

With the two different color types that can be used in this shader, you will need to add two techniques:

```
technique TransformSpecularPerVertexMetallic
{
    pass P0
    {
        // shaders
        VertexShader = compile vs_1_1 TransformSpecular(true);
        PixelShader  = NULL;
    }
}
technique TransformSpecularPerVertexColorful
{
    pass P0
    {
        // shaders
        VertexShader = compile vs_1_1 TransformSpecular(false);
        PixelShader  = NULL;
    }
}
```

You should notice that the only difference between these two techniques (other than the name) is the value that is passed into the shader. Since the technique names have changed, you'll need to update your main code to handle the new technique:

```
effect.Technique = "TransformDiffusePerVertexMetallic";
```

With the diffuse lighting with branching statements out of the way, you should now add a new shader to deal with specular highlights. Add the method found in Listing 12.2 to your HLSL code.

### LISTING 12.2   Transform and Use Specular Highlighting

```
VS_OUTPUT_PER_VERTEX TransformSpecular(
    float4 inputPosition : POSITION,
    float3 inputNormal : NORMAL,
    uniform bool metallic
    )
```

**LISTING 12.2**   Continued

```
{
    //Declare our output structure
    VS_OUTPUT_PER_VERTEX Out = (VS_OUTPUT_PER_VERTEX)0;
    // Transform our position
    Out.Position = mul(inputPosition, WorldViewProj);

    // Transform the normals into the world matrix and normalize them
    float3 Normal = normalize(mul(inputNormal, WorldMatrix));

    // Make our diffuse color metallic for now
    float4 diffuseColor = MetallicColor;

    // Normalize the world position of the vertex
    float3 worldPosition = normalize(mul(inputPosition, WorldMatrix));

    // Store the eye vector
    float3 eye = EyeLocation - worldPosition;

    // Normalize our vectors
    float3 normal = normalize(Normal);
    float3 light = normalize(DiffuseDirection);
    float3 eyeDirection = normalize(eye);

    if(!metallic)
        diffuseColor.rgb = cos(normal + eye);

    // Store our diffuse component
    float4 diffuse = saturate(dot(light, normal));

    // Calculate specular component
    float3 reflection = normalize(2 * diffuse * normal - light);
    float4 specular = pow(saturate(dot(reflection, eyeDirection)), 8);

    // Return the combined color
    Out.Color = AmbientColor + diffuseColor * diffuse + specular;

    return Out;
}
```

This is by far the largest shader this book has covered thus far. It starts out just like the last one by transforming the position and the normal, and then by setting the diffuse color to the metallic color constant. From here on, it begins to change, though. First, the position of each vertex in the world is stored. This is done since the eye position is already in world space, while the vertex is in model space. Since the eye direction will be used to calculate the specular highlights, each member needs to be in the same coordinate system.

Next, each of the vectors are normalized, which will clamp the unit length to 1.0f. Now the Boolean variable can be checked, and the color updated based on the newly normalized vector to simulate the random animating color. The diffuse component is stored using the same formula as always. Finally, the specular component is calculated. See the DirectX SDK docs on the mathematics of lighting for more information on this formula.

Once the light components have been calculated, the shader returns the combined color using the same mathematics of lighting formulas. With the specular shader now written, you can add the following techniques to allow access to it:

```
technique TransformSpecularPerVertexMetallic
{
    pass P0
    {
        // shaders
        VertexShader = compile vs_1_1 TransformSpecular(true);
        PixelShader  = NULL;
    }
}


technique TransformSpecularPerVertexColorful
{
    pass P0
    {
        // shaders
        VertexShader = compile vs_1_1 TransformSpecular(false);
        PixelShader  = NULL;
    }
}
```

Before running the application once more, you should update your main code to use the specular highlight shader:

```
effect.Technique = "TransformSpecularPerVertexMetallic";
```

You should now see your teapot appear shiny as it spins around. See Figure 12.1.

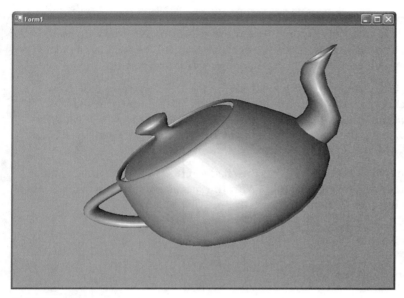

**FIGURE 12.1**   Teapot using per-vertex specular highlights.

## SHOP TALK

### UPDATING TO USE PER-PIXEL SPECULAR HIGHLIGHTS

As you can see, the teapot looks much more realistic with the shiny surface formed by the specular highlights. You can obviously tell the lighting calculations are performed per vertex. The lighting doesn't appear to smoothly light the entire curved surface of the teapot. Since the shader written for this application was a vertex shader, this is to be expected. In order to get an even more realistic effect, why not have the light be calculated per pixel rather than per vertex?

Since this lighting calculation requires more instructions than allowed for pixel shader 1.x, you will need to ensure that your application supports at least pixel shader version 2.0. You can update your main code that checks this logic as follows:

```
if ((hardware.VertexShaderVersion >= new Version(1, 1)) &&
    (hardware.PixelShaderVersion >= new Version(2, 0)))
```

You will still need a vertex shader to transform your coordinates, as well as to pass on the data needed to your pixel shader. Add the shader programs shown in Listing 12.3:

*SHOP TALK*

**LISTING 12.3**   Shader Programs

```
struct VS_OUTPUT_PER_VERTEX_PER_PIXEL
{
    float4 Position : POSITION;
    float3 LightDirection : TEXCOORD0;
    float3 Normal : TEXCOORD1;
    float3 EyeWorld : TEXCOORD2;
};

// Transform our coordinates into world space
VS_OUTPUT_PER_VERTEX_PER_PIXEL Transform(
    float4 inputPosition : POSITION,
    float3 inputNormal : NORMAL
    )
{
    //Declare our output structure
    VS_OUTPUT_PER_VERTEX_PER_PIXEL Out = (VS_OUTPUT_PER_VERTEX_PER_PIXEL)0;
    // Transform our position
    Out.Position = mul(inputPosition, WorldViewProj);
    // Store our light direction
    Out.LightDirection = DiffuseDirection;
    // Transform the normals into the world matrix and normalize them
    Out.Normal = normalize(mul(inputNormal, WorldMatrix));
    // Normalize the world position of the vertex
    float3 worldPosition = normalize(mul(inputPosition, WorldMatrix));
    // Store the eye vector
    Out.EyeWorld = EyeLocation - worldPosition;

    return Out;
}


float4 ColorSpecular(
 float3 lightDirection : TEXCOORD0,
 float3 normal : TEXCOORD1,
 float3 eye : TEXCOORD2,
 uniform bool metallic) : COLOR0
{
    // Make our diffuse color metallic for now
    float4 diffuseColor = MetallicColor;
```

**LISTING 12.3    Continued**

```
    if(!metallic)
        diffuseColor.rgb = cos(normal + eye);

    // Normalize our vectors
    float3 normalized = normalize(normal);
    float3 light = normalize(lightDirection);
    float3 eyeDirection = normalize(eye);
    // Store our diffuse component
    float4 diffuse = saturate(dot(light, normalized));

    // Calculate specular component
    float3 reflection = normalize(2 * diffuse * normalized - light);
    float4 specular = pow(saturate(dot(reflection, eyeDirection)), 8);

    // Return the combined color
    return AmbientColor + diffuseColor * diffuse + specular;
};
```

The code here is similar to the per vertex version. The vertex shader does the transformation and stores the required data for the pixel shader to use later. The pixel shader in turn does all of the math calculations to determine the resulting color. Since the pixel shader is run per pixel rather than per vertex, this effect will be much more fluid and realistic. Add the following technique to your shader file:

```
technique TransformSpecularPerPixelMetallic
{
    pass P0
    {
        // shaders
        VertexShader = compile vs_1_1 Transform();
        PixelShader  = compile ps_2_0 ColorSpecular(true);
    }
}
```

Switching your application to use this technique instead will produce a much more realistic result. See Figure 12.2.

**FIGURE 12.2**    Teapot with per-pixel specular highlights.

The sample included on the CD allows you to seamlessly switch between the per-vertex and per-pixel versions of this application, along with switching between the metallic and colorful versions.

## In Brief

- Simple vertex and color animation
- Texture blending
- Advanced lighting mechanisms

In the next chapter, the animation system of Managed DirectX will be discussed.

# Rendering Skeletal Animation

You don't see modern games render a bunch of static items; instead you see rich environments that are fluid. Characters are fully animated, with much of the animation coming from a motion capture studio. Models are designed with "bones" that can be positioned and animated to simulate motion. Aside from these complex animations, there are also other simple animation types, dealing mainly with scaling, rotation, and translation. This chapter will cover rendering meshes with animation data, including

- Loading frame hierarchy
- Generating any skeletal information
- Rendering each frame
- Advancing the animation time
- Using indexed animation for better performance

## Creating the Frame Hierarchy

Most meshes (even those not created with animation built in) have some type of hierarchy; an arm attached to the chest, a finger attached to the arm. In the Direct3D extensions library, you can load these hierarchies and maintain them yourself.

In order to store this information, there are two abstract classes that will be used to maintain the hierarchy: Frame and MeshContainer. Each Frame can contain zero to many sibling frames, as well as a potential child frame. Each frame can also contain zero to many mesh containers.

Before we get into all that, though, a new project will need to be created. Go ahead and get it created with the default options, the device variable declared, and the window style set, just like you've done with all of the other Direct3D applications.

Declare the following variables in your application:

```
private AnimationRootFrame rootFrame;
private Vector3 objectCenter;
private float objectRadius;
private float elapsedTime;
```

The AnimationRootFrame structure will hold the root frame of the hierarchy tree, as well as the animation controller class. The next two variables will hold the center of the loaded mesh, with the other storing the radius of the bounding sphere that can encase the full mesh. These will be used to position the camera so that the entire model will be seen. The last variable will store the elapsed time of the application, which will be used to update the animation.

Since each animated mesh is different, Direct3D will not force a particular way to load the hierarchy on you. Instead, you will need to derive a new class from the AllocateHierarchy object. Add the following class to your application:

```
public class AllocateHierarchyDerived : AllocateHierarchy
{
    Form1 app = null;
    /// <summary>
    /// Create new instance of this class
    /// </summary>
    /// <param name="parent">Parent of this class</param>
    public AllocateHierarchyDerived(Form1 parent)
    {
        app = parent;
    }
}
```

So far, the class doesn't do anything. The constructor stores an instance of the main form so that it can be used to call methods later, but right now the application won't even compile. There are two methods that must be implemented in this class before it can be compiled, since they are marked abstract. The two methods are used to create the frames and mesh containers that will be used to store the hierarchy. Since both of these classes are marked abstract as well, they cannot be created, so you will need to add new derived versions of the classes to your application. There will be extra information stored for each class to help our rendering later as well. Add the following class to your application:

```
public class FrameDerived : Frame
{
    // Store the combined transformation matrix
    private Matrix combined = Matrix.Identity;
    public Matrix CombinedTransformationMatrix
    {
        get { return combined; } set { combined = value; }
    }
}
```

In addition to the normal data a frame can store, each frame in this application will also store the combined transformation matrix of this frame and all of its parents. This will be useful when setting the world matrices later. Now you will need to include the derived mesh container class found in Listing 13.1.

**LISTING 13.1** The MeshContainer Class

```
public class MeshContainerDerived : MeshContainer
{
    private Texture[] meshTextures = null;
    private int numAttr = 0;
    private int numInfl = 0;
    private BoneCombination[] bones;
    private FrameDerived[] frameMatrices;
    private Matrix[] offsetMatrices;

    // Public properties
    public Texture[] GetTextures() { return meshTextures; }
    public void SetTextures(Texture[] textures) { meshTextures = textures; }

    public BoneCombination[] GetBones() { return bones; }
    public void SetBones(BoneCombination[] b) { bones = b; }

    public FrameDerived[] GetFrames() { return frameMatrices; }
    public void SetFrames(FrameDerived[] frames) { frameMatrices = frames; }

    public Matrix[] GetOffsetMatrices() { return offsetMatrices; }
    public void SetOffsetMatrices(Matrix[] matrices){offsetMatrices = matrices; }

    public int NumberAttributes {get{return numAttr;}set{numAttr = value;}}
    public int NumberInfluences {get{return numInfl;}set{numInfl = value;}}
}
```

Each mesh container will hold a little more information, including the bone combination table, the number of attributes, the number of influences, and offset matrices. Each of these will be used while rendering our animated mesh.

With all of the derived classes implemented, the abstract methods currently missing can be added. First, add the CreateFrame overload to your allocate hierarchy derived class:

```
public override Frame CreateFrame(string name)
{
    FrameDerived frame = new FrameDerived();
    frame.Name = name;
    frame.TransformationMatrix = Matrix.Identity;
    frame.CombinedTransformationMatrix = Matrix.Identity;

    return frame;
}
```

For each frame that needs creating, this code will store the name of the frame, as well set the transformation and combined transformation matrices to the identity matrix. Behind the scenes, the frames siblings, children, and mesh containers will be filled in by the runtime, so you need not worry about that.

There's a lot more work that needs to go on for creating a mesh container. Add the override found in Listing 13.2 to your application.

**LISTING 13.2**    Creating a New MeshContainer

```
public override MeshContainer CreateMeshContainer(string name,
    MeshData meshData, ExtendedMaterial[] materials,
    EffectInstance effectInstances, GraphicsStream adjacency,
    SkinInformation skinInfo)
{
    // We only handle meshes here
    if (meshData.Mesh == null)
        throw new ArgumentException();

    // We must have a vertex format mesh
    if (meshData.Mesh.VertexFormat == VertexFormats.None)
        throw new ArgumentException();

    MeshContainerDerived mesh = new MeshContainerDerived();

    mesh.Name = name;
    int numFaces = meshData.Mesh.NumberFaces;
```

**LISTING 13.2**  Continued

```
Device dev = meshData.Mesh.Device;

// Make sure there are normals
if ((meshData.Mesh.VertexFormat & VertexFormats.Normal) == 0)
{
    // Clone the mesh
    Mesh tempMesh = meshData.Mesh.Clone(meshData.Mesh.Options.Value,
        meshData.Mesh.VertexFormat ¦ VertexFormats.Normal, dev);

    meshData.Mesh = tempMesh;
    meshData.Mesh.ComputeNormals();
}

// Store the materials
mesh.SetMaterials(materials);
mesh.SetAdjacency(adjacency);
Texture[] meshTextures = new Texture[materials.Length];

// Create any textures
for (int i = 0; i < materials.Length; i++)
{
    if (materials[i].TextureFilename != null)
    {
        meshTextures[i] = TextureLoader.FromFile(dev, @"..\..\" +
            materials[i].TextureFilename);
    }
}
mesh.SetTextures(meshTextures);
mesh.MeshData = meshData;

// If there is skinning info, save any required data
if (skinInfo != null)
{
    mesh.SkinInformation = skinInfo;
    int numBones = skinInfo.NumberBones;
    Matrix[] offsetMatrices = new Matrix[numBones];

    for (int i = 0; i < numBones; i++)
        offsetMatrices[i] = skinInfo.GetBoneOffsetMatrix(i);
```

**LISTING 13.2**  Continued

```
        mesh.SetOffsetMatrices(offsetMatrices);

        app.GenerateSkinnedMesh(mesh);
    }

    return mesh;
}
```

This looks quite a bit more complicated than it really is. The first thing that needs to be done is to verify that this mesh is something the application will support. Obviously, if there is no mesh included in the mesh data structure, there will be a problem, so an exception is thrown. If the mesh that is included isn't using a valid vertex format, another exception is thrown.

Assuming that the mesh data itself is valid, a new mesh container is created. The name is set, and the number of faces the mesh contains is stored, along with the device. The code could also use the app variable to access the windows forms device, but that's marked as private.

With code that should look familiar, the mesh is checked for normal data. If it does not exist, it is added to the mesh. Our animated mesh will be lit and will require this normal data.

Next, you store the materials and adjacency information that was passed into this method into the mesh container for later use. Since the materials will include texture information, a new array of textures is created. The correct texture is then loaded into each member of the texture array, and that array is stored in the mesh container.

Finally, the code checks if there is any skeletal information in the mesh container. Assuming there is, the number of bones is stored, and an array of offset matrices (one for each bone) is created. We store the bone offset matrices in this array, and make a call to our (so far) non-existent GenerateSkinnedMesh method from our form. With everything complete, you can now return this mesh container.

Although in reality, everything isn't complete. The application still won't compile since the method that is called while creating the mesh container does not exist. Add the GenerateSkinnedMesh method from Listing 13.3 into your main class.

**LISTING 13.3**  Generating Skinned Meshes

```
public void GenerateSkinnedMesh(MeshContainerDerived mesh)
{
    if (mesh.SkinInformation == null)
        throw new ArgumentException();

    int numInfl = 0;
    BoneCombination[] bones;
```

**LISTING 13.3**   Continued

```
    // Use ConvertToBlendedMesh to generate a drawable mesh
    MeshData m = mesh.MeshData;
    m.Mesh = mesh.SkinInformation.ConvertToBlendedMesh(m.Mesh, MeshFlags.Managed
        | MeshFlags.OptimizeVertexCache, mesh.GetAdjacencyStream(), out numInfl,
        out bones);

    // Store this info
    mesh.NumberInfluences = numInfl;
    mesh.SetBones(bones);

    // Get the number of attributes
    mesh.NumberAttributes = bones.Length;

    mesh.MeshData = m;
}
```

This method should never be called if there isn't any skeletal information, so if there isn't, an exception is thrown. We store the mesh data temporarily and then use ConvertToBlendedMesh to generate a new mesh with per-vertex blend weights and a bone combination table. This method is the root of what allows the mesh to be animated. Finally, we store the number of influences in this mesh, the bone combination table, and the number of attributes.

# Loading Meshes with Animation

The basic hierarchy of the mesh has been established. Now, all you need to do is write some code to actually use it. Before you do that, though, you will need to initialize your graphics device. You should use a method similar to the programmable pipeline examples earlier, so use the method found in Listing 13.4.

**LISTING 13.4**   Initializing Your Graphics

```
public bool InitializeGraphics()
{
    // Set our presentation parameters
    PresentParameters presentParams = new PresentParameters();

    presentParams.Windowed = true;
    presentParams.SwapEffect = SwapEffect.Discard;
    presentParams.AutoDepthStencilFormat = DepthFormat.D16;
    presentParams.EnableAutoDepthStencil = true;
```

**LISTING 13.4**   Continued

```
bool canDoHardwareSkinning = true;
// Does a hardware device support shaders?
Caps hardware = Manager.GetDeviceCaps(0, DeviceType.Hardware);
// We will need at least four blend matrices
if (hardware.MaxVertexBlendMatrices >= 4)
{
    // Default to software processing
    CreateFlags flags = CreateFlags.SoftwareVertexProcessing;

    // Use hardware if it's available
    if (hardware.DeviceCaps.SupportsHardwareTransformAndLight)
        flags = CreateFlags.HardwareVertexProcessing;

    // Use pure if it's available
    if (hardware.DeviceCaps.SupportsPureDevice)
        flags |= CreateFlags.PureDevice;

    // Yes, Create our device
    device = new Device(0, DeviceType.Hardware, this, flags, presentParams);
}
else
{
    // No shader support
    canDoHardwareSkinning = false;

    // Create a reference device
    device = new Device(0, DeviceType.Reference, this,
        CreateFlags.SoftwareVertexProcessing, presentParams);
}

// Create the animation
CreateAnimation(@"..\..\tiny.x", presentParams);

// Hook the device reset event
device.DeviceReset += new EventHandler(OnDeviceReset);
OnDeviceReset(device, null);

return canDoHardwareSkinning;
}
```

Once again, you want to try to run in hardware first, and then fallback to the reference device if you must. The animation file used for this example will require at least four vertex blend matrices in order to render completely in hardware, so that's what the code will check for. Assuming it can, the best possible device will be created; otherwise, the reference device is created.

Once the device has been created, our animation should be loaded. The method that is being used hasn't been defined yet, but you will add that in just a moment. Before you do that, you should add the device reset event handler, as this method will have no other dependencies. Add the event handler from Listing 13.5 into your class.

**LISTING 13.5**   Handling Device Reset

```
private void OnDeviceReset(object sender, EventArgs e)
{
    Device dev = (Device)sender;

    // Set the view matrix
    Vector3 vEye = new Vector3( 0, 0, -1.8f * objectRadius );
    Vector3 vUp = new Vector3( 0, 1, 0 );

    dev.Transform.View = Matrix.LookAtLH(vEye, objectCenter, vUp);

    // Setup the projection matrix
    float aspectRatio = (float)dev.PresentationParameters.BackBufferWidth
        / (float)dev.PresentationParameters.BackBufferHeight;

    dev.Transform.Projection = Matrix.PerspectiveFovLH( (float)Math.PI / 4,
        aspectRatio, objectRadius/64.0f, objectRadius*200.0f );

    // Initialize our light
    dev.Lights[0].Type = LightType.Directional;
    dev.Lights[0].Direction = new Vector3(0.0f, 0.0f, 1.0f);
    dev.Lights[0].Diffuse = Color.White;
    dev.Lights[0].Commit();
    dev.Lights[0].Enabled = true;
}
```

As you can see, the view matrix is set, placing the camera far enough away to see the entire object, and is looking at the center of the object. The projection matrix is created with a large enough far plane to see the entire model as well. There is also a single directional light created in order to see the model correctly.

Now you are ready to add the animation creation code:

```
private void CreateAnimation(string file, PresentParameters presentParams)
{
    // Create our allocate hierarchy derived class
    AllocateHierarchyDerived alloc = new AllocateHierarchyDerived(this);

    // Load our file
    rootFrame = Mesh.LoadHierarchyFromFile(file, MeshFlags.Managed,
        device, alloc, null);

    // Calculate the center and radius of a bounding sphere
    objectRadius = Frame.CalculateBoundingSphere(rootFrame.FrameHierarchy,
        out objectCenter);

    // Setup the matrices for animation
    SetupBoneMatrices((FrameDerived)rootFrame.FrameHierarchy);

    // Start the timer
    DXUtil.Timer(DirectXTimer.Start);
}
```

This method seems pretty simple, but in reality all it does is call other methods, so naturally it should seem pretty simple.

First, the derived allocate hierarchy class you created is instantiated. This is passed on to the LoadHierarchyFromFile method, along with the file name of the mesh you wish to load, any options, and the Direct3D device. When this method is called, you will notice that your CreateFrame and CreateMeshContainer overrides will be called numerous times, depending on the number of frames and mesh containers in your mesh. The AnimationRootFrame object that is returned will hold the root frame of the hierarchy tree, as well as the animation controller, which will be used to, well, control the animation for this mesh.

After the hierarchy has been created, you can calculate the bounding sphere of the entire frame by passing the root frame into this CalculateBoundingSphere method. This will return the radius of this sphere, as well as the center of the mesh, which has already been used to position the camera.

Finally, before the mesh is ready to be animated, you must set up the bone matrices. This will be the first method that will "walk" the frame hierarchy tree and will be the foundation for each of the others. Add the methods found in Listing 13.6.

**LISTING 13.6**  *Setting Up Bone Matrices*

```
private void SetupBoneMatrices(FrameDerived frame)
{
    if (frame.MeshContainer != null)
    {
        SetupBoneMatrices((MeshContainerDerived)frame.MeshContainer);
    }

    if (frame.FrameSibling != null)
    {
        SetupBoneMatrices((FrameDerived)frame.FrameSibling);
    }

    if (frame.FrameFirstChild != null)
    {
        SetupBoneMatrices((FrameDerived)frame.FrameFirstChild);
    }
}

private void SetupBoneMatrices(MeshContainerDerived mesh)
{
    // Is there skin information?  If so, setup the matrices
    if (mesh.SkinInformation != null)
    {
        int numBones = mesh.SkinInformation.NumberBones;

        FrameDerived[] frameMatrices = new FrameDerived[numBones];
        for(int i = 0; i< numBones; i++)
        {
            FrameDerived frame = (FrameDerived)Frame.Find(
                rootFrame.FrameHierarchy,
                mesh.SkinInformation.GetBoneName(i));

            if (frame == null)
                throw new ArgumentException();

            frameMatrices[i] = frame;
        }
        mesh.SetFrames(frameMatrices);
    }
}
```

As you can see, walking the frame hierarchy isn't all that difficult. If you have a sibling, you simply call the method you are currently in once more with yourself. If you have children, you do the same. You don't need to call yourself with all of your children, just the first, since the first child will have each subsequent child listed as its sibling. In this case, we want to store each frame based on its bone name.

## USING THE DIRECTX TIMER

The animation system will require a relatively high precision timer. Rather than reinvent the wheel, this code will assume you are using the DirectX timer that ships in the SDK. You can add this file to your project by clicking Add Existing Item, navigating to the common folder, and choosing the dxutil.cs source file.

The overload that accepts the frame isn't overly interesting, since its only job is to walk the hierarchy tree and pass the mesh container along to the second overload. Here, an array of our frames is created, one for each bone in our mesh, assuming there is skeletal information in the first place. Each frame is retrieved by searching through the entire list looking for the one with the correct bone name. Once that is found, it is stored for later use.

Now would be the perfect time to update the main method to ensure that your initialization code will be called. Use the main method found in Listing 13.7.

**LISTING 13.7**    Main Entry Point

```
static void Main()
{
    using (Form1 frm = new Form1())
    {
        // Show our form and initialize our graphics engine
        frm.Show();
        if (!frm.InitializeGraphics())
        {
            MessageBox.Show("Your card can not perform skeletal animation on " +
                "this file in hardware. This application will run in " +
                "reference mode instead.");
        }
        Application.Run(frm);
    }
}
```

# Rendering Animated Meshes

What you want to do now is to render your animated character. The rendering method itself appears deceptively simple, so add the code from Listing 13.8 to your class now.

**LISTING 13.8**    Rendering Your Animated Character

```
protected override void OnPaint(System.Windows.Forms.PaintEventArgs e)
{
    ProcessNextFrame();

    device.Clear(ClearFlags.Target | ClearFlags.ZBuffer,
        Color.CornflowerBlue, 1.0f, 0);

    device.BeginScene();

    // Draw our root frame
    DrawFrame((FrameDerived)rootFrame.FrameHierarchy);

    device.EndScene();

    device.Present();

    this.Invalidate();
}
```

As you can see, the method is quite simple. Process the next frame, clear the device, draw the root frame, and you're done. A lot of things need to happen in these steps, though. First, look at the things that need to be done to process the next frame:

```
private void ProcessNextFrame()
{
    // Get the current elapsed time
    elapsedTime = DXUtil.Timer(DirectXTimer.GetElapsedTime);

    // Set the world matrix
    Matrix worldMatrix = Matrix.Translation(objectCenter);
    device.Transform.World = worldMatrix;

    if (rootFrame.AnimationController != null)
        rootFrame.AnimationController.AdvanceTime(elapsedTime, null);

    UpdateFrameMatrices((FrameDerived)rootFrame.FrameHierarchy, worldMatrix);
}
```

First, the current elapsed time is stored. Next, the world matrix for the root frame is created. Simply translate to the object's center, and update the device. Assuming this mesh has animation, you should advance the time, using the stored elapsed time. Finally, each of combined transformation matrices needs to be updated. Look at the following method:

```
private void UpdateFrameMatrices(FrameDerived frame, Matrix parentMatrix)
{
    frame.CombinedTransformationMatrix = frame.TransformationMatrix *
        parentMatrix;

    if (frame.FrameSibling != null)
    {
        UpdateFrameMatrices((FrameDerived)frame.FrameSibling, parentMatrix);
    }

    if (frame.FrameFirstChild != null)
    {
        UpdateFrameMatrices((FrameDerived)frame.FrameFirstChild,
            frame.CombinedTransformationMatrix);
    }
}
```

In this method, the current frame's combined transformation matrix is calculated by multiplying the frame's transformation matrix along with its parent's transformation matrix. Each of the siblings uses the same parent matrix that the current frame does. Each of the children should use the current frames combined transformation matrix to combine with their own. This forms a "chain" of matrices where the final child has its own transformation matrix, combined with each of its parents.

The next frame has been processed, so now you can actually draw it. The DrawFrame method is actually quite simple, and should look at least somewhat familiar:

```
private void DrawFrame(FrameDerived frame)
{
    MeshContainerDerived mesh = (MeshContainerDerived)frame.MeshContainer;
    while(mesh != null)
    {
        DrawMeshContainer(mesh, frame);

        mesh = (MeshContainerDerived)mesh.NextContainer;
    }

    if (frame.FrameSibling != null)
```

```
    {
        DrawFrame((FrameDerived)frame.FrameSibling);
    }

    if (frame.FrameFirstChild != null)
    {
        DrawFrame((FrameDerived)frame.FrameFirstChild);
    }
}
```

You simply walk the tree like normal, only this time, you will attempt to draw every mesh container the frame has a reference to. This method is where the bulk of the work will take place. Use Listing 13.9 to add this method to your application.

**LISTING 13.9** Rendering a Mesh Container

```
private void DrawMeshContainer(MeshContainerDerived mesh, FrameDerived frame)
{
    // Is there skin information?
    if (mesh.SkinInformation != null)
    {

        int attribIdPrev = -1;

        // Draw
        for (int iattrib = 0; iattrib < mesh.NumberAttributes; iattrib++)
        {
            int numBlend = 0;
            BoneCombination[] bones = mesh.GetBones();
            for (int i = 0; i < mesh.NumberInfluences; i++)
            {
                if (bones[iattrib].BoneId[i] != -1)
                {
                    numBlend = i;
                }
            }

            if (device.DeviceCaps.MaxVertexBlendMatrices >= numBlend + 1)
            {
                // first calculate the world matrices for the current set of
```

**LISTING 13.9** Continued

```
                    // blend weights and get the accurate count of the number of
                    // blends
                    Matrix[] offsetMatrices = mesh.GetOffsetMatrices();
                    FrameDerived[] frameMatrices = mesh.GetFrames();
                    for (int i = 0; i < mesh.NumberInfluences; i++)
                    {
                        int matrixIndex = bones[iattrib].BoneId[i];
                        if (matrixIndex != -1)
                        {
                            Matrix tempMatrix = offsetMatrices[matrixIndex] *
                                frameMatrices[matrixIndex].
                                CombinedTransformationMatrix;

                            device.Transform.SetWorldMatrixByIndex(i, tempMatrix);

                        }
                    }

                    device.RenderState.VertexBlend = (VertexBlend)numBlend;
                    // lookup the material used for this subset of faces
                    if ((attribIdPrev != bones[iattrib].AttribId) ||
                        (attribIdPrev == -1))
                    {
                        device.Material = mesh.GetMaterials()[
                            bones[iattrib].AttribId].Material3D;

                        device.SetTexture(0, mesh.GetTextures()[
                            bones[iattrib].AttribId]);

                        attribIdPrev = bones[iattrib].AttribId;
                    }

                    mesh.MeshData.Mesh.DrawSubset(iattrib);
                }
            }
        }
        else // standard mesh, just draw it after setting material properties
        {
            device.Transform.World = frame.CombinedTransformationMatrix;
```

**LISTING 13.9** Continued

```
ExtendedMaterial[] mtrl = mesh.GetMaterials();
for (int iMaterial = 0; iMaterial < mtrl.Length; iMaterial++)
{
    device.Material = mtrl[iMaterial].Material3D;
    device.SetTexture(0, mesh.GetTextures()[iMaterial]);
    mesh.MeshData.Mesh.DrawSubset(iMaterial);
}
    }
}
```

This method looks at least somewhat intimidating. Once it's broken down, though, you'll see it really isn't that complicated. First, the skin information member is checked. If this mesh container has no skeletal information, the mesh will be rendered exactly like our meshes have been in the past. If there is skeletal information, however, the rendering path is much different.

For every attribute entry (set of materials, textures, and so on) in this mesh, a number of operations will need to be performed. First, you must scan through the bone combination table and determine the number of blend weights the mesh will use. The file being used in the example on the included CD uses a maximum of four blend weights, which is what the device creation tests against; however, this code still ensures that the device has the capabilities to blend this many matrices, in case the mesh file has been changed.

Once you've determined that your device can render your mesh with these blend weights, you will need to set the world transforms. For each item you find in the bone id member of your bone combination table, you will combine the offset matrix with the frames combined transformation matrix and set the currently indexed world matrix transform to this resulting matrix. This will allow Direct3D to render each blended vertex with the appropriate world transforms.

Once that's been completed, you set the vertex blend render state to the number of blends this mesh expects. Finally, you set the material and texture of this subset and draw it.

With that, you are ready to run the application. You should expect to see a model walking toward you. See Figure 13.1.

## USING ANIMATED MESHES WITH NO SKELETON

Just because a mesh has no skeletal information does not mean the mesh has no animation. If the only animation included in the mesh is a standard matrix operation (for example, scale, translate, or rotate), there is no need for any bones or skeleton. However, the animation system will still update the matrices for your mesh, so rendering them like normal will still produce the desired results.

**FIGURE 13.1**   An animated mesh.

## SHOP TALK

### USING AN INDEXED MESH TO ANIMATE THE BONES

We talked earlier about how rendering vertex data with an index buffer could improve performance by reducing the number of triangles that need to be drawn, and the memory consumption of the triangles already there. In complex characters such as the one being rendered here, the performance benefits of using an indexed mesh are quite noticeable. On top of that, the code is a little shorter as well.

Before you can update the mesh to be an indexed mesh, you will need to make a few changes elsewhere. First, you'll need to add a new member to your derived mesh container class:

```
private int numPal = 0;
public int NumberPaletteEntries
{
    get { return numPal; } set { numPal = value; }
}
```

This will store the number of bone matrices that can be used for matrix palette skinning when we convert our mesh. Next, since we will no longer be using standard vertex blending for our animation, you will need to update the initialization method that ensures your device has this support. Instead, replace that check, with this one:

```
    if (hardware.MaxVertexBlendMatrixIndex >= 12)
```

All that's required now is to replace the generate mesh call (to generate our indexed mesh instead), and then the actual drawing call will need to be replaced. First, see Listing 13.10 for the mesh generation:

**LISTING 13.10**    Generating a Mesh

```
public void GenerateSkinnedMesh(MeshContainerDerived mesh)
{
    if (mesh.SkinInformation == null)
        throw new ArgumentException();

    int numMaxFaceInfl;
    MeshFlags flags = MeshFlags.OptimizeVertexCache;

    MeshData m = mesh.MeshData;

    using(IndexBuffer ib = m.Mesh.IndexBuffer)
    {
        numMaxFaceInfl = mesh.SkinInformation.GetMaxFaceInfluences(ib,
            m.Mesh.NumberFaces);
    }
    // 12 entry palette guarantees that any triangle (4 independent
    // influences per vertex of a tri) can be handled
    numMaxFaceInfl = (int)Math.Min(numMaxFaceInfl, 12);

    if (device.DeviceCaps.MaxVertexBlendMatrixIndex + 1 >= numMaxFaceInfl)
    {
        mesh.NumberPaletteEntries = (int)Math.Min((device.DeviceCaps.
            MaxVertexBlendMatrixIndex+ 1) / 2,
            mesh.SkinInformation.NumberBones);

        flags |= MeshFlags.Managed;
    }

    BoneCombination[] bones;
    int numInfl;

    m.Mesh = mesh.SkinInformation.ConvertToIndexedBlendedMesh(m.Mesh, flags,
        mesh.GetAdjacencyStream(), mesh.NumberPaletteEntries, out numInfl,
```

**LISTING 13.10**   Continued

```
        out bones);

    mesh.SetBones(bones);
    mesh.NumberInfluences = numInfl;
    mesh.NumberAttributes = bones.Length;
    mesh.MeshData = m;
}
```

Here, the first thing we do is get the maximum number of face influences in this mesh. Once we have that number, we make sure it is at least 12 (since 12 would be the magic number of 4 vertex blends for each vertex in a triangle). Assuming our device supports this (which our initialization method does check), we calculate the number of palette entries we expect to use (which is either the number of bones, or half the max face influences supported).

Now, we can convert our mesh to an indexed blended mesh and store the same data we used in our non-indexed version. Look at the changes to the draw call. For brevity, this will only include the code inside the block where the skin information member isn't null (see Listing 13.11):

**LISTING 13.11**   The draw Call

```
if (mesh.NumberInfluences == 1)
    device.RenderState.VertexBlend = VertexBlend.ZeroWeights;
else
    device.RenderState.VertexBlend = (VertexBlend)(mesh.NumberInfluences - 1);

if (mesh.NumberInfluences > 0)
    device.RenderState.IndexedVertexBlendEnable = true;

BoneCombination[] bones = mesh.GetBones();

for(int iAttrib = 0; iAttrib < mesh.NumberAttributes; iAttrib++)
{
    // first, get world matrices
    for (int iPaletteEntry = 0; iPaletteEntry < mesh.NumberPaletteEntries;
        ++iPaletteEntry)
    {
        int iMatrixIndex = bones[iAttrib].BoneId[iPaletteEntry];
        if (iMatrixIndex != -1)
        {
            device.Transform.SetWorldMatrixByIndex(iPaletteEntry,
```

SHOP TALK

**LISTING 13.11** Continued

```
                    mesh.GetOffsetMatrices()[iMatrixIndex] *
                    mesh.GetFrames()[iMatrixIndex].
                    CombinedTransformationMatrix);

            }
        }

        // Setup the material
        device.Material = mesh.GetMaterials()[bones[iAttrib].AttribId].Material3D;
        device.SetTexture(0, mesh.GetTextures()[bones[iAttrib].AttribId]);

        // Finally draw the subset
        mesh.MeshData.Mesh.DrawSubset(iAttrib);
    }
```

This method is much less complicated. First, you set the vertex blend render state to the number of influences minus one. Next, if there are influences (which you should expect in a skeletal animation), set the render state to enable indexed vertex blending.

With that, the rest of the code is similar to the last method. For each palette entry, set the corresponding world matrix at that index to the combined offset matrix and frames combined transformation matrix. Once the world matrices are set, you can set the materials, textures, and draw each subset.

Using the indexed blended mesh rather than the normal mesh can show an increase in performance of 30% or even more, depending on the data.

# In Brief

In this chapter we covered the basics of animation, specifically skeletal animation. Topics included

- Creating and loading a frame hierarchy
- Walking this hierarchy to update and render the meshes
- Using the animation controller
- Converting our animated character to an indexed mesh

In the next chapter, we will discuss how to use sound in your applications.

# PART IV

# Sound and Input

# Discovering the Wonders of Sound

All of the 3D graphics in the world won't make a great game. Aside from the obvious game play issues, you also need to create an atmosphere in order to be compelling. Fancy graphics and pretty environments help, but the world doesn't really come alive until you've added sound. Could you imagine playing Pac-Man without hearing the trademark "wakka wakka wakka" while you're running around? What fun would Undying be without the amazing use of creepy sounds? During the course of this chapter you'll learn how to use rich sound and include it in your applications. The topics that will be covered include

- Loading and playing static sounds

- Playing sounds in a 3D world

- Playing sounds with special effects

## Including the Sound Namespace

Well, it's been a while since you've needed to add any new references to one of the applications. Naturally the sound resources that you will need to use do not reside in the Direct3D namespace; you will instead need to use the Microsoft.DirectX.DirectSound namespace. For each of the examples in this chapter, you will need to add a reference to this assembly for the project, as well as add a using clause for this namespace.

# Loading and Playing a Static Sound

In the simplest case, what do you want to do for a sound? You want to have some type of audio data, and you want to output this audio data to all of the speakers attached to the system. Sounds easy enough, but how do you do that in a DirectX application? For the simple case just described, it is exceedingly simple.

Much like Direct3D has a Device class that controls the actual graphics hardware, DirectSound has a Device class that controls the actual sound hardware. Since both of these classes share the same name (in different namespaces), it's important to remember that if you are referencing both Direct3D and DirectSound in the same code file, you may need to fully qualify any references to a "Device" variable.

DirectSound also has buffers that are used to hold the audio data it needs to play the sounds, much like Direct3D used buffers to hold geometry or pixel data. There are only two types of buffers in DirectSound, either the stock "Buffer" object, or the more robust "SecondaryBuffer" object (which also derives from Buffer).

So since the simple case is so simple, you can just write it now, and take a look at it. First, create a new project and get the DirectSound references and namespaces in, and then add the following variable declarations:

```
private Device device = null;
private SecondaryBuffer sound = null;
```

You will have one device that is used to talk to the sound hardware, and you will have one buffer you can use to play the actual audio data that will be loaded. Now, you can write the "InitializeSound" method, which will load and play a sound. Since this method will reference an audio file, you will need to provide one. The file used in this method was copied from the DirectX SDK. You can copy this file from the included source on the CD. Add the following method:

```
public void InitializeSound()
{
    device = new Device();
    device.SetCooperativeLevel(this, CooperativeLevel.Normal);
    sound = new SecondaryBuffer(@"..\..\drumpad-crash.wav", device);
    sound.Play(0, BufferPlayFlags.Default);
}
```

As you can see, the code is quite simple. You create a new device (by using the parameter-less constructor; the other overloads for this object will be discussed later in this chapter), and then set the cooperative level on the device. I know what you're thinking: What exactly is a cooperative level?

The sound hardware in your machine is shared among many different applications. Windows may beep at you when an error has occurred. Messenger may beep when a friend has logged in, and all of these things can happen while you're listening to your favorite songs. The cooperative level is used to determine how your application behaves with others, hence its name. The choice selected here is the default option. It has the best multitasking and resource sharing behavior. You may look in the DirectX SDK documentation for details on the other priority levels; for the needs of this application, you can stick with normal.

After you have set the cooperative level, and are prepared to play nice with the rest of the system, you can create the buffer. You will load the buffer from a file (the code on the included CD uses a simple sound that ships with the DirectX SDK), and finally just play it. The first parameter of the play call is the priority, which is only valid if you've created your buffer deferred (which you haven't). You play the buffer using the default flags, and you're off. Now, you just need to actually call this method from somewhere, so how about replacing the main code with this:

```
static void Main()
{
    using (Form1 frm = new Form1())
    {
        frm.InitializeSound();
        Application.Run(frm);
    }
}
```

The simple case really is that simple. Just a few lines of code and the sound plays when the application starts up; it doesn't get much easier than that. If you look at the constructor for the SecondaryBuffer though, you'll notice that it takes quite a few different sets of parameters. You should look at those now. The following two overloads cover the basic variations of the constructors:

```
public SecondaryBuffer ( System.String fileName ,
    Microsoft.DirectX.DirectSound.BufferDescription desc ,
    Microsoft.DirectX.DirectSound.Device parent )

public SecondaryBuffer ( System.IO.Stream source , System.Int32 length ,
    Microsoft.DirectX.DirectSound.BufferDescription desc ,
    Microsoft.DirectX.DirectSound.Device parent )
```

All of the constructors for the secondary buffer take in the device that will be used to play the actual audio data. As you can see, the constructors can take either a filename for the audio data you wish to load, or a stream that contains the audio data. There is only one constructor available that does not take in a BufferDescription object as well (which happens to be the one you used). A default BufferDescription is used in that case, because all buffers need to have a description when they are created.

So what does the BufferDescription do? As the name implies, it describes the various options of the buffer you are creating. The properties of this object are found in Table 14.1.

**TABLE 14.1**

**Buffer Description Properties**

| PROPERTY | DESCRIPTION |
| --- | --- |
| BufferBytes | A read-write property for the size of the new buffer in bytes. If you are creating a primary buffer, or a buffer from a stream or sound file, you can leave this member at zero. |
| CanGetCurrentPosition | A read-write Boolean property that allows you to specify if you want an accurate position of the playing cursor. |
| Control3D | A read-write Boolean property indicating whether or not your buffer can be manipulated in 3D space. This option can not be used if your buffer has a stereo (two channel) format, or if the ControlPan option is set to true. |
| ControlEffects | A read-write Boolean property indicating that this buffer can or cannot use effects processing. In order to use these effects, you must have an 8- or 16-bit PCM format audio data, and are not allowed more than two channels (stereo). |
| ControlFrequency | A read-write Boolean property indicating your buffer's frequency can be modified when true. |
| ControlPan | A read-write Boolean property indicating if your buffer can support panning. Cannot be used with the Control3D flag. |
| ControlPositionNotify | A read-write Boolean property indicating whether or not your buffer will support position notification. |
| ControlVolume | A read-write Boolean property indicating whether or not your buffer will be able to control the volume. |
| DeferLocation | A read-write Boolean property indicating that your buffer can be assigned to either play in hardware or software at play time. This flag must be set to true for any buffer that will use voice management. |
| Flags | A bitwise combination of the BufferDescriptionFlags enumeration. The values for these items in the enumeration are matched as the Boolean properties of this object for ease of use. For example, rather than saying `desc.ControlPan = true;` `desc.ControlEffects = true;` you could say `desc.Flags = BufferDescriptionFlags.ControlPan ¦ BufferDescriptionFlags.ControlEffects;` |
| Format | A read-write property specifying the wave format of the audio data you are creating. If you load your buffer from a file or a stream, this object will be filled for you when the constructor returns, informing you of the format of the buffer you just created. |

**TABLE 14.1**

Continued

| PROPERTY | DESCRIPTION |
|---|---|
| GlobalFocus | A read-write Boolean property indicating whether or not your buffer is global. By default, sounds will only play if your window has the focus on the system. By setting this member to true, your sound will continue to play even while your application does not have focus. |
| Guid3DAlgorithm | A read-write GUID property used to specify the algorithm used for 3D virtualization. You may use any of the DSoundHelper.Guid3Dxxxx GUID constants listed in Managed DirectX for the built-in behaviors. |
| LocateInHardware | A read-write Boolean property indicating whether or not this buffer is required to be located in hardware. If true and the necessary hardware support isn't available, creating this buffer will fail. |
| LocateInSoftware | A read-write Boolean property indicating whether or not this buffer is required to be located in software. If true, this buffer will always be located in software, regardless of the availability of hardware resources. |
| Mute3DAtMaximumDistance | A read-write Boolean property indicating whether or not to stop playing a sound if the maximum distance has been exceeded. This only applies to software buffers. |
| PrimaryBuffer | A read-write Boolean property indicating whether or not this buffer is a primary buffer. |
| StaticBuffer | A read-write Boolean property indicating whether or not to place the buffer in hardware memory if it is available. If no hardware is available, the call will still succeed, but the buffer will be placed in software. You may not have ControlEffects true when specifying this flag. |
| StickyFocus | A read-write Boolean property indicating whether or not "sticky" focus is in use. As already mentioned when discussing the global focus flag, the default for DirectSound is to stop playing your buffer if your window does not have focus. If the sticky focus flag is set to true, your buffer will still play if the currently focused window is not already using DirectSound. If it is, it will revert back to default behavior. |

As you can see, there are quite a few options for a buffer. This next example will use a few of them to show you what they do. It will be based off the simple one you've already done; however, this one will rotate the sound back and forth between left and right by controlling the pan of the sound.

In order to do this, you'll need to use a buffer description object like you've just described. Add the following code after your call to SetCooperativeLevel:

```
BufferDescription desc = new BufferDescription();
desc.ControlPan = true;
desc.GlobalFocus = true;
```

You are essentially telling DirectSound that you will be creating a buffer and will want to allow the pan to be controlled. Also, you want the buffer to be global across the entire system.

You will also need to modify the creation of the buffer to use the constructor that takes the buffer description you just created. To improve the effect, you will have the buffer loop forever while it is being played. Modify the code as follows:

```
sound = new SecondaryBuffer(@"..\..\drumpad-crash.wav",desc, device);
sound.Play(0, BufferPlayFlags.Looping);
```

Running the application now will cause the sound to play, and loop continuously, but the pan value of the buffer is never actually updated anywhere. For a nifty effect, why don't you update it every 50 milliseconds or so. In the design view for your form, add a timer control, and set the interval to 50. Add the following code for the timer event (double-clicking the timer in design view will bring up the event handler method):

```
private void timer1_Tick(object sender, System.EventArgs e)
{
    // Adjust the pan
    sound.Pan *= -1;
}
```

The pan value is an integer value that specifies the stereo position of the sound; the farther negative the value, the more the sound comes out of the left speaker. The more the value is positive, the more it comes out of the right speaker. A value of zero (the default) says to come out of both speakers equally. Since the default is zero, the code above will not actually do anything (since 0 * -1 is still 0). Now set the initial pan value to the left speaker and start the timer. Add this code directly after the play call in InitializeSound:

```
sound.Pan = -5000;
timer1.Enabled = true;
```

Run the example now. You should now hear the sound file being played back and forth across your two speakers for an interesting effect. It's really quite simple to use sounds for your application.

# Using Sounds in 3D

Many multimedia computer systems nowadays have high-end speaker systems attached to high-end audio cards. It isn't uncommon for a system to have the ability to use full surround sound, and it won't be long before 5.1 systems are the norm for computers, particularly for the gamers.

The DirectSound API already has the ability to play sounds in 3D space, and can use these features if the computer supports them today. The options are controlled with the Buffer3D object (for controlling the actual source of the sound) and the Listener3D object (for controlling the position and orientation of the listener). You'll notice that the constructors for these objects each take in a buffer that is used to create the 3D version of the audio. These buffers must be created with the Control3D flag set to true.

So what benefits do you gain from implementing 3D sound into your application? Naturally you get a richer experience. When you go to the movie theater nowadays, the sound is normally played digitally, and they always have a surround sound system. Imagine if you were playing a game, and a door opened behind you, if there were speakers behind you, you would *expect* the sound to come from those speakers, not the two in front of you. Games today require the full experience, and this includes 3D sound.

There are two items you can deal with when you want to manipulate the sounds in 3D. You can manipulate the actual source of the sound, or you can manipulate the "ears" that are hearing the sound. First, you can look at moving around the sound itself, by using the Buffer3D object.

This object is only designed to control the 3D settings for the buffer. All of the methods for playing the buffer, and so on, still reside on the original buffer object. The properties you can update with this object are located in Table 14.2.

## TABLE 14.2

**Buffer3D Properties**

| PROPERTY | DESCRIPTION |
|---|---|
| ConeAngles | A read-write property that is used to set or get the angles for the inside or outside of the projection cone. Both angles are specified in degrees. Sounds within the inside cone angle are at normal volume, while sounds outside of the outside cone angle are at the outside volume. |
| ConeOrientation | A read-write property that controls the orientation of the sound's projection cone. DirectSound will automatically normalize the vector. The vector information used should be the center of the sound cone. |
| ConeOutsideVolume | A read-write property that controls the volume of sounds that lie outside the angle of the sound cone. |
| Deferred | A read-write Boolean property that determines if property changes will happen instantly or if they will be deferred until the listener updates settings. The default is false, and the properties are updated immediately. |
| MaxDistance | A read-write property that determines the maximum distance from the listener before the sound is no longer attenuated. |
| MinDistance | A read-write property that determines the minimum distance from the listener before the sound begins to be attenuated. |

**TABLE 14.2**

Continued

| PROPERTY | DESCRIPTION |
|----------|-------------|
| Mode | A read-write property that determines the 3D mode for sound processing. The default value is Mode3D.Normal. You may also use Mode3D.Disable, which disables processing of 3D Sound, or Mode3D.HeadRelative, which uses the listener's properties to determine the relative changes for processing sound, rather than using the absolute parameters. |
| Position | A read-write property that determines the current position of the sound source in world space. |
| Velocity | A read-write property that determines the velocity of the sound source, in meters per second by default. |

There is also another property that allows you to modify all of these parameters at once. It is called AllParameters, and you can update all of the options at once using this property. It should be a simple matter to update the last example using the pan property to use 3D processing instead, so you can try that now.

The audio file you've used thus far happens to be a stereo file; it contains two separate channels for the left and right speakers. In order to use 3D processing, you will need to use a mono audio file (or one with only one channel). The code here (and on the included CD) will use a different file from the DirectX SDK that is a mono file instead for this example. Make sure you copy that file to your source code location.

Add a reference to the Buffer3D object you will use to control the 3D buffer:

```
private Buffer3D buffer = null;
```

You should update the InitializeSound method to use 3D processing rather than the pan control you used before:

```
public void InitializeSound()
{
    device = new Device();
    device.SetCooperativeLevel(this, CooperativeLevel.Normal);

    BufferDescription desc = new BufferDescription();
    desc.Control3D = true;
    desc.GlobalFocus = true;

    sound = new SecondaryBuffer(@"..\..\drumpad-bass_drum.wav", desc, device);
    buffer = new Buffer3D(sound);
    sound.Play(0, BufferPlayFlags.Looping);

    buffer.Position = new Vector3(-0.1f, 0.0f, 0.0f);
```

```
        timer1.Enabled = true;
}
```

As you can see, you replaced the pan control with the 3D control, as well as changed the audio file to one that was mono. You then created the Buffer3D object from the already created sound buffer. After you play the buffer (ensuring it will loop continuously), you set the position just to the left of the listener (which defaults to 0, 0, 0). Finally, you should update the timer code. Rather than just move back and forth, though, you should really make this buffer move around. Replace the timer code with this:

```
private void timer1_Tick(object sender, System.EventArgs e)
{
    // Adjust the position
    buffer.Position *= mover;
    if ((Math.Abs(buffer.Position.X) > MoverMax) && (mover == MoverUp))
    {
        mover = MoverDown;
    }
    if ((Math.Abs(buffer.Position.X) < MoverMin) && (mover == MoverDown))
    {
        mover = MoverUp;
    }
}
```

This code uses a few new variables and constants here that are used to make the position move around. Add them to your class so that you can compile:

```
private const float MoverMax = 35.0f;
private const float MoverMin = 0.5f;
private const float MoverUp = -1.05f;
private const float MoverDown = -0.95f;
private float mover = MoverUp;
```

When the application first starts up, you'll notice the sounds moving back and forth quickly between your speakers, then it slowly sounds like the sounds get far away, and just when it sounds like they may move out of listening range, they start coming back toward you. The application will continue doing this until you quit it.

# Manipulating the Listener

The Listener3D object is created and used much like the Buffer3D object is. However, instead of manipulating the actual sound source (of which there can be many), you are dealing directly with the listener, of which there is only one per device. For this reason, you cannot use a SecondaryBuffer when creating a listener object; you can only use a Buffer object, and then only if it is a primary buffer.

Before you write the code using the listener object, you should take a look at the properties and settings you can modify on it, much like you did with the 3D buffer object. You will find these properties in Table 14.3.

**TABLE 14.3**

**Listener3D Properties**

| PROPERTY | DESCRIPTION |
| --- | --- |
| CommitDeferredSettings | If any of the settings were deferred on any 3D sound buffers, or the listener, this method will commit all new values at the same time. This method will have no effect if there were no deferred changes made. |
| DistanceFactor | A read-write property that controls the number of meters in a vector unit. |
| DopplerFactor | A read-write property that controls the multiplier for the Doppler effect. Any buffer that has velocity will automatically get Doppler shift effects, and these effects are cumulative. |
| Deferred | A read-write Boolean property that determines if property changes will happen instantly or if they will be deferred until the listener updates settings. The default is false, and the properties are updated immediately. |
| Orientation | A read-write property that controls the orientation of the listener. DirectSound will automatically normalize the vector. |
| RolloffFactor | A read-write property that determines the rolloff factor. This factor determines the rate of attenuation over distance. |
| Position | A read-write property that determines the current position of the listener in world space. |
| Velocity | A read-write property that determines the velocity of the listener, in meters per second by default. |

You should take the existing example where the sound buffer is moving, and update it to move the listener instead. You can get rid of the 3D buffer object you were using, and replace that variable with the following two:

```
private Listener3D listener = null;
private Microsoft.DirectX.DirectSound.Buffer primary = null;
```

You need to have a primary buffer in order to create the listener object. You'll also notice that since the class name "Buffer" is also in the system namespace, you will need to fully qualify the buffer variable name. Since you don't have the "buffer" variable anymore, you'll need to update the InitializeSound method as well. Replace the code that is used to create the 3D sound buffer with this:

```
BufferDescription primaryBufferDesc = new BufferDescription();
primaryBufferDesc.Control3D = true;
primaryBufferDesc.PrimaryBuffer = true;
```

```
primary = new Microsoft.DirectX.DirectSound.Buffer(primaryBufferDesc, device);
listener = new Listener3D(primary);
listener.Position = new Vector3(0.1f, 0.0f, 0.0f);
```

Here similar things are done. You create a primary buffer, and use that to get the listener object, then set the listener's position to a slightly left value. Finally, you just need to update the timer code to move the listener rather than the buffer that's no longer in the code:

```
private void timer1_Tick(object sender, System.EventArgs e)
{
    // Adjust the position
    listener.Position *= mover;
    if ((Math.Abs(listener.Position.X) > MoverMax) && (mover == MoverUp))
    {
        mover = MoverDown;
    }
    if ((Math.Abs(listener.Position.X) < MoverMin) && (mover == MoverDown))
    {
        mover = MoverUp;
    }
}
```

As you can see, you did nothing more than replace buffer with listener. This example should sound identical to the last one, since the same basic principle is being applied.

### SOUND LISTENERS EFFECT

It's also important to note that the listener object only affects buffers created with the control 3D flag. If you create buffers without this flag they will be played at equal volume from all speakers.

# Using Effects with Your Sounds

Aside from 3D manipulation of sounds, another technique used to bring out the realism of the games you play would be the effects added to already existing sounds. For example, walking across a wood floor would sound totally different in a small room from the way it would

### BUFFERS THAT SUPPORT EFFECTS

Effects can only be used on a secondary buffer. The required method to apply the effects to the buffer only resides on this object.

sound if you were in a large empty concert hall. Yelling in a cavern may cause your voice to echo among the cavern walls. These effects are an integral part of the immersion you are trying to create when developing a game, or any good interactive multimedia application.

Luckily, the act of using these special effects is pretty straightforward and there are quite a few of these effects already built into the DirectSound API. Revisiting the old example you created that was controlling the pan, update that to control some effects. Remove the timer since you won't be using that anymore. Then change the InitializeSound method as follows:

```
public void InitializeSound()
{
    device = new Device();
    device.SetCooperativeLevel(this, CooperativeLevel.Normal);

    BufferDescription desc = new BufferDescription();
    desc.ControlEffects = true;
    desc.GlobalFocus = true;

    sound = new SecondaryBuffer(@"..\..\drumpad-crash.wav",desc, device);

    EffectDescription[] effects = new EffectDescription[1];
    effects[0].GuidEffectClass = DSoundHelper.StandardEchoGuid;
    sound.SetEffects(effects);

    sound.Play(0, BufferPlayFlags.Looping);
}
```

## SETTING EFFECTS

Effects can only be set on a buffer that is stopped. If the buffer is playing when SetEffects is called, an exception will be thrown. You can use the Status property on the buffer to detect if it is playing. If it is, you can call the Stop method to ensure that it has stopped before applying the effects.

The big changes here are the ability to control the pan being removed, and change it to controlling the effects. Then you create an array of effect descriptions (currently with just one member), and assign that member to be the standard echo effect. You then pass in the effects that you have just created and start playing the buffer.

That's really all there is to setting the basic effects. If you run the application now you will be able to hear the echo that wasn't there before. It's also possible to add "stacks" of these effects on top of each other. If we wanted to have the sound played with an echo effect along with a flanger effect, followed by a distortion effect, you could update the method as follows:

```
EffectDescription[] effects = new EffectDescription[3];
effects[0].GuidEffectClass = DSoundHelper.StandardEchoGuid;
effects[1].GuidEffectClass = DSoundHelper.StandardFlangerGuid;
effects[2].GuidEffectClass = DSoundHelper.StandardDistortionGuid;
sound.SetEffects(effects);
```

Well, you've managed to take the drum cymbal sound and make it sound like an airplane engine; at least that's what this sounds like to me. The effects also do not have to be different; you could just as easily pass in three flanger effects for the example above. As you can already tell, there are a few built-in effect types already, but what are they? You can find the effects listed in Table 14.4.

## TABLE 14.4
### Built-in Effect Types

| EFFECT | DESCRIPTION |
| --- | --- |
| Chorus | The chorus effect doubles the voices by echoing the original sound with a slight delay and slightly modulating this delay. |
| Compression | The compression effect is essentially a reduction in the signal above certain amplitudes. |
| Distortion | The distortion effect is implemented by adding harmonics to the signal, so that as the level increases, the top of the waveform becomes either squared off, or clipped. |
| Echo | The echo effect will cause the entire sound to be played again (at a lower volume) after a set delay. |
| Environment Reverberation | The environment reverberation effect is implemented with the Interactive 3D Audio Level 2 (I3DL2) specification. It only controls the listener portions of this specification. |
| Flange | The flange effect is like the chorus effect in that it also is implemented with an echo; however, the delay is very short, and varies over time. |
| Gargle | This effect simply modulates the amplitude of the signal. |
| Parametric Equalizer | This effect is much like the equalizer in your car or stereo. It amplifies or attenuates signals of a certain frequency. |
| Waves Reverberation | This effect is intended to be used with music. It causes a nice reverb effect to be applied to your sound. |

It is also possible to take any of the effects you've applied to the buffer and change any or all of the settings currently applied. You can do this with the GetEffects method on the secondary buffer. In order to better hear the changes you're making, get rid of all the effects you're currently playing except for the echo effect. Now, add the following section of code immediately after the call to SetEffects:

```
EchoEffect echo = (EchoEffect)sound.GetEffects(0);
EffectsEcho param = echo.AllParameters;
param.Feedback = 1.0f;
param.LeftDelay = 1060.2f;
param.RightDelay = 1595.3f;
param.PanDelay = 1;
echo.AllParameters = param;
```

## UPDATING EFFECT PROPERTIES

Even though SetEffects may only be called when the buffer is stopped, you can manipulate any of the effects that are currently loaded in real time as the buffer is playing.

Here, you use the GetEffects method to create an instance of the EchoEffect object, which holds all of the data for the echo effect that is currently being used. You then change a few properties on the echo effect, and you're done. Listen to the audio with and without this code running, the changes to the effect should be immediately obvious. Any effect that you load can have its options manipulated in this way.

# In Brief

- Loading and playing static sounds
- Playing sounds in a 3D world
- Playing sounds with special effects

In our next chapter, we will finally begin to look at controlling user input with the keyboard, mouse, or joystick.

# Controlling User Input

Thus far, the book has covered 3D graphics in depth, and it has now covered sound as well. Aside from briefly in Chapter 6, "Using Managed DirectX to Write a Game," user control hasn't been discussed at all. Even that control only dealt with the keyboard, while ignoring the mouse, or even joysticks and game pads. Not to mention the force feedback possibilities. This chapter will cover the DirectInput API, and how to use it to get the data the user input devices are giving you. The topics being covered include

- Controlling the keyboard

- Controlling the mouse

- Controlling joysticks and game pads

- Force feedback

## Detecting the Devices You Can Use

Just like last chapter, you will need to ensure that you add references to DirectInput in order to use the code that will be discussed in this chapter. You will need to add a reference to Microsoft.DirectX.DirectInput as well as add a using clause for this namespace. Once this is done for the project(s), you are ready to begin. ·

Unless your computer is a server system, mounted inside a "rack" (a headless system), chances are your computer has at a minimum two input devices: a keyboard and a mouse.

With the multitude of USB devices on the market today, though, you may very well have quite a few input devices. It's not uncommon for a laptop, for example, to have multiple mice attached. You could theoretically have upward of 100 different user input devices attached to your system at any given time.

With all of these different input devices available to you, what can you do to detect the various devices available on your system? Do you remember way back early in the book when you talked about the Manager class that exists in Direct3D? DirectInput has a similar class that you can use to find out just about anything you will need to about the devices attached (or even not attached) to your system.

The easiest thing you can do is to detect all of the devices available on the system. You can use the devices property on the manager object to do this enumeration. First though, you'll need to create a tree view on our form, and set its dock parameter to fill so that it covers the entire form. You will also need some constants for the "root" key names you will use for the tree view. Add these constants to your application:

```
private const string AllItemsNode = "All Items";
private const string KeyboardsNode = "All Keyboard Items";
private const string MiceNode = "All Mice Items";
private const string GamePadNode = "All Joysticks and Gamepad Items";
private const string FeedbackNode = "All ForceFeedback Items";
```

Based on these constants, you can see that you will need to create five different nodes in the tree: one for all the items on your system, and then one section each for mice, keyboards, joysticks, and force feedback items. Everything in the "All Items" node should be duplicated in other nodes as well.

You should fill this node first. You will create a single function to do them all called "LoadDevices". The only object of this function will be to fill the tree view with the items currently on the system. You should add the method found in Listing 15.1 now.

**LISTING 15.1**   Adding Your Devices to the TreeView

```
public void LoadDevices()
{
    TreeNode allNodes = new TreeNode(AllItemsNode);
    // First get all devices
    foreach(DeviceInstance di in Manager.Devices)
    {
        TreeNode newNode = new TreeNode(string.Format("{0} - {1} ({2})",
            di.InstanceName, Manager.GetDeviceAttached(di.InstanceGuid)
            ? "Attached" : "Detached", di.InstanceGuid));
```

**LISTING 15.1** Continued

```
        allNodes.Nodes.Add(newNode);
    }
    treeView1.Nodes.Add(allNodes);
}
```

As you can see, the device enumerator class (DeviceList) that is returned from the Devices property returns a list of DeviceInstance structures. This structure contains all of the useful information on the devices, including the instance GUID (to use when creating the device), the product name, and the type of device.

You can also use another of the manager class methods here to check if the device is attached. It is entirely possible to have a device "available" on your system that isn't currently attached. It's important that you only use devices that are attached to your system.

Lastly, you add each device that was found into the parent node, and add that parent node into the tree view itself; all in all, it's quite simple. However, what if you wanted to only look for certain types of devices, for example, only the keyboards that are attached to the system? Add the code in Listing 15.2 directly below your all devices check in LoadDevices.

**LISTING 15.2** Adding Keyboards to Your TreeView

```
// Now get all keyboards
TreeNode kbdNodes = new TreeNode(KeyboardsNode);
foreach(DeviceInstance di in Manager.GetDevices(DeviceClass.Keyboard,
    EnumDevicesFlags.AttachedOnly))
{
    TreeNode newNode = new TreeNode(string.Format("{0} - {1} ({2})",
        di.InstanceName, Manager.GetDeviceAttached(di.InstanceGuid)
        ? "Attached" : "Detached", di.InstanceGuid));

    kbdNodes.Nodes.Add(newNode);
}
treeView1.Nodes.Add(kbdNodes);
```

The code here is remarkably similar to the all devices code, with the major exception being the actual enumeration being done. Rather than using the Devices property, you will use a new method on the manager class, GetDevices, which allows you to further specify the types of devices you will want to enumerate. In this case, you want all keyboard objects, and only the ones that are attached to the system. The mice and game pad code is pretty much the same, just using a different device class value:

```
// Now get all mice
TreeNode miceNodes = new TreeNode(MiceNode);
foreach(DeviceInstance di in Manager.GetDevices(DeviceClass.Pointer,
    EnumDevicesFlags.AttachedOnly))
{
    TreeNode newNode = new TreeNode(string.Format("{0} - {1} ({2})",
        di.InstanceName, Manager.GetDeviceAttached(di.InstanceGuid)
        ? "Attached" : "Detached", di.InstanceGuid));

    miceNodes.Nodes.Add(newNode);
}
treeView1.Nodes.Add(miceNodes);

// Now get all joysticks and gamepads
TreeNode gpdNodes = new TreeNode(GamePadNode);
foreach(DeviceInstance di in Manager.GetDevices(DeviceClass.GameControl,
    EnumDevicesFlags.AllDevices))
{
    TreeNode newNode = new TreeNode(string.Format("{0} - {1} ({2})",
        di.InstanceName, Manager.GetDeviceAttached(di.InstanceGuid)
        ? "Attached" : "Detached", di.InstanceGuid));

    gpdNodes.Nodes.Add(newNode);
}
treeView1.Nodes.Add(gpdNodes);
```

Notice that the mouse device class is Pointer? Pointer isn't restricted to mice; it's just the most common type. Screen pointers fall into this category as well. What if you wanted to enumerate only devices with the force feedback ability? It's not specific to any one device type necessarily; it's a feature you want to support. This check is quite simple as well:

```
// Now get all Force Feedback items
TreeNode ffNodes = new TreeNode(FeedbackNode);
foreach(DeviceInstance di in Manager.GetDevices(DeviceClass.All,
    EnumDevicesFlags.ForceFeeback))
{
    TreeNode newNode = new TreeNode(string.Format("{0} - {1} ({2})",
        di.InstanceName, Manager.GetDeviceAttached(di.InstanceGuid)
        ? "Attached" : "Detached", di.InstanceGuid));

    ffNodes.Nodes.Add(newNode);
}
treeView1.Nodes.Add(ffNodes);
```

The overall structure of the code remains the same; you've just changed the enumeration once more. Now you want to enumerate all device classes, but only those that support force feedback.

**OPENING THE CONTROL PANEL**

There is also a method on the Manager class called "RunControlPanel" that (much like its name implies) opens the control panel. This is useful for allowing customization of the devices you have on your system.

# Using the Keyboard Device

Each of the devices you can use in DirectInput have their own Device object, much like each graphics card and sound card have their own device objects. There are normally more DirectInput devices than the others though.

Creating a device requires a GUID to be passed in that is the same as the instance GUID you receive when enumerating your devices. It can also be a member of the SystemGuid object if you only want to create the default keyboard or mouse device. The devices that are created are generic enough to retrieve data from any device support by DirectInput.

Our first look at the device will start with the most common device, the keyboard. You will obviously need a device variable to use, so go ahead and declare one now:

```
private Device device = null;
```

Now, there are two ways you can use DirectInput. You can use a loop (the normal "game loop" mechanism) and get the current state of the device each frame. You can also set DirectInput up to notify you when the device state has changed so that you can update the game's state. This code will investigate the former mechanism first. Add the following initialization function:

```
private bool running = true;
public void InitializeInput()
{
    // Create our keyboard device
    device = new Device(SystemGuid.Keyboard);
    device.SetCooperativeLevel(this, CooperativeLevelFlags.Background |
        CooperativeLevelFlags.NonExclusive);
    device.Acquire();

    while(running)
    {
        UpdateInputState();
        Application.DoEvents();
    }
}
```

As you can see here, this is the entire "input" loop. You first create the device, using the standard keyboard GUID. If you remember from the DirectSound section, you must set the cooperative level of the devices, since they are shared throughout the system. The various flags that can be used (and combined) for the cooperative levels can be seen in Table 15.1.

**TABLE 15.1**

**DirectInput Cooperative Levels**

| FLAG | DESCRIPTION |
|------|-------------|
| Background | The device can be used in the background, and can be acquired at any time, even if the associated window isn't the active window. |
| Foreground | The device can only be used if the window is in the foreground. When this window loses focus, any acquired device will be unacquired. |
| Exclusive | The device requires exclusive access. While acquired exclusively, no other application can acquire the device exclusively. Nonexclusive acquires are still allowed. For security reasons, exclusive and background flags are not allowed to be used together on certain devices, like keyboards and mice. |
| NonExclusive | The device can be shared among many applications and does not require exclusive access. |
| NoWindowsKey | Disables the windows key. |

For this application you can use the foreground and non-exclusive flags. Before you can actually receive any data from the device, you will first need to acquire it. This allows you to retrieve the data from the device.

Finally, you go into a loop; as long as the application is running, you will update the input state of the device and call DoEvents (to allow the system to stay responsive). Before you write the UpdateInputState method, you will need to have something to hold the text you'll be writing. Create a text box on your form, with the multiline property and read-only property set to true, and the Dock property set to fill. Now you can add the following method to update this textbox:

```
private void UpdateInputState()
{
    // Check the keys currently pressed first
    string pressedKeys = "Using GetPressedKeys(): \r\n";
    foreach(Key k in device.GetPressedKeys())
        pressedKeys += k.ToString() + " ";

    textBox1.Text = pressedKeys;
}
```

Only two last things you need to do before you can try this application out. If you notice, the loop will run forever until the running variable is false, but that variable is never set to false anywhere. You want the application to quit when the form is closed, so you should set the variable to false there:

```
protected override void OnClosed(EventArgs e)
{
    running = false;
}
```

It might help if you actually call this InitializeInput method sometime as well. Update the main method as follows:

```
static void Main()
{
    using (Form1 frm = new Form1())
    {
        frm.Show();
        frm.InitializeInput();
    }
}
```

With all of these things out of way, you can now run this application. Notice how anytime you press a key, it shows up in the text box. You can also notice that all of the keys are named already, with no extra code required from you. The keys show up only while they are held down, and as soon as you let them go, they disappear from the UI again.

## HOLDING DOWN TOO MANY KEYS

Most keyboards can only maintain the state of five or so keys simultaneously. Holding more than this number of keys will result in the extra keys being "ignored."

While you can see that this method works, since there wasn't a game loop running already, the looping seems a little out of place. What would be better is for DirectInput to notify you when the device state has changed so that you can do the checks then. You can start a separate thread to wait for these notifications from DirectInput. Create a new method to initialize input from Listing 15.3.

**LISTING 15.3**    Initializing DirectInput and a Second Thread

```
private System.Threading.AutoResetEvent deviceUpdated;
private System.Threading.ManualResetEvent appShutdown;
public void InitializeInputWithThread()
```

## LISTING 15.3    Continued

```
    {
        // Create our keyboard device
        device = new Device(SystemGuid.Keyboard);
        device.SetCooperativeLevel(this, CooperativeLevelFlags.Background |
            CooperativeLevelFlags.NonExclusive);

        deviceUpdated = new System.Threading.AutoResetEvent(false);
        appShutdown = new System.Threading.ManualResetEvent(false);

        device.SetEventNotification(deviceUpdated);
        System.Threading.Thread threadLoop = new System.Threading.Thread(
            new System.Threading.ThreadStart(this.ThreadFunction));
        threadLoop.Start();
        device.Acquire();
    }
}
```

The basic premise of this method is the same as the last one; however, you've declared two wait handle variables. One of these is an AutoResetEvent that you will pass in to DirectInput; the other is a ManualResetEvent that you will use to notify the thread when the application is shutting down. You will also need a thread to sit around and wait for one of these events to be fired, so you create that as well and start that thread. So what does the thread function actually look like?

```
private void ThreadFunction()
{
    System.Threading.WaitHandle[] handles =
        { deviceUpdated, appShutdown };

    // Continue running this thread until the app has closed
    while(true)
    {
        int index = System.Threading.WaitHandle.WaitAny(handles);
        if (index == 0)
        {
            UpdateInputState();
        }
        else if (index == 1)
        {
            return;
        }
    }
}
```

This function is pretty much par for the course when dealing with multithreaded applications, and since you're not dealing with writing robust multithreaded code in this book, you can skip most of the mumbo jumbo. If the DirectInput device signals the event to notify you that the device has been updated, you call the UpdateInputState method; if our other event has been fired, return from this function, which will abort the thread.

Just like our looping method, you need to do two more things to "finish" this way. You need to set our event on application shut down by firing that event. Replace the OnClosed override with this one:

```
protected override void OnClosed(EventArgs e)
{
    if (appShutdown != null)
        appShutdown.Set();
}
```

You also need to modify our main function to call our new initialize method. Update the main function once more as follows:

```
static void Main()
{
    using (Form1 frm = new Form1())
    {
        frm.Show();
        frm.InitializeInputWithThread();
        Application.Run(frm);
    }
}
```

Most of the time, though, you don't want to get a list of the currently pressed keys; you want to detect if a certain key was pressed. In this scenario, you want to get the state of the keys and check this state against what you're looking for. For example, to see if the escape key was pressed, you would do something like

> **OPENING THE DEVICE-SPECIFIC CONTROL PANEL**
>
> Just like the manager class, there is a method on the device class called "RunControlPanel" as well. This method will open the device-specific control for that device. If you have a keyboard device created, this method will open the keyboard properties; for a mouse device, this will open the mouse properties. It can be useful to allow calibration or changing of the options.

```
KeyboardState state = device.GetCurrent KeyboardState();
if (state[Key.Escape])
{
    /* Escape was pressed */
}
```

# Using the Mouse Device

All of the DirectInput devices use this same device class, so the differences between using the mouse and keyboard are quite simple. You will need to update the device creation method in InitializeInput() to use a mouse GUID rather than the keyboard:

```
device = new Device(SystemGuid.Mouse);
```

In order to get the application working, the only other thing you will really need to change is the piece of code where you actually get the data, since the keyboard data doesn't make much sense for the mouse. Update the UpdateInputState method as follows:

```
private void UpdateInputState()
{
    // Check the mouse state
    MouseState state = device.CurrentMouseState;
    string mouseState = "Using CurrentMouseState: \r\n";

    // Current location of the mouse
    mouseState += string.Format("{0}x{1}x{2}\r\n", state.X,
        state.Y, state.Z);

    // Buttons
    byte[] buttons = state.GetMouseButtons();
    for(int i = 0; i < buttons.Length; i++)
        mouseState += string.Format("Button {0} {1}\r\n",
            i, buttons[i] != 0 ? "Pressed" : "Not Pressed");

    textBox1.Text = mouseState;
}
```

Here, instead of using a "helper" function to get the current data, you just take a complete snapshot of the mouse data currently. You then output the current X, Y, and Z of the mouse (the Z axis normally refers to the mouse wheel), as well as any of the buttons.

Running the application now, you'll notice that the majority of the time, the "position" of the mouse is reported as 0x0x0, even while you move it around. It's obvious you are really moving the mouse, so why isn't the UI being updated? In actuality, it is; however, the mouse data is being reported in relative units, as opposed to absolute values. That means the values reported for the different axes of the mouse are relative to the last frame. If you want to have the mouse data reported in absolute values, you can update your device's properties as follows (do this immediately after device creation):

```
device.Properties.AxisModeAbsolute = true;
```

While the application is running, it's quite obvious to see it being updated as the mouse moves around; however, the data returned for the axes initially is some crazy number. It is up to the application to keep track of this data to ensure that the mouse moves correctly in the application. The majority of applications will use the relative axis mode that is the default.

# Using Game Pads and Joysticks for User Input

While the basic idea of the joystick device is quite similar to the mouse and keyboard (since they do share the same device class), there are a few other things that need to happen for these, since they are much less standardized. You can pretty much guarantee that there will be two buttons on a mouse, and the keyboard will have at least 36 keys. Joysticks and game pads, on the other hand, come in all shapes and sizes. You may have one with two axes and two buttons, and then another with 3 axes, 10 buttons, two throttles, a pedal, and who knows what else.

There's also no default SystemGuid member for creating a joystick. You will need to enumerate the joysticks first. Update the device creation function using Listing 15.4.

**LISTING 15.4**    Initializing DirectInput for Joysticks

```
public bool InitializeInput()
{
    // Create our joystick device
    foreach(DeviceInstance di in Manager.GetDevices(DeviceClass.GameControl,
        EnumDevicesFlags.AttachedOnly))
    {
        // Pick the first attached joystick we see
        device = new Device(di.InstanceGuid);
        break;
    }
    if (device == null) // We couldn't find a joystick
        return false;

    device.SetDataFormat(DeviceDataFormat.Joystick);
    device.SetCooperativeLevel(this, CooperativeLevelFlags.Background |
        CooperativeLevelFlags.NonExclusive);
```

**LISTING 15.4**    Continued

```
    device.Properties.AxisModeAbsolute = true;
    device.Acquire();

    while(running)
    {
        UpdateInputState();
        Application.DoEvents();
    }

    return true;
}
```

Here you do the enumeration discussed at the beginning of this chapter to try to find an attached joystick or game pad. Since you didn't create the device with a system GUID, you will need to inform DirectInput about the type of device this is so that it knows how to interpret the data. You do this with the SetDataFormat method. A return value for the method has also been added so that the caller can know if the device creation has failed (because there is no device to create). With this, you will need to update the main function to handle this case:

```
static void Main()
{
    using (Form1 frm = new Form1())
    {
        frm.Show();
        if (!frm.InitializeInput())
            MessageBox.Show("Couldn't find a joystick.");
    }
}
```

Now, joysticks normally have a few axes that can be manipulated, and the range of these axes is unknown normally. You should treat all of the axes the same, with a "resolution" of 10,000 units. It's entirely possible that the device doesn't support this resolution, but DirectInput will fake it for you. You need to find the axes on the joystick and update the range. Add this code immediately after the device has been created:

```
// Enumerate any axes
foreach(DeviceObjectInstance doi in device.Objects)
{
    if ((doi.ObjectId & (int)DeviceObjectTypeFlags.Axis) != 0)
    {
        // We found an axis, set the range to a max of 10,000
        device.Properties.SetRange(ParameterHow.ById,
```

```
                    doi.ObjectId, new InputRange(-5000, 5000));
    }
}
```

Any device's objects can be enumerated in this fashion. Doing this on a keyboard, for example, will return an object for every key on the keyboard. Here, you only care about the axes that are found, and then you update the property of that object (doing so by ID) to ensure that the range falls within the values specified. The last thing you need to do is to update the UI. Update that method as follows:

```
private void UpdateInputState()
{
    // Check the joystick state
    JoystickState state = device.CurrentJoystickState;
    string joyState = "Using JoystickState: \r\n";

    joyState += string.Format("{0}x{1}",
        state.X, state.Y);

    textBox1.Text = joyState;
}
```

You could spend the time to use the preceding enumeration and detect every item in the joystick and update the UI, but the exercise doesn't really teach you anything you don't already know, so for this example, only update the x and y axes, which most all joysticks should have. The method looks remarkably like the mouse method, since the two aren't that dissimilar.

## SHOP TALK

### CONTROLLING THE RANGE

Game pads (and non-analog joysticks in general) will normally jump from one extreme of the range to the other. In the example earlier, when the game pad is "at rest", the value would naturally be 0. If you pressed the pad to the left, the x axis would go instantly to the minimum range value, while pressing right goes instantly to the maximum range value. There isn't any "smooth" movement of the values as you move the axis to the left; the values simply jump from one extreme to the other.

Most joysticks fall into one of two categories: a digital joystick or an analog joystick. The digital joystick is what was just described. There isn't a range of motion for pressing the axis to the left; it either happens or it does not. Analog joysticks, on the other hand, have this range built in. A good example of this is the flight controller sticks. There is a wide range of motion when moving the axes on these joysticks, and that wide range of motion can be seen when tracking the data.

# Using Force Feedback

Using force feedback in your application adds to the immersion a player experiences while using your application. Driving a car around at over 100 miles per hour, suddenly ramming into a tree, and having the joystick you're using jerk out of your hand from the force is an experience you just can't match. So, how can you add this to your applications?

One of the first things that needs mentioning is that force feedback effects will require you to have exclusive access to the device. Luckily, these joysticks can be acquired with exclusive mode and in the background. You will use a similar method to create the device for this example as you did for the joystick. Replace the existing InitializeInput method with the one found in Listing 15.5.

**LISTING 15.5** Initializing a Device for Force Feedback

```
private ArrayList effectList = new ArrayList();
public bool InitializeInput()
{
    // Create our joystick device
    foreach(DeviceInstance di in Manager.GetDevices(DeviceClass.GameControl,
        EnumDevicesFlags.AttachedOnly | EnumDevicesFlags.ForceFeeback))
    {
        // Pick the first attached joystick we see
        device = new Device(di.InstanceGuid);
        break;
    }
    if (device == null) // We couldn't find a joystick
        return false;

    device.SetDataFormat(DeviceDataFormat.Joystick);
    device.SetCooperativeLevel(this, CooperativeLevelFlags.Background |
        CooperativeLevelFlags.Exclusive);
    device.Properties.AxisModeAbsolute = true;
    device.Acquire();

    // Enumerate any axes
    foreach(DeviceObjectInstance doi in device.Objects)
    {
        if ((doi.ObjectId & (int)DeviceObjectTypeFlags.Axis) != 0)
        {
            // We found an axis, set the range to a max of 10,000
            device.Properties.SetRange(ParameterHow.ById,
```

**LISTING 15.5**   Continued

```
                    doi.ObjectId, new InputRange(-5000, 5000));
        }
    }

    // Load our feedback file
    EffectList effects = null;
    effects = device.GetEffects(@"..\..\idling.ffe",
        FileEffectsFlags.ModifyIfNeeded);
    foreach(FileEffect fe in effects)
    {
        EffectObject myEffect = new EffectObject(fe.EffectGuid, fe.EffectStruct,
                device);
        myEffect.Download();
        effectList.Add(myEffect);
    }

    while(running)
    {
        UpdateInputState();
        Application.DoEvents();
    }

    return true;
}
```

There are a few changes that have been made here. You've switched to exclusive access, since it's required for use with force feedback. You've also updated our enumeration to only return force feedback devices. You do the range setting once more, and finally get into the force feedback effects.

You can create the force feedback effect from a file. In actuality, each effect from a file can be an array of separate feedback effects. The code included on the CD (and in this text) will use the idling.ffe file that ships with the DirectX SDK. You will also find a copy with the source on the CD. After you've loaded the effect list from the file, you scan through each individual force feedback effect and create your effect object. You download this effect to the actual device so that it can use it and check its status, and finally add it to the local array list.

Now that you have the set of effects loaded, you will want to actually use them on the device. You should add a method that checks to see whether the effect is currently playing, and if it isn't, to start playing it. This will ensure that as long as our application is running, the effect will be playing:

```
private void PlayEffects()
{
    // See if our effects are playing.
    foreach(EffectObject myEffect in effectList)
    {
        if (!myEffect.EffectStatus.Playing)
        {
            // If not, play them
            myEffect.Start(1, EffectStartFlags.NoDownload);
        }
    }
}
```

## USING THE FORCE EDITOR

The Force Editor utility that ships with the DirectX SDK can be used to create any force feedback effect that you want. While it is possible to create these effects manually in your code, why hard code them into your application when you can just save them into a file, and use them from there?

You should add a call to PlayEffects into our UpdateInputState method as well so that it actually gets called.

# In Brief

- Controlling the keyboard
- Controlling the mouse
- Controlling joysticks and game pads
- Force feedback

In our next chapter, we will look at multiplayer opportunities by introducing peer-to-peer networking.

# PART V

# 2D Graphics

# Using Direct3D for 2D Graphics

This chapter will cover rendering 2D graphics in Direct3D, including

- Creating a full screen device.
- Using the Sprite class.
- Rendering sprites.

## Creating a Full Screen Rendering Device

Rendering complex 3D scenes is by definition "complex." While it is true that the vast majority of games being released currently use 3D graphics, there are still plenty of game types out there where the "fancy" graphics aren't necessary. It seems that more often than not these days, games that should be written in 2D are still written in 3D, just because you "have to."

Given that Direct3D can render complex 3D scenes, it should be no surprise that it is also quite capable of rendering a fully two-dimensional scene.

Creating a full screen device is not that much different from creating a windowed device. The same basic principles apply; there are just a few extra properties that will need to be filled out. Create a windows forms application that can be used to render the 2D graphics. You will need to add the using clauses, declare the device variable, and set the windows style before the application, like has been done in previous chapters.

Once the project has been created, you will need to add two constants for the full screen size:

```
public const int ScreenWidth = 800;
public const int ScreenHeight = 600;
```

These constants will represent the width and height of the full screen window that will be used for rendering. With the constants declared, you can now add the updated initialization method found in Listing 16.1.

**LISTING 16.1**   Initializing Your Full Screen Device

```
public void InitializeGraphics()
{
    // Set our presentation parameters
    PresentParameters presentParams = new PresentParameters();
    presentParams.SwapEffect = SwapEffect.Discard;

    // Start up full screen
    Format current = Manager.Adapters[0].CurrentDisplayMode.Format;

    if (Manager.CheckDeviceType(0, DeviceType.Hardware, current, current, false))
    {
        // Perfect, this is valid
        presentParams.Windowed = false;
        presentParams.BackBufferFormat = current;
        presentParams.BackBufferCount = 1;
        presentParams.BackBufferWidth = ScreenWidth;
        presentParams.BackBufferHeight = ScreenHeight;
    }
    else
    {
        presentParams.Windowed = true;
    }
    // Create our device
    device = new Device(0, DeviceType.Hardware, this,
        CreateFlags.SoftwareVertexProcessing, presentParams);
}
```

The beginning of this method should appear familiar. You'll notice that there is no depth buffer being declared for this device. Since the only objects being rendered will be 2D, and thus at the same depth, keeping the depth buffer provides no benefit. In actuality it's a performance hit, since the depth check will be performed for each sprite.

It's normally a safe assumption that the current display mode format of the default adapter is a valid format for a full screen device. Before blindly assuming this is the case, you should perform the check done here by calling the CheckDeviceType method. If this device type is supported, update the presentation parameters to specify a full screen device.

Naturally the windowed property must be false, since the device will run full screen, not in a window. The full screen properties are all maintained by the back buffer properties in your presentation parameters structure. The width and height of the back buffer should be set to the full screen size you wish to use, so the constants that were declared earlier are used here. The format is set to the default adapters display mode that was stored and checked to be supported.

If for some reason the check fails, you don't want the sample to just quit, so you can revert to windowed mode by setting the appropriate member in your presentation parameters structure. Once this structure has been filled out, you can actually create the device.

Since you will be rendering your scene in full screen mode, you will need an easy way to quit the application. Using the Escape key is a common way to quit, so add the following override to your code:

## HANDLING DEVICE CREATION FAILURES

It is entirely possible (although improbable) that the device creation will fail. Even though the format of the device was checked before creation, the back buffer sizes were not. An 800×600 screen is pretty common, and it would be uncommon to not have this support. For the full code of enumerating every possible display mode size, see Chapter 2, "Choosing the Correct Device."

## USING THE FULL SCREEN DEVICE

The full screen device isn't specific to drawing 2D graphics. Any device can be created in full screen mode, much like was done in this code. Follow the same pattern when creating your 3D device to render your 3D applications in full screen mode.

The earlier chapters covering 3D graphics focused mainly on windowed mode, given the larger difficulty in debugging code in full screen mode.

```
protected override void OnKeyUp(KeyEventArgs e)
{
    if (e.KeyCode == Keys.Escape) // Quit
        this.Close();

    base.OnKeyUp (e);
}
```

# Rendering Sprites

Direct3D already has an object that can be thought of as a sprite, namely the texture. However, textures must be rendered onto some type of primitives in order to be seen by the user. The Sprite class handles this work for you. Add the following variables for your application:

```
private Texture spriteTexture;
private Sprite sprite;
private Rectangle textureSize;
```

These obviously store the texture that will be used to render the sprite, as well as the sprite itself. You will also need to know the size of the texture in order to render it correctly, so that will be stored as well. At the end of your initialization method, directly after the device has been created, you will need to initialize these variables as follows:

```
// Create our texture
spriteTexture = TextureLoader.FromFile(device, @"..\..\logo.tga");

using (Surface s = spriteTexture.GetSurfaceLevel(0))
{
    SurfaceDescription desc = s.Description;
    textureSize = new Rectangle(0, 0, desc.Width, desc.Height);
}
sprite = new Sprite(device);
```

You will find the logo.tga file located on the enclosed CD. After the texture has been created, we will need to determine its size. We retrieve the underlying surface and use the description of this surface to store our texture's size. Finally, we create an instance of the sprite class.

Each instance of the sprite class can draw zero to many sprites, by using various textures. Rather than duplicate our sprite class and textures, we will create a new class to handle our multiple sprites. Add the class found in Listing 16.2.

## LISTING 16.2   The Custom Sprite Class

```
public class GraphicsSprite
{
    // static data for our sprites
    private static readonly Vector3 Center = new Vector3(0, 0, 0);
    private static readonly Random rnd = new Random();

    // Instance data for our sprites
    private Vector3 position;
    private float xUpdate = 1.4f;
```

**LISTING 16.2** Continued

```
    private float yUpdate = 1.4f;

    public GraphicsSprite(int posx, int posy)
    {
        position = new Vector3(posx,posy,1);
        xUpdate += (float)rnd.NextDouble();
        yUpdate += (float)rnd.NextDouble();
    }

    public void Draw(Sprite sprite, Texture t, Rectangle r)
    {
        sprite.Draw(t, r, Center, position, Color.White);
    }
}
```

Sprites can be rotated (even though this code won't perform this operation). When you draw the sprites, one of the parameters that must be passed in is the center of the sprite for rotation calculation. Rather than creating a new vector every time draw is called, it's easier to just store this here. The code should also add a little randomness to the sprites so that they don't appear to run the exact same way every time.

The class will need to store some data about each sprite it will be responsible for, namely the current position of the sprite and the speed at which it's moving. Separate speeds for both x and y will be stored so that the sprite won't be forced to move in 45-degree angles. Each is assigned a base value, but that will be randomly incremented.

The constructor takes the initial position of this sprite, and updates the speeds randomly. The only method left is where the actual drawing will take place. As you can see, the method is extremely simple. The method takes in the sprite and texture we will be using, as well as the size of the texture we stored. The color parameter is used to determine how to "shade" the rendered texture. Full white (as done here) will render the texture as it appears normally. Using red will give the texture a red tint as it's rendered. This color can be thought of like the materials you use for the meshes.

With the wrapper sprite class, the code can be updated to include drawing of the sprites. Before that happens, though, you will need to add a new variable to store the sprites you'll be rendering:

```
System.Collections.ArrayList ar = new System.Collections.ArrayList();
```

For ease of use, the ArrayList class can't be beat. Of course, an empty array list won't do much good, so you'll need to add some sprites. Add the following code into your initialization method directly after you've created your sprite:

```
// Add a few sprites
ar.Add(new GraphicsSprite(0,0));
ar.Add(new GraphicsSprite(64,128));
ar.Add(new GraphicsSprite(128,64));
ar.Add(new GraphicsSprite(128,128));
ar.Add(new GraphicsSprite(192,128));
ar.Add(new GraphicsSprite(128,192));
ar.Add(new GraphicsSprite(256,256));
```

Feel free to modify the number and location of the sprites you'll be adding. With sprites in the collection, the application can finally render something. In the OnPaint override after the BeginScene call, add the following code to render your sprites:

```
// Begin drawing our sprites with alpha blend
sprite.Begin(SpriteFlags.None);
// Draw each sprite in our list.
foreach(GraphicsSprite gs in ar)
    gs.Draw(sprite, spriteTexture, textureSize);
// Notify Direct3D we are done drawing sprites
sprite.End();
```

Before any sprites can be drawn, you need to tell Direct3D that you are about to render them. The Begin method accomplishes this. Then for every sprite in the collection, the Draw method is called. Every Begin call must be matched with an End call, so naturally one is included here.

With that out of the way, you could now run the application. One of the first things you'll probably notice is that the sprites don't seem to move, even though we're storing some speed information about them. Obviously, if nothing is ever done with this information, it's pretty useless. Add the method found in Listing 16.3 into the GraphicsSprite class.

**LISTING 16.3**   Updating Sprites

```
public void Update(Rectangle textureSize)
{
    // Update the current position
    position.X += xUpdate;
    position.Y += yUpdate;
    // See if we've gone beyond the screen
    if (position.X > (Form1.ScreenWidth - textureSize.Width))
    {
        xUpdate *= -1;
    }
```

**LISTING 16.3** Continued

```
if (position.Y > (Form1.ScreenHeight - textureSize.Height))
{
    yUpdate *= -1;
}

// See if we're too high or too the left
if (position.X < 0)
{
    xUpdate *= -1;
}
if (position.Y < 0)
{
    yUpdate *= -1;
}
}
```

In the update method, the position of the sprite is updated by the two separate speed variables. The position is then checked against the boundaries of the screen to make sure the sprite hasn't moved off screen, and if it has (or is about to), the direction is reversed. This will cause a "bouncing around the screen" effect on the sprites. This method will still need to be called, though, so add the following to the beginning of the OnPaint override:

```
// Before we render each sprite, make
sure we update them
foreach(GraphicsSprite gs in ar)
    gs.Update(textureSize);
```

Much like the actual draw calls, Update is called on each sprite in the collection. Running the application now will have your sprites bouncing all over your screen.

## RENDERING SPRITES WITH ALPHA

If you are using the texture that is included on the CD, you've probably noticed the white around the texture that covers everything. This texture has alpha (or transparency) information stored in it, which will cause the border to be transparent. Turning on support for this feature is quite simple. Change the following method:

```
sprite.Begin(SpriteFlags.None);
```

Instead, use this:

```
sprite.Begin(SpriteFlags.AlphaBlend);
```

Rendering the scene now will produce much more favorable results. See Figure 16.1.

**FIGURE 16.1** Bouncing sprites.

# Animating Your Sprites

Most applications that render 2D sprites will not simply render a static image continuously. The majority of times, they will render a series of consecutive images that form what appears to be animation. Since the basic principle of this rendering is the same as the static image written earlier, that code will be used as the starting point. Go ahead and make a copy of that code for this new application.

The major differences between this application and the last will be in the helper class being used to render the sprites. The initialization will be mostly the same, although the filename that the source code included with the CD uses has been changed to sprites.tga to emphasize the fact that there are multiple sprites stored in this one file.

First, since these will be small animated sprites flying around the screen, rather than the large static one, it makes more sense to have the position of these sprites initialized randomly. Update the constructor for the sprite class as follows:

```
public GraphicsSprite()
{
    position = new Vector3(rnd.Next(Form1.ScreenWidth-SpriteSize),
        rnd.Next(Form1.ScreenHeight-SpriteSize), 1);

    xUpdate += (float)rnd.NextDouble();
```

```
    yUpdate += (float)rnd.NextDouble();

    column = rnd.Next(NumberSpritesCol);
    row = rnd.Next(NumberSpritesRow);

    if ((column % 3) == 0)
        xUpdate *= -1;

    if ((row % 2) == 0)
        yUpdate *= -1;
}
```

The position of the sprite onscreen is determined by taking the width and height of the screen, subtracting the size of the sprite, and getting a random integer between zero and that value. However, the sprite size hasn't been defined yet. For the sprite that is stored on the included CD, the size of each frame of animation is 50×45. Define these constants now:

```
private const int SpriteSizeWidth = 50;
private const int SpriteSizeHeight = 45;
```

Once the position has been determined, the velocity is set to a random value between zero and one. You could multiply this value by two to simulate "quicker" sprites if need be. The sprites in this example are formed by a series of 50×45 images, each located in the file sequentially. The file is composed of five of these sprites per column, and a total of six rows. Store this information using constants:

```
private const int NumberSpritesRow = 6;
private const int NumberSpritesCol = 5;
```

You will also need to declare the variables that will be used to store the current animation frame:

```
private int column = 0;
private int row = 0;
```

Since the code is randomly picking the position, it may as well randomly pick a starting point for the animation as well. Once that is done, you don't want every sprite to be moving in the same direction (at random speeds), so some of the sprites' initial velocity will be reversed.

Now that the constructor for your sprite class has been changed, the code should no longer compile. You will need to replace the end of the initialization where the sprites were added with this:

```
// Add a few sprites
for(int i = 0; i < 100; i++)
    ar.Add(new GraphicsSprite());
```

This makes it much easier to add sprites to your application. Feel free to modify the number of sprites added at any time.

The update method will need to be modified next. Since you already know the size of each sprite, having the texture size as a parameter to this function is pointless. Also, you will need to update the animation frame being rendered anyway. Replace your method with the method found in Listing 16.4.

**LISTING 16.4**   Updating Your Animated Sprites

```
public void Update()
{
    // Update the current position
    position.X += xUpdate;
    position.Y += yUpdate;
    // See if we've gone beyond the screen
    if (position.X > (Form1.ScreenWidth - SpriteSizeWidth))
    {
        xUpdate *= -1;
    }
    if (position.Y > (Form1.ScreenHeight - SpriteSizeHeight))
    {
        yUpdate *= -1;
    }

    // See if we're too high or too the left
    if (position.X < 0)
    {
        xUpdate *= -1;
    }
    if (position.Y < 0)
    {
        yUpdate *= -1;
    }

    // Now update the column
    column++;
    if (column >= NumberSpritesCol)
    {
        row++;
        column = 0;
    }
```

**LISTING 16.4**  Continued

```
    if (row >= NumberSpritesRow)
    {
        row = 0;
    }
}
```

The beginning of this method is very similar to the last version, only it uses the sprite size instead of the passed-in texture size. However, at the end, the animation frame needs to be updated. Since the frame is stored simply as the column and row that should be rendered, the method simply increments the column. If you've reached the end of one column of sprites, move to the next row. If you've reached the end of the rows of sprites, move back to the beginning.

Again, with the method signature for the update code having been changed, the application will no longer compile. You can simply remove the parameter from your calls into update:

```
foreach(GraphicsSprite gs in ar)
    gs.Update();
```

The last thing that you should need to do for this application is to modify the Draw method and the call to this method. First, replace your Draw method with the following:

```
public void Draw(Sprite sprite, Texture t)
{
    sprite.Draw(t, new Rectangle(column * SpriteSizeWidth, row * SpriteSizeHeight,
        SpriteSizeWidth, SpriteSizeHeight), Center, position, Color.White);
}
```

As you can see here, the size has been removed from the parameter list. Instead, the source rectangle of the sprite is calculated using the animation frame data we have stored. Now you can update your OnPaint override to call this updated method:

```
foreach(GraphicsSprite gs in ar)
    gs.Draw(sprite, spriteTexture);
```

Running the application now, you should see some animated sprites flying around your screen. See Figure 16.2.

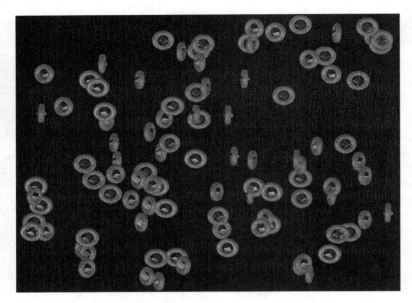

**FIGURE 16.2**   Animated sprites.

# In Brief

- Switching to full-screen mode.
- Rendering sprites.
- Rendering animated sprites.

In the next chapter we will look at each of the items covered in this chapter, only DirectDraw will be used instead.

# Using DirectDraw for 2D Rendering

One of the downsides of using Direct3D to render simple 2D applications is the hardware requirements. Direct3D is by its nature more complex than DirectDraw, and the minimum hardware requirements just for creating a Direct3D device can be too high for some systems. For example, laptops that are only a little over a year old at times don't have the capabilities of creating a Direct3D device, yet they can easily create a DirectDraw Device.

Even with the pervasive support Direct3D has in the graphics cards today, DirectDraw has even more. If you need to render 2D graphics with the minimum hardware requirements, DirectDraw will meet your needs quite nicely. In this chapter, we will cover the same types of rendering we did in the previous chapter, just using DirectDraw instead. These actions will include

- Creating a full screen device.

- Rendering sprites.

- Animating sprites.

# Creating a Full Screen DirectDraw Device

Before you can create your DirectDraw device, a new project will need to be created. Since this will still be an application where items will need to be rendered, windows forms should still be used. Use these steps to get started:

1. Create a new Windows Forms project named whatever you like.

2. Add a reference to Microsoft.DirectX.dll and Microsoft.DirectDraw.dll.

3. Include a new using clause for Microsoft.DirectX.DirectDraw into your main code file.

4. Set the window style to Opaque and AllPaintingInWmPaint, just like you did for 3D applications.

5. Add a private variable for your DirectDraw device.

You'll notice that most of these steps are similar to what was done for the 3D applications that were built in earlier chapters, with the major difference being the references that were added.

In DirectDraw you don't have textures that are used to represent your 2D images; instead you have "surfaces." A surface is essentially a data store for a rectangular image. When rendering a single sprite with a full-screen device, you will need a total of three surfaces. Add these to your application now:

```
private Surface primary = null;
private Surface backBuffer = null;
private Surface sprite = null;
```

Obviously the sprite surface will be where the actual image being rendered is stored. The first two parameters are something new, though. Since the screen itself is essentially a rectangular surface that you will be rendering to, you will use a surface to access this as well. Rendering directly to the video screen is never a good idea, because then you can have problems with what is called "tearing," which is when part of two (or more) different rendered scenes end up on the screen at the same time. To ensure this behavior doesn't happen, all of the rendering should happen in a stored back buffer, and then be copied to the primary buffer in one chunk. This is handled for you automatically in Direct3D (see Chapter 1, "Introducing Direct3D"), but you must handle it yourself in DirectDraw.

Before you go on, you should once again ensure that you handle the Escape key to quit. Since the application will be running in full screen mode, you want an easy way to quit. Add the following code to ensure your application exits on escape:

```
protected override void OnKeyUp(KeyEventArgs e)
{
    if (e.KeyCode == Keys.Escape) // Quit
```

```
        this.Close();

    base.OnKeyUp (e);
}
```

Now that an easy method to quit has been established, you can create your initialization method. Add the method found in Listing 17.1 to your application.

**LISTING 17.1**    Initialize a DirectDraw Device

```
public void InitializeGraphics()
{
    SurfaceDescription description = new SurfaceDescription();

    device = new Device();
    // Set the cooperative level.
    device.SetCooperativeLevel(this, CooperativeLevelFlags.FullscreenExclusive);
    // Set the display mode width and height, and 16 bit color depth.
    device.SetDisplayMode(ScreenWidth, ScreenHeight, 16, 0, false);

    // Make this a complex flippable primary surface with one backbuffer
    description.SurfaceCaps.PrimarySurface =
        description.SurfaceCaps.Flip =
        description.SurfaceCaps.Complex = true;
    description.BackBufferCount = 1;

    // Create the primary surface
    primary = new Surface(description, device);

    SurfaceCaps caps = new SurfaceCaps();
    caps.BackBuffer = true;
    // Get the backbuffer from the primary surface
    backBuffer = primary.GetAttachedSurface(caps);

    // Create the sprite bitmap surface.
    sprite = new Surface(@"..\..\logo.bmp",
        new SurfaceDescription(), device);

    // Set the colorkey to the bitmap surface.
    // which is what the ColorKey struct is initialized to.
    ColorKey ck = new ColorKey();
    sprite.SetColorKey(ColorKeyFlags.SourceDraw, ck);
}
```

As you can see, this method is slightly more complicated than the Direct3D version. After your DirectDraw device has been created, you will need to call the SetCooperativeLevel method, which notifies DirectDraw how you plan on cooperating with other applications wishing to share the graphics card resources. Since this application will be full screen, there's no need to share the resources. Using the option FullScreenExclusive tells DirectDraw this.

After the device has been created and the cooperative level has been set, you can now change the display mode. The first two parameters are the width and height of the updated display mode, respectively. The third parameter is the color depth you want the display mode to be in. 16-bit color is the most commonly used format. 32-bit color gives you a larger array of colors to use, but uses double the amount of resources. The fourth parameter is the refresh rate the monitor should use; for most applications simply using zero for the monitor default should be sufficient. The last parameter indicates whether this mode is a standard VGA mode. It's a rare case when this would be used.

With the device in a good state now, it's time to create our surfaces. First, the primary surface should be created. Each surface that is created must be created with a surface description describing that surface. In this case, the primary surface description will include the options of PrimarySurface (naturally), Flip, and Complex. These options inform DirectDraw that not only will this be the primary surface, it will be flippable and complex. Complex surfaces have other surfaces attached, and in this case, the attached surface will be the back buffer surface. This is the reason for the back buffer count of one for this description.

With this surface description, you can now create the primary surface. From that surface, the back buffer surface can be retrieved by calling the GetAttachedSurface method on the primary surface. With the first two surfaces created, the last item that needs to be created is the actual sprite surface. The code included on the CD uses the dx5_logo.bmp that ships as part of the DirectX SDK as the sprite to render. Since the surface will be created from the file, no extra information is needed for creating this surface, thus the "empty" surface description.

## SHOP TALK

### TRANSPARENCY IN DIRECTDRAW

DirectDraw does not support the alpha blending features that exist in Direct3D. In the Direct3D version of this application, we used simple alpha blending techniques to ensure that the "background" of our sprite was rendered transparent. DirectDraw has no support for doing alpha blending, so transparency is rendered by using a "color key." This color key essentially turns one particular color in a sprite transparent. While this is useful and works quite well for 2D applications, it has its drawbacks, the most notable of which is that you cannot use the color specified as the color key anywhere in your image.

In this application, the image being used has a black background, so black will be used as the color key. Since the color key structure initializes to zero, which happens to be the color key for black, no further work needs to be done other than to set the color key on the sprite.

The initialization method uses a few constants that haven't been declared yet. Go ahead and add those now:

```
public const int ScreenWidth = 800;
public const int ScreenHeight = 600;
private static readonly Rectangle SpriteSize =
    new Rectangle(0,0,256,256);
```

The screen width and height constants have been used before. Since the image file that will be used as the sprite is of known size, storing this size is easier than determining the size later. If you did want to calculate the size, you could simply look at the Width and Height members of the surface description structure after the surface has been created.

You will need to call the initialize method at some point, and the main method is the ideal place. Update this method much like the Direct3D applications were used:

```
static void Main()
{
    using (Form1 frm = new Form1())
    {
        // Show our form and initialize our graphics engine
        frm.Show();
        frm.InitializeGraphics();
        Application.Run(frm);
    }
}
```

Now, once again you will need a wrapper class that will be used to maintain your sprites' information. Add the following class to your application:

```
public class GraphicsSprite
{
    // static data for our sprites
    private static readonly Random rnd = new Random();

    // Instance data for our sprites
    private int xPosition = 0;
    private int yPosition = 0;
    private float xUpdate = 1.4f;
    private float yUpdate = 1.4f;

    /// <summary>
    /// Constructor for our sprite
    /// </summary>
```

```
/// <param name="posx">Initial x position</param>
/// <param name="posy">Initial y position</param>
public GraphicsSprite(int posx, int posy)
{
    xPosition = posx;
    yPosition = posy;

    xUpdate += (float)rnd.NextDouble();
    yUpdate += (float)rnd.NextDouble();
}
}
```

This class will store the current position of the sprite's upper-left corner. You will notice that in this case, two separate integer values are stored, rather than the Vector3 that was used in the Direct3D example. Since DirectDraw only deals with screen coordinates, the position will be integer values rather than the floats used in Direct3D. Since there is no depth in a DirectDraw application, the third member isn't needed at all.

The class will still store the velocity for each direction separately, in order to have the sprites bounce around the screen. The constructor for the class will take the initial position of the sprite, as well as randomly incrementing the velocity in each direction, so all sprites don't follow the same pattern.

Now, you should update your sprite class to handle the movement and drawing. Add the two methods found in Listing 17.2 to your sprite class.

**LISTING 17.2**  Updating and Drawing Your Sprites

```
public void Draw(Surface backBuffer, Surface spriteSurface,
    Rectangle spriteSize)
{
    backBuffer.DrawFast(xPosition, yPosition, spriteSurface, spriteSize,
        DrawFastFlags.DoNotWait ¦ DrawFastFlags.SourceColorKey);
}

public void Update(Rectangle spriteSize)
{
    // Update the current position
    xPosition += (int)xUpdate;
    yPosition += (int)yUpdate;
    // See if we've gone beyond the screen
    if (xPosition > (Form1.ScreenWidth - spriteSize.Width))
```

**LISTING 17.2** Continued

```
    {
        xUpdate *= -1;
    }
    if (yPosition > (Form1.ScreenHeight - spriteSize.Height))
    {
        yUpdate *= -1;
    }

    // See if we're too high or too the left
    if (xPosition < 0)
    {
        xUpdate *= -1;
    }
    if (yPosition < 0)
    {
        yUpdate *= -1;
    }
}
```

The drawing call takes in the back buffer surface that you will render to (remember, you don't want to render directly to the screen), as well as the sprite's surface and its size. The DrawFast call from the back buffer simply draws the sprite at the location specified, using the full sprite as the source material (the size). The flags tell DirectDraw that it shouldn't wait if the draw cannot be completed immediately, and that the source color key should be used for transparency (which was set up when the sprite was created).

The update method is virtually identical to the Direct3D version. The position of the sprite is updated by the velocity, and the direction is reversed if the sprite has come to a border. With the sprite class now

## UNDERSTANDING THE DIFFERENCES BETWEEN DRAW AND DRAWFAST

When the calls to Draw and DrawFast are hardware accelerated (which is most likely the case in any modern graphics card), there is no difference between these two calls. However, if there is a case where the methods are called using software, the DrawFast method will be approximately 10% faster than the Draw method.

This speed increase does not come without a cost, though. The DrawFast method is much less robust. The Draw method allows the sprite being rendered to be stretched or shrunk. It allows many different drawing operations as well. For simple drawing operations like this one, you will always want to use DrawFast.

complete, you will need to maintain a list of sprites for your application. The same method that was used for the Direct3D example will be used here, so add the following variable to your main class:

```
System.Collections.ArrayList ar = new System.Collections.ArrayList();
```

You'll still need to add some sprites to your collection now, and you can use the same code that was used before. Add the following to the end of your initialization method:

```
// Add a few sprites
ar.Add(new GraphicsSprite(0,0));
ar.Add(new GraphicsSprite(64,128));
ar.Add(new GraphicsSprite(128,64));
ar.Add(new GraphicsSprite(128,128));
ar.Add(new GraphicsSprite(192,128));
ar.Add(new GraphicsSprite(128,192));
ar.Add(new GraphicsSprite(256,256));
```

The only thing left is to add the rendering to our main class. This application will use the same mechanism for the rendering, so add the following override into your windows form class:

```
protected override void OnPaint(System.Windows.Forms.PaintEventArgs e)
{
    Microsoft.DirectX.DirectXException.IgnoreExceptions();
    foreach(GraphicsSprite gs in ar)
        gs.Update(SpriteSize);

    backBuffer.ColorFill(0);
    foreach(GraphicsSprite gs in ar)
        gs.Draw(backBuffer, sprite, SpriteSize);

    primary.Flip(backBuffer, FlipFlags.DoNotWait);
    this.Invalidate();
}
```

The very first thing this method does is to turn off all Managed DirectX exception throwing. This will be explained briefly, but you should use this method with extreme caution, as it will disable *all* exception throwing from Managed DirectX.

Now each sprite is updated based on the stored size, much like the 3D version of this application. Next, in place of the Clear method the Direct3D application used, the back buffer will simply be filled with a solid color. In this case, black will be used.

Next, each sprite in your collection will be rendered to the back buffer. With everything now rendered into the back buffer, you are ready to update the screen. Simply call the Flip method on the primary buffer, passing in the back buffer where everything has been rendered. This will update the screen with the contents of the back buffer. Finally, invalidate the window's contents, so that the OnPaint override will be called again immediately, and there is a constant state of rendering going on.

Running the application now should show similar results to the Direct3D version of this application.

# Animating Your Sprites

To follow the same pattern that was used in the previous chapter, you should now make a copy of this code so that it can be updated to show some animated sprites.

The major changes will once again happen in the sprite class. The same constants that were used before can be used now:

```
private const int NumberSpritesRow = 6;
private const int NumberSpritesCol = 5;
private const int SpriteSizeWidth = 50;
private const int SpriteSizeHeight = 45;
```

The source code included on the CD uses the file sprites.bmp for the sprites to be rendered, which is the same file used in the previous chapter, just with different dimensions and no alpha channel.

You will need to store the animation frame as well, which is a combination of a row and column. Add those variables to your sprite class:

## DISABLING EXCEPTION HANDLING

As written, this application can be expected to throw two separate exceptions. The first is the WasStillDrawingException, which will happen if you attempt to flip the primary surface or draw to the back buffer while the system is busy completing a previous draw operation. In Direct3D, this scenario is simply ignored if you are using the SwapEffect.Discard flag for your device. Ignoring this exception simply emulates that behavior.

The second exception that can be expected is the InvalidRectangleException. In Direct3D, if your sprites happen to be slightly offscreen, it doesn't really matter since the device deals in world space, which is essentially infinite. In DirectDraw, this isn't the case, and trying to render a sprite when the rectangle will go out of the bounds of the screen is not allowed. You could alter the logic of the application to ensure that this scenario never happens, but for our simple example, ignoring this case is desirable.

## USING NON-SQUARE SURFACES

In Direct3D textures are normally required not only to be square, but to also have each side have a length that is a power of two. Most of the modern cards out today have support for textures that don't fit these parameters, but even those that do can suffer a performance loss for using "irregularly" shaped textures.

In the previous chapter, the animated sprites file was "enlarged" to be a square with a power-of-two length, with the remaining area being filled with "unused" data just to ensure that the texture could be loaded on most cards. DirectDraw does not enforce these rules on the surfaces it creates, thus the sprite in this example is of the exact size needed to hold the data.

```
private int column = 0;
private int row = 0;
```

Now, you will need to update the constructor, to randomly place the sprite somewhere on the screen, with a random animation frame:

```
public GraphicsSprite()
{
    xPosition = rnd.Next(Form1.ScreenWidth-SpriteSizeWidth);
    yPosition = rnd.Next(Form1.ScreenHeight-SpriteSizeHeight);

    xUpdate += (float)rnd.NextDouble();
    yUpdate += (float)rnd.NextDouble();

    column = rnd.Next(NumberSpritesCol);
    row = rnd.Next(NumberSpritesRow);

    if ((column % 3) == 0)
        xUpdate *= -1;

    if ((row % 2) == 0)
        yUpdate *= -1;
}
```

The Draw method will also need updating:

```
public void Draw(Surface backBuffer, Surface spriteSurface)
{
    backBuffer.DrawFast(xPosition, yPosition, spriteSurface,
            new Rectangle(column * SpriteSizeWidth, row * SpriteSizeHeight,
        SpriteSizeWidth, SpriteSizeHeight), DrawFastFlags.DoNotWait |
        DrawFastFlags.SourceColorKey);
}
```

As you see, we calculate the source rectangle based on the animation frame and the sprite size. Once again, the sprite is drawn using the source color key transparency. Finally, you will need to make the Update method handle the animation as well. See Listing 17.3:

LISTING 17.3   Updating Your Animated Sprites

```
public void Update()
{
    // Update the current position
    xPosition += (int)xUpdate;
```

**LISTING 17.3**   Continued

```
    yPosition += (int)yUpdate;
    // See if we've gone beyond the screen
    if (xPosition > (Form1.ScreenWidth - SpriteSizeWidth))
    {
        xUpdate *= -1;
    }
    if (yPosition > (Form1.ScreenHeight - SpriteSizeHeight))
    {
        yUpdate *= -1;
    }

    // See if we're too high or too the left
    if (xPosition < 0)
    {
        xUpdate *= -1;
    }
    if (yPosition < 0)
    {
        yUpdate *= -1;
    }

    // Now update the column
    column++;
    if (column >= NumberSpritesCol)
    {
        row++;
        column = 0;
    }
    if (row >= NumberSpritesRow)
    {
        row = 0;
    }
}
```

With the sprite class finally updated, your main class should have a few compilation errors now. First, replace your sprite creation code:

```
// Add a few sprites
for(int i = 0; i < 100; i++)
    ar.Add(new GraphicsSprite());
```

The last two items that need updating are both in the rendering code, but are removing the size parameter that is passed into the sprite methods. You can replace this method with the following:

```
protected override void OnPaint(System.Windows.Forms.PaintEventArgs e)
{
    DirectXException.IgnoreExceptions();
    foreach(GraphicsSprite gs in ar)
        gs.Update();

    backBuffer.ColorFill(0);
    foreach(GraphicsSprite gs in ar)
        gs.Draw(backBuffer, sprite);

    primary.Flip(backBuffer, FlipFlags.DoNotWait);
    this.Invalidate();
}
```

As you can see, the differences between Direct3D and DirectDraw aren't as all-encompassing as some people seem to think. While it's true that porting a fully 3D application to DirectDraw is next to impossible, it would be relatively simple to port any 2D application from one to the other.

# In Brief

- Switching to full screen exclusive mode.

- Rendering a single image as a sprite onscreen.

- Rendering animated sprites.

In the next chapter we will look at peer-to-peer networking.

# PART VI

# Adding Networking

# Implementing Peer-to-Peer Networking Using DirectPlay

# 18

In this chapter, we will look at the peer-to-peer networking aspects of DirectPlay, including the following:

- DirectPlay addresses

- The peer object

- The event model of DirectPlay

- Sending data to other members of your session

## Understanding DirectPlay Addresses

Playing single-player games can be fun and exciting, but it's nothing compared to playing against real live people. Even game consoles that were notoriously single player have begun offering online play and matchmaking services. It's rare to see top-of-the-line games coming out nowadays without some form of multiplayer features. There is also an entire class of quite popular games that have no single-player options at all; they are only multiplayer.

Managed DirectX includes the DirectPlay API that can be used for implementing a networking layer. Before we begin the code for this chapter, we will once again need to ensure that we have the right references for DirectPlay. Ensure that you have the Microsoft.DirectX.DirectPlay reference included in your projects, as well as the using clause. All of the code in this chapter assumes this has already been done.

If you have a computer that can connect to the Internet, your computer already has a TCP/IP address. Each computer needs to have a unique "address" that distinguishes it from other computers on a network. While it's true that TCP/IP addresses are not unique, they are unique within a single network. TCP/IP addresses are the standard address of the Internet.

DirectPlay also needs a way to distinguish one computer from another, and each networked computer must have a unique address. The act of creating a unique DirectPlay address isn't all that difficult. Let's look at the code:

```
Address address = new Address();
address.ServiceProvider = Address.ServiceProviderTcpIp;
```

As the preceding code implies, there is more than one service provider that DirectPlay can use. We've chosen in this instance to use the TCP/IP provider, which is by far the most common service provider available in computers today. The service providers available to DirectPlay by default are

- TCP/IP
- IPX
- BlueTooth
- Serial connections
- Direct modem-modem connections

We will deal with only the TCP/IP service provider when dealing with DirectPlay. I won't spend the time to go into details of the other service providers; if you don't know about them already, chances are you won't need to write any applications using them. Besides, the DirectPlay object model is designed to work the same, regardless of the service provider in use. All of the code we write using the TCP/IP service provider applies directly to any of the other service providers.

## USING URLS AS ADDRESSES

Addresses can also be specified in URL (Uniform Resource Locator) form, much like Web addresses. If you've seen an address like http://www.mycompany.com, you've seen an URL. The first "section" of the URL is the protocol type, in this case http (or Hypertext Transfer Protocol). The Web pages you see are normally HTML (Hypertext Markup Language), thus the name of the protocol. In DirectPlay, these URLs take on a construct; for example, the address we just created could also be specified as

```
x-directplay:/provider=%7BEBFE7BA0-628D-11D2-
    AE0F-006097B01411%7D;hostname=
    www.mygameserver.com;port=9798
```

If you'll notice, the type of this URL is x-directplay, or a DirectPlay address. The rest of the address specifies the components of the address, the service provider GUID, the host name, and the port. There is an URL property on the address object that you can use to get the current URL of the address, or set it to a new value.

*SHOP TALK*

## USING TCP/IP ADDRESSES

There are four constructors for the address object, the majority of which deal with the TCP/IP service provider. The parameterless constructor that we've already used is the only constructor that doesn't set the service provider automatically. The other three constructors will each set the service provider to TCP/IP. These constructors are as follows:

```
public Address ( System.String hostname , System.Int32 port )
public Address ( System.Net.IPAddress address )
public Address ( System.Net.IPEndPoint address )
```

Each of these constructors performs the same operation, just with different data sets. The first creates a TCP/IP address, sets the host name to the string provided, and sets the port to the number specified. The host name can be a computer name, an Internet address (for example, www.mycompany.com), or an IP address (for example, 192.168.2.1). Each TCP/IP connection happens on a particular port (for example, Web browsers request data on port 80), and the second parameter allows you to specify this port. Each of the other two parameters can take existing TCP/IP addresses (provided in the .NET Runtime) and convert them into the equivalent DirectPlay address.

In our first example of code, we never mentioned any "hostname" or "port." How exactly can you add these members to an address? It's quite simple actually. The address object has a method to add various components such as the hostname and port. Each component has a name (a string value) and associated data, either a string, a GUID, an integer, or a byte array. The address class itself has the standard key names attached to itself. Here is the code to manually attach the hostname and port to an existing address:

```
Address address = new Address();
address.ServiceProvider = Address.ServiceProviderTcpIp;
address.AddComponent(Address.KeyHostname, "www.mygameserver.com");
address.AddComponent(Address.KeyPort, 9798);
```

In actuality the parameterized constructors for the Address class do this exact set of steps, replacing the host name and port with the values you specify. There are many default key names that can be used (for example KeyPhoneNumber for direct modem-to-modem connections), plus you can make up your own keys.

It's important to realize that the hostname component in particular is really only important when you are connecting to another computer. DirectPlay is smart enough to figure out your own hostname, so this key is not needed for local addresses.

# Creating a Peer Connection

With the basics of addressing out of the way, we can move on to actually getting a connection made, and really start to network. The types of networking that DirectPlay supports would be peer-to-peer and client/server. In this chapter, we will discuss the peer-to-peer connections.

So what is a peer-to-peer connection? As the name implies, each member (or peer) of a session is connected to every other member (or peer) in the session. For small sessions, this method works quite well. There are many examples of peer-to-peer networks that are quite popular today. Many of the file-sharing programs out there today (Kazaa, Napster, and so on) are peer-to-peer networks.

Before you can begin a peer-to-peer session in DirectPlay, you must first decide a few things. What service provider do you want the connection to use? Will you be "hosting" this connection, or will you connect to an existing session? You can think of the first peer in a session as the "master" peer, or host of the session.

The main class that we will use for our session is (I'm sure you've guessed it) the Peer object. It's always easier to see things visually while looking at code, so let's start writing some now. Declare a variable for our peer object, and our addresses:

```
private Peer connection = null;
private Address deviceAddress = null;
```

You'll notice that we have our address declared. We will maintain this address to hold the connection information for our local machine. We also maintain a peer object for our connection.

In the design view for your form, create two buttons in the upper right corner. The first will be to "Host" a session, while the second will be to "Connect" to an existing session. Add a third button to the upper right corner of your form; this will be to send any data throughout the session. This third button should be disabled at first (we don't want to send any data before we are in a session). Finally, create a large label to fill up the bottom portion of the UI. This will be our status screen. With the plumbing work out of the way, we're ready to start networking.

We will create one initialization function to set up our peer object and any default state. Let's examine the function in Listing 18.1 now.

**LISTING 18.1**   Initializing a Peer Object

```
private void InitializeDirectPlay(bool host)
{
    // Create our peer object
    connection = new Peer();

    // Check to see if we can create a TCP/IP connection
```

**LISTING 18.1**  Continued

```
    if (!IsServiceProviderValid(Address.ServiceProviderTcpIp))
    {
        // Nope, can't, quit this application
        MessageBox.Show("Could not create a TCP/IP service provider.", "Exiting",
            MessageBoxButtons.OK, MessageBoxIcon.Information);
        this.Close();
    }
    // Create a new address for our local machine
    deviceAddress = new Address();
    deviceAddress.ServiceProvider = Address.ServiceProviderTcpIp;
}
```

This method will get much larger before we're done. For now though, what is it doing? Well, first we create our peer object using the default constructor. There is one other constructor available that takes in initialization flags that we didn't use. These flags can be one or more of the values found in Table 18.1.

**TABLE 18.1**

**Peer Creation Flags**

| FLAG | DESCRIPTION |
| --- | --- |
| DisableParamaterValidation | Using this flag will disable the parameter validation for this connection. This will increase performance; commonly, retail versions of applications will set this flag. |
| DisableLinkTuning | Using this flag will disable DirectPlay from attempting to tune the rate it sends data. All messages will be pushed into the network as soon as possible. |
| HintLanSession | Opens a larger send window for games running on a LAN. |
| None | Default options, same as using the default constructor. |

These options can be quite useful, but for this simple application, they're a little overboard, so we'll just use the default constructor. We want to use the TCP/IP service provider for this application, but how do we know if this provider exists on this machine? Well, we can check, and that's what this IsServiceProviderValid method will do. Look at this method:

```
private bool IsServiceProviderValid(Guid provider)
{
    // Ask DirectPlay for the service provider list
    ServiceProviderInformation[] providers =
        connection.GetServiceProviders(true);

    // For each service provider in the returned list...
    foreach (ServiceProviderInformation info in providers)
```

```
    {
        // Compare the current provider against the passed provider
        if (info.Guid == provider)
            return true;
    }

    // Not found
    return false;
}
```

This method will retrieve every available service provider on the system and return an array of information about each one. If we had passed in "true" as the parameter, rather than false, it would enumerate *all* providers, including those that weren't available at the time. Part of the information returned is the GUID of the service provider, which we can compare to the one we're passing in. If we find this GUID in the returned array, we can assume this service provider exists; otherwise, it does not.

Finally, if we find that the service provider for TCP/IP is not valid, we will inform the user and quit the application. Otherwise, we will create our device address using the TCP/IP service provider. You must also ensure that you dispose of the peer object when you are finished with it; otherwise there is a good chance bad things will happen when shutting down your application. There is already a default override for Dispose, so you can simply add the following code to the beginning of this method:

```
if (connection != null)
    connection.Dispose();
```

Now we need to implement our code for hosting or joining a session.

# Getting into a Session

We have two buttons on our form for either hosting or connecting to an existing session. Once we try to do either of these actions, we will need to disable these buttons so that we can't try to do more than one action at a time. The event handlers for these two buttons would be

```
private void button1_Click(object sender, System.EventArgs e)
{
    button1.Enabled = false;
    button2.Enabled = false;
    InitializeDirectPlay(true);
}
```

```
private void button2_Click(object sender, System.EventArgs e)
{
    button1.Enabled = false;
    button2.Enabled = false;
    InitializeDirectPlay(false);
}
```

As you see, they are both remarkably similar. The only difference between the two is the parameter they pass in to the InitializeDirectPlay method; one uses true to host, the other uses false to connect. We could simplify this by having each button use the same event handler:

```
private void button_Click(object sender, System.EventArgs e)
{
    button1.Enabled = false;
    button2.Enabled = false;
    InitializeDirectPlay((sender == button1));
}
```

Much nicer; this eliminates the duplicated code and achieves the exact same behavior. If the sender of the event happens to be the first button (our hosting button), it will call InitializeDirectPlay with true; otherwise, it will call it with false. Hook each button's event in this way. We never actually did anything with the parameter for this method, though. We should look at that now.

Before we can either host a session or connect to an existing one, we will need a way to "recognize" a session. DirectPlay includes an application description structure that will contain all of the information we need to describe an application. Let's look at the code we'll use for our application description; add this to the end of the InitializeDirectPlay method:

```
// Set up an application description
ApplicationDescription desc = new ApplicationDescription();
desc.SessionName = "MDXBookPeerSession";
desc.GuidApplication = new Guid(41039, 1702,1503,178, 101,
    32, 13, 121, 230, 109, 59);
```

The most important member of this structure is the GuidApplication member. This GUID uniquely identifies your application, and all instances of your application must use the same GUID for this member. The other member we set is the session name. This is useful for when there are many sessions available to help identify yours. You will find all of the members of the ApplicationDescription structure in Table 18.2.

**TABLE 18.2**

**ApplicationDescription Members**

| MEMBER | DESCRIPTION |
| --- | --- |
| GuidApplication | Uniquely identify your application. |
| GuidInstance | A unique identifier for your session, generated by DirectPlay. This is to identify separate instances of your application running simultaneously. |
| MaxPlayers | The maximum number of users allowed in a given session. Setting this value to zero (the default) will allow an unlimited number of players. |
| CurrentPlayers | The number of users currently in the session. |
| Flags | Used to define the session behavior, may be one or more of the following flags: <br>■ ClientServer<br>■ FastSigned<br>■ FullSigned<br>■ MigrateHost<br>■ NoDpnServer<br>■ NoEnumerations<br>■ RequirePassword |
| SessionName | User-defined name of the session. |
| Password | The password needed to join the session. This value must be null unless the RequirePassword flag is set. |

With the application description created now, we are ready to get into a session. Since we need to have a session exist before we can connect to it, we will deal with the hosting code first. Add the following to the end of the initialize method:

```
if (host)
{
    try
    {
        // Host a new session
        connection.Host(desc, deviceAddress);
        // We can assume after the host call succeeds we are hosting
        AddText("Currently Hosting a session.");
        EnableSendDataButton(true);
    }
    catch
    {
        AddText("Hosting this session has failed.");
    }
}
```

As you can see, the Host call is relatively straightforward. We've used the simplest overload for our call that takes only the application description and our local address. There are, however, eight separate overloads for the Host method. Each of these overloads take in the application description, and either one or more address objects, as these are the only required parameters. You may also pass in an object to be used as a player context variable (we'll describe these shortly). You may also pass a member of the HostFlags enumeration. There is currently only one member of this enumeration, which allows DirectPlay to open a windows dialog to query for any missing addressing information.

## PASSWORDS ARE NOT ENCRYPTED

Be careful when using passwords with these sessions. Whatever data you pass in to this member will be sent across the network in plain text, with no encryption. If you want to safeguard your passwords, you will need to encrypt them manually before sending them out.

We wrap our Host call into a try/catch block to allow for the case when the method fails for some reason. We could catch only exceptions derived from the DirectPlayExcetion class, but for this simple example, we'll simply catch them all. There are two methods we haven't seen before that will simply update the UI. We'll look at these now:

```
private void AddText(string text)
{
    label1.Text += (text + "\r\n");
}
private void EnableSendDataButton(bool enable)
{
    button3.Enabled = enable;
}
```

No need to go into these methods as they are quite self-explanatory. Running this application now and hitting the host button will start a DirectPlay peer-to-peer session, display a status message to this affect, and enable the send data button. With all that done, all we need now is another peer to connect to our session. Add the following clause to the end of the initialize method:

```
else
{
    try
    {
        connection.FindHosts(desc, null, deviceAddress, null,
            0, 0, 0, FindHostsFlags.OkToQueryForAddressing);

        AddText("Looking for sessions.");
    }
    catch
```

```
    {
        AddText("Enumeration of sessions has failed.");
    }
}
```

Once again, we wrap our method in a try/catch block to be notified of any errors, as well as update our UI based on what we are doing. However, we aren't calling the Connect method; we are calling the FindHosts method. In some cases, it is possible to directly connect to an existing session; however, in most cases you will need to search for any existing hosts first.

Much like the Host method, the FindHosts method takes in the application description, as well as the local device address. The second parameter is the host's address, which we don't happen to know right now, so we can just use null for this parameter. The fourth parameter for this method is any application-defined data you want to pass in to the server. The server can use this information in anyway it wants.

The next three parameters control the behavior of how the hosts are enumerated. They control the number of times to send out the enumeration packets, how often it should wait before retrying another enumeration, and finally the time out value of the enumerations. By specifying zero for each of these parameters, the default values for the service provider will be used. The last parameter can be one or more members of the FindHostsFlags enumeration. The possible values of this enumeration are listed in Table 18.3.

### TABLE 18.3

**Possible FindHostFlags Values**

| VALUE | DESCRIPTION |
| --- | --- |
| None | Using this flag will implement the default behavior. |
| NoBroadcastFallback | If you use this flag, the service provider that supports broadcasting these capabilities will be disabled. You can use the GetSpCaps method on the Peer object to determine if your service provider supports broadcasting. |
| OkToQueryForAddressing | Specifying this flag will allow DirectPlay to display a windows dialog to provide any addressing information not already provided in the method call. |
| Sync | The default behavior for this method is to return immediately (asynchronous operation). Using this flag will change this behavior, and the method will not return until the enumeration has completed. |

If you try running the application now, you'll notice that clicking the connect button causes a dialog will show up asking for the remote machine's address. You can leave this blank to search the entire subnet of the network you are on. You can also specify the name or IP address of the machine you want to connect to. You'll notice that the FindHosts method returns no parameters, and currently there is no way to actually find out what hosts we've found.

# Using the Event Model

The majority of actions you perform in a DirectPlay session happen asynchronously. The method will return almost instantly, and then DirectPlay will go to work doing the action you requested. After this action has been completed, or when there is something DirectPlay needs to inform the application about, an event will be fired on a separate thread. These events are how we find out everything we need to know.

In our preceding call to FindHosts, the method will return right away, but behind the scenes, DirectPlay is busy looking for any available sessions. Whenever one is found the FindHostResponsee fired. Since we want to know about the hosts we find, we should hook this event. Add the following line directly after you've created your new peer object in the InitializeDirectPlay method:

```
connection.FindHostResponse += new
    FindHostResponseEventHandler(OnFindHost);
```

You'll also need to add the actual method that will be used to handle this event. You will find this in Listing 18.2.

**LISTING 18.2**   Event Handler for a Found Host

```
private void OnFindHost(object sender, FindHostResponseEventArgs e)
{
    lock(this)
    {
        // Do nothing if we're connected already
        if (connected)
            return;

        connected = true;
        string foundSession = string.Format
            ("Found session ({0}), trying to connect.",
            e.Message.ApplicationDescription.SessionName);

        this.BeginInvoke(new AddTextCallback(AddText),
            new object[] { foundSession });

        // Connect to the first one
        ((Peer)sender).Connect(e.Message.ApplicationDescription,
            e.Message.AddressSender,
            e.Message.AddressDevice, null, ConnectFlags.OkToQueryForAddressing);
    }
}
```

As you can see, our event handler includes a FindHostsReponseEventArgs object that will include the data about the host that was found. Examining the rest of this method tells us a lot about how multi-threaded programming should happen.

First, it's entirely possible for two different hosts to be found by DirectPlay. It's also possible that your application could be notified about each on two separate threads at the exact same time. Having two separate threads manipulating the same data at the same time is a big no-no, so we want to avoid that. We do this by using the lock keyword from C# (which is really just Monitor.Enter and Monitor.Exit calls wrapped in a try/finally block). Once the lock block has been entered by one thread, no other thread can enter that block until the first one has left the block.

We can only connect to one host at a time, so we will use a Boolean variable to check if we are already connected (you will need to declare this variable in your class; feel free to declare it publicly). If we are, there's nothing more to do in this method; we can just return. If we aren't, however, the first thing we will do is update this variable so that new enumerations won't interrupt us while we really do try to connect.

Now we want to update our UI to let the user know that we have found a session, and we are going to try to connect to it now. However, this event has been fired on a thread that is *not* the main UI thread where the control was created. It is not legal to modify or update controls on any thread other than the thread on which it was created. Doing so can result in failures, or even worse, deadlocks. The BeginInvoke method we use will call any delegate with the set of parameters we specify on the thread where the control was created for us. BeginInvoke happens asynchronously, much like DirectPlay. There is also an Invoke method that takes the same parameters, but runs synchronously. The definition for our delegate would be

```
private delegate void AddTextCallback(string text);
```

Nothing special, and we'll only use it to call our already existing AddText method. It is never a good idea to let a DirectPlay thread be blocked (for example, by using the synchronous Invoke method, or by displaying a modal message box). Always try to get the data you need and let the event end as quickly as possible.

Finally, we are ready to try and connect to this session. The connect call has four overloads, and once again, we used the simplest of them to get our connection started. You'll notice that we use the application description we received from the FindHostsEventArgs object to pass in to the Connect call. Actually, the majority of parameters we pass in to this method are retrieved from this object: the hosts address (the "sender" of the find hosts response), as well as the local address.

The last two parameters we pass in are application defined. The first is any user-defined data you want to pass into the connect call. This could be data that the host uses to determine which "team" you are on, for example; it is completely up to the application. The last parameter allows DirectPlay to query for addressing information, which probably isn't necessary since we are receiving full addressing information from the callback. The Sync flag is also allowed here to change the default behavior of the call to behave synchronously.

Other overloads of the Connect method contain one or more parameters we didn't need to use in this instance. One is an out parameter that is the asynchronous handle of the call. In DirectPlay, all calls that run asynchronously can return a handle to the call. You can use this handle to cancel the operation via the CancelAsyncOperation method if needed. We don't plan on canceling our operations, so this isn't necessary. The last two possible parameters are both user-defined context variables. Context variables can be used to store application-specific data.

## SHOP TALK

### DEFINING ENOUGH ADDRESSING INFORMATION

When you are running a full-screen game, you don't expect to see an "ugly" windows dialog popping up when you try to join a network game. You expect that any information needed to join this game will be entered inside of the game's user interface.

When you are designing a networking layer for a full-screen application, you will most likely never want to pass in the OkToQueryForAddressing flags on the Connect, Host, or FindHosts methods. Using this flag will allow DirectPlay to display its own custom windows dialog, which more than likely will not match your application's UI.

If you use these methods without this flag and it throws an AddressingException, more than likely there is some component of the address you are missing. In the TCP/IP case, this could be the host name of the server you're trying to reach, or the port the session should be run on. During implementation, make sure you know everything your service provider needs to perform the action, and make sure your addresses have the necessary components.

## Performing Actions in Our Session

We've made our connect call, but much like after our find hosts call, we don't really know what the outcome of that call was. Naturally, there is an event to handle this as well. Add the following handler to our InitializeDirectPlay method:

```
connection.ConnectComplete += new
    ConnectCompleteEventHandler(OnConnectComplete);
```

We also need the event handler method implementation, so add this as well:

```
private void OnConnectComplete(object sender, ConnectCompleteEventArgs e)
```

```
{
    // Check to see if we connected properly
    if (e.Message.ResultCode == ResultCode.Success)
    {
        this.BeginInvoke(new AddTextCallback(AddText),
            new object[] { "Connect Success." });

        connected = true;

        this.BeginInvoke(new EnableCallback(EnableSendDataButton),
            new object[] { true } );
    }
    else
    {
        this.BeginInvoke(new AddTextCallback(AddText), new object[] {
            string.Format("Connect Failure: {0}", e.Message.ResultCode) });

        connected = false;

        this.BeginInvoke(new EnableCallback(EnableSendDataButton),
            new object[] { false } );
    }
}
```

So this is where we can check to see if our connection call actually succeeded. The result code will tell us the result of the operation, and if that was a success, we've been connected to the session. In this case, we want to update our UI, and enable the send data button. If the connect call failed, we still update our UI; however, instead we disable the send data button, and set our connected variable to false. Setting this to false allows the FindHosts handler to try to connect to other sessions that it finds. You'll also notice that we don't have the delegate to enable or disable our send data button declared. You can declare it as follows:

```
private delegate void EnableCallback(bool enable);
```

You can run two instances of the application now and get them to connect to one another and be joined in the same session. On the first instance, click the Host button, and it should inform you that you are currently hosting the session. You can click the Connect button on the second instance, and after the dialog asking you about the remote host, you should see that it found your session and connected to it.

What we need now is a way to actually send some type of data to the session. We already have our send data button that currently doesn't do anything, so let's add this event handler for it:

```
private void button3_Click(object sender, System.EventArgs e)
{
    NetworkPacket packet = new NetworkPacket();

    packet.Write(byte.MaxValue);
    connection.SendTo((int)PlayerID.AllPlayers, packet,
        0, SendFlags.Guaranteed);
}
```

When sending data to a session in DirectPlay, it is common to use a network packet. You can write any information into this packet you want, providing it is a value type, an array of value types, or a string. You cannot pass in reference types to this method. We don't really care what we pass in for this application; we just want to send some value, so we'll just send in a single byte.

The actual send call is relatively straightforward. The first parameter is the player identifier of the user we want to send the data to. You can use any player or group identifier you wish, or (as we've done here) send it to all players. Don't worry; we'll discuss groups later. We naturally will also want to specify the network packet we will be sending. The third parameter is the timeout value for this packet. Values of zero (like we pass here) will never time out, unless of course the session itself drops. The last parameter we use for this call is one or more members of the SendFlags enumeration. Valid values for this enumeration are in Table 18.4:

## TABLE 18.4

**Possible SendFlags Values**

| VALUE | DESCRIPTION |
| --- | --- |
| Sync | Change the default behavior of this method from asynchronous operation to synchronous operation. |
| NoCopy | This flag is only valid on the overloads that accept the GCHandle structure as the network packet. This GCHandle must be allocated and pinned for this flag to be used. This will allow DirectPlay to use the data in the GCHandle directly, without making a separate copy. You may free the GCHandle on the SendComplete event. This flag cannot be used with the NoComplete flag. |
| NoComplete | Using this flag will cause the SendComplete event not to be fired. You may not use this flag if the NoCopy or Guaranteed flag is used. |
| CompleteOnProcess | When using this flag, the SendComplete event will only fire once the target connections receive method has processed the data. Normally, this event will fire as soon as the data is sent, but before the receiving connection has processed the message. Using this flag will add some extra overhead to the packet being sent. You must also use the Guaranteed flag when using this flag. |
| Guaranteed | Sends this message by a guaranteed method of delivery. Unless, of course, the connection is dropped. |
| PriorityHigh | Sends this message with a high priority. Cannot be used when you specify PriorityLow as well. |

**TABLE 18.4**
Continued

| VALUE | DESCRIPTION |
|---|---|
| PriorityLow | Sends this message with a low priority. Cannot be used when you specify PriorityHigh as well. |
| NonSequential | The default behavior of DirectPlay is for messages to be received in the same order in which they were sent. If the messages arrive at the computer out of order, they will be buffered and re-ordered until DirectPlay has the ability to deliver them sequentially. Specifying this flag changes this default behavior and allows the messages to be delivered in the same order they arrive in. |
| NoLoopBack | Specifying this flag will cause the receive data event not to be fired when you're sending to a player or group that includes your local player. |
| Coalesce | Using this flag will allow DirectPlay to combine packets when sending. |

As you can infer from the comments on the NoCopy flag, there are several overloads that take a GCHandle and buffer size variables. Since this is an asynchronous method, there are also overloads that return the asynchronous handle via an out parameter. Some of the overloads also include an application-defined context variable as well.

Now that data is being sent when we click our button, we will obviously need to include an event handler for when the data is received. Add this with the rest of the event hooks:

```
connection.Receive += new
    ReceiveEventHandler(OnDataReceive);
```

Here is the code for the actual event handler:

```
private void OnDataReceive(object sender, ReceiveEventArgs e)
{
    // We received some data, update our UI
    string newtext = string.Format
        ("Received message from DPlay UserId: 0x{0}",
        e.Message.SenderID.ToString("x"));

    this.BeginInvoke(new AddTextCallback(AddText),
        new object[] { newtext });
}
```

For this simple application, we don't actually care what the data we've received is, although we can get it from the ReceiveEventArgs object. Instead, we will just get the DirectPlay user identifier and update our UI to notify the user that a message was received.

Get two different instances of the application running (either on the same machine or on separate machines, it really doesn't matter). Have one be the host, while the other connects to it. Clicking the Send Data button should update the UI on both the sender as well as the receiver. This happens because we did not pass in the NoLoopBack flag when we called our SendTo method. The data is sent to everyone, including you.

Now, try this. While both instances are still running, quit the session that is the host. Now click the Send Data button on the remaining instance. You'll notice that an unhandled exception has occurred, which will cause your application to crash.

# Handling Lost Sessions

When the host of the session quit, the connection was then dropped. There was no longer any host, so the connection couldn't be maintained any longer. DirectPlay sent a message to all connected clients informing them of this; however, we never included a handler for this event. Let's do this now:

```
connection.SessionTerminated += new
    SessionTerminatedEventHandler(OnSessionTerminate);
```

The session-terminated event can be fired when the host has quit (like we did previously) or for just about any other reason why you can no longer be in the session. For example, if you unplugged your network cable, shortly later you would receive this event because no one in the session could be contacted. We should add the code for this handler now:

```
private void OnSessionTerminate(object sender, SessionTerminatedEventArgs e)
{
    // The session was terminated, close our peer object, re-enable our buttons
    this.BeginInvoke(new DisconnectCallback(OnDisconnect), null);
}
```

Hmmm, we've got a new delegate we're calling, plus an entirely new method. Why exactly did we do it this way? First, we'll declare the delegate and the method used:

```
private delegate void DisconnectCallback();
private void OnDisconnect()
{
    // Re-enable the UI
    button1.Enabled = true;
    button2.Enabled = true;
    button3.Enabled = false;
    // Notify the user
    AddText("The host has quit, you have been disconnected.");

    // Dispose of our connection, and set it to null
    connection.Dispose();
    connection = null;
}
```

Now you can see the reason for the new delegate and method. We need to do quite a bit here. First, we switch the button states back to the defaults so that we can be allowed to host a new session or join a different session. We then update the UI to inform the user, and finally, since this connection is no longer valid, we dispose it and set it to null.

## SHOP TALK

### HANDLING HOST MIGRATION

I know what you must be thinking. Just because the first person in the session quit, why does the entire session need to be disbanded? That seems pretty stupid. Luckily, this isn't *always* the case. DirectPlay has a feature called "Host Migration" that will automatically pick a new host out of the remaining peers if the original host happens to quit. In the design view of our form, add a check box between the Connect and Send Data buttons. The text for this button should be "Migrate the host".

Now we'll need to update a few different places in our application to enable host migration. First, we'll need to see whether our box has been checked before we host, since the peer that calls Host must include the host migration flag if the option is going to be used. Add the following line before the call to Host:

```
// Should we allow host migration?
desc.Flags = checkBox1.Checked ? SessionFlags.MigrateHost : 0;
```

As you see, if the box is checked, we include the migrate host flag; otherwise, we do not. You will also need to include the checkbox control in the OnDisconnect method and the first two button event handlers. You should enable/disable this control just like you do the connect and host buttons.

Lastly, it would be nice if the UI was updated when the host has quit and the host migration has been kicked off. Naturally, there is an event for this as well. Add this handler:

```
connection.HostMigrated += new
    HostMigratedEventHandler(OnHostMigrate);
```

The handler for this event is as follows:

```
private void OnHostMigrate(object sender, HostMigratedEventArgs e)
{
    // The host has been migrated to a new peer
    this.BeginInvoke(new AddTextCallback(AddText),
        new object[] { "The host was migrated." });
}
```

Here, we don't actually do anything other than update the UI. However, if your application had host-specific options, you would want to enable them in this method by checking the NewHostId member of the HostMigratedEventArgs object.

# In Brief

- DirectPlay addresses
- The peer object
- The event model of DirectPlay
- Sending data to other members of your session
- Host migration

In our next chapter, we will look at multiplayer opportunities using the client/server topology and start sending much more interesting data.

# Creating a Client/ Server Session

Peer-to-peer sessions can work quite well when you're dealing with a small subset of users. However, when you're looking to maintain a network session with hundreds or even thousands of simultaneous players, you really need a dedicated server. In a peer-to-peer session, all data sent from one peer to the other peers can be duplicated for every peer in the session. For small groups, this isn't prohibitive, but even a small chunk of data can be quite large when it's sent 10,000 times.

DirectPlay includes two other networking classes much like the peer object: the client and the server objects. You can think of each of these as a subset of the functionality that exists in the peer object, considering that the peer object is essentially both a client and a server. In this chapter you will create a client/server application that delves a little deeper into the workings of DirectPlay, including

- Creating dedicated servers running on particular ports

- Connecting to these servers using the client interface

- Tracking player joining and disconnecting

- Sending game-specific data

## Creating a Dedicated Server Session

Obviously, you will need to create a server before the client. Without the server, what exactly could the client do? In practice, you may find working on both the client and server portions of the code in tandem beneficial. That model will be followed here, but before you get to that point, you have to meet a "bare minimum" standard of working. You can define this as being able to host a dedicated session and having a client connect. So now you can get started with your server.

The majority of dedicated server applications pick an Internet port that they (and only they) run. For example, Web servers almost always listen on port 80 for any Web requests. FTP servers use port 21. Only one application may listen to any given port at one time, so it's common for the application to pick a unique port to run with. The first thousand ports are considered "reserved," but you may feel free to use any available port to listen on.

For this dedicated server application, you should pick a port you feel comfortable using. The code in the text will use port 9798 to listen on. There won't be any options for the server; it will just run and update its status via the UI. The only action the server will be able to perform other than what you program into it will be shutting down.

Naturally then, you'll want a windows form for the UI status update. Go ahead and create a windows form application, and make sure your references and using clauses have been defined for DirectPlay. You will want a form with a fixed dialog border style and a label. The label can be set to a dock mode of fill so that it covers the entire form.

You will first need a declaration for the server object (which, as mentioned earlier, is similar to the peer object):

```
private Server connection = null;
```

You will need to add the initialization function. Since it's not possible for a server object to connect to any other session, there is no need to have a Boolean parameter for this method. Add the method found in Listing 19.1 to your application.

### LISTING 19.1    Initializing a Server

```
public void InitializeServer()
{
    // Create our server object
    connection = new Server();

    // Check to see if we can create a TCP/IP connection
    if (!IsServiceProviderValid(Address.ServiceProviderTcpIp))
    {
        // Nope, can't, quit this application
        MessageBox.Show("Could not create a TCP/IP service provider.", "Exiting",
            MessageBoxButtons.OK, MessageBoxIcon.Information);
        this.Close();
    }
    // Create a new address for our local machine
```

**LISTING 19.1**   Continued

```
Address deviceAddress = new Address();
deviceAddress.ServiceProvider = Address.ServiceProviderTcpIp;
deviceAddress.AddComponent(Address.KeyPort, SharedCode.DataPort);

// Set up an application description
ApplicationDescription desc = new ApplicationDescription();
desc.SessionName = "MDX Book Server Session";
desc.GuidApplication = SharedCode.ApplicationGuid;
desc.Flags = SessionFlags.ClientServer ¦ SessionFlags.NoDpnServer;

try
{
    // Host a new session
    connection.Host(desc, deviceAddress);
    // We can assume after the host call succeeds we are hosting
    AddText("Currently Hosting a session.");
}
catch
{
    AddText("Hosting this session has failed.");
}
}
```

You'll notice that this is similar to the hosting method for your peer session. The definitions for the IsServiceProviderValid and AddText methods aren't provided here, since they were already provided in the previous chapter. There are three significant changes in this section of code that didn't exist in the peer-to-peer session, though.

First, you'll notice that the port component has been added to the address. The yet-to-be-defined SharedCode.DataPort constant has been used for the port. Since the client (as well as the server) will require this constant, you should create a separate code file that will be used for both the server and client code bases. Create a new code file that will be used to share code between the server and client:

```
public class SharedCode
{
    public static readonly Guid ApplicationGuid = new Guid
        (15741039, 1702,1503,178, 101, 32, 13, 121, 230, 109, 59);

    public const int DataPort = 9798;

}
```

For now, you'll notice that there are two constants included here. Each of these constants will be needed by both the client and server. In the peer-to-peer session, the peer code was encapsulated in a single executable, so this "sharing" of code wasn't necessary. Since you will have separate executables for the client and server here, this shared code is necessary.

The last major change is the flags you're using for the application description. The flags for ClientServer and NoDpnServer are being used for the application. The first flag is relatively self-explanatory. You want this session to be a client/server session. The second flag, however, requires a little more explaining.

As discussed earlier, only a single application may listen on a given port at any given time. You cannot have two applications each trying to listen on port 9897, for example. The first call will succeed, and the second (and each subsequent) call will fail, so long as the first application is still listening on that port. However, running multiple servers on a machine, even on the same port, is a scenario that is supported by DirectPlay.

To facilitate this behavior, DirectPlay has an external application, "dpnsrv.exe ", that is spawned whenever a session is created for the first time. This application's only job is to be the one application that is listening to the specified port (or the default port if none is specified) and forwarding any client enumerations to the correct "real" host. While potentially useful in some scenarios, it isn't recommended that you use this application for your session. Using the NoDpnServer flag informs DirectPlay not to use the "dpnsrv.exe " application, and you will handle everything yourself.

Before you are ready to have the server up and running, you will need to make sure you call the initialization method, as well as making sure you dispose your connection object when the application quits. Update your main method as follows:

```
static void Main()
{
    using (Form1 frm = new Form1())
    {
        frm.Show();
        frm.InitializeServer();
        Application.Run(frm);
    }

}
```

You will also need to update the disposing override for your form and add the following code to dispose your connection object:

```
if (connection != null)
    connection.Dispose();
```

In order to see the difference between using the NoDpnServer flag and not using it, first compile your application and run it. You should see your status inform you that you are hosting a session. Now run the application a second time, without closing the first instance. You should be informed that hosting the session has failed. This is because the second instance was trying to listen on a port that was already opened for listening by another application. Now, remove the flag and try the same steps. You can now successfully host two instances of your server. In order to be "dedicated," though, you will only ever want one. Place the flag back in your code.

# Connecting a Client

With the bare minimum for the server session created, you can now do the small amount of work to get a client connected to this server. While it is technically possible to add the code for the client into the same executable as the server, in order to have a dedicated server, you will want the code separated. In order to do this, you will create an entirely new second windows forms application.

The client UI will be similar to the servers. You should have one large label covering the majority of the screen. The difference is that you should leave some room for buttons along the top of the form, since you will use these buttons to have the client perform particular actions. You also will want the clients to be able to have a name for this session, and you will want this name to be changeable. For now, just create the label covering most of the form, as well as a textbox above this label where you will be able to modify the client's name.

You will also need to ensure that you have access to the shared data between the server and the client, so you will need to add a link to the shared code file you created for the server. When adding the existing item, be sure to click the small arrow on the open button, and select the Link File option if the code file is in a different folder. Otherwise, simply selecting the Open option will create a copy of the file in your local folder, and it will no longer be shared between the two applications.

With that minor plumbing out of the way, you can start writing the client code. You will first need to create your local variables:

```
private Client connection = null;
private bool connected = false;
```

Much like the peer-to-peer session, you will need a variable to track whether or not you've been connected to a session. You also need to maintain the connection object as well. Once again, you will need to have an initialization method implemented, only this time it will only try to find existing hosts. Add the method from Listing 19.2 to your client application.

**LISTING 19.2**   Initializing a Client Connection

```
public void InitializeClient()
{
    // Create our client object
    connection = new Client();
    // Hook the events we want to listen for
    connection.ConnectComplete += new
        ConnectCompleteEventHandler(OnConnectComplete);

    connection.FindHostResponse += new
        FindHostResponseEventHandler(OnFindHost);

    // Check to see if we can create a TCP/IP connection
    if (!IsServiceProviderValid(Address.ServiceProviderTcpIp))
    {
        // Nope, can't, quit this application
        MessageBox.Show("Could not create a TCP/IP service provider.", "Exiting",
            MessageBoxButtons.OK, MessageBoxIcon.Information);
        this.Close();
    }
    // Create a new address for our local machine
    Address deviceAddress = new Address();
    deviceAddress.ServiceProvider = Address.ServiceProviderTcpIp;
    // Create a new address for our host machine
    Address hostaddress = new Address();
    hostaddress.ServiceProvider = Address.ServiceProviderTcpIp;
    hostaddress.AddComponent(Address.KeyPort, SharedCode.DataPort);

    // Set our name
    PlayerInformation info = new PlayerInformation();
    info.Name = textBox1.Text;
    connection.SetClientInformation(info, SyncFlags.ClientInformation);

    // Set up an application description
    ApplicationDescription desc = new ApplicationDescription();
    desc.GuidApplication = SharedCode.ApplicationGuid;

    try
    {
        // Search for a server
        connection.FindHosts(desc, hostaddress, deviceAddress, null,
            0, 0, 0, FindHostsFlags.None);
```

**LISTING 19.2** Continued

```
        AddText("Looking for sessions.");
    }
    catch
    {
        AddText("Enumeration of sessions has failed.");
    }
}
```

There is actually quite a bit of new information here. You will need to add the implementations of AddText and IsServiceProviderValid from where you've seen them before. The minimum client will first search for existing hosts to connect to and then try to perform the connection, so you will first hook the two events shown, much like you did in the peer-to-peer sample. You also check the service provider validity before creating the addresses.

Ah, and in this instance it really is addresses. You first create the local device address, which will simply be an address with the TCP/IP service provider. However, you also want to create a distinct address for the server that will be used to try to find any sessions. You know for certain that any host you want to connect with will be run on the port specified in SharedCode.DataPort, so you add that component to the address. If you also knew the host name of the server, you could add that component to this address as well.

The next small section is completely new. Each "member" of a session in DirectPlay can have associated information attached to it, and this data can contain the name of the "player," or some set of application defined data. For this example, you will only want to set the name of the client, so you use whatever the text from the text box happens to be (which right now is probably "textbox1"). That's a horrible name for a client, so you should update the text box before you get to this code. At the end of your forms constructor, add the following line:

```
textBox1.Text = System.Environment.UserName;
```

This sets the text box (and thus your initial client name) to the username of your computer. A way to change this username will be added later in this chapter.

Next you set up the application description. You'll notice that the only member you need to set for this case is the application GUID. You use the shared GUID for this member, since the server and client must have the same application GUID in order to connect to one another. Finally, you make the call to FindHosts, and assuming that succeeds, update the UI to inform the user that you're searching for sessions.

**ONLY SEARCHING LOCAL SUBNET**

You'll notice that in this instance you did not use the FindHostsFlags.OkToQueryForAddressing flag. For this example, you can expect the server to exist on the same subnet you are on (which is the default searching area for DirectPlay). If this isn't the case for your network, you should use this flag, or add the host name of the server into a component of its address.

You will also need the two event handler methods you've declared thus far. You will find them in Listing 19.3.

**LISTING 19.3** Joining a Session Event Handlers

```
private void OnFindHost(object sender, FindHostResponseEventArgs e)
{
    lock(this)
    {
        // Do nothing if we're connected already
        if (connected)
            return;

        connected = true;
        string foundSession = string.Format
            ("Found session ({0}), trying to connect.",
            e.Message.ApplicationDescription.SessionName);

        this.BeginInvoke(new AddTextCallback(AddText),
            new object[] { foundSession });

        // Connect to the first one
        ((Client)sender).Connect(e.Message.ApplicationDescription,
            e.Message.AddressSender,
            e.Message.AddressDevice, null, ConnectFlags.OkToQueryForAddressing);
    }
}

private void OnConnectComplete(object sender, ConnectCompleteEventArgs e)
{
    // Check to see if we connected properly
    if (e.Message.ResultCode == ResultCode.Success)
    {
        this.BeginInvoke(new AddTextCallback(AddText),
            new object[] { "Connect Success." });

        connected = true;

        this.BeginInvoke(new EnableCallback(EnableSendDataButton),
            new object[] { true } );
    }
    else
```

**LISTING 19.3**  Continued

```
    {
        this.BeginInvoke(new AddTextCallback(AddText), new object[] {
            string.Format("Connect Failure: {0}", e.Message.ResultCode) });

        connected = false;

        this.BeginInvoke(new EnableCallback(EnableSendDataButton),
            new object[] { false } );
    }
}
```

These methods should look familiar as they're similar to the peer-to-peer connection strate-gies. You first try to find any hosts available, and as soon as one is found, attempt to connect to it. With that, you are close to having the bare minimum for the client being connected. Like the server before, the only things left are calling the initialize method and disposing the connection when the application is complete. The call to dispose won't be included here, since it's already been covered for the server, and the code is identical, but make sure you do it in your application. Finally, update the main method as follows:

```
static void Main()
{
    using (Form1 frm = new Form1())
    {
        frm.Show();
        frm.InitializeClient();
        Application.Run(frm);
    }

}
```

With that, your client should be ready to go. Go ahead and start a server session, and then open up a client. You should see the server update its UI to say that it is hosting, and the client should look for sessions, find your server, and connect. Now you can try to add some-thing a little more exciting.

# Detecting Users Joining and Leaving Your Session

Now that clients are connecting to the server, it would be nice to update the UI on the server side to indicate when a client has connected (and left, for that matter). However, currently no way to do this has been discussed. As luck would have it, there are two events you can hook to give you this information. In your initialization method for the server, you will need to add the following event hooks:

```
connection.PlayerCreated += new
    PlayerCreatedEventHandler(OnPlayerCreated);

connection.PlayerDestroyed += new
    PlayerDestroyedEventHandler(OnPlayerDestroyed);
```

Whenever a player either joins or leaves the session, the appropriate event will be fired. The implementations of the event handlers are pretty similar as well. Add them from Listing 19.4 to your server application.

**LISTING 19.4**  Player Management Event Handlers

```
private void OnPlayerCreated(object sender, PlayerCreatedEventArgs e)
{
    try
    {
        string playerName = ((Server)sender).GetClientInformation
            (e.Message.PlayerID).Name;

        string newtext = string.Format
            ("Accepted new connection from {0}, UserID: 0x{1}",
            playerName, e.Message.PlayerID.ToString("x"));

        this.BeginInvoke(new AddTextCallback(AddText),
            new object[] { newtext });
    }
    catch { /* Ignore this, probably the server */ }
}

private void OnPlayerDestroyed(object sender, PlayerDestroyedEventArgs e)
{
    string newtext = string.Format
        ("DirectPlayer UserID: 0x{0} has left the session.",
        e.Message.PlayerID.ToString("x"));

    this.BeginInvoke(new AddTextCallback(AddText),
        new object[] { newtext });
}
```

The player-destroyed handler is quite simple, as all it does is update the UI to notify you that the user has left the session. The player-created handler has a method that has never actually been discussed before, though. In the client's application, you set the client name with a call to SetClientInformation; in the server you retrieve this name with the call to GetClientInformation. When a server first starts a session, a default "hidden" player is created. Since there is no client associated with this player, the call to SetClientInformation will naturally fail. You can simply ignore that case for this example since it is expected.

## SHOP TALK

### CONTROLLING WHO JOINS YOUR SESSION

It's entirely possible that there are certain users who you do not want joining your session. However, as it stands right now, it looks like just about anyone could join any DirectPlay session, assuming they knew even a small amount of information, such as the application GUID and the port the application is running on. Naturally, there has to be a way to prevent "rogue" applications from joining your session without needing to require a password.

Before the player-created event you just hooked is fired, there is another event fired: IndicateConnect. The event arguments object for this event (IndicateConnectEventArgs) includes a property, RejectMessage, that defaults to false. Based on the information you've received in this event handler, you can decide whether or not you want to allow this connection. If you do wish to allow the connection, you can simply do nothing, and the connection will be allowed. However, if you decide that this user shouldn't be allowed to connect to your session, you can simply set the RejectMessage property to true. Doing this will deny the client access to your session.

What if you don't even want your session to be found, though? You already know that when a host is found, you receive a FindHostsResponse event; however, before that event is fired on the client, the server will receive a FindHostsQuery event. You can use the same strategy as used previously to stop the clients from even receiving the FindHostsResponse event. You can have total control over who is allowed to see and join your session using a combination of these two events.

Peer session hosts have these same abilities.

## Sending Data Packets

You've already written some code for sending a simple data packet in the peer-to-peer session, but all you really did was send a single byte of data, and it didn't even really matter what that data was. In a real networking session, the traffic that will be sent between the server and the clients will be much more varied, and intended to perform specific actions.

To model more accurately what a "real" application might do, you should add a few options to the client that facilitate sending various data packets to the server. You can include the following actions for your client:

- Check the number of players currently in the session.

- Wave to other players in the session.

- Send "private" data to the server.

- Run away from the other players in the session.

- Change the client's name.

Obviously, both the client and server applications will need to know about these actions, so you will add the following enumeration to the shared code file that will track the type of data packet you will be sending to the server:

```
public enum NetworkMessages
{
    CheckPlayers,
    Wave,
    SendData,
    RunAway,
    ChangeName,
}
```

You have one value for each of the actions you want the client to perform. You could have just as easily created a list of constants to use, but the grouping of the enumeration made it more attractive for this simple case. Now you will need a way for the client to actually perform these actions. In your client application, create five buttons at the top of your form, one for each of these actions. In order to simplify the sending of the data, you will hook and create a single event handler for all of the buttons. The event handler method can be found in Listing 19.5.

**LISTING 19.5**   Sending Data Based on Button Clicks

```
private void button_Click(object sender, System.EventArgs e)
{
    // We want to send some data to the server
    NetworkPacket packet = new NetworkPacket();

    // Write the correct message depending on the button pressed
    switch(((Button)sender).Name)
    {
        case "button1":
```

**LISTING 19.5**   Continued

```
            packet.Write(NetworkMessages.CheckPlayers);
            break;
        case "button2":
            packet.Write(NetworkMessages.Wave);
            break;
        case "button3":
            packet.Write(NetworkMessages.SendData);
            break;
        case "button4":
            packet.Write(NetworkMessages.RunAway);
            break;
        case "button5":
            if (textBox1.Text.Length > 0)
            {
                packet.Write(NetworkMessages.ChangeName);
                packet.Write(textBox1.Text);

                PlayerInformation info = new PlayerInformation();
                info.Name = textBox1.Text;
                connection.SetClientInformation(info,
                                SyncFlags.ClientInformation);
            }
            else
            {
                // Don't try to do anything if there is no name
                return;
            }
            break;
    }
    connection.Send(packet, 0, SendFlags.Guaranteed);
}
```

The first thing done here is to create a new network packet that will hold the data you want to send. Then you do a switch statement on the button's name. Unfortunately, C# doesn't currently have the ability to do a switch statement on a reference type such as the button itself, so this is the next best thing. You could have also done a series of if statements comparing the sender with each button, as well.

Depending on the name of the button pressed, you then write the appropriate message into the network packet. If the message happens to be the change name message, and there is a string in the text box, you not only write the correct message into the packet, you also write the new name and update your client information.

Finally, you send the data to the server. You will notice that there is no user id parameter to send the data to a particular user. In a client/server session, the client can *only* send data to the server; it isn't possible to send data to any other client directly.

With the client capable of sending data now, it would probably be a good idea to update the server so that it actually knows what to do with the data it's receiving. Naturally, before you can receive any of the data, you will need to hook the event that is fired. Add the following line to your initialize server method:

```
connection.Receive += new
    ReceiveEventHandler(OnDataReceive);
```

Now, what you want to accomplish in this event handler is pretty simple. You want to detect the type of message being sent and react accordingly. You can do this with the handler found in Listing 19.6.

**LISTING 19.6**   Handling Received Data for the Server

```
private void OnDataReceive(object sender, ReceiveEventArgs e)
{
    NetworkMessages msg = (NetworkMessages)e.Message.ReceiveData.Read
        (typeof(NetworkMessages));

    NetworkPacket returnedPacket = new NetworkPacket();

    string newtext = string.Empty;
    switch (msg)
    {
        case NetworkMessages.ChangeName:
            string newname = e.Message.ReceiveData.ReadString();
            newtext = string.Format
                ("DPlay UserId 0x{0} changed name to {1}",
                e.Message.SenderID.ToString("x"), newname);

            // The user wants inform everyone they ran away
            returnedPacket.Write(NetworkMessages.ChangeName);
            returnedPacket.Write(e.Message.SenderID);
            returnedPacket.Write(newname);
            // Now send it everyone
            connection.SendTo((int)PlayerID.AllPlayers, returnedPacket, 0,
                SendFlags.Guaranteed | SendFlags.NoLoopback);
            break;
```

**LISTING 19.6**   Continued

```
case NetworkMessages.CheckPlayers:
    newtext = string.Format
        ("Received CheckPlayers from DPlay UserId: 0x{0}",
        e.Message.SenderID.ToString("x"));

    // The user wants to know how many players are in the session
    returnedPacket.Write(NetworkMessages.CheckPlayers);
    // subtract one user for the server user
    returnedPacket.Write(connection.Players.Count - 1);
    // Now send it only to that player
    connection.SendTo(e.Message.SenderID, returnedPacket, 0,
        SendFlags.Guaranteed);

    break;
case NetworkMessages.RunAway:
    newtext = string.Format
        ("Received RunAway from DPlay UserId: 0x{0}",
        e.Message.SenderID.ToString("x"));

    // The user wants inform everyone they ran away
    returnedPacket.Write(NetworkMessages.RunAway);
    returnedPacket.Write(e.Message.SenderID);
    // Now send it everyone
    connection.SendTo((int)PlayerID.AllPlayers, returnedPacket, 0,
        SendFlags.Guaranteed | SendFlags.NoLoopback);
    break;
case NetworkMessages.SendData:
    newtext = string.Format
        ("Received SendData from DPlay UserId: 0x{0}",
        e.Message.SenderID.ToString("x"));

    // No need to reply, 'fake' server data
    break;
case NetworkMessages.Wave:
    newtext = string.Format
        ("Received Wave from DPlay UserId: 0x{0}",
        e.Message.SenderID.ToString("x"));

    // The user wants inform everyone they waved
    returnedPacket.Write(NetworkMessages.Wave);
    returnedPacket.Write(e.Message.SenderID);
```

**LISTING 19.6** Continued

```
            // Now send it everyone
            connection.SendTo((int)PlayerID.AllPlayers, returnedPacket, 0,
                SendFlags.Guaranteed | SendFlags.NoLoopback);
            break;
    }
    // We received some data, update our UI
    this.BeginInvoke(new AddTextCallback(AddText),
        new object[] { newtext });
}
```

## READING DATA IN THE CORRECT ORDER

Note that you must always read the data in the exact same order you wrote it into the packet. Trying to read data in any other order will most likely cause errors in your application.

This method is definitely not as complex as it may look. In fact, it's actually quite simple. One of the properties of the event arguments is the network packet that was received. Much like you called the Write method to put data into the packet, you will call the Read method to extract that same data out.

The read method takes a single type member that will be the type of data that is returned by the method. Since you want to first determine the type of message that was sent, you call read using the type of the enumeration. You also know that in certain cases, you will want to reply either to a specific client or to all clients with a "new" network packet, so go ahead and create that now. Now, you just need to use a switch statement on the received message type and perform the action it requests.

The easiest action is the SendData member. Since this is intended to just be a "private" message to the server, no response is needed, so you can simply update the server's UI to reflect that the message was received.

The Wave and RunAway actions are both virtually identical to each other. When either of these messages are received, you first update the server UI like normal; however, after that you begin filling the new network packet. You first write the exact same message you just received into it, followed by the user id of the player who sent the message originally. You do this so that when you send this message back to the clients, they know which client performed the action described. Finally, you send this packet back to all clients in the session, for them to react as they see fit. Notice that you include the NoLoopBack flag for this send. Without this flag, sending the messages would cause the server to get into an infinite loop (since each handling of a particular message results in that same message being sent again).

The CheckPlayers action is different from the rest. This is the client requesting information from the server, so no one other than the client needs to see the response from the sever. Once again you write the message id into the new network packet; however, next you write the number of players currently in the session (the one "phantom" server player is removed). You then send the new packet directly to the sender of the request, so no other players in the session can see this message from the server (unless they too request it). You also make sure you update the UI for the server.

The last action is most similar to the wave and run away actions. You'll notice a new method you call on the network packet here as well. In retrieving the new name of the client, you call the ReadString method. Assuming you used the write method to put the string into the network packet, this method should be able to extract the string directly from the network packet. The only major difference between this action and the wave and run away actions is that after writing the message id and the sender id, you also write the new name of the client in the packet as well.

# Making the Client React

It's clear now that the client will also need to hook the receive data event since you've updated the server to actually send data as well. Add the same hook you used for the server into your client application. The actual event handler for the client will be similar as well. Add the event handler found in Listing 19.7 to your client application.

LISTING 19.7    Handling Received Data on the Client

```
private void OnDataReceive(object sender, ReceiveEventArgs e)
{
    NetworkMessages msg = (NetworkMessages)e.Message.ReceiveData.Read
        (typeof(NetworkMessages));

    string newtext = string.Empty;
    int playerID = 0;

    switch (msg)
    {
        case NetworkMessages.ChangeName:
            playerID = (int)e.Message.ReceiveData.Read(typeof(int));
            string newname = e.Message.ReceiveData.ReadString();
            newtext = string.Format
                ("DPlay UserId 0x{0} changed name to {1}",
                playerID.ToString("x"), newname);

            break;
        case NetworkMessages.CheckPlayers:
            int count = (int)e.Message.ReceiveData.Read(typeof(int));
```

**LISTING 19.7**    Continued

```
            newtext = string.Format
                ("Server reports {0} users on the server currently.",
                count);
            break;
        case NetworkMessages.RunAway:
            playerID = (int)e.Message.ReceiveData.Read(typeof(int));
            newtext = string.Format
                ("Server reports DPlay UserId 0x{0} has ran away.",
                playerID.ToString("x"));

            break;
        case NetworkMessages.Wave:
            playerID = (int)e.Message.ReceiveData.Read(typeof(int));
            newtext = string.Format
                ("Server reports DPlay UserId 0x{0} has waved.",
                playerID.ToString("x"));

            break;
    }
    // We received some data, update our UI
    this.BeginInvoke(new AddTextCallback(AddText),
        new object[] { newtext });

}
```

You can see that this is essentially a simplified version of the server's handler. All you ever do is get the message and update the UI to notify the user about what's going on. You also don't even bother listening for the SendData action, since the server will never send that message.

# Handling the Server Lost Event

The last thing you will need to cover is ensuring that the client can react correctly if the server is lost. You've handled this in the peer-to-peer session already, and the code here is identical. First, you add a hook for the SessionTerminated event:

```
connection.SessionTerminated += new
    SessionTerminatedEventHandler(OnSessionTerminate);
```

Plus you'll need the actual event handler:

```
private void OnSessionTerminate(object sender, SessionTerminatedEventArgs e)
{
    this.BeginInvoke(new DisconnectCallback(OnDisconnect), null);
}
private void OnDisconnect()
{
    EnableSendDataButtons(false);
    AddText("Session terminated.");
    connected = false;

    // Dispose of our connection, and set it to null
    connection.Dispose();
    connection = null;
}
```

All you really want to do in this scenario is make sure you dispose the connection and nullify the object. However, it's good practice to inform the user by updating the UI and disabling the buttons.

# In Brief

- Creating dedicated servers running on particular ports
- Connecting to these servers using the client interface
- Tracking player joining and disconnecting
- Sending game-specific data

In our next chapter, we will look at advanced networking topics, including data throttling, bandwidth detection, statistics, launching applications, and even voice communication.

# Understanding Advanced Networking Features

## IN THIS CHAPTER

This chapter will cover various features of DirectPlay that
will allow us to enhance our networking performance and
features, including

- A detailed look at all events and why they occur.

- Bandwidth and lag detection.

- Sending queue.

- Lobby-launching applications.

- Using Voice chat in your application.

## Having a Detailed Look at the Event Model

You've dealt with the basics of client/server sessions, and
peer-to-peer as well. However, thus far you haven't really
gotten into the advanced features of networking or how to
use them. This chapter will begin to look further into how
you should create an efficient networking layer.

You've looked at a few of the possible events that can be
fired during the course of a networking session, but
haven't yet looked at the exhaustive list and why they
actually occur. Some of these events will not occur for
certain class types, so the text will be sure to mention
which class the event applies to. Without further ado,
the events:

- ApplicationDescriptionChanged—Applies to Peer, Server, and Client. This event is fired when the application description has been changed; for example, possibly the name has been changed. If you care, you will need to get the new application description when you receive this event.

- AsyncOperationComplete—Applies to Peer, Server, and Client. This event is fired when an asynchronous operation has been completed. Any of the DirectPlay methods that can return an asynchronous operation handle (for example, the Connect method or the Receive method) will notify the application when they have completed via this event. It is also possible to cancel these methods by using the CancelAsyncOperation method and passing in either the handle or a flag to cancel all operations of a particular type. You should remember that certain operations are automatically cancelled by other actions. For example, the FindHosts method is automatically cancelled when you connect to a session.

- ConnectComplete—Applies to Peer and Client. We've already covered this event when dealing with our client and peer sessions. This event is fired after attempting to connect to a session, even if that connection was not successful. You can check the ResultCode member of the event arguments object to determine whether or not the connection was successful. For example, if the host rejected your connection, you would expect the result code to be HostRejectedConnection.

- FindHostQuery—Applies to Peer and Server. This event is fired when a new connection has called FindHosts and is attempting to find your session. If you do not capture this event or if you do not modify the RejectMessage property of the event arguments, the caller of FindHosts will successfully enumerate this session. Setting the RejectMessage property to true before leaving this event handler will cause the enumeration to be rejected, and the caller will not be able to see this session. A common practice is to use the ReceivedData from the FindHosts call to determine if this enumeration should be successful.

- FindHostResponse—Applies to Peer and Client. This event is fired once a host is found. The event arguments object returned in this event will contain enough information to connect to the server that was found, including the hosts address object and the application description. Since the enumerations happen continuously, if you do not connect to a host immediately, it's possible (and probable) that the same host will be found multiple times.

- GroupCreated—Applies to Peer and Server. DirectPlay allows the creation of groups, which naturally are a collection of players and even other groups. The hosts of a server session or any peer in a peer-to-peer session can call the CreateGroup method to create a new group. After this method has been called and the group has been created, this event will be fired.

- GroupDestroyed—Applies to Peer and Server. When a group is about to be destroyed, this event will be fired. A group can be destroyed in multiple ways, either because DestroyGroup was called, or because the session is ending. If the AutoDestruct flag was used when creating this group, the group will also be destroyed when the creating player has left the session. You can check the Reason property in the event arguments object to determine why the group was destroyed.

- GroupInformation—Applies to Peer and Server. When a group's information has been changed (due to a call to SetGroupInformation), this event will be fired to all members of that group. This event will only provide the id of the group; you will be responsible for retrieving the new group information.

- HostMigrated—Applies to Peer. This event is fired in a peer-to-peer session when the current host has left the session. The new host's player id will be included with this event. This event will only be fired if the host migration flag is passed in when the Host call is made.

- IndicateConnect—Applies to Peer and Server. This event is fired when a player is trying to join your session. Much like the FindHostQuery event, you can reject this event to cause the connection to fail.

- IndicateConnectAborted—Applies to Peer and Server. Once the IndicateConnect event has been fired, normally the next event you would see would be the PlayerCreated event. However, if for some reason the connection was aborted before this event had occurred (for example, the line was dropped), you will receive this event. While this event may not be common, it is important to understand why you might receive it.

- PeerInformation—Applies to Peer. Like the other information events, this is fired when a peer's information has been changed. You will be responsible for retrieving the new information after this event is fired if you need it.

- PlayerAddedToGroup—Applies to Peer and Server. After a group has been created, players (or other groups) can be added to it. When this occurs, this event will be fired with the group's id, as well as the player (or group) id.

- PlayerCreated—Applies to Peer and Server. After the IndicateConnect event has been processed, you will receive this event next informing you that the new player has been created. You may set the player context variable (any application-specific object) during this event (it is a property of the event arguments object). Any time you receive an event from this player (such as receive) you will also receive this player's context variable as well.

- PlayerDestroyed—Applies to Peer and Server. You will receive this message when any player has left the session. Even if the session itself is exiting, you will always receive one destroyed message for every created message you received.

- PlayerRemovedFromGroup—Applies to Peer and Server. Much like the PlayerAddedToGroup event, you will receive this event when a player has been removed from a group. This removal can come from a call to RemovePlayerFromGroup, or from the player leaving the session.

- Receive—Applies to Peer, Server, and Client. This event is fired anytime new data has been received. You will receive a network packet including the data that you have just received, as well as the player id and player context variables of the sending player. This is where the majority of your work will take place. Since it is common to do a lot of work on each receive, it is common to have a separate thread perform these actions so that the DirectPlay threads are not blocked. Also note that you will receive this event for any data you send to a group you belong to, unless the NoLoopback flag is enabled.

- SendComplete—Applies to Peer, Server, and Client. This event is fired when an asynchronous send operation that you initiated has completed. Exactly when you receive this event depends on how the data was sent. If you used the CompleteOnProcess flag, you will receive this event only after the receiving player has processed the message. If you used the NoComplete flag, this event will not be fired at all. Otherwise, this event will be fired when the data has successfully been sent from this session.

- SessionTerminated—Applies to Peer and Client. This event is fired anytime a session is terminated. You may examine the ResultCode member to determine why the session was terminated. This event may also contain user-defined data that could (for example) tell a client to connect to a new server.

- ClientInformation—Applies to Server and Client. Like the other information events, this is fired when a client's information has been changed. You will be responsible for retrieving the new information after this event is fired if you need it.

- ServerInformation—Applies to Server and Client. Like the other information events, this is fired when a server's information has been changed. You will be responsible for retrieving the new information after this event is fired if you need it.

# Detecting Bandwidth and Network Statistics

At least currently, network bandwidth can be a difficult problem to work around. The majority of people on the internet today still have "low speed" modem-based connections. Even those with high-speed or broadband connections (which are steadily increasing) have a maximum upload and download speed. The goal of the network programmer is to ensure that there is little enough information going through the wire so as to not take up all available bandwidth, while at the same time ensuring that enough data is passed through to maintain the information needed.

The application you are writing for has a lot of effect on this as well. For example, if you are writing the server code for a massive online multiplayer game, then you would expect that server to have a fat pipe, with tons of available bandwidth. It's expected to maintain connections with thousands of clients simultaneously, each of them constantly sending data to the server. Plus, the server itself must send out data to each client quite often as well. Tuning the data throughput for this application is much different than, say, for the client of this server. The client only sends a small amount of data, and only to one spot, the server. It also only receives a small amount of data from that same server.

DirectPlay's API is generic enough to allow you to connect the information you need in order to make decisions on how much data you are passing across clients. If you wanted to get an idea of the current stats of your session, you could call the GetConnectionInformation method on your session. For a server or peer object, you must pass in the player id for the player you wish to receive this information on; the client will return the information about its connection with the server. Let's look at a sample output of this data:

```
Connection information:
PacketsDropped: 0
BytesDropped: 0
PacketsRetried: 0
BytesRetried: 0
PacketsSentNonGuaranteed: 1
BytesSentNonGuaranteed: 0
PacketsSentGuaranteed: 99
BytesSentGuaranteed: 1344
PeakThroughputBps: 116
ThroughputBps: 80
RoundTripLatencyMs: 4
MessagesReceived: 79
PacketsReceivedNonGuaranteed: 0
BytesReceivedNonGuaranteed: 0
PacketsReceivedGuaranteed: 79
BytesReceivedGuaranteed: 1836
MessagesTimedOutLowPriority: 0
MessagesTransmittedLowPriority: 0
MessagesTimedOutNormalPriority: 0
MessagesTransmittedNormalPriority: 99
MessagesTimedOutHighPriority: 0
MessagesTransmittedHighPriority: 1
```

As you can see, there is a wealth of information here. You can easily see the number of packets (and bytes) that were dropped (only non-guaranteed packets would be dropped).

You can see the number of packets (and bytes) that were retried (guaranteed packets that failed to reach the destination). The number of packets (and bytes) you send, both guaranteed and non-guaranteed, is included as well.

The next few members are really where this information is useful. You can see the peak throughput of the pipe in bytes per second, as well as the average throughput. You could use this information to determine whether you are sending too much data, or possibly not enough. For example, if the average throughput was 100 bytes per second, and you're sending 30K of data per second, you are killing the bandwidth. However, if the opposite were the case, you'd have plenty of extra bandwidth to fill with extra information.

Another useful piece of information you can see here is the average round trip latency. This is the approximate time it takes any packet to be received by the remote system and returned to you. Long round trip latencies are another indication that you may be oversaturating the bandwidth of either your connection or possibly the remote systems.

We round out this information by seeing the number of guaranteed and non-guaranteed packets (and bytes) we have received from the remote system. Finally, we get an indication of the number of messages we have had time out or have transmitted for each of the three priority levels (normal, low, and high).

This is all well and good, but in reality some period of time needs to pass in order to make any sound judgments on the current state of the network. A way to determine the state of the network at any given time would help eliminate this statistic tracking.

DirectPlay will not send messages to a remote computer faster than it can process them. If it detects that the remote computer isn't responding fast enough, it will queue the messages on the sender, and not send them until a more appropriate time. During this time, depending on the send options, the packets may be coalesced or timed out. If you are receiving a lot of time outs in your send complete event handler, you will know the remote system is having a tough time keeping up with the data you are sending.

You can also check the amount of data in the send queue directly by calling the GetSendQueueInformation method. Much like the GetConnectionInformation method, the server and peer objects expect the player id of the user who will check the send queue, while the client will not expect this id. In each of these objects, two integer out parameters will be returned from the call. The first is the number of messages currently waiting in the send queue. The second is the number of combined bytes these messages take up. You may control the priority of the data you are checking by passing in the appropriate member of the GetSendQueueInformationFlags enumeration as well. If you detect the send queue filling up, it's a very good indication that you need to send less data to this client.

You may also use the properties returned from the SendComplete event to help in determining potential lag. You can find the total amount of time it took to send the packet, as well as the first frame's round-trip time.

The most important thing to remember when trying to tune your network performance is to eliminate unnecessary data being passed across the wire. Don't send strings unless it's necessary. Never send a Boolean variable if you have more than one, and most of the time don't send even one. Rather than sending four Boolean variables, send one byte that is bit-masked for the various Boolean constants. For example, let's say you have four Booleans:

```
private bool IsRunning = true;
private bool IsMale = false;
private bool IsWarrior = true;
private bool IsGhost = false;
```

Now, say that you need to send each of these every frame, and so you add them all to your network packet. Just for these 4 variables, your network packet is now 16 bytes. Obviously that's highly inefficient, and we can get it down to a single byte. Look at this:

```
private const byte IsRunning = 0x1;
private const byte IsMale = 0x2;
private const byte IsWarrior = 0x4;
private const byte IsGhost = 0x8;
private byte SendData = IsRunning | IsWarrior;
```

Now, the SendData member is only a single byte and holds the same information that our 4 Boolean variables did. A single byte can hold 8 Boolean values (saving 31 bytes in the process). If you need more than 8, move up to the short type, which can hold up to 16 Boolean variables (saving 62 bytes). You can go up to the long type, which will hold a whopping 64 Boolean variables (and save a whopping 252 bytes).

Always use the smallest data type possible to minify the amount of traffic you will need to generate. If you don't need a full 32-bit integer, don't use the int type; switch to the short type. The more data you can get in the smaller packets, the more available network bandwidth you will have.

# Launching Applications Using a Lobby

Anyone who's ever played games someplace such as MSN Games by Zone.com (http://zone.msn.com) understands the concept of a lobby, even if you don't realize it. A lobby is essentially where a group of players get together before they actually start playing the game. The game can then be "launched" from the lobby and all of the players in that lobby will automatically start the game and connect to each other.

Looking at the DirectPlay assemblies, you may have noticed that this is the first assembly that has "sub-namespaces." To group functionality inside this assembly, there are two extra namespaces included: Lobby and Voice. We will get to the Voice functionality later in this chapter, so for now we will concentrate on the Lobby namespace.

There are two main classes in the Lobby namespace that will control how you interact with lobby-aware applications: Application and Client. The Client class is used to enumerate and launch lobby-enabled applications on your local system. The Application class is used by the application that supports the lobby. Each of these classes has an event model that is similar to the one used by the Peer, Server, and Client classes, as well.

The easiest thing to do is to list the programs that are currently able to be launched via a lobby, and then launch them, so let's try that first. Create a new windows form application, adding a list box with the dock parameter set to fill, so that it encompasses the entire form. Also make sure that you have included the reference to the DirectPlay assembly and included the using clause for the lobby namespace as shown here:

```
using Microsoft.DirectX.DirectPlay.Lobby;
```

As we've already mentioned, the Client class will control enumerating and launching a lobby-enabled application, so we will need to declare this variable:

```
private Client connection = null;
```

Before we forget, we should also make sure we dispose of this object when the application quits. Add the following to the Dispose override:

```
if (connection != null)
    connection.Dispose();
```

You'll notice that the class name (Client) exists both in the core DirectPlay namespace as well as the Lobby namespace. You'll need to make sure that you include both of these namespaces in your using clauses to fully qualify these variables. You may also notice that the other class (Application) also exists in the System.Windows.Forms namespace, so you will need to fully qualify any references to that as well.

Now, let's fill our list box with the names of the applications that are registered as being lobby-aware. Add the following code to your forms constructor:

```
// Fill the list box
connection = new Client();
foreach(ApplicationInformation ai in connection.GetLocalPrograms())
{
    listBox1.Items.Add(ai.ApplicationName);
}
```

As you see, this is a relatively simple operation. After we create our lobby client object, we simply enumerate through each of the local programs registered and write the name of that application into our list box. Launching these applications is equally easy; add an event handler for the double-click event of the list box. Use the code found in Listing 20.1.

**LISTING 20.1**    Launching an Application

```
private void listBox1_DoubleClick(object sender, System.EventArgs e)
{
    if (listBox1.SelectedItem == null)
        return;

    foreach(ApplicationInformation ai in connection.GetLocalPrograms())
    {
        if (ai.ApplicationName == (string)listBox1.SelectedItem)
        {
            ConnectInformation ci = new ConnectInformation();
            ci.GuidApplication = ai.GuidApplication;
            ci.Flags = ConnectFlags.LaunchNew;
            connection.ConnectApplication(ci,
                System.Threading.Timeout.Infinite, null);

            break;
        }
    }
}
```

Now, this section of code isn't the most efficient, since we potentially enumerate through the entire list once more, but it's easy to read. If there is an item currently selected, we will go through the list of registered programs until we find the one that is currently selected. Once we find it, we initialize a ConnectInformation structure with the GUID of the application and flags instructing it to launch a new instance.

**CONNECTING TO AN EXISTING SESSION**

It's also possible to "connect" to an already running application that is waiting for a lobby connection. In order to do this, you must fill out the ConnectionSettings structure and change the flags to ConnectFlags.LaunchNotFound. This will still launch a new instance if a running one was not found.

If you try to compile this application, you will notice that the main method will complain that the Application class is ambiguous. It says this because there are two classes named Application, one in System.Windows.Forms, and another in Microsoft.DirectX.DirectPlay.Lobby. Replace the main method with this one to eliminate this error:

```
static void Main()
{
    using (Form1 frm = new Form1())
    {
        frm.Show();
        System.Windows.Forms.Application.Run(frm);
    }
}
```

Once the application has been successfully launched, a connection handle will be returned to you from the ConnectApplication method. With this handle you can send data to the application via the Send method, which will fire an event in the launched application's Lobby.Application object. You may also call the ReleaseApplication method, which signals that you are done with the application. This will *not* cause the launched application to quit; it will simply disconnect the lobby client object from the application. The connection handle is no longer valid after this call has been made.

# Making Your Application Lobby Aware

The Application class in the Lobby namespace is how you can actually receive information after you've been launched from a lobby, as well as how you register your application as being lobby-aware. The act of registering your application is quite simple; we will look at this first.

In order to register your application, you will first need to create a ProgramDescription structure. At the very least, you will need to fill out the application GUID and name parameters, as well as the executable path and filename members. The others are optional. Then you can call either the RegisterProgram or UnregisterProgram method, depending on the operation you wish to perform.

We never actually looked at the constructor for the Application object yet though. While it's possible to create the object without any parameters, the majority of time you will want to detect whether you have been launched from a lobby client. Let's look at the overload with the most parameters, as every other overload is a subset of this one:

```
public Application ( System.Int32 connectionHandle ,
    Microsoft.DirectX.DirectPlay.Lobby.InitializeFlags flags ,
    Microsoft.DirectX.DirectPlay.Lobby.ConnectEventHandler connectEventHandler )
```

The connection handle parameter is an out parameter that will be returned to you. If you were launched by a lobby client, this handle will be the same as the one returned from the ConnectApplicaton method. However, if you were not, you can expect this member to be zero. The InitializeFlags enumeration allows you to disable parameter validation, but for this context is wholly uninteresting. The last parameter is something we haven't seen before. This allows you to actually hook the Connect event before the object is created, mainly because the constructor can actually fire this event.

Once you've detected that you've been launched from a lobby client, you need to call the RegisterLobby method on the appropriate DirectPlay connection object you are using. In the Connect event handler, you can also detect whether there were any connection settings passed in, and if so, use them to get into a session. The ConnectionSettings structure that is included in the event arguments object has all the information you need to either host or join an existing session.

# Adding Voice Chat to Your Sessions

Sitting around and typing chat messages while playing your favorite online games seems to be a common occurrence. Even though these players can type quite quickly, and use a form of shorthand many times, the fact remains that in many types of games, the act of stopping to type a chat message leaves you vulnerable, even if only briefly. What you need is a hands-free way to communicate that allows you to keep playing the game. As humans, we've relied on voice communication for thousands of years, and unless you're using sign language, it's completely hands-free.

Adding voice chat into your application can be *quite* simple, although with a little extra work you can have full control over everything. To handle this simple case first, let's take the peer-to-peer session application we wrote in Chapter 18, "Simple Peer-to-Peer Networking," and add voice to it. No fancy options, just allow everyone in the session to speak with everyone else.

Before we begin, we will need to add a few things to the project file. First, the voice communication used in DirectPlay goes through DirectSound, so we will need to include a reference to the DirectSound assembly. Since there is are Server and Client classes in our voice namespace as well, we should also add the following using clauses:

```
using Voice = Microsoft.DirectX.DirectPlay.Voice;
using Microsoft.DirectX.DirectSound;
```

In order to actually use voice during a session, we will need both a client and a server object. The server will be responsible for starting the voice session, while the client will naturally connect to the server's session. In a peer-to-peer session, where the host is also a member of the session, that peer will need to be both the server and a client of the voice session. Let's add our variable declarations:

```
private Voice.Client voiceClient = null;
private Voice.Server voiceServer = null;
```

Naturally, without a server, the client has nothing to connect to, so we should go about creating a server first. Find the section of code where we first host our peer-to-peer session. Directly after the EnableSendDataButton call in the InitializeDirectPlay method, add the following code:

```
// Create our voice server first
voiceServer = new Voice.Server(connection);

// Create a session description
Voice.SessionDescription session = new Voice.SessionDescription();
session.SessionType = Voice.SessionType.Peer;
session.BufferQuality = Voice.BufferQuality.Default;
session.GuidCompressionType = Voice.CompressionGuid.Default;
session.BufferAggressiveness = Voice.BufferAggressiveness.Default;

// Finally start the session
voiceServer.StartSession(session);
```

As you can see, when we create our voice object, we also need to pass in the DirectPlay object that will act as the transport for the voice communication. This will allow the voice to be transmitted along with the other data in your session. Before we can actually start a session, though, we need to have a basic way to describe the session.

Since we are in a peer-to-peer networking session, we choose the peer session type for our voice communication. This sends all the voice data directly between all of the players. Other types of sessions are

- Mixing—In this mode, all voice communication is sent to the server. The server then mixes the combined voice data and forwards it on to the clients. This dramatically reduces CPU time and bandwidth on the client, but subsequently raises each for the server.

- Forwarding—All voice communication will be routed through the session host in this mode. It will lower bandwidth for each client, but drastically increase the bandwidth for the host. Unless the host has a large amount of bandwidth, this option won't help you much.

- Echo—Voice communication will be echoed back to the speaker.

Another option we can set in the session description is the codec we want to use for voice communication. We've chosen the default codec here, but there are actually numerous codecs you can use. This code fragment will print out each of them in the output window:

```
foreach(Voice.CompressionInformation ci in voiceServer.CompressionTypes)
{
    Console.WriteLine(ci.Description);
}
```

The compression information structure contains enough data to determine which code you wish to use. You may also use any of the ones listed in the CompressionGuid class.

The remaining options we set for the session are the quality and aggressiveness of the buffer we are using for the voice communication. We simply want to use the default options for these.

With the server created and a session started, it will be important to ensure that we actually stop the session and dispose of our object when we are finished. Add the following code to your dispose override (before calling dispose on your peer object):

```
if (voiceServer != null)
{
    voiceServer.StopSession();
    voiceServer.Dispose();
    voiceServer = null;
}
```

Nothing all that fancy here; we simply stop the session and dispose of our object. However, we only have half of our voice communication implemented. Sure, we have a server running, but what about the clients? Add the function found in Listing 20.2 into your application.

LISTING 20.2    Connect to a Voice Session

```
private void ConnectVoice()
{

    // Now create a client to connect
    voiceClient = new Voice.Client(connection);

    // Fill in description object for device configuration
    Voice.SoundDeviceConfig soundConfig = new Voice.SoundDeviceConfig();
    soundConfig.Flags = Voice.SoundConfigFlags.AutoSelect;
    soundConfig.GuidPlaybackDevice = DSoundHelper.DefaultPlaybackDevice;
    soundConfig.GuidCaptureDevice  = DSoundHelper.DefaultCaptureDevice;
    soundConfig.Window = this;
```

**LISTING 20.2**   Continued

```
// Fill in description object for client configuration
Voice.ClientConfig clientConfig = new Voice.ClientConfig();
clientConfig.Flags = Voice.ClientConfigFlags.AutoVoiceActivated ¦
     Voice.ClientConfigFlags.AutoRecordVolume;

clientConfig.RecordVolume = (int) Voice.RecordVolume.Last;
clientConfig.PlaybackVolume = (int) Voice.PlaybackVolume.Default;
clientConfig.Threshold = Voice.Threshold.Unused;
clientConfig.BufferQuality = Voice.BufferQuality.Default;
clientConfig.BufferAggressiveness = Voice.BufferAggressiveness.Default;

// Connect to the voice session
voiceClient.Connect(soundConfig, clientConfig, Voice.VoiceFlags.Sync);

voiceClient.TransmitTargets = new int[] {
        (int)Voice.PlayerId.AllPlayers };
}
```

This looks a lot more intimidating than it is. First, we create our voice client object, once again passing in our DirectPlay connection object to be used as the transport. Before we can actually connect to our session, though, we need to set up the configuration for both our sound card as well as the client.

The SoundDeviceConfig structure is used to tell DirectPlay Voice information about the sound devices you wish to use for the voice communication. In our case, we want to automatically select the microphone line, and use the default playback and capture devices. If you remember back to our DirectSound chapter, the cooperative level was set based on the window, so we pass that in as well.

Next, we want to establish the runtime parameters for the client, and that is done with the ClientConfig structure. We set our flags so that the record volume is automatically adjusted to give the best sound quality, as well as to signify that we want to automatically start sending voice communication when sound is actually picked up from the microphone. When you use the AutoVoiceActivated flag, you must also set the threshold value to unused, as we did previously. If the voice communication is "manually" activated, the threshold value must be set to the minimum level needed to start the voice communication.

Finally, we set our playback and recording volumes to the defaults, along with the buffer quality and aggressiveness, much like we did with the server. We then connect to the hosting session. We use the synchronous parameter here because for simplicity I didn't want to create the event handlers yet. Once we've been connected to the session, we set the transmit targets to everyone, signifying that we want to talk to the world.

With the code to create a client and set the transmit targets, we are left with two remaining items. First, we need to deal with cleanup. Before your voice server object is disposed, add the following:

```
if (voiceClient != null)
{
    voiceClient.Disconnect(Voice.VoiceFlags.Sync);
    voiceClient.Dispose();
    voiceClient = null;
}
```

Simple stuff; we disconnect from the session (using the synchronous flag once more), and then dispose our object. The last remaining item is to actually *call* our ConnectVoice method from somewhere. Since both the host and the clients of the DirectPlay session will need to create this voice client, you will put the call in two places. First, place the call after the StartSession method on your server to allow the host to create its voice client. Next, in the OnConnectComplete event handler, if the connection was successful, put the call in that block as well:

### CHECKING AUDIO SETUP

It's entirely possible that if you haven't ever run the voice wizard, the Connect call will fail with a RunSetupException exception. If this is the case, you can easily catch this exception and run setup. You can run setup quite easily with the following code fragment:

```
Voice.Test t = new Voice.Test();
t.CheckAudioSetup();
```

After the setup has been run, you can try your connection once more. This setup should only need to be run once.

```
if (e.Message.ResultCode == ResultCode.Success)
{
    this.BeginInvoke(new AddTextCallback(AddText),
        new object[] { "Connect Success." });

    connected = true;

    this.BeginInvoke(new EnableCallback(EnableSendDataButton),
        new object[] { true } );

    ConnectVoice();
}
```

# In Brief

In this chapter we covered the more esoteric aspects of DirectPlay, including

- A detailed look at all events and why they occur.
- Bandwidth and lag detection.
- Sending queue.
- Lobby launching applications.
- Using Voice chat in your application.

In our final chapter, we will look at putting most everything we've learned thus far together.

# Achieving Maximum Performance

**21**

Items covered will include

■ Boxing and unboxing

■ The event model and its detriments

■ Understanding the cost behind certain methods

## Using Value Types as Objects

One of the biggest questions people ask about writing managed code for things like games is "Is it fast enough?" Speed is very important to an industry that prides itself in getting high-quality games that look near photo-realistic, all in essentially real time. The basic answer is yes, so long as you know how to write high-performance code. Of course, that's the same answer that was given when the switch from assembly to C was made, and that turned out all right.

The .NET Runtime and the C# language have changed the way people write code. They have opened up the world of programming to new developers, and expanded the productivity of the ones that have been around for a while. They handle so many things for you that it's quite easy to forget how much some operations may cost. Look at the real-world example in the following paragraph.

The Billboard sample that ships with the DirectX SDK has multiple versions: an unmanaged version written in C++, along with two managed versions, one written in C# and the other in VB.NET. Since each of the DirectX SDK samples includes the frame rate while you are running, you can easily tell which of the applications is running faster, and by approximately how much. Comparing the C++ Billboard sample with the C# Billboard sample, you'll notice the C# version runs at approximately 60% of the speed of the C++ sample.

Considering that the other samples run at similar speeds between the managed and unmanaged variations, there must be something special about this particular sample that causes this slowdown. Naturally, there is, and the culprit is boxing and unboxing.

The term "boxing" refers to what the .NET runtime does to convert a value type (for example a structure) into an object. The reverse of this process is obviously called "unboxing." In order to perform this operation, the .NET runtime will allocate a portion of the heap large enough to hold your value type, and then copy the data from the stack (where the value type resides) to the newly allocated heap space.

Now, when looking at the Billboard managed sample, you may notice that each tree that will be drawn has a corresponding structure that maintains the information needed to draw the tree. Since the trees are alpha blended, and will need to be drawn in a certain order (from back to front), each tree is sorted every frame. You'll see the code in the sample do this:

```
trees.Sort(new TreeSortClass());
```

This class implements IComparer, which is needed for comparison. If you look at the implementation of this class, though, you'll see quickly that the comparison method takes two objects in as the parameters, while we are using a structure. This structure must be boxed before it can be passed on to the compare method. Then, as soon as the compare method is started, the object is unboxed to be able to manipulate the data.

The sort method will be called approximately 4,300 times per frame. Each of these calls will perform a total of two boxing operations, followed immediately by two unboxing operations. The structure itself is defined as such:

```
public struct Tree
{
    public CustomVertex.PositionColoredTextured v0, v1, v2, v3;
    public Vector3 position;
    public int treeTextureIndex;
    public int offsetIndex;
};
```

Now, if you calculate the structures size, you'll see that it is quite large: 116 bytes. So, calculate the data that is being allocated and copied during a single sort operation. Multiply the number of bytes that will need to be allocated per object (116), by the number of objects (2), by the number of calls per frame (4,300), and you will come up with a whopping 997,600 bytes that will need to be allocated for *every* frame. This just covers the allocation for the boxing operation; it doesn't even consider the copy operation to get the data into the newly allocated object.

Even after the copy operation has taken place, as soon as the method has been entered, the very first thing that is done is to take all the data that has just been boxed, and unbox it. Which means the exact same allocation and copy will need to be performed a second time, with the exception being that this allocation will be performed on the stack.

So, in reality, for every frame the billboard sample is running, on average 1,995,200 bytes are allocated between the stack and heap and then copied back and forth between them. This doesn't even consider the fact that this large amount of tiny allocations (since each allocation will be 116 bytes) will cause the garbage collector to kick in quite a few times for a generation zero collection. Seeing this data, it is easy to understand why this sample lacks the performance of the C++ sample.

The point of this exercise is that many developers using managed languages don't understand the costs behind the code they are writing. The .NET Runtime gives you enormous power and flexibility, but given the "newness" of the API, it's still overly common to see people take advantage of these features without fully understanding the costs associated with them. I'm quite sure the "average" developer wouldn't realize that the simple sorting algorithm in the Billboard sample would be allocating and copying close to two megabytes of data *per frame*.

# Understanding the Performance Implications of the Event Model

There's a similar scenario that is specific to Managed Direct3D. You've already learned that each resource that is created hooks the device events for at least disposing, and in many cases, device lost and device reset as well. Each of these event hooks can do a few things that can be disastrous to your performance if you aren't aware of them.

First, there is the actual memory allocation. Every time you create a vertex buffer, for example, aside from the normal vertex buffer allocations, just to cover the event handlers, there are three extra allocations of delegates. Couple this with the fact that these event handlers act as hard links to the object itself, and you can see that these objects will never be destroyed until the device itself is. Look at this piece of sample code:

```
public void WasteVideoMemory()
{
    VertexBuffer waste = new VertexBuffer(device, 5000,
        0, VertexFormats.None, Pool.Default);
}
```

It looks like a piece of dead code. Sure, a vertex buffer is created, but it's never used, so obviously the garbage collector will kick in and collect it. This is what you might expect anyway; however, nothing could be further from the truth.

In reality, even this simple piece of code does quite a bit outside of just creating a vertex buffer. After the vertex buffer has been created, the DeviceLost, DeviceReset, and Disposing events from the device are all hooked. These event handlers will maintain a link between the device and the vertex buffer. Even though this vertex buffer is never used anywhere, the garbage collector will never try to collect it because the *device* still maintains a reference to the object via the event handler.

If a method similar to the preceding one was called numerous times, you would slowly erode away the amount of free video memory you have (since the object was created in the default memory pool). Since you never maintained a reference yourself to this vertex buffer, once it has lost scope, you can never remove it. In a short time you would run out of memory, and be puzzling to figure out why.

Another side effect of this behavior is shutdown time. There have been a few people who have reported "bugs" in the Managed Runtime due to a misunderstanding between how they thought things should work and the reality of what really goes on. It's normally the same story, "I'm doing such and such, and my application locks up when I exit." The scenario is invariably something like this:

```
device.SetRenderTarget(0, mySwapChain.GetBackBuffer(0, BackBufferType.Mono));
// Render some stuff
```

This code does pretty much exactly the same thing the previous code did. It creates a "new" object (in this case, a surface) that is never used again. Running this line of code thousands of times creates thousands of surfaces that are orphaned and only accessible from the device. When the device is finally disposed on application shutdown, the device signals to each of its dependencies (these thousands of surfaces) that they need to dispose themselves now as well. This "event unwinding" takes a period of time; the more orphaned objects, the longer it takes. Most times, the customer's application hasn't locked up; it's simply trying to handle the events.

There are two ways around this type of behavior. The first one is the easiest to implement. You can simply use the using statement on objects you expect to have a short lifetime. The preceding statement should be

```
using(Surface backBuffer = mySwapChain.GetBackBuffer(0, BackBufferType.Mono))
{
    device.SetRenderTarget(0, backBuffer);
    // Render some stuff.
}
```

Making sure you eliminate the shortly used objects and replace them with using statements as shown previously can drastically improve the performance of your application if you do a lot of the small allocations.

This doesn't solve the problem of the event hooks, though. Each object will still be created with the device hooks, and the extra allocations for the event handlers could still be detrimental to your application's performance. The events and handlers are in Managed DirectX to allow you, as the developer, to not worry about object scopes and lifetimes. Depending on the needs of your application, though, it may be helpful for you to maintain the object lifetimes yourself.

In the DirectX 9.0 release of Managed DirectX, you were stuck with this behavior, even if you didn't want or need it. With the SDK Update, you now have the choice of turning the event handling in Managed DirectX completely off. See the following code:

```
Device.IsUsingEventHandlers = false;
device = new Device(...);
```

The default value for this property is true, and it can be changed at any time. Switching it to false before you create the device and never touching it again will turn off all event handling in your application.

## DISSECTING THE USING STATEMENT

If you are unaware of what the using statement does, it will automatically dispose of the object created in the initialization clause. The C# compiler breaks the above statement into code like this:

```
Surface backBuffer;
try
{
    backBuffer = mySwapChain.GetBackBuffer(0,
    ➥BackBufferType.Mono);
    device.SetRenderTarget(0, backBuffer);
    // Render some stuff
}
finally
{
    if (backBuffer != null)
        backBuffer.Dispose();
}
```

## UNDERSTANDING THE EVENT HANDLING

Using this property will only turn off the automatic hooking of events. All events that Direct3D fires will still be fired, so you can hook them yourself. You must use caution when disabling the automatic event handling. You will have much more control over your application, but that extra control will require you to ensure that you manage your object lifetimes correctly.

It's entirely possible to use the event handling routines for the majority of your application, but turn them off in certain cases. For example, this code is perfectly valid:

```
// Device is currently using event handlers
Device.IsUsingEventHandlers = false;
using(Surface backBuffer = mySwapChain.GetBackBuffer(0, BackBufferType.Mono))
```

## FORCING YOUR APPLICATION TO USE A SINGLE THREADING DEVICE

With the ability to turn off the event hooking by resources, the Managed DirectX runtime was updated to always turn on the Multithreaded flag on device creation. If you know you will be handling all of the object lifetimes manually on a single thread, you can turn this feature off as well. Update the following flag in the presentation parameters structure that you use to create your device:

```
presentParams.ForceNoMultiThreadedFlag = true
```

```
{
    device.SetRenderTarget(0, backBuffer);
    // Render some stuff.
}
// Allow device events to be hooked again
Device.IsUsingEventHandlers = true;
```

This code would turn off the event handler hooks while this temporary surface is created, but turn them back on afterward. Depending on your needs, you may want to turn the event hooking off completely or just partially. You will *always* get better performance handling the object lifetimes yourself than letting the system handle it.

# Understanding the Cost of Methods

One of the most important aspects of ensuring that you write applications with the best performance is to always know the cost of any method you call. While memorizing all the different permutations of APIs you can call and the performance they take is unreasonable, you should have at least a vague idea about the cost of any method.

In Managed DirectX there are a few cases where seemingly harmless code can cause problems. For example, any method that takes a string as an argument in Managed DirectX has a cost of allocating a new unmanaged string type and copying the string data over.

Take the case where you are using HLSL to render your scene, and numerous times throughout each frame, you switch the technique being used, such as

```
myEffect.Technique = "TransformWorldSpace";
//Render some stuff
myEffect.Technique = "TransformAndAddGlow";
// Render some other stuff
```

Each time you switch the technique, you are allocating some memory and copying the technique name over. A much better solution to this problem would be to cache the handles returned, such as

```
// On device creations, cache technique handles
EffectHandle handle1 = myEffect.GetTechnique("TransformWorldSpace");
EffectHandle handle2 = myEffect.GetTechnique("TransformAndAddGlow");
```

```
// Later on, for every render
myEffect.Technique = handle1;
//Render some stuff
myEffect.Technique = handle2;
//Render some stuff
```

Another common case of not understanding the cost of methods was covered earlier when dealing with resources. The difference between locking a resource and returning an Array or a GraphicsStream is quite drastic.

# In Brief

- The horrors of boxing and unboxing.
- Understanding the cost of all methods.
- The pitfalls of using the event model.

# PART VII

# Appendices

# Using the Diagnostics Assemblies

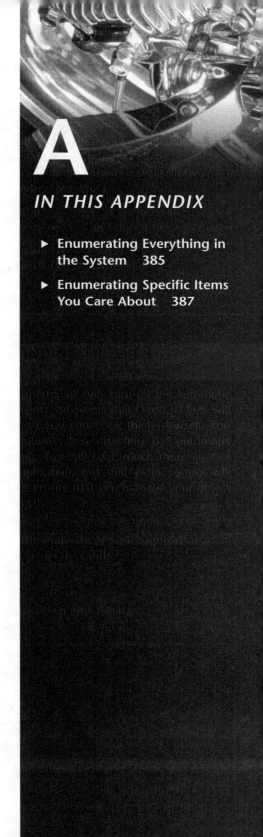

You've just released your game to the public. Your test team has done a remarkable job, but you never got the chance to test your application on every possible set of systems out there. It seems that approximately 5% of all people who have paid for your game can't play it for some reason, and you don't know why. You've got a sneaky suspicion that it is a certain type of video card, but you can't be sure. What if you had a way to report the current items installed on the system in your game, and return the list to you? The Diagnostics namespace can be used for this. In this appendix we will cover these topics, including

- Enumerating every option the diagnostic software knows about and reporting them

- Checking for certain options we care about

## Enumerating Everything in the System

The diagnostics namespace is built on the same code base that the DxDiag tool as ships in the operating system and versions of DirectX. If you've ever run this tool, it can tell you just about everything you ever wanted to know about your system.

The diagnostics data is arranged in a hierarchal fashion. You have containers, which can contain zero-many properties, as well as zero-many children containers. Enumerating all objects is simple to do with a recursive function. In Listing A.1, look at the function that is included with the DirectX SDK DxDiagOutput sample:

**LISTING A.1**   Outputting Diagnostic Data

```
static void OutputDiagData(string parent, Container root)
{
    try
    {
        foreach (PropertyData pd in root.Properties)
        {
            // Just display the data
            Console.WriteLine("{0}.{1} = {2}", parent, pd.Name, pd.Data);
        }
    }
    catch
    {
    }

    try
    {
        foreach (ContainerData cd in root.Containers)
        {
            // Recurse all the internal nodes
            if (parent == null)
                OutputDiagData(cd.Name, cd.Container);
            else
                OutputDiagData(parent + "." + cd.Name, cd.Container);
        }
    }
    catch
    {
    }

    // We are done with this container, we can dispose it.
    root.Dispose();
}
```

If there are any properties in this container, we will enumerate each of them, and display them to the user, as well as the value they contain. The values will always be either a string, Boolean, or integer value, depending on the property. You can check the pd.Data.GetType() method to determine the type if it is important to you.

After we've dealt with the properties for this container, we need to check whether this container contains any children containers. If it does, we enumerate each of those, and for every one we find, we simply call this method once more recursively.

The only thing left to do for this to be useful is to create the first container and make the initial call into this method. The container object contains only one constructor that takes one Boolean value. This value is used to determine whether the diagnostics should include WHQL (Windows Hardware Quality Labs) information as well. Retrieving this information can be time consuming, so unless you need it, it's probably better to pass in false here. The DirectX SDK sample uses this entry into the executable (see Listing A.2):

**LISTING A.2**   Starting the Application

```
static void Main(string[] args)
{
    try
    {
        // Just start our recursive loop with our root container.  Don't worry
        // about checking Whql
        OutputDiagData(null, new Container(false));
    }
    catch
    {
        // Something bad happened
    }
}
```

If you built this diagnostics functionality into your application and could detect when a failure had occurred, you could automatically send this data back from your customers' machine to you, allowing you to narrow down the causes of problems. You could package the data up into a small XML file, and use that as a parameter into a Web service on your Web site to collect the failures. Be sure to inform your users if you will be sending machine-specific information to your servers, and allow them to opt out of the action completely. If they do allow you to send the data to your servers, make sure your privacy and data retention policies are known to the user as well.

# Enumerating Specific Items You Care About

If you've run DxDiag, or even the sample app from the DirectX SDK, you know that enumerating *everything* that DxDiag knows about can take quite some time. What if you don't care about the vast majority of the stuff listed, and only want to maintain information on a small subset of items? Luckily, the diagnostic namespace can be used for this as well.

Let's say the first thing you wanted to know was what version of DirectX the system running your application was using. No need to go through all of the work enumerating everything when you only care about something so simple. Here is the code you would use to determine this:

```
Container parent = new Container(false);
Container child = parent.GetContainer("DxDiag_SystemInfo").Container;
int dxVersionMajor = (int)child.GetProperty("dwDirectXVersionMajor").Data;
int dxVersionMinor = (int)child.GetProperty("dwDirectXVersionMinor").Data;
string dxVersionLetter = (string)child.GetProperty("szDirectXVersionLetter").Data;
Console.WriteLine("DX Version:{0}.{1}{2}",dxVersionMajor,dxVersionMinor,dxVersionLetter);
```

Here, we create the root container (without any WHQL information). We then get a child container from this root named DxDiag_SystemInfo. We then get three different properties of the DirectX version: the major version number, the minor version number, and then any "letter" associated with this version of DirectX (since DirectX is notorious for releasing versions such as DX8.1b).

You may be wondering where these property names came from, and although it isn't obvious initially, all of these names are discoverable. As we were enumerating the properties and containers, you can see that we printed out the name of each as we went. You would need to write the enumeration code at the very least (or use the DX SDK sample) to determine the container and property names for the information you want to get.

The property names prefixes also give you the default data type for the object. They are all given names that match Hungarian notation for C developers. Items with the prefix "sz" denote strings. Items with the prefix "b" are Boolean values. All other prefix values denote integer values.

Using the Diagnostics namespace can be an invaluable way to help track down issues in your application. Your application should use it for error reporting, at the very least for debugging purposes. It's even possible to use this in your shipping game to help support when trying to figure out why your game refuses to run on certain customers' computers. The time saved by detecting common errors (old outdated drivers, for example) and allowing support to fix them quickly is significant. Who knows, it's possible a bug could be found in your game that only happens on certain video cards; you wouldn't have been able to tell without getting this information from multiple customers having similar problems.

It's better to plan for problems early than to wait and be sorry later.

# Playing Music and Videos

The Managed DirectX SDK included APIs to talk with each of the DirectX APIs, with the exception of DirectMusic and DirectShow. While the reasons for this decision could be debated, we understood early on that at the very least, developers were going to want (and need) a way to play DirectShow content, namely movies and encoded music (such as mp3s and wma files). We wanted a simple and easy-to-use interface for accessing this basic functionality, and thus the AudioVideoPlayback namespace was born. In this appendix we will cover this namespace, including

■ Simple playback of an audio file

■ Simple playback of a video file

■ Playing a video file in your own window

■ Using a video file as a texture in your 3D application

## Playing Back an Audio or Video File Simply

In order to use the audio and video playback namespace, you will first need to add a reference to this namespace into your application. You may also want to include a using clause for the namespace in your code file.

Our goal when we designed these classes was to make them extremely simple to use, so if we wanted to play a file, it should be accomplished with just one line of code. If you wanted to play an audio file called "piano.mp3", let's say, the code would look like this:

```
Audio someAudio = new Audio("piano.mp3", true);
```

There are two main classes that are included in this namespace: the video class and the audio class. These names are pretty self-explanatory. Each class's constructor has two overloads; the first parameter of each overload is the name of the file you wish to play. The other constructor for each class contains a Boolean value that determines whether or not this file should begin playing automatically. The default option is false, and the file will not begin playing until you call Play on it.

As you can see by our call, we are creating an audio object, and we want it to begin playing automatically. For the simplest of cases, this is all that is required for you to do. Using the constructor without the Boolean parameter, or specifying false for the parameter when you call the constructor, will cause the file to be loaded, but it will not be played.

The constructors aren't the only way to create (or load) these files, though. The most similar method would be the static FromFile method, which takes the same parameters as the constructor does and returns a new instance of the class. There is also a static FromUrl method, which behaves exactly the same as the FromFile method, with the exception that it can be used to load the data from a Web site (or any valid URL). If possible, this data will be streamed from this URL to your system, so playback should begin much quicker than waiting for the entire file to be downloaded.

There are also Open and OpenUrl methods on the classes themselves that take the same parameters as their static counterparts. They will replace the data in an already created object with the data from the new file or URL you specify.

# Using the Features of Video Files

In the previous example, we used an audio file as our "test" to show how simple it was to load and play the content. What if we wanted to do the same thing with the video file "butterfly.mpg" instead? Simple enough; just use the following:

```
Video someVideo = new Video("butterfly.mpg", true);
```

If you ran code similar to this in your application, the very first thing you would notice is that the video plays in an entirely new window. While this may be adequate for you, what if you didn't want that? What if you already had a window where you wanted to display your movie? Of course, this is quite simple to do; however, it requires an extra couple lines. First, you will want to skip the auto play feature. Instead, use code like this:

```
Video someVideo = new Video("butterfly.mpg");
someVideo.Owner = this;
someVideo.Play();
```

The default option is not to auto-play the data, so we use the constructor that takes a single argument. We then set the owner of the video file, which can be any Windows Forms control. For example, it could be your main form itself, or a picture box that is a child of your form. Finally, we play the video. Notice now that the video is played inside the window you specified in the owner property?

You can also control the audio of a video (if it contains audio data) directly from the video object. You will notice that the video object has a property "Audio" which will return the Audio object associated with this video. You may use this just like you would any other audio object.

# Using Video as Textures

Another common feature for video files that users must have is the capability to play these movies onto a 3D texture inside the application they are building. Many of the developers use movie files as the "cut-scenes" during their game, and need some way to show the movie in full screen mode. The Audio Video playback classes can handle both cases quite well.

For the simplest case of a developer wanting to use a full screen movie as a cut-scene in the game they are writing, we made it as simple as could be. Simply load the video file into your Video object, set the "Fullscreen" property to true, and play the video. Nothing could be simpler...well, unless there was a constructor that took these parameters.

For the more difficult scenario where the developer has some set of geometry they want to texture using a video, we've come up with a different solution. First, there is an event you will want to hook, TextureReadyToRender. This event will be fired every time there is a new frame in the video file that is ready to be rendered as a texture.

The TextureRenderEventArgs member that is passed into the event handler contains the newly created texture that is ready to be rendered. This event may be fired from many different threads, so ensure that you do not have multiple threads accessing variables simultaneously. Who knows what craziness you can end up with doing that? All you need to do to start the video playing and the event firing is call the method RenderToTexture on the video object. You should begin receiving the events and textures immediately.

The sample that ships with the DirectX SDK renders the entire scene at the same frame rate as the movie being played; it only renders each frame when a new texture is ready. In many cases, this is adequate for the developers, since movies being rendered as a texture is a fairly uncommon occurrence. However, you may still want to use the texture in your "real time" rendering application, so how would you go about that?

First, you will need to detect whether your video texture has been created in the system memory pool or the default pool (since you won't have control over this). You can do this by checking the level description of the first level of the texture.

If the texture was created in the default pool (most common), you will need to use the Direct3D device's method GetRenderTargetData on the surface of the texture and a surface of your own created in the system memory pool. You cannot render textures created in the system memory pool, so you will also need to create a texture in the default memory pool to use for rendering. Something like

```
SurfaceDescription ds = e.Texture.GetLevelDescription(0);

if (ds.Pool == Pool.Default)
{
    systemSurface = device.CreateOffscreenPlainSurface(ds.Width, ds.Height,
        ds.Format, Pool.SystemMemory);
}

texture = new Texture(device, ds.Width, ds.Height,
    1, Usage.Dynamic, ds.Format, Pool.Default);
```

This code will check to see whether your video texture has been created in the default memory pool, and if it has, it will create an off-screen plain surface to hold the texture data, plus a texture in the default memory pool that we can use to render our scene. After this is executed, there are two methods on the device that we need to use to get the data from one texture to the next:

```
using(Surface videoSurface = e.Texture.GetSurfaceLevel(0))
{
    using(Surface textureSurface = texture.GetSurfaceLevel(0))
    {
        device.GetRenderTargetData(videoSurface, systemSurface);
        device.UpdateSurface(systemSurface, textureSurface);
    }
}
```

As you can see here, we get the render target data from our video texture and move it into our temporary system memory surface. From there, we move it into our real texture. We can then use the texture we created in the default pool as the texture to render our scene.

Since the texture will be accessed by more than one thread, you will need to ensure that only one thread at a time has access to this texture by using the lock semantics on it.

The Audio and Video playback classes are not designed to be fully featured implementations of DirectShow. They do not offer many of the in-depth features, such as video capture or filter graph management. They are designed for the simplest cases of loading audio and video data, and playing this data back; nothing more. They are quick and easy to use, but should not be considered a full and robust solution, nor a "replacement" to the DirectShow APIs already out there.

There are no planned updates for this namespace or references.

# Index

# J–K

# L

# N

**namespaces**

audio and video playback, 1-2

diagnostics, enumeration and, 1-4

DirectSound, 261

buffers, 262

Device class, 262

Lobby (DirectPlay), 366

Microsoft.DirectX.DirectSound, 261

**networking, 359**

bandwidth detection, 362-365

event model, 359-362

events

ApplicationDescriptionChanged, 360

AsyncOperationComplete, 360

ClientInformatin, 362

ConnectComplete, 360

FindHostQuery, 360

FindHostResponse, 360

GroupCreated, 360

GroupDestroyed, 361

GroupInformation, 361

HostMigrated, 361

IndicateConnect, 361

IndicateConnectAborted, 361

PeerInformation, 361

PlayerAddedToGroup, 361

PlayerCreated, 361

PlayerDestroyed, 361

PlayerRemovedFromGroup, 362

Receive, 362

SendComplete, 362

ServerInformation, 362

SessionTerminated, 362

statistics, 362-365

**networking, 359.** *See also* **DirectPlay**

**NoDirtyUpdate flag, locking buffers, 141**

**non-square surfaces, 313**

**NoOverwrite flag, dynamic buffers, 140**

# O

**objects**

Buffer3D, properties, 267-268

BufferDescription, properties, 264-265

Listener3D, 269-271

Meshes, stock objects, 70

Peer object, 322

SimplificationMesh, 149

texture, 44-49

**obstacles, Dodger game, 96-108**

collection class, 100

constants, 97

drawing, 99

**optimization, mesh data, 121-123**

**Optimize function, 121**

# S

*How can we make this index more useful? Email us at indexes@samspublishing.com*

*How can we make this index more useful? Email us at indexes@samspublishing.com*

# Your Guide to Computer Technology

**inform IT**

**www.informit.com**

# KICK START

< QUICK >
< CONCISE >
< PRACTICAL >

## Microsoft .NET Compact Framework Kick Start

**By Erik Rubin and Ronnie Yates**

0-672-32570-5
$34.99 US/$54.99 CAN

## ASP.NET Kick Start

**By Stephen Walther**

0-672-32476-8
$34.99 US/$54.99 CAN

## ASP.NET Data Web Controls Kick Start

**By Scott Mitchell**

0-672-32501-2
$34.99 US/$54.99 CAN

## Microsoft Visual C# .NET 2003 Kick Start

**By Steven Holzner**

0-672-32547-0
$34.99 US/$54.99 CAN

## Microsoft Direct3D Programming

**By Clayton Walnum**

0-672-32498-9
$34.99 US/$54.99 CAN

## Microsoft Visual Basic .NET 2003 Kick Start

**By Duncan Mackenzie**

0-672-32549-7
$34.99 US/$54.99 CAN

## C#Builder Kick Start

**By Joe Mayo**

0-672-3258-9
$34.99 US/$54.99 CAN